# Yesterday's Faces

# Yesterday's Faces
## Volume II
## Strange Days

## Robert Sampson

Bowling Green University Popular Press
Bowling Green, Ohio 43403

*A portion of Chapter III: "Bumudemutumuro" appeared in slightly different form in* The Age of the Unicorn *No. 8, Vol. II, No. 2. The discussion of Jules De Grandin appeared in* The Weird Tales Collector *No. 5 (1979) as "The Very Much So Clever Fellow." The Semi-Dual discussion appeared in* The Mystery Fancier *as "Detection By Other Means, Vol. 6, No. 1, Jan/Feb 1983."*

To Randy Cox, a fellow seeker for yesterday's faces.

# Acknowledgments___

My warm thanks to the following publishers, copyright holders, collectors and friends who assisted so much in the preparation of this volume.

*Dave Arends* who graciously made available his S&S *Detective Story* collection and went to unprecedented lengths in identifying the series characters of that magazine, mile after mile of them.

*Paul Bonner and the Conde Nast Publications, Inc.* for permission to quote from the Street & Smith magazines, *Detective Story Magazine*, the *People's Magazine* and *The Popular Magazine*.

*J. Randolph Cox*, whose library data files were thrown wide open to me, and whose Craig Kennedy information brought order to chaos.

*Winston Dawson*, without whom the Semi-Dual story could never have been written, and who responded, cheerfully and factually, to dozens of inquiries.

*Nils Hardin* for the loan of his scientific detective magazines and for permission to quote from that treasure chest which was *Xenophile*.

And to *Ed Keniston* for days in the attic and nights in the darkroom.

*Glenn Lord* for permission to quote from the Solomon Kane and King Kull stories by Robert E. Howard.

*Richard Minter* whose support shines through every page of this book.

*Will Murray* for his comments on Polaris and uncounted letters of information and encouragement.

*Gene Reed* for the loan of the Kline and Cummings novels of his collection.

*Leonard Robbins* who made available original unpublished bibliographic materials from his personal files.

*John Roy* for permission to quote from his book, *A Guide to Barsoom* (Ballentine Books, 1976).

*Fred J. Siehl* who provided copies of *All-Story* and *Argosy* from his collection with a superb disregard for the perils of cross-country mailings.

*Syracuse University* and the *George C. Arents Research Library*, and particularly *Carolyn A. Davis*, for assistance in obtaining copies of stories available in no other place.

*Robert Weinberg,* for more than a decade of help, and *Blazing Publications Inc.* for permission to quote from *Argosy All-Story Argosy, Detective Fiction Weekly, Dime Detective.*

# Contents

# Introduction

This, the second volume of *Yesterday's Faces*, continues the story of series characters in pulp magazine fiction.

The pulp magazine, that denigrated art form, barely existed at the turn of the century. In twenty years, multitudes of pulps would jostle wildly on the newstand. But in 1900, only *The Argosy* represented the coming swarms.

*The Argosy* offered fiction of an accessible and speculative sort, printed on cheap pulp paper. It could be found in the company of a handful of semi-pulps—the general fiction magazines that were aimed at that ambiguous target, the American Family. The contents of these magazines resembled a plate of scrambled eggs: Non-fiction, poetry, sickly humor, occasional photographs, all mingled with fiction of singular blandness.

These few magazines were overwhelmed by the quality magazines: *The Saturday Evening Post, The Atlantic, The Ladies' Home Journal* and *The Woman's Home Companion*. These were dressed in fine paper and scented with cultural excellence. Around their skirts swarmed the lesser magazines, each gripping its morsel of the reading public.

Off in the corner, very humble, giggled the dime novels.

The dime novels were pamphlets of some thirty pages, whose illustrated covers reeled with peril and violence. They occupied the niche later to be seized by the pulps. The dime novels were the spiritual ancestors of the pulps, as the general fiction magazines were the physical ancestors.

The dime novels were raucous, simple, shallow, inexpensive, and everywhere. Because they were neither respectable nor literary, they had no qualms about using simple materials. The stories were filled with action, the characters uncomplex. Coincidence resolved what the author could not.

From the dime novels precipitated story forms and character types that would deeply influence the course of pulp magazine development.

To begin with, the dime novels were strongly character oriented. Frank Merriwell, Jesse James or Nick Carter caught readers' imaginations and, more to the point, assured a profitable level of sales. The personality sold issues, every week. The personality endured through endless series, piling up libraries of fiction—the *Nick Carter Weekly, Buffalo Bill Stories, Young Sleuth Library, Tip Top....*

Lethal, chaste, capable, those figures fleshed out the readers' ideal, the fictional daydream being a vehicle of the inner wish. In the behavior of these successful series characters, you can trace the ideals and attitudes of the time. Buffalo Bill adventured across the prairie, but he embodied the standards of the middle class and confirmed their assumptions concerning

1

merit and virtue.

Eventually the dime novels were absorbed by the pulps. The form vanished. The character types, narrative techniques, story themes persisted.

The pulps were voracious. They swallowed everything—Sherlock Holmes and Shakespeare, western adventure and the speculation of astronomers. Great masses of material, whatever tickled the public taste, was taken up, reworked into hotly moving fiction, and rushed out for sale at the corner kiosk. Since the public enjoyed series heroes, series heroes were provided in abundance. Not all of these derived directly from the dime novels. Slick paper magazines and books made their own contributions, if unwittingly. The pulps absorbed successful character types wherever they appeared.

In Volume 1 of this study, we met a number of series characters who exerted great influence on the development of pulp magazine fiction. These included such notable men as Hopalong Cassidy (1906), the lightning-quick gun fighter in a West that never was; the Lone Wolf (1914) and Cleek (1910), brilliant criminals who reformed for love and thereafter fought evil; and the Just Men (1905), those deadly unknowns who administered justice when the Law stood helpless.

While these justice figures and bent heroes tested the dimensions of their worlds, other series characters were making their appearance. They arrived at about the same time—for our story, although it is presented in sequential chapters, tells of concurrent events. Literary history is not a braided rope but a slowly woven tapestry, formed line by line and year by year, whose bright dots of color and incomprehensible lines gradually take coherent shapes, given time enough and skill.

In this volume, we will examine several more types of series characters whose personalities and adventures shaped the plastic stuff of popular fiction. Here, for example, are investigators of mysteries—the scientific detectives, who function in a rational world, using the instruments of science. And a second group, the occult investigators, who prefer non-rational means to achieve their wonders.

Next we will meet Edgar Rice Burroughs' two major characters: Tarzan, who is the superman in harsh Eden, and John Carter, the first great figure of the interplanetary romance.

And, finally, we will follow out the remarkable development of the planetary romance as it unfolded through the magazines of the 1920s.

It was long ago. But these echoes shake our reading still.

Huntsville, Ala.                                              Robert Sampson
January 1984

# I—Willemite Fluorescing

**1**

"It seems," said Dr. John Watson, "a very delicate test."

He stood in a hospital laboratory, examining the experimental results achieved by a Mr. Sherlock Holmes. The two had just met. Holmes frequently borrowed the laboratory facilities to conduct his experiments, he being a dedicated dabbler in chemistry.

Although no one appreciated it at the time, other large matters met in that same laboratory. There you can observe the ghosts of science, detection and medicine formally touching hands in public. How casually they are introduced. You might overlook their presence—except that we are so wise, ninety years later, and see so much.

Yes, cried Holmes, it was a delicate test. Enthusiasm gripped him. A beautiful test. Beautiful. In the beaker, brown precipitate sheeted downward. Look at this. It would have hanged ————————. It would have convicted ————————. For the first time, a test clearly demonstrates that a bloodstain is human.

His lean face shone. It was Chapter 1 of "A Study in Scarlet," *Beaton's Christmas Annual* for 1887, and the famous friendship has begun over a beaker of blood stain.

That long-drawn romance of science and detection had formally declared itself, too.

It had started—this matter of scientific detection—some years earlier than Sherlock Holmes. Roots underlie roots. But Conan Doyle's medical training, shining through The Sacred Writings, brought together laboratory glassware and a man who knew how to use it. There is not much science in the Sherlock Holmes series. But Holmes made possession of laboratory apparatus respectable. The public was fascinated.

Once you define the form, however rudimentary, then evolution begins and eventually you stand amazed at the results. It would be realistic to look for the roots of scientific detection in the dime novels. Seek to identify that character who first used a new device to solve the mystery of the vanished bonds or to identify the Spectre Indian Chief. Something like that. The dime novels missed no flicker of public interest. Let a single headline appear and—lo!—somebody wrote a series about it:

*FEARLESS WOODA AND HIS STEAM TELEVISION; or,*
*Investigating the Strange Melodies from*
*Northfield*

Whatever the first root, science and technology came roaring into the public awareness in the final decades of the 1800s. The detective story, now becoming a popular form, was bound to make the obvious connection.

What the public considered science was, in reality, applied engineering. So the scientific detective story, as it developed, would be apt to substitute gadgets for science. The public taste was for things that flew and rolled. Give the public submarines, air ships, steam men, mysterious drugs striking the victim into a state precisely resembling death. Give them hypnotism and powered vehicles howling along the road at 40 mph. Real science—that's what the public wanted.

If you are going to have a scientific detective, he can flower in several ways. First is the way of the cold intellect: scientific, heartless, dispassionate, analytical. Second, there is the medical road—very popular—with the hero a doctor and of the elite, being also aware of the possibilities in dilute solutions and botanical abnormalities. Finally, there is the easier road of the detective who uses scientific devices and procedures to solve his puzzles.

Bless those fine devices.

They permit the detective to slice open the mystery as if he were carving a melon. The device can be a tool to clarify a clue. Or the detective may use it to start him on a long chain of pseudodeductive logic. Or the device so scares the villain that he leaps up, on the final page, to confess all, his blood-stained hands clasping and unclasping.

While not always the case, but frequently enough, the scientific gadget in a detective story is really a magic wand.

Hey, presto. The puzzle is unwound.

Scientific deduction. Wonderful, wonderful, beautiful, beautiful science.

Back in London, Holmes and Watson took up rooms at Baker Street. There Holmes installed a table of chemical apparatus and, amid curious glassware and reagents, committed powerful odors. Soon every successful detective would operate a private laboratory. Each would be competent in the art of chemistry, physics and the detection of subtle poisons.

How contagious it all was. By the time we reach down time to the *Doc Savage Magazine* in 1933, the main characters of that admirable series will be operating five private laboratories and hauling still another one around in suitcases. It would be a far cry from Holmes' table of stewing retorts.

After Holmes, other detectives adopted the personal laboratory rather quickly. By 1904, Nick Carter has not only established a lab but uses it in the creation of advanced gadgets:

> ...a small bomb about the size of an almond, containing a very powerful explosive, more effective than nitroglycerine, invented by Nick and prepared by a secret process in his own laboratory. When exploded, the force acted in only one direction, making it perfectly safe for a person to stand within two feet of the object to be blown open.[1]

Nick and his boys were always up to date. Their series was as sensitive as litmus paper to fine alterations in public interests. Let a new concept or device appear and it was, at once, scooped up into a Nick Carter adventure. Through the pages of *Nick Carter Weekly* (and all the other dime novels, for that matter), you can trace the penetration of science and technology into Turn-of-the-Century America:

> —Nick Carter uses an X-ray machine to photograph an Ace of Diamonds, conveniently metallic, concealed in the villain's pocket. (And a splendid radiation burn that fellow must have received.)
> —Nick cracks an otherwise perfect murder after receiving an accidental telephone call that has been transmitted by induction between two uninsulated telephone wires.
> —Nick receives a valuable clue to a murder by scanning a silent movie film, made in New York City, and observing the fiend photographed in the act.

It is clear that the scientific devices are being used as fascinating gadgets. In both the Holmes and Carter stories, the science is decorative. But it would soon grow integral to the story.

Science, of course, is various things to various people. To some, it may suggest white-coated men in a place of lofting glass, where the vermitzer machine buzzes bluely and the air is scented with ozone and caged animals.

To others, less movie minded, science is an organized system of thinking and experimentation to disclose facts of the natural world. It is an accumulation of reverifiable physical facts. It is a method of procedure, a technique of thinking logically from the obvious to the unexpected.

All this based on demonstrated fact. "Give me facts," cried Holmes. His personal method is purely observation of fact, leavened by knowledge, with conclusions ordered in a neat chain. Very persuasive. Imitators instantly picked up Holmes' patter (behold page after page of Nick Carter deducing from a dust grain), and draped themselves in dazzling garments of intellect.

Given facts and the disciplined reasoning techniques of science and you could—well, you could, for example, sit in a chair and reason out a mystery. No guns. No disguises. No rushing into peril. Just pure mental application.

As, for example, demonstrated by that interesting character created by Baroness Orczy—the Old Man in the Corner. He sits in an English tea shop, picking at a tangle of string, and explaining the most complex criminal problems.

Hardly any figure could be further from the hero of an action story. The old man, exceedingly shabby, ugly, compulsively knots and unknots his length of string as he deluges newspaperwoman Polly Burton with his monologue:

> Mysteries! There is no such thing as a mystery in connection with any crime, providing that intelligence is brought to bear upon its investigation.[2]

Those are his first recorded words, appearing in 1901, when Holmes was in full cry. Like Holmes, the unnamed Old Man is a creature of reason. His grasp of detail is awesome, his knowledge comprehensive. He carries a walletful of pictures of the principals involved in the crimes he discusses. His intellect hovers like a hawk over the fields of others' passions.

The more peculiar the hero, the more he seems separated from society. The Old Man is no exception. He is consciously debarred from active participation in society—just why is never explained. He might work with the police. But, really, they wouldn't have him, he says. Anyway, his sympathy is more usually with the criminal.

The Old Man represents the intellectual method whittled to a point: the insistence on facts, then reconstruction of the most probable sequence of events by an intelligence that is, at once, isolated and of exceeding power, regardless of the shabby exterior and grotesque face.

An even more renowned practitioner of the purely intellectual method appeared in 1905. This paragon was Professor Augustus S.F.X. Van Dusen, Ph.D., LL.D., F.R.S., M.D., and M.D.S. He was familiarly called The Thinking Machine. Van Dusen first reached the public in a six-part short story ("The Problem of Cell 13") serialized in the *Boston American* newspaper, beginning with the October 30, 1905, issue.[3]

The Professor is as close to pure intelligence as is possible for mortal human. In person, he resembles a citizen of the remote future. He is tiny, a little feeble man with an immense head—he wears a size 8 hat. His hair is straw colored. His eyes are blue slits behind thick glasses. "... the face was white with the pallor of the student; his mouth was a bloodless slit."[4]

He is, in short, the image of those creatures with bulging heads who used to appear on the covers of *Amazing Stories*, hurling rays at beautiful Earth girls.

Professor Van Dusen is more formidable than any death-ray slinger. He boils with impatience. He is testy, tart, searing in speech. His normal voice is one of perpetual irritation. He is so intensely busy. And everything—everything—interrupts!

In all respects, he is the outstanding scientist and logician of his day.

The name, The Thinking Machine, was bestowed on him by the Russian world chess champion. Van Dusen, who had never played chess, defeated the Russian after a single day's instruction. The game over, the Professor irritably gave up chess and strode back to his laboratory and more pleasurable academic disputes.

For above all, Van Dusen is a scientist. He maintains a personal laboratory and, in it, he immerses himself for half weeks at a time, working continuously through the hours. Only rarely does he focus his intellect on secular problems.

Almost always, these problems are brought to him by Hutchinson Hatch, a newspaper man "lean, wiry, hard as nails." Hatch is the filter through which most problems are presented to Van Dusen. Once the Professor becomes interested, it ends up Hatch's duty to go forth in search of those few facts that complete the chain of logic.

"I want facts. Facts," Van Dusen cries, glaring enigmatically around.

Once the facts are in place and the solution obvious to any intelligent being (except the reader, Hatch and the police), then The Thinking Machine arranges for the necessary raids and arrests. These are handled by Detectives Mallory and Cunningham, two burly competent professionals, tough but prosaic. They are willing to be ordered about by an inscrutable genius. They accept his thorny personality because he does solve cases. You intelligent readers will already know that The Professor has only contempt for the brains of the police. But considering the cases he accepts, it is no wonder that the police so frequently find themselves helpless.

These cases include, for example, murder by vacuum, disappearance from a locked guarded office, horrors in a haunted house, more horrors in a disappearing house. There is leakage of privileged information from a stock-broker's office; theft of radium from an impregnable laboratory; an automobile that habitually vanishes along an isolated, wall-lined road guarded by a policeman at each end. And there was the case where footprints led across the snow to the center of a huge empty lot, then stopped short ....

Back against the chair cushion goes Van Dusen's head. His eyes lift upward. His slender white fingers press together at the tips. An almost visible nimbus of thought crackles about him, as intellect, nourished by facts, orders events in a rational universe.

> Every scientist knows that we gain knowledge through observation and clear thinking. And clear thinking—or logic—tells us that two and two make four, not sometimes, but all the time.[5]

The Thinking Machine stories were written by Jacques Futrelle, an American author born in Georgia, who died during the Titanic disaster. (Six new Thinking Machine stories were lost when the old ship went down.)

Forty-eight short stories are known. Most were published in newspapers and Sunday magazine sections, beginning in 1905. Many—not all—were collected in two books: *The Thinking Machine* (1907) and *The Thinking Machine on the Case* (1908). The Professor also makes a brief appearance at the end of the novel *The Chase of the Golden Plate* (1906). And a Thinking Machine novelette, "The Haunted Bell," is included in the 1909 *The Diamond Master*.

During 1912 *The Popular Magazine* had begun publication of a new series of Van Dusen stories. Under the series title, "The Thinking Machine," four short stories appeared: "The Tragedy of the Life Raft" (August 1), "Five Millions by Wireless" (August 15), "The Case of the Scientific Murderer" (September 1), and "The Jackdaw" (September 15).

More recently, seven stories were reprinted in *Ellery Queen's Mystery Magazine*: Spring 1942, February and November 1949; June and October 1950; June 1952, and December 1958.[6] "The Problem of Cell 13" has been reprinted time without end in everything.

In their time, the Thinking Machine stories were immensely popular. Futrelle was occupied to the hilt in writing them. Age has hardly dimmed their flavor. Through them, supernatural overtones boom weirdly and the situations are frequently impossible.

"Don't say that," flares the Professor. "You make me angry when you say that. Nothing is impossible. Nothing."

Perhaps he was correct. Certainly the impossible, rationally explained, became a popular story form in years to come, exploited by many hands, and a particular stock in trade of John Dickson Carr.

However great Van Dusen's influence with police and press, he remains, like the Old Man in the Corner, a deliberate isolate. Except for his infrequent cases—when he mingles effectively with the outside world—he stands apart. His back is three-quarters turned to daily life, his mind immersed in technical problems.

In spite of this stance, he occupies a unique position. The police acclaim him. International science accepts him as arbiter of disputes. Even academia, that dark and bloody ground, submits to the vigor of his intellect. Worldly status lifts the Professor. You wonder how he has the opportunity to indulge himself in the classic posture of the justice figure, who stands remote outside society, as if it were contained in a very small glass globe; reaching in to fix matters; then retiring again, huge, to more private concerns.

**2-**

Toward the end of the 1800s, science was in the air. A rising tide of discovery, new knowledge, evolving technology, foamed through the final decades and came boiling out into the new century, indiscriminately hurling forth argosies of wonders. Each day brought new invention. And some of these, huge with unanticipated consequences, already clawed the social fabric, so that pundits roared with dismay and the newspaper-reading public marveled at crystal towers to come.

Popular fiction, that bright mirror, gleamed with new images.

> ... the stories are important in that they reflect the public mind and attitude. They reflect a transition in values. Early twentieth century America was a period of faith in science, technology, industry, a time of confidence in man's ability to solve the problems of the world.[7]

Part of that confidence, as we have seen, was in the ability of applied science to solve almost any crime. As a way of thought, the scientific method was not limited to genius professors and manipulators of string. Another kind of scientific detective had already sprung to popularity.

To call upon heads wiser than our own, Ellery Queen indicates that, in 1894, in England, the first example of this new species was published: *Stories from the Diary of a Doctor* by L.T. Meade and Dr. Clifford Halifax.[8] The book brought to focus (if it did not create) the medical mystery. Queen calls the book "pseudo-scientific."

But the public takes what it wants, pseudo-scientific or not. Books about doctors were popular then, as now. Combine that form with the mystery—with 90% of England gone Holmes mad—and you bring forth a steaming new literary line.

Great medical sleuths came early. One of the greatest arrived almost at once—Dr. John Evelyn Thorndyke, whose adventures are contained in 27 novels and short story collections, 1907 to 1942. Thorndyke was created by R. Austin Freeman (1862-1943), himself a licensed physician (eye-ear-nose-throat). He practiced both in Africa (where he lost his health) and England (where he enjoyed no particular success). Eventually he gave up medicine for writing. With publication of *The Red Thumb Mark* (1907)—his fourth book—he found the vein that he was to follow successfully.

*The Red Thumb Mark* appeared in the new morning of the formal detective story. Freeman created the scientific detective story and planted the field later reaped by legions of medical detectives.

*The Red Thumb Mark*, itself, turns about the device of forged fingerprints, a sophisticated concept even today. The idea flickered through the 1930-1940 pulp fiction—the general approach being that a hero, knocked unconscious, would rouse to find suspicious crumbs of gelatine under his fingernails and his fingerprints all over the murdered man's possessions. In these action stories, nothing at all is made of Freeman's concern that, since it is perfectly possible to forge fingerprints, then the presence of fingerprints at the scene of a crime does not definitely establish a person's presence there without other corroborative evidence.[9]

Beginning with the short story "The Case of Oscar Brodski" (later collected into the 1912 *The Singing Bone*), Freeman devises a new narrative twist. The story is split into two parts: the first shows commission of the crime; the second follows Thorndyke (as related by his associate, Jervis), as he clears up the matter.

This is the inverted detective story—the reader knowing almost everything, Thorndyke knowing nothing. Yet Thorndyke invariably astonishes. It is a tricky technique, full of dangers for the writer. You watch with admiration as Freeman brilliantly handles it through many other stories.

Dr. Thorndyke may seem a strange individual to figure in a discussion of pulp magazine fiction. In almost no way can the Freeman/Thorndyke work be considered representative of the type. While there is action during Thorndyke's investigations, and even a death trap or so, the primary thrust is intellectual.

In spite of this radical approach, and Freeman's insistence on technical accuracy, the Thorndyke stories appeared intermittently in the pulps. Most of his short stories first appeared in the English *Pearson's Magazine*. A scattering of these was later reprinted in the United States in *Argosy, Flynn's, Amazing Detective Stories*, and, later, *Ellery Queen's Mystery Magazine* and *The Saint Mystery Magazine*.

"The Stolen Ingots" was published in the September 15, 1923, *Argosy-All Story*. A box of gold ingots has miraculously changed into a box of gilded lead bars at some time during transit. Using ship manifests and applying his knowledge of specific gravities of lead and gold, Thorndyke locates the stolen shipment. A simple matter. Inspector Badger and Jervis share the discomforts of a sea chase to catch the plotters. They are, as usual, at sea in more ways than one.

The October 20, 1923, *Argosy-All Story*, included "A Fisher of Men," which is filled with particularly satisfying Thorndyke scenes. As usual, he is perniciously omniscient. He baits the police and his associate, Jervis, with a pleasantly ironic tone. Our amusement at his little ways is qualified; he would do the same to us from that Olympian height of detachment appropriate to one who recognizes the significance of a *Clausilia biplacata*—an almost extinct species of shell—and, what's worse, knows the two places in England where it can be found. In summary, Thorndyke deduces a man's disappearance from the articles contained in a traveling shaving kit (his performance is pure Sherlock Holmes). After this feat, he proceeds confidently, and with faultless accuracy, into the deeps of England to dig up a missing case of blue diamonds buried along the river. "You are a wonderful man, Thorndyke," Jervis remarks. "You foresee everything." And so he does.

*Flynn's* reprinted a number of the Dr. Thorndyke cases. These appeared intermittently from 1924 to at least 1927. All stories have not been traced. At this period in its life, *Flynn's* was offering a curious mixture of English and American detective fiction. The proportions varied from issue to issue. Such prominent figures as J.G. Reeder (Edgar Wallace), Reggie Fortune (H.C. Bailey), Dr. Hailey (Anthony Wynne), and other high notables of the period moved through the magazine.

Among these splendors, the Thorndyke stories brightly shine. The stories are clean, solid, modern—hard oak and crystal. Nothing is faked. The science is rigorously exact. The prose strides firmly on, the story unfolding with a leisurely inevitability. There are an agreeable number of violent deaths and the narratives brim with corpses found, almost complete, the circumstances being suspicious.

Typical cases include a variety of interesting subjects:

"Nebuchadnezzar's Seal," *Flynn's*, January 31, 1925, weaves together antique faking, murder by cyanide, a series of elaborate deductions based on impressions left by a cane tip and the theft of Old King N's original seal.

In "The Green Check Jacket," *Flynn's* March 28, 1925, Thorndyke's microscopic examination of dust reveals it to contain specific *foraminifera* (microscopic shells), and he forms a hypothesis which swiftly exposes a double murder concealed in a prehistoric flint mine.

"Left by Flame," *Flynn's*, March 12, 1927, refers to the few fragments remaining of an unfortunate fellow who stood unwisely close to an exploding bomb. Evidence indicates that he was holding his left hand in his left hand. Thorndyke thinks otherwise.

For all his merits, Thorndyke lacked that crowd-pleasing flair which, in the 1930s, would bloom forth in titles such as:

The *Dr. Thorndyke Magazine* or *John Thorndyke, Super Detective.*

At Flynn's he was popular, although not loudly celebrated, but he was treasured by a dedicated circle of readers. Hugo Gernsback (who first published *Amazing Stories* in 1926) resurrected the first Thorndyke short story, "The Blue Sequin." This had been published in *Pearson's Magazine* (1908). Gernsback republished it as "The Blue Spangle" in the June 1930 issue of *Amazing Detective Tales,* a retitling of the *Scientific Detective Monthly.* In this story, a woman is found dead in her compartment on an English train, a horrible wound in her head. No one could have entered the compartment, yet there she lies. An artist is suspected for no good reason other than because he had seen her last and quarreled with her. Instantly, Thorndyke has no less than six possible ways she could have died. Use of his caliper-gauge, microscope, and some mild mystification concerning ox-gall reveal the true story.

The Thorndyke short stories were published in several books, the most complete edition being the *Dr. Thorndyke Omnibus* (1932) which reprinted all but two of the short stories. These were finally reprinted in *Ellery Queen's Mystery Magazine* and are rare enough in the United States to bear mentioning here.

"Percival Bland's Proxy," originally written in 1918, was reprinted in the Spring 1942 *EQMM*. It is a formal "inverted" mystery. In Part I, we watch Bland fake his own death—establishing a false identity, buying a skeleton, framing the circumstances of a fire, dressing the skeleton and adorning it with slabs of beef and cow hide, then firing his rooming house. Alas for dedicated deceit. In Part II, Thorndyke and Jervis see through the gull in a microsecond—poor Bland has purchased the skeleton of a negro female. We then receive a pithy Thorndyke lecture on what a fire actually does to a cadaver, as opposed to a bare skeleton. And Mr. Bland, sorrowing, seats himself behind those cold hard walls.

The second story, reprinted in the May 1949 *EQMM*, is "The Missing Mortgagee," also an inverted story, also written in 1918. Part I shows a young man in the toils of a greasy money lender. When that wicked person accidentally tumbles over a cliff, the young man switches identity with him, recovers his note and the deceased's wallet, and lights out for a new life. Unfortunately, the young man's life is insured by that company which employs Dr. Thorndyke as a consultant. Thorndyke speedily discovers that the corpse (faceless because of the sea's action) is not that of a 35-year old man but of an old wretch with false teeth and a heart condition. Little good the discovery does anyone; the young man escapes to France. But then, the wicked partner does not get the insurance. Or did he want it? Well ....

In accomplishing his marvels, Thorndyke generously uses all those scientific devices that make glad the heart. Through his stories pass a sparkling series of telephoto cameras, X-ray machines, microscopes, equipment of the chemical laboratory and the dissection room. Personally, Thordyke travels with a little green case loaded with miniaturized equipment. You never know when you might need a hand lens or scapel or a microscope the size of a flea. It is all sound, useful equipment.

For Thorndyke, above all other considerations, is a professional. He does not consider himself a detective but a specialized medical investigator. Wrote Freeman: "He is a medico-legal expert and his methods are of medico-legal science."[10]

Which is to say that he applies medical knowledge and laboratory techniques to criminal problems—explaining events and identifying the remains of the deceased, and generating enough evidence to convince the most hardheaded jury.

He is, by the way, an independent consultant, rather than a formal private investigator. He has no official position with the police who are rather wary of him and his sudden miracles. An insurance company retains him as a consultant to provide expert medical opinion in cases of violent death—or suspicious death—which frequently comes to the same thing.

In person, Dr. John Thorndyke stands out like a tower of stone. Erect, strongly built, he draws the eye. From him blazes force of character. He radiates dignity—not that pompous egoism of the mediocre man contaminated by power, but that informed assurance, attributed to Roman senators, which is attained by unrelenting service to standards of merit.

His face is handsome. Freeman saw no reason to make his detective unique because of either ugliness or eccentricities, both of which suggest problems of the psyche. So Thorndyke looks good, indeed. His face is often described as "symmetrical," the brows level, the nose straight. Over the years, his hair gradually became a dark iron-gray. Says one of the narrators during the series: "It was a strangely calm—even immobile face ... it conveyed a feeling of attentiveness and concentration, and especially of power."

Jervis, a part-time Watson, notes that when Thorndyke is struck by some particularly barbed insight, the impassivity becomes still more rigid, freezing to an immobility as "uncommunicative as the granite face of an Egyptian statue."

Thorndyke's personality is difficult. Outwardly he seems friendly enough, a warm, pleasing man. This face he meticulously maintains even when he feels neither outgoing nor warm. Beneath it all lies a calm reserve. Few people penetrate there. He stands back, just a little, never giving fully; his self-control is exquisite and he is delicately cautious.

The natural climate of his mind is a slightly chilled calm. This creeps into the stories. When Thorndyke is off scene, you can hear the jangle of life. At Thorndyke's first words, precision steps forward, order arrives and the disciplined imagination. Reality, tangled and abashed, sits up straight in its chair. For Thorndyke is all that a scientist should be—which is rarely what scientists are.

Not for Thorndyke, the Thinking Machine's state of harsh irritation. Thorndyke is imperturbable. Unassailed by situation, he can regard a dismembered corpse with the identical detachment he gives to a study of cane marks on a path. His mind reasons powerfully, accurately:

> "He doesn't think like any other man," says his assistant, Polton. "[He has] a different kind of intelligence. Ordinary men have to reason from visible facts. He doesn't. He reasons from facts which his imagination tells him exist, but which nobody can see." (*A Silent Witness*)

Thorndyke seeks truth. Only truth. Regardless of whose dog gets kicked. When he is satisfied as to a point, that point has verified not once but twenty times.

> *Thorndyke*: "My hypothesis was perfectly sound, perfectly consistent in all its parts, and perfectly congruous with all the known facts, but it did not follow therefore that it was true. It was entirely unverified...." (*A Silent Witness*)

That hyper-cautious, scrupulously rigid precision is characteristic of formal scientific work. And it is this trait which gives solid completeness to a Thorndyke summation. He has tested and proven each fact. His evidence is always over-determined. If Thorndyke has a fault, it is a tendency to be over-precise, too elaborately exact. You can rarely quibble with him, as a result. His evidence is as conclusive as that of his later imitators in fiction is almost always shoddy.

Those great men we meet in fiction seem to require a reflector against which their blaze is magnified. The great man's associates are liable to be of lesser luster than himself. At least it is so in fiction. Traces of this appear in Thorndyke's relations with those around him. It is to Freeman's credit (with the Sherlock Holmes characters ever before him) that he developed so many strong secondary characters to support the good doctor's work.

While different people narrate portions of most Thorndyke stories, the narrator who appears most frequently is Dr. Christopher Jervis, colleague and friend. He is in more of the short stories, in the novels less often. There are enough unresolved problems about his life that you have some problem in constructing a coherent biography.

The most important parts are available. Jervis and Thorndyke were classmates together in medical school, Thorndyke being slightly the elder. After graduation, Jervis was not quite able to find his niche. When introduced in *The Red Thumb Mark*, he is unemployed and in lean financial shape. He meets Thorndyke by accident—Jervis is standing outside Thorndyke's residence, at 6A King's Bench Walk, admiring the Christopher Wren architecture, when the great man walks up. (In all later stories, the address is given as 5A King's Bench Walk.)

A somewhat different version of their meeting is given in the novelette "Thirty-One New Inn." In his introduction to *The Best Dr. Thorndyke Detective Stories* (1973), E.F. Bleiler indicates that this novelette was the first story about Thorndyke. It was not, however, published until after *The Red Thumb Mark* had appeared. When "Thirty-One New Inn" was published in the January 1911 *Adventure*, a paragraph was added referring to the Thorndyke-Jervis meeting in *The Red Thumb Mark*.

These niceties to one side, it is in Chapter 10 of "Thirty-One New Inn" that Thorndyke offers Jervis the position of his "junior or assistant." Jervis finds this far more satisfactory than filling in for other doctors who are temporarily absent from their practice, and so their association begins.

(To complicate matters more, "Thirty-One New Inn" was expanded and published, in 1911, as the novel *The Mystery of 31, New Inn*. Literary history is full of interesting variations.)

In later stories, Jervis becomes Thordyke's junior colleague in the practice. The sheer volume of work surprises him. Forensic medicine is far from general practice. Thorndyke does make house calls, however. He must view corpses and the murder scene, and he investigates with an eye to detail that would delight Nick Carter.

It is pleasant to note that Jervis is intelligent and well-informed. True, he suffers from slowness of wit whenever Thorndyke is around—that is an occupational hazard of Watsons. In other aspects, he is tall and married to a charming, unobtrusive wife who rarely enters the stories.

Jervis has no talent for deductive reasoning, however competent he is medically. Occasionally Thorndyke will prod him to think in that deductive manner so easy to heroes of medical detective stories. But Thorndyke, in these moods, is also patronizing. The lessons end sourly. Jervis bristles. He cannot deduce and refuses to be bludgeoned into doing so.

Of all Thorndyke's circle, the major figure is not Jervis but Polton—Nathaniel Polton, a first-water genius. Polton serves as part-time housekeeper and cook and full-time laboratory assistant. His mechanical inventiveness rivals that of Tom Swift. He can build anything "from an astronomical clock to a microscope objective." In addition, he is an analytical chemist, a photographic specialist of rare competence, is talented in metal-working and carpentry. Generally gifted, he sets the pattern for a one-man scientific support staff.

This pattern, established here, will repeat itself through the years in other magazines, other series. Polton-like figures appear constantly. Thus Lord Peter Wimsey turns to his servant, Bunter, for photographic marvels. Thirteen years later, Professor Brownlee will be the technical arm of the *Spider* magazine, whipping up antidotes and sleeping gases and analyzing buckets of germs with rare zeal and rarer speed.

The technical support character is a significant addition to the form. It places the unofficial investigator on the same plane with the police technical facilities. It gives the hero lots more time to dart about shooting and detecting. It also adds to the effect of technical wheels grinding out wonders behind the scenes. And, conveniently, it allows the hero access to all sorts of technical accomplishments that do not have to be justified in detail.

In person, Polton is either a very old man, heavily wrinkled, or else he is a relatively young, man, also heavily wrinkled. There is some confusion between early and late novels and the point is evaded, rather than cleared up. It is possible to ignore the discrepancy. Polton is a genius, his natural habitat in that laboratory workshop on the third floor of 5A, where modest miracles are performed daily. His biography is a major feature of the 1940 *Mr. Polton Explains*, a fascinating book, filled with a love of clockwork.

Various other characters look into the Thorndyke series from time to time. There are Superintendent Miller, and Inspectors Badger and Blandy, all Scotland Yard men. Wonder of wonders, they do not come to Thorndyke to solicit his ministrations in matters too complex for them to handle. Not at all. These are close-mouthed policemen, visiting Thorndyke as he investigates as a private individual, and no more apt to offer official information than the police anywhere. They are tough, competent professionals, respecting Thorndyke without that ill-advised adoration which other authors find necessary to raise the status of their hero.

For his part, Thorndyke is even more closemouthed with the police than he is with Jervis—and he tells Jervis next to nothing. ("Thorndyke will never tell you anything until he can tell you everything.")

The lawyer, Mr. Brodribb, appears frequently. He is fat, rosy, a sort of crusty Pickwick, but—like most people in a Freeman story—a professional, competent and wary in his speciality. It gives great satisfaction to read fiction where the minor characters are not fools.

Robert Anstey, King's Counsel, is another figure. A cheerful, witty man, he affects a light, teasing manner toward Thorndyke's technical medical activities. He can be critical of Thorndyke and offers a point of view far different from that of Jervis. That altered angle of view adds to the sharpness with which we see Thorndyke. It freshens the atmosphere and brings out character depth in a way that the Watson's essentially uncritical view can never do.

Characters like Dr. Thorndyke are influential in ways more subtle than providing an easily copied example. Key figures in fiction exert their influence by limiting possibilities. They are so right—they work so well—that it is hard to imagine similar characters in radically different situations. Like immense suns, major characters are so hotly powerful that they warp all space near them. They polarize their immediate surroundings, existing so intensely that their example virtually dictates how their type of story will be handled.

Characters, narrative style, plot development, incident selection—all become part of the convention of How Best To Handle This Type Of Story. The inertia of success is formidable. So the matter of derivative characters is more complex than it looks. It is not so much a matter of direct copying, as it is the writer's attempt to employ an appealing character type within the conventions unwittingly imposed by the original major character.

**3-**

From 1905-1911, almost every year saw new figures flame up and begin detecting scientifically. Or something close to it. In 1908, Algernon Blackwood's John Silence arrived, a psychic detective who was adept at medicine, scientific thinking and disembodied spirits. Next appeared Luther Trant (1909) and Craig Kennedy (1910), both massively dedicated to detecting by use of scientific equipment. Carnaki (1910) and Dr. Wycherley (1911) both combined scientific apparatus and psychic sensitivity in their specialities.

Through the magazines tumbled an array of doctors and professorial types detecting for all they were worth. If they were not leading characters, then they contrived to be foils or villains or secondary figures aiding the police:

> "Yes, yes. I'm a doctor. Here, let me look at the poor fellow. Good God! He's dead—killed by the bite of a rare Tibetan Snow Viper. It seems incredible!"

Wonderful, forgettable men. You found them in *Pearson's Magazine, The Strand, Hampton's Magazine, Short Stories*, the new *Blue Book* (formerly *Monthly Story Magazine*), *Cosmopolitan, McClure's, People's Ideal Fiction, Argosy*...

The uproar caused by the discovery of X-rays—

LADIES! X-RAY-PROOF CLOTHING AVAILABLE HERE!!

... was nothing compared to the uproar that developed when the popular press discovered the theories of Dr. Sigmund Freud. Since Freud was a psychologist—as well as a perverted fiend—and since psychologists were, by profession, hypnotizers all (except William James and he was from Boston), psychology found itself prominently featured in popular fiction.

Well, it was not psychology, exactly . . .

Detectives who were, only five minutes before, professors and doctors, were suddenly fitted with fresh new titles. "Psychologists" they were, as, by the early 1920s, they would all become "Criminologists." But Psychologists, now, using the latest of scientific equipment, their wonders to perform.

Those of you still reading so long after your bedtime will recall that Dr. Thorndyke used all manner of advanced equipment, although, in his stories, the main emphasis was placed on people and their problems. With the coming of Luther Trant, in 1909, the equipment received a very great deal more attention.

According to the *Foreword* of *The Achievements of Luther Trant* (1910):

> The methods which the fictitious *Trant* . . . here uses to solve the mysteries . . . are real methods; the tests he employs are real tests . . . . *Luther Trant*, therefore, nowhere in this book needs to invent or devise an experiment or an instrument for any of the results he here attains; he has merely to adapt a part of the tried and accepted experiments of modern scientific psychology.

The stories are more interesting than mere accounts of equipment manipulation. Before the first wire is hooked up, Trant must feel his way through the complicated messes people have built with their lives. Only when he understands the situation does the equipment come out. The hardware confirms the deduction. Only then.

Although you may find yourself convinced that the hardware wrote some the plots.

Trant represents the test and evaluation school of psychology. The psychologist does not listen to you describe the inside of your head, as does the psychiatrist or the psychoanalyst. The psychologist humps his muscles against statistical deviations and is enthralled by response times and correlation factors. Among his specialized tools are those measuring physical response to emotional stress. From these, Luther Trant's usual equipment is drawn.

Trant, himself, is a young man of exhausting vigor, surrounded by an almost audible discharge of energy. In person, he is a stumpy red-head, well muscled. His movements are quick, his voice decisive and abrupt, the words rushing after his swooping mind.

Eagerness plucks at him. Enthusiasm seethes his blood. It is important that he press on rapidly; there is so much experience to engulf. He can barely wait. His mismatched eyes glitter with urgency (the right eye is much bluer) and that small scar under the right eye flushes red. It is all so clear: Best that we demonstrate it this way . . . .

Restless, compelled, he stepped directly from the farm into university life and found his field at once. He gulped down courses, working through the night, tireless, fascinated, penetrating, brilliant.

Early he caught the attention of Professor Reiland of the University Psychology Laboratory. Just before Trant's graduation, the Professor accepted him as his assistant. But holding Trant as an assistant was equivalent to restraining a jet liner with thread. That eager mind, fuming with ideas, would not linger long in any quiet place.

Thus the background of Luther Trant, America' first scientific detective. He was created by Edwin Balmer and William MacHarg. Brothers-in-law, Chicago newspapermen, their non-fiction pieces scatter through the periodicals of the day. Their professionalism shows in the Trant stories: the writing is smoothly neutral, like well-kneaded dough. It is competent, straightforward copy, unsmudged by obeisance to turn-of-the-century affectations. The dialogue is simple and realistic in an age when fictional characters adorned their thought with phrases extended well beyond speaking limits.

As far as is known, Balmer and MacHarg wrote a dozen Trant stories. These first appeared in *Hampton's Magazine* during 1909-1910. The first story, "The Man In the Room," was published in the May 1909 issue. At monthly intervals thereafter followed "The Fast Watch," "The Red Dress," "The Private Bank Puzzle," "The Man Higher Up," "The Chalchihuiti Stone," "The Empty Cartridges," and 'The Odor of Death." The series continued into 1910 with publication of "The Axion Letters" (January), "The Eleventh Hour" (February), "The Hammering Man" (May), and "A Matter of Mind Reading" (October).

Nine cases were collected in the 1910 *The Achievements of Luther Trant*, omitting "The Hammering Man," "The Odor of Death," and "A Matter of Mind Reading."

After 1910, the shining career of Trant vanished from the public print. The series would have remained in obscurity, an interesting artifact of bygone days, but for the enthusiasm of Hugo Gernsback.

Gernsback found these device-oriented cases fascinating. During 1926-1928, he reprinted at least three of them in *Amazing Stories*, the first magazine entirely devoted to science-fiction. Trant, the applied technologist, did not quite fit into the world of *Amazing Stories*, whose high extrapolations spurned Hardware for the joys of Fantastic adventure. But Trant did exactly fit into Gernsback's new magazine, the *Scientific Detective Monthly*.

The covers of the first two issues of this publication (January and February 1930) were illustrated by scenes from Trant achievements. In both cases, the defiant wretch sits wired to remarkable apparatus. This blares his guilt to those standing stern-faced around him. How conclusive it all seems.

*Scientific Detective Monthly* reprinted five Trant cases. But the magazine did not prosper and, with the June 1930 issue, the title changed to *Amazing Detective Tales*. Under that title, four additional cases were reprinted. Unfortunately *Amazing Detective Tales* was no more successful than *Scientific Detective* and the magazine was discontinued after the

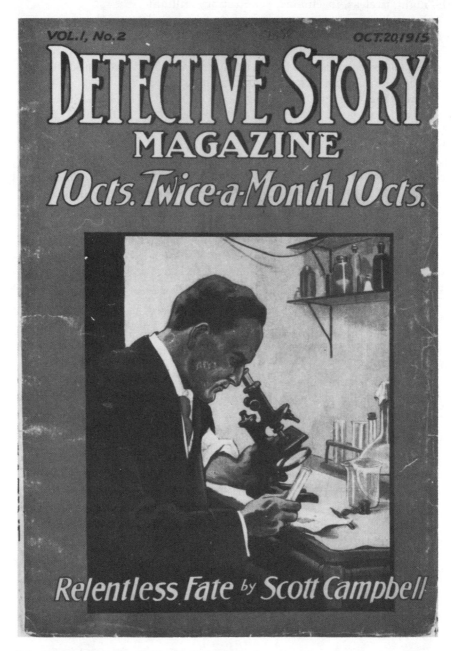

*Detective Story Magazine*, October 20, 1915. Science, the new magic, and mystery fiction, the new fad, combined to fill magazines with scientific detectives and their microscopes.

*Scientific Detective Monthly*, February 1930. Luther Trant, in the dark coat, used laboratory apparatus to confirm his deductions. Other series emphasized the equipment to the eventual destruction of the story form.

October 1930 issue. Once more, Luther Trant returned to the shadowland of obsolete investigators, recalled only by archivists tunneling in the past.

In fictional time, the Trant stories occur, more or less in sequence, over a six-month period, from mid-October to the end of the following March. ("The Red Dress" and "The Odor of Death" appear out of sequence, being placed in late Spring and Summer, if we are to go by internal dating.) Minor deviations to one side, the series begins with Trant still at the University, progresses through his first successes, ends with his establishment as a "Practical Psychologist."

His first case, "The Man In the Room," opens amid leafless trees and frost. Trant, restive, stalks the campus, fiercely lecturing his companion, Professor Reiland. Under Trant's eye, the scar glows. His voice rises. The principal of psychological testing should be—must be—applied to civil criminal cases, not left as laboratory demonstrations. That authorities should fumble so when available devices could readily demonstrate . . . .

The time of demonstration is upon him. In University Hall, lies the body of Dr. Lawrie, dead in a gas-thick room. On his desk is a tray of charred paper. In the University accounts is a $100,000 shortage. Suicide to avoid prosecution? After five minutes on the scene, Trant thinks not.

Another man was in that room, turning on the gas, moving the body, burning the paper. If true, only three suspects. Can Dr. Lawrie's daughter help? But she is almost prostrated by shock, barely able to respond to Trant's proposed word association test.

From the psychology laboratory, the pendulum chronoscope, a sensitive, voice-actuated device measuring the delay between a word spoken and the response of the testee. By tricky arrangement, Trant surreptitiously tests out the suspects during questioning of the daughter.

Responses indicate that one man has guilty knowledge.

Confrontation.

Confession.

Dr. Lawrie died of heart failure, was framed to hide another's theft. Science triumphs.

The story establishes the series' direction. As in the Thorndyke adventures, equipment augments but does not replace the deductive mind. First, the investigation, the methodical sifting through tangled motives and evidence fragments. After some glimpses of the truth, then the demonstration—the equipment is used to validate the deduction.

The technique is brilliant. But alas, usable courtroom evidence is slim. With luck, the guilty will confess under the strain of exposure. If they do not, conviction may be doubtful.

Following his initial achievement, Trant offers his services to the police to clear up a murder case now one month old. Bronson, the city prosecuting attorney, was killed that long ago. Although the police have arrested sixteen suspects, they are not far along in their case. The story is "The Fast Watch."

Captain Crowley, North Side Police Station, derisively doubts that Trant can help. Fortunately Inspector Walker listens. After a brief personal investigation of the murder scene and background, Trant is prepared. With some banana oil and a galvanometer he swiftly breaks an alibi based on the dead man's stopped watch.

A galvanometer? That's a device measuring the amount of current passing through the hand-held electrodes and modified by the amount of moisture on a person's palm. A fearful person sweats. Sweat and you go to jail.

Now Trant's name gets to the newspapers. From this point on, clients come to him because they have read his name or he has been recommended by the people of the preceding case.

In "The Red Dress" he conducts a test series to determine suggestibility and diagnoses a case of hyperaestheia—acute nervous stimulation. The crime is the kidnapping of a rich man's nephew. Trant discovers that it is all in the family.

"The Private Bank Puzzle" occurs late in November. Trant is now living at the University Club, with offices on the 12th floor of the First National Bank Building, "towering sixteen floors."

A test for memory dysfunction and an obsolete borrowed typewriter disclose (to the trained mind) an attempt to rob the bank. Trant's explanation clears one young man of suspected robbery; a second receives a chance for restitution; and a fine old cashier receives a generous retirement.

By this time, the stories have snuggled down into their characteristic form, a gentle drowse. Not in this fiction do high-powered automobiles hurtle urgently through the streets or brave men struggle sweatily at death's lip. Not for Bulmer and MacHerg are chapters areel with action and gasping adjectives. No, no.

No movement disturbs the narrative tranquility. Each story is approximately 12,000 words long, divided into six reasonably distinct parts, each placid, each murmurous with conversation.

First a brief Introduction, 500 words, perhaps: dialogue, distress, ending in a call to Trant.

Next follows a lengthy discussion between Trant and client. Often the longest section of the story, this averages 4,000 words. Here is given most of the background, most of the clues, had you the wit to seize them. If the story requires the presence of a girl in peril of losing her fellow (he is falsely accused), she appears here.

In the third part, Trant may investigate for 2,000 words. Not always. He may merely walk into the next room, thus providing a burst of physical action.

It is now time for science. Since demonstration of equipment is why the story was written, many words are used in this part—often as many as 3,500—describing the polished surfaces, the glittering dials. When the reader foams over with anticipation, a page or two of procedure from a psychological test manual is then dramatized.

Now we move into the fifth, or Revelatory Action, segment. In this part, there is occasional action. The villain, revealed, sneers or weeps, denies, laughs, or quakes all over. In these 500-750 words is concentrated most of the action, such as standing up fast or bumping over a chair.

The obligatory action scene completed, Trant explains all, using 2,000-3,000 words. While the detail is fascinating, the story endings leave you waiting for the bell to end class.

"The Man Higher Up"—a most educational story of science serving law—concerns customs frauds, murder, smuggling and white-collar crime. In this most reprinted of the Trant series, our hero goes after The Boss of it all, the man higher up. With the aid of a devoted German psychologist, unfortunately named Professor Schmaltz, Trant collects a quantity of equipment with hard-to-spell names:

—the plethysmograph to measure blood volume fluctuation in the finger;

—the pneumograph to measure alterations in breathing rate.

And, in short order, the master mind stands revealed, his fat lips sagging apart, his gang tumbling in the Law's grip.

"The Chalchihuitl Stone" mixes monoideric somnambulism, a green turquoise, and an attempted swindle based on a native marriage to a 4-year old girl. In "The Axton Letters," Trant differentiates between auditory and visual memory by analysis of personal correspondence, and prevents a swindler from pillaging a sweet girl's estate.

The electric psychometer ("the soul machine") is really an improved galvanometer. When you're hooked up to this thing, your emotional stress causes a mirror to shift light across a screen. The tenser you get, the further the light swings. Using this device, in "The Eleventh Hour," Trant clears an innocent man of murder charges and exposes a sinister Oriental execution plot. The victim deserved to die, and it is a matter of record that Sin Chung Ming did it.

In mid-1910, the science detective story form paused to test the air. Through Luther Trant, this branch of the detective story had adapted to American interests and the peculiarities of American tastes. Behold the young professional man, rising by personal exertions. He moves familiarly among the monied classes, an outsider accepted for his abilities. Up he has mounted on scientific wings. Not gossamer wings, either, but sound structures of polished steel and extracts from German experimentalists. Decidedly he has mounted. Proving that knowledge, most certainly, is power.

And scientific knowledge, almost invincible power.

Measurement of the soul. Mind reading. The infallible machine remorselessly recording each involuntary self-revelation. Each man becomes his own accuser; the guilty stand self-revealed. It is the American way.

One year ahead, the scientific detective would become a national fad. Already broad hints of that popularity trembled the air. Still, golder showers were as hard to foresee in 1910 as at present. The Trant series had enjoyed only modest success—only that—and it faded swiftly.

Indeed the stories did drag. They displayed less vigor than the museum's display of pottery shards. And Trant did lecture so. That was the best and worst of it: the series was slow and educational.

The next obvious step was to improve the narrative pace. And this happened almost immediately.

It happened with the December 1910 issue of *Cosmopolitan*, which introduced Craig Kennedy, The American Sherlock Holmes.

The initial Craig Kennedy series ran in *Cosmopolitan* from December 1910 through October 1912, the short stories appearing monthly under the overall title of "The Adventures of Craig Kennedy, Scientific Detective." (Minor variations in this title have been noted.) In November 1912, the series switched to *Hearst's Magazine*, where at least four stories appeared ("The Campaign Grafter," "The Kleptomanic," "The Opium Joint" and "The Vampire"). In April 1913, the series returned to *Cosmopolitan* and continued through at least December of that year.

The series became popular, then wildly popular. Within two years of magazine publication, the stories were collected in both American and English hardback editions. Rather rapidly, a large library of Craig Kennedy developed. It would be printed and reprinted in various editions and sets until well into the 1930s. A total of about 25 books appeared.

Kennedy began appearing in the pulp magazines during 1912 and continued until 1935. Titles include *The Popular Magazine* (1912-1914), *Adventure* (February 1914), *Street & Smith Detective Story Magazine* (1918-1928), *Everybody's* (1923-1924), *Flynn's* (1924-1925), *Argosy-All Story Weekly* and *Argosy* (1925-1935), *Detective Fiction Weekly* (1928-1929), *Clues* (1929-1930), *Scientific Detective Monthly* and *Amazing Detective Tales* (1930), *Complete Detective* (1932-1935), *Dime Detective* (1933), *Popular Detective* (1934-1935), *World Man-Hunters* (1934) and *Weird Tales* (1935). The list is by no means complete.[11]

All these words spilled from the mind of Arthur Benjamin Reeve, born in Patchoque, New York, October 15, 1880. He created Craig Kennedy while an undergraduate at Princeton, first using the name (not the character) in the *Nassau Literary Magazine*. Graduating from Princeton in 1903, Reeve briefly attended the New York Law School. There it occurred to him to combine "science and law in a Nick Carter who should have both the University and Third Avenue Theatre melodrama in his make-up."[12]

Law was not to be Reeve's profession. He entered journalism and, while on the editorial staff of *The Survey* (1907), discovered a series of articles on scientific crime detection. So stimulated (his account does not mention Luther Trant) he wrote the first Craig Kennedy detective story and received his first rejection. "The story" (he wrote later) "became a commuter."

Eventually the story stopped at *Cosmopolitan,* caught on, and fortune burnt hotly from that point. Very hotly. According to Reeve:

... including reprints, foreign editions and so on, ... well over three and one-half million copies of my books have been sold, ... with magazine, newspaper syndicate, book, motion picture and play circulation ...

these same stories have had a circulation far in excess of the population of the earth.[13]

Reeve was a very very careful man when marketing his works. By judicious care in selling "The Radio Detective," a short story, he pointed out that he was able to squeeze seven different sales from it in various forms— book, newspaper syndication, motion-picture rights, renovelization of the motion-picture, reprints of the renovelization—and so was able to realize a cumulative profit of about $15.00 a word on a story that had originally sold to *Boy's Life* at 2¢ a word.

A most meticulous, careful man. His picture appears on the cover of the January 31, 1925 *Flynn's*, as introduction to still another Craig Kennedy series. Reeve is paunchy, balding, middle-aged. But the eyes behind the glasses assess you with cold precision.

Reeve grew prize-winning dahlias and died in Trenton, New Jersey, August 9, 1936, of a bronchial condition.

Mr. Reeve's thoroughness with sale of his works explains many series anomalies that tumble unwary readers on their faces, roaring and swearing vengeance. Reeve was forever tinkering. Under his master hand, a short story expands to a novel. The novel splinters to gleaming shards of peacock blue and poppy red and gold, and every splinter leaps into independent life.

So it is not strange that "The Scientific Gunman" (*Popular*, 1914), a Craig Kennedy story, shivers strangely and ends as a novel titled *Guy Garrick* (1914). Or that *Amazing Detective Tales* and *Scientific Detective Monthly* are heavy with reprints of Kennedy adventures. Or that *Gold of the Gods* (1915), a novel, is an immensely expanded version of the final three chapters of *The Social Gangster* (1916), itself a collection of previously published short stories.

You must commend Reeve for his businesslike manner, even when you condemn him for selling you the same story warmed over five times.

The subject of all these pages is Craig Kennedy, Professor at Columbia University, confidant of the police, and a fee-earning consulting detective.

Illustrations show Kennedy to be a handsome, tall man who would be right at home selling ties and escorting Gibson girls. He wears Coolidge collars and an intense expression appropriate to a scientist. Sad to relate, Reeve gives almost no physical description of Kennedy. From bits dropped along the way, we learn that he is firm chinned, lean, has exceptional physical strength, irregularly shows a flash of humor. All standard characteristics. A physical image of the man eludes us. He is as faceless as an ice cube.

That lack of detail is entirely characteristic of Reeve, who rarely unbent sufficiently to describe any character. If one of his creatures roused his dislike, he would assign him greasy hair or a weak chin. He succeeds only slightly better with the girls, frequently observing that they are beautiful and have fine faces.

The lack of description goes hand-in-hand with a lack of character development. The stories swarm with names. There are virtually no characters. These have almost no character traits. Names, names, names sprinkle the text: This one is guilty; that one is innocent. Try and separate them.

Most stories are narrated in the first person by Walter Jameson, Kennedy's roommate, a reporter for the *Star* and another faceless golem. Walter is an American Bunny Manders, an inconsequential lightweight. Why Kennedy bothered to associate with Walter is a mystery beyond solution. Poor Walter has the personality of a blank tablet. He is a successful writer of special features for the *Star*'s Sunday magazine section. It is his only gift. Otherwise, he displays only a crushing capacity for the obvious, and trails after Kennedy, wide-eyed and inept, a spectacle of fuzzy bewilderment.

From story to story, various other regulars look in. First-Deputy Barney O'Connor (New York Police Department) and Dr. Leslie (NYC Coroner) show up frequently, giving Kennedy the legal backing required by an unofficial investigator. Burke (US Secret Service) stops by when cases involve counterfeit money or stolen official secrets—that sort of thing. Burke is faceless. O'Connor is Irish, so we may presume that he is red-headed, brawny, with a pug nose. They are all sort of thick. Especially Walter.

What we have, then, is the standard mixture of the astute private investigator, complete with stooge, who performs his marvels supported by the usual amiable officials. All this is written in prose from which most sensory cues have been stripped, after which each sentence has been ironed flat.

Not to say that the stories are dull. Not at all. They begin furiously. And dialogue in the first sentence: Trouble, problem, anxiety:

This poor woman is terribly worried about her daughter.

Perpetual motion has been discovered.

"You've heard of such things as cancer houses ...."

"I suppose you have read ... of the mysterious burning of our country house."

The stories leap off, savagely screeching their tires. Names fly in all directions. People rush in. Soon someone is dead or sick or victimized. The police have discovered nothing. But Kennedy—traveling with at least two large, paper-wrapped packages of equipment—consults a dial and his fine eyes light up.

He never explains a blessed thing to Walter, though.

In early stories, Kennedy shows a positive genius for getting trapped by lethal groups. No matter; it is only a small problem. He need only think of some scientific principle and out he pops, unwrinkled, unconcerned.

And now the final clue is in his hands. The entire cast is assembled in Kennedy's laboratory. The police stand by, their stern looks concealing deep confusion. Kennedy sets the electromechanograph to buzzing and— BEHOLD—right there, right before everyone, the guilty party is identified. Good gracious. It is a regular scientific seance, using laboratory equipment in lieu of a crystal ball.

The first Kennedy story to be published was "The Case of Helen Bond" (*Cosmopolitan*, December 1910). This would later be reprinted in *Amazing Detective Tales* (August 1930) as "The Scientific Cracksman." With this initial story, the tone and style of the series for the next fourteen years is established.

A rich old boy is found dead before his open safe. Although the door has been neatly punched full of holes around the lock, nothing is missing but the will. At the request of the old man's nephew, Kennedy and Walter drive out to the "great lonely house on Long Island." Investigation discloses that the cracksman had covered his fingers with rubber cement, daringly plugged his drill into the electric light fixture, then bored into the safe.

At this point, Kennedy sets up his dynamometer ("My mechanical detective") to determine how much pressure was exerted on the jimmy in forcing the safe door. And very little pressure was required, too.

Having introduced the laboratory equipment, the story now turns to personalities. Kennedy wishes to interview Helen Bond, fiancee of the nephew. But Helen is in a sad state of shock and so, to fill up another two pages, Kennedy steps outside to collect automobile tire tracks. "Craig," cries Walter, "that's the thumbprint of an automobile!"

And indeed he is right. Although it is not clear why Kennedy should be collecting tire prints at this time; he explains as little as Sherlock Holmes.

By this time, Walter is all aquiver with confusion. His condition grows worse when Kennedy takes him to visit Miss Bond, using the pretext that they are nerve specialists come to diagnose her illness.

Giving that cover story, Kennedy persuades her to don a long rubber glove, stiffened with leather, that somehow allows liquid to interact with a dial, thereby affording intimate glimpses of the subject's blood pressure. This device has the inspiring name of "plethysmograph." A second apparatus measures "association time." As Walter mans the stop-watch, Kennedy then administers a word association test.

By this time, the most sluggish reader has understood that Helen Bond knows all about the robbery, since she is the only possible suspect, other than the nephew. And sure enough, under Kennedy's clever questioning, it is revealed that she—*she*—committed the crime. Using techniques taught her by a notorious Apache chief, she donned rubber cement, drilled the safe, jimmied the door. When the rich old boy entered and saw her at work, he promptly had a heart attack and perished.

Let it be explained that the will gave the old man's $50,000,000 fortune to establish a school of preventive medicine. Helen intended to carry away the will and forge in a new paragraph bequeathing her $20,000,000 because, as she explains in a trembling voice: "I need a fortune, for then I could have the town house, the country house, the yacht, the motors, the clothes, the servants that I need ...."

So touching is her appeal that Kennedy and Walter swear to conceal her part in the matter. They hide the original will in a tin box and find it again with great rejoicing.

To clear up a few dangling ends: The tire tracks were made by Helen's electric runabout, which she drove to the mansion the night of her robbery. And the Apache chief, that sinister cliche of 1910, was mentioned only to explain Miss Bond's remarkable technical skill with safes. But enough. No other probing is required of this effort, distorted as it is, and sickly and opportunisitic. We may cross the street to avoid greeting it, but remember, please, it sold to *Cosmopolitan* and launched Kennedy's career.

In his article on "Scientific Detectives" in the *Encyclopedia of Mystery and Detection*, Sam Moskowitz remarks that "Helen Bond" borrows the plot and device to record lapsed time that was used in the Trant adventure, "The Man In the Room."[14] In defense of Reeve's limp effort, the only two points of similarity seem to be that the victim died of a heart attack and that word association testing was used to get at the truth. The lapsed-time measuring device Trant employed (the pendulum chronoscope) was activated by voice; Kennedy's device is not described at all, save as a "delicate stopwatch," a phrase exceedingly vague. Kennedy also hooks Miss Bond to the blood-pressure device in the belief that, if one scientific device is good, two are superb. "Helen Bond" may not have been a carbon copy of "The Man In the Room," but you can hardly argue Reeve's ignorance of the Balmer/MacHarg story. They are blood relations, if not twins.

In subsequent stories, Reeve ranges away from Trant's psychological-laboratory devices into the wonderland of Scientific Machinery. This is understood to be a generic term for any gadget which could be wedged in among the fleeting scenes.

In "The Silent Bullet" (*Cosmopolitan*, January 1911), a silenced .32 revolver is used to kill the victim in a busy office. In this story, we first meet Inspector Barney O'Connor and the first scientific seance is held in Kennedy's laboratory. "The Bacteriological Detective" (February 1911) features murder by the introduction of typhoid germs into drinking water. The March, "The Deadly Tube," tells of a tube of radium bromide that an unkind husband, seeking divorce, has introduced into the springs of his wife's bed, causing rude changes to her beauty. Not only does Kennedy discover the tube, but uses an acoustiphone (listening device) to hear the husband's angry confidences to a crony.

On the stories ran. And on. And on. You may find them collected in such books as *The Silent Bullet* (1912), *The Poisoned Pen* (1913) and *The Dream Doctor* (1914). All are built to the same blueprint. Themes and settings vary. Scientific equipment and more-or-less scientific principles crowd the paragraphs. The crimes are mixed:

An arsonist runs amok. Kennedy is trapped in a room filling with ether vapor. This he damps with carbon dioxide. Thereafter, he uses a telantograph (long-distance, hand-writing transmission device) to reveal the crook, who gets shot in the arm with a rock-salt bullet. For Kennedy is a non-lethal fellow.

Now counterfeiting: Bertillon's methods are discussed, and the plot includes surgical modification of fingerprints and paraffin injections to change facial contours.

Fake medium: Searching for clues, Craig and Walter visit one medium after the other, giving a running commentary on their tricks and frauds. Human hairs are analyzed under the microscope and Walter experiences the effect of hashish at first-hand.

Forgery: Forged checks abound and the accused has been framed. It is all cleared up by the telectrograph (for electrical transmission of photographs) and a color comparison microscope.

Murder in the hotel: A spy has got the plans for "Corregidor at Manila" and comes within this much of giving them to the Japanese. During this story, Kennedy hurls out information. We learn the test for residual chloroform in tissue, and watch Kennedy extemporize a microphone from two telephone carbon transmitters and the glass of a framed picture. We also learn of a wonderful device used by Apaches: a thin glass ball of drugs held in a handkerchief. Crush this beneath the victim's nose and down he falls. These little darlings are called "endormeurs," French, we are told, for "sleep-makers."

Then smuggling—with murder thrown in and Apache knuckle knives and a photophone (a beam of light used to carry the vibrations of the voice).

And a fine case of swindling, involving transmutation of copper to gold and a gloriously crackpot theory of the periodic table. A man is blinded by ultra-violet rays, and there is all manner of excitement. A pulmotor is used to resuscitate gas victims. Kennedy detects a disguised identity by the unique vein patterns on the back of a man's hand and discourses on the heredity of eye color.

And what, you may ask, gave this heinous crime away? Why it was the fake transmutation machine, all lighted up scientifically and pouring forth ultra-violet rays. (Thus blinding the gullible soul sitting there watching gold appear.)

How did Kennedy know? He had in his hand this bit of willemite, you see. When bombarded by ultra-violet rays—rays totally invisible to the eye—the willemite glows or fluoresces. An infallible indicator, a scientific wonder, the material responding to invisible energies, just as the mind of the investigator blazes forth on the mystery and, behold, it glows with truth.

In "The Dream Doctor" (August 1913), pyschoanalysis is introduced— or so legend has it. Legend is not quite correct. It would be useful to consider this story in some detail, for it is a rather famous one, typical of early Kennedys.

As background to the action, it should be explained that Walter has been assigned by his editor to follow Kennedy for a month, writing up his experiences daily. Reeling with joy, Walter bolts to the apartment on the Heights he shares with Kennedy. There the great man sits reading "one of the latest untranslated treatises on the new psychology" by Freud. Apparently this is *Die Traumdeutung—The Interpretation of Dreams—* which did not receive an English translation until 1913. (If, instead, it were *Three Essays on the Theory of Sexuality*, then the title alone would keep it from mention in a decent American magazine that entered the home.)

While Walter is explaining his assignment, Kennedy receives a phone call from the coroner, Dr. Leslie. Come to Municipal Hospital at once. There they learn that a broker named Price Maitland was found dying on the streets. In his pocket was a brief, semi-coherent typewritten note with suicidal sound. For several pages, the doctors discuss Maitland's symptoms:

> The tissues seemed to be thickly infiltrated with a reddish serum and the blood-vessels congested.

Kennedy diagnoses it as death by cobra venom. Dr. Leslie relates the reaction to Maitland's wife, who seems to think his unfortunate condition was forewarned in a horrible dream she had the previous night. She is in a severe emotional state. After secretly taking a sample set of impressions from her typewriter and some typing paper, Kennedy and Walter leave to visit Dr. Ross.

Ross is Mrs. Maitland's doctor. He feels that she is sexually suppressed and discloses that he uses cobra venom to test for blood diseases. He gives Kennedy a sample of venom and Kennedy surreptitiously takes another set of typewriter key impressions and paper. He also gets a detailed account, from Dr. Ross, of Mrs. Maitland's latest dream (for she has had a string of spooky ones). In her recent dream, she was attacked by a bull that changed into a serpent and looked much like Arnold Masterson—a well-known clubman presently undergoing Dr. Ross' venom treatment.

In a matter of three lines, Kenendy and Walter arrive at Masterson's apartment. Under questioning, he admits that he was once engaged to Mrs. Maitland but that she broke it off to marry another. He provides Kennedy with a short typewritten statement of his travels after she broke his heart, and then suavely ushers them out.

These interviews leave Walter miserably bewildered, a sad spectacle. Kennedy, however, smiles his lean smile and rubs his hands together and is full of secrets. He instructs the coroner to assemble everyone associated with the case in Kennedy's laboratory that evening.

And, because coroners are such obliging fellows, there they all are after dinner, seated in the chair customarily used by the students. Behind the lecturn, Kennedy stands—and begins to lecture.

To begin with, he discusses cobra venom and its peculiar properties of being harmless when swallowed but deadly in a wound. That subject at length exhausted, he turns to typewriting, describing how the key image can positively be tied to a given machine, using such scientific equipment as the Lovibond tintometer to evaluate ink intensity, the vernier micrometer caliper to measure paper thickness, and an alignment test plate to analyze the placement of each typed character in a line.

Insufficient science having not yet been invoked, he next turns to Mrs. Maitland's dreams. There follow three pages that concentrate rather neatly one element of Freud's dream theory. The latent content of Mrs. Maitland's dreams seems to be that she regretted jilting Masterson and would sort of like her husband to die, so that she would be free to receive Masterson's embraces again.

*Kennedy*: "... your dream of fear was ... what we call the fulfillment of a suppressed wish."

As she dissolves into her hankie, Masterson rouses up roaring: "Kennedy, you are a fake—nothing but a damned dream doctor...."

Kennedy's lips quietly curls. Before you realize it, Masterson is standing there loaded with handcuffs. For it was his typewriter that wrote Maitland's suicide note. This is the only evidence that is brought forth, and it firmly proves that Masterson's typewriter wrote the note. How it was proved that Masterson used the typewriter to type the note remains all vague and blurry, rather like a dream fulfilling a suppressed wish.

The way Kennedy sees it, Masterson caught Maitland in a crowd, scratched him with a poisoned needle, shoved the suicide note into his pocket. Motive: to win Mrs. Maitland.

So off goes Masterson to wherever unsuccessful murderers go when they are caught. And Kennedy, having completed his "soul analysis," strides onward to ever more interesting cases. The next one concerns an actress found dead in a beauty shop, her lips shining, shining ....

What a defense lawyer would do to Kennedy's evidence doesn't bear thinking about. All the scientific flim-flam to one side, there is only one scrap of formal evidence, and that accuses the typewriter, rather than the owner of the typewriter. As far as linking a murderer with his crime, Kennedy has failed completely.

He does not realize this, however. Nor does Walter or the coroner or, as far as we know, Arthur Reeve. Nick Carter would have been vastly entertained at the sight of a detective unable to distinguish between the operation of gadgets and rigorous evidence.

It is precisely here, in their formal moments, that these stories fail to unify. Kennedy stands there, voice thundering, "Thou Art the Man." And likely he is right. But who could know by the evidence presented. Never is there that hard, incontestable fact to make the Prosecuting Attorney nod with pleasure and the jury nod with agreement. We can only hope that the police, unencumbered by tintometers and alignment test plates, found more concrete evidence during their less spectacular investigations.

While his stories were appearing in *Cosmopolitan, Pearson's* and *Popular*, Reeve had become involved with silent movie serials. Aided by various collaborators, he worked on about fifteen serials and full-length features between 1915 and 1936. In six of these, Kennedy was featured.

The first three serials were essentially vehicles for Pearl White. They were titled *The Exploits of Elaine* (1915), *The New Exploits of Elaine* (1915), and *The Romance of Elaine* (1916). Chunks of these plopped into the Reeve pressure cooker and came steaming forth as books: *The Exploits of Elaine* (1915) and *The Romance of Elaine* (1916); a third book, *The Triumph of Elaine* (1916), was published only in England and contained most of *The Romance*, plus an additional five chapters.

The Elaine books differ sharply from Reeve's other fiction of the time.

They throw a merciless glare upon his literary opportunism.

These are pseudo books, neither novel, sketch, nor short story. Examination suggests that they are scripts of the serial chapters, lightly coated with prose. The total effect is that of an illustrated bubble gum advertisement.

Madly onward the action lurches. Brief scenes burst one after the other, firecrackers on a string, eight to ten explosions a chapter. The chapters have no continuity, no development. Action is the key, blind action, crude and raw. The point of view skips crazily among the scenes.

The sequence of action is typical of serials: thrust, counter-thrust, another thrust, an additional counter-thrust. In the serial, the visual images furnish sufficient continuity to glue these bits together. The book simply ignores continuity, jerking violently from scene to scene with transitions indicated by a line of dots.

. . . . . . . .

It is intolerably scrappy work, cynical and exploitative, a disgrace to the character and the author.

. . . . . . . .

This pitiful travesty illustrates some of the incestuous relationships existing between silent films, stage melodrama, dime novels and popular fiction. Here are similar chase-and-struggle plots, thrilling scenes chopped off unresolved to create greater suspense, mysterious objects whose meaning will be explained later, and the same trivial plots and single-trait characters. One form fed the other. The process was repetitive and unashamed, as in the Elaine adventures.

In the initial book, *The Exploits of Elaine*, the heroine (who almost certainly had a last name, although it is not mentioned) is menaced by The Clutching Hand, a lawyer attempting to steal her inheritance by means foul. Elaine loves Craig and he loves her, in a chaste, hands-off sort of way. (After the Elaine books, she dissolves back into the silver screen and love does not trouble Professor Kennedy again.)

Peril piles on peril as Elaine and Kennedy evade collapsing walls, explosions, clouds of sinister smoke, henchmen leering and electrical fizzes. At long last, after endless to-do, The Clutching Hand is killed. But his treasure horde is not recovered.

Now begins the second book. Kennedy and Walter are sorting The Clutching Hand's private papers. It is Chapter 1 of *The Romance of Elaine* and here follow a few specific scenes from that chapter:

> —Kennedy and Walter discover among the papers a drawing of a fireplace, done in secret ink.
> ——Elaine, home in bed, is menaced by a weird figure at her window. She fires her pistol to no effect, but finds on the ground outside, a small box containing a mysterious ivory figure.

—Wu Fang, mastermind of Chinese evil, has secured a map to The Clutching Hand's treasure. This has been concealed in a secret passage under Elaine's home. Wu and his sinister aide, Long Sin, slink off by night to snatch the treasure.

—Kennedy discovers that the fireplace in Elaine's living room is the spitting image of the fireplace in the drawing. Investigating, he opens a secret door into the depths. He descends with Walter, breathless, behind.

—Down beneath, they surprise the Chinese at work. Wu Fang hurls a smoke bomb and escapes.

—Kennedy observes that the oriental fiends were attempting to open a safe down there in the passageways. He drills into the safe, an unwise act releasing poison gas. He crumples senseless and Walter does too.

—Long Sin re-enters, lifting his glittering knife over their unconscious figures.

—Elaine, arriving in the tunnel at that exact moment, grapples with Long Sin. The passageway collapses around them.

—Long Sin escapes through a hole in the lawn.

—Servants dig out Elaine, Kennedy, and they also dig out Walter.

—In his secret headquarters, Wu Fang examines a box snatched by The Clutching Hand's secrets. It contains only a cryptic ring.

So much for Chapter 1. You can almost hear the piano accompanying each thrilling incident. In the following chapters, Kennedy is poisoned by aconite, revived by digitalin. Has a gunfight with Long Sin while whizzing up an elevator shaft. Pursues Long Sin across a rope, which is cut, hurling Kennedy into the deeps. Wu Fang learns that the ring triggers the lock of a secret safe under Elaine's home (a second safe, apparently); this he opens, finding prodigies of treasure. Kennedy and Walter are trapped in a flaming barn and it seems that they must perish .... Elaine is trapped by Wu Fang and it seems that she must ....

But enough. It is the distilled essence of the Saturday serial, a wild parody of the dime novel modifed for silent screen projection. It is wonderful, in a sort of wild-eyed way, for all the elements of an action story are here, a mass of jagged pieces shoveled into a coherent action adventure, given time enough, motivation, character development and coherent thought. In seventeen years, Street & Smith would magic such materials into huge magazine sales. But that would require more literary enterprise than was expended in the fabrication of *The Romance.*

It would be improper to carry the reader of these comments to a high peak of excitement, then leave him trembling and distraught, combing the used book stores for a copy of *The Romance of Elaine.*

WHAT HAPPENED FURTHER!!

Wu Fang makes Kennedy and Walter look feckless for five chapters, after which they capture Long Sin and send Wu Fang flying. By now, Kennedy has discovered the secret of the ring and the concealed treasure. Meanwhile, the Navy has begun a separate story by testing his Teleautomatic Torpedo; it is a little radio-controlled device that blows ships silly, no one of the time having heard of electronic counter-measures. A gang of foreign spies has directed Wu Fang to steal models of the torpedo. He does. But Kennedy catches up with him and, shades of

Conan Doyle, they tumble, struggling, off the edge of a pier. After a dramatic pause, Wu Fang floats to the surface, cruel steel buried in his heart. Of Kennedy there is no sign. Walter covers his face. But Elaine, her lovely face pale, can only hope that somewhere, somewhere . . . .

That is Chapter 5. For the remainder of the book, Elaine and Walter and the torpedo models have a terrible time, as they battle Del Mar, a foreign spy and heartless fiend. Kennedy is there all the time, disguised under a large beard. Eventually the torpedo wipes out Del Mar and his slinking crew and, as they sink flaming into the deep, the spy scribbles a final note:

Tell my emperor I failed because Craig Kennedy was against me.

Now that is a real personal tribute.

In spite of the Elaine books, the Kennedy star continued to rise. Between 1916 and 1924 Reeve published nine books, contributed to numbers of moving pictures, and sold serials to *Street & Smith's Detective Story Magazine.* The titles noted include "Craig Kennedy and the Film Tragedy" (4-part serial, July 16 through August 6, 1918), "The Sinister Shadow" (short story, August 27, 1918) and "The Soul Scar" (4-part serial, September 17 through October 8, 1918). During the same period, his short stories were also appearing in such diverse publications as *Everybody's, Country Gentleman* and *Flynn's.*

The *Everybody's* stories mark the end of Craig Kennedy's first phase. Six of these were published:

"Thicker than Water" (September 1923) features a blood test to determine a child's true parentage, and an individual who left his forehead print on the window glass is identified by the pore marks. October 1923: "Dead Men Tell Tales": Kennedy resurrects a woman pronounced dead until he injects her heart with a solution of epinephrin and connects her to a pulmotor. Subsequent stories are "The Radio Wraith" (November), "The Hawk" (December). The January 1924 "The Jazz Addict" is a moralistic tale about drug addiction, and not, as you may suspect, about a fan of King Oliver's Creole Jazz Band. The final story, "The Counterfeit Beauty" (February) involves disappearing women in the toils of a disguise master.

These stories are very similar to those of the *Cosmpolitan* group, being filled with scientific gadgets that are more or less convincingly applied. But major changes now appear in the image of Professor Kennedy, scientific detective. During the next sequence of stories in *Country Gentleman* and *Flynn's*, the gadgetry is firmly reduced. So is the action. The stories become whodunit problems, frequently bogged down in seas of conversation. The scenes are often far from New York City. All are problem stories, all are slow, the resolution of each turning on a single fact.

As if to compensate for these deficiencies, groups of stories are written around specific themes. Beginning in the September 27, 1924, issue of *Flynn's* is a four-part series titled "Craig Kennedy and the Elements." These are the old-fashioned elements: "Air" (September 27), "Fire" (October

11), "Earth" (October 25) and "Water" (November 8). The relationship of the story to the element is virtually nil and only by the most ungraceful contortions does Reeve manage the connection. In "Water" Kennedy has deduced that a stolen diamond is hidden in a child's handkerchief pocket. Therefore he peels a lemon before the boy and, when his mouth waters (oh yes, isn't it pitiful?) whips out the handkerchief, revealing the diamond.

The following series is as disconcerting. This is "Craig Kennedy and the Compass." The stories, December 13, 20, 27 and January 3, 1925, are identified, respectively as "North," "South," "East" and "West," and provide tedium in all directions.

In the story "West," Kennedy and Walter, on vacation in New Hampshire, discover an unoccupied cabin that has about it "something sinister that provoked foreboding thoughts." Some months before, a fellow had been mysteriously shotgunned there. After six pages of talk and background, Kennedy identifies the murderer. The essential fact is that cows face the sun as they eat and therefore a photograph supposedly taken in the morning was actually made in the evening. So much for scientific detection.

A third series, "Craig Kennedy and the *Six* Senses," began in the January 31, 1925, *Flynn's* and continued weekly, Febuary 7, 14, 21, 28 through March 7.

"Every Crime," said Kennedy, "depends for its solution on one of the five senses," thus neatly justifying the package in which these trifles are wrapped. Reeve struggles to fit his stories to the stated matrix, sometimes succeeding.

In "Sight," Kennedy does the detection while serving as foreman of a jury, far far from his lab. The case is one of those Perry Mason affairs—the accused has been framed and it all gets cleared up after last-moment courtroom revelations, very dramatic. The cavalcade of legal wonders includes evidence from a photograph of lunar mountains and testimony of a blind astronomer. During these proceedings, we learn that Kennedy is Professor of Science and Crime at Columbia, an academic rank entirely suited to his talents.

"Smell" (February 7) is one of those mid-1920s problem pieces where a group of people come together and discuss matters to rags. Any action is accidental. So here sit Kennedy and Walters with members of the fancy All-Night Club, discussing the curious case of the man found murdered in a fish-glue factory. By a singular coincidence the murderer is present and, even more coincidentally, lacks a sense of smell.

In "Touch" (February 14), a husband who has abandoned his family and changed his name is identified by his touch on a telegraph key.

The March 7, "Sixth Sense" is entirely immobile, like a pyramid. A wealthy man has vanished, and at his home lounges a gang of reporters waiting for a news break. From their conversation, Kennedy gleans sufficient information to locate the missing man—a suicide locked into a secret room. The crucial clue is the thickness of a 8A file. The sixth sense, by the way, proves to be Common Sense. Isn't that nice?

While "The Compass" and "The Senses" dragged out their weary ways in *Flynn's*, a loosely comparable story group was appearing in the 1924-1925 *Country Gentleman*. Enough similarities exist between the series to make an overly suspicious individual conclude that *Flynn's* bought the *Country Gentleman's* rejects.

As appropriate to *Country Gentleman's* special slant, these Kennedy cases occur out among the fields and chickens. No sophisticated clubmen lounge here; in all directions stand only hard-working sons of the soil. The narratives are invigorated by country air and trip along more briskly than those published in *Flynn's*.

In "The Hypocrites" (not a typical story), a blizzard at the Canadian border traps Kennedy and Walter with a singularly mixed group: a rum-runner, a salesman, his girl, and a preacher. Believing themselves about to die, the rum-runner and the salesman are converted to more wholesome lives. Eventually Kennedy leads them all to safety in Vermont. Hymns rise skyward as they go, the scene being spun of delicately tinted pink sugar. Once in Vermont, Kennedy arrests the preacher—no preacher at all but the disguised leader of an alien smuggling ring.

"Woman's Wiles" are what ensnare the cauliflower growers of Long Island. The Treasurer of the Farmer's Co-operative seems to have decamped with $8,000 and a big-city vamp. ("Her eyes were pools of beauty, deep and intriguing one minute, angelic blue the next . . . .") Even worse, a man lies murdered among crates of acid-drenched cauliflower. But Kennedy straightens it all out quickly enough. And as for the vamp, she is burnt white by love. Says so right at the end of the story.

During "The Long Arm" Kennedy performs circuit analysis on a boy's home-built radio and traps a pair of slick swindlers. "Harvest Home," altogether more violent, features murder under the prize apple tree, the deadly device being a white-phosphorous lewsite bomb. "The Barn Burner" has torched five Long Island barns and a lynch mob drives their Fords in deadly searching. Futile effort. Only Kennedy knows who hired the touch-off men.

"Frozen Paper" is about paper that will not burn. It must be supernatural. Luminous ghosts appear—one of them being Kennedy. Walter is skairt of dark basements, weird noises, glowing ghosts, exaggerates his fears for laughs, and generally behaves as if he were in blackface.

There is no great pleasure in savaging stories as poor as these. It is the commentator's responsibility to search for causes and discuss relationships, not to snarl at work published so many generations ago. Still you expect much more. Kennedy almost lives. The stories almost flash to life. Almost.

But they don't. They lie there, flaccid, distorted. You feel that they were published by virtue of past glory. While Reeve was never an outstanding artist, these stories fall well beneath his modest best.

The 1924-1925 material comprises about twenty-five short stories. Ten of these may be found in the book *Craig Kennedy on the Farm* (1925).[15] The

*Flynn's* cases were reprinted in the 1926 *The Fourteen Points: Tales of Craig Kennedy, Master of Mystery.* As a group, all stories are markedly inferior to the earlier *Cosmopolitan* series. Far less complex, far more static, they have been stripped of all that fascinating scientific apparatus that won Kennedy his reputation. The structure of the stories has also been modified. The terminal seance and Kennedy's concluding lecture on aspects of modern science have almost entirely evaporated. The endings come more suddenly than ever: "You are guilty," Kennedy roars. The accused snarls. The story ends. Quick quick—before the lack of evidence is noticed.

That Reeve altered his formula so drastically suggests a change in popular taste. During the Post-World War I period, science did not shine with its former luster, a stately angel beckoning to wonders. The War had discredited many things: science and technology, as well as government, patriotism, and faith in elected officials. Moreover, the public's fascination with science detectives had continued for more than ten years. New faces, bedecked in fascinating new styles, now peered from popular magazines. The science detective fad had worn thin:

> Nearly all the stories were based on the dramatization of some contemporary mechanism or scientific invention, and these inventions have long since been outmoded.[16]

So said Kunitz and Haycraft in 1942. In truth, the devices had been outmoded before the stories entered book form, so quickly obsolete is yesterday's technology. The process was even more accelerated because Kennedy's science was simplified to the level of the Sunday supplements. Nor were his professional techniques ever as rigorous as those of Dr. Thorndyke.

Whatever the cause, by the mid-1920s the glorious torrent of 'graphs and 'ometers used in Kennedy's cases has slacked to an occasional drop. Henceforth, he will detect, but rarely will he science detect. The scientific detective label will remain with him to the end.

Not only had Reeve changed his approach to his fiction, but he had also modified the language of the narrative. Into the stories, he packed an increasing load of 1920s catch phrases and jargon. These occur as frequently in the narrative as in the dialogue. The prose assumes a loose, colloquial tone. The paragraphs become quaint period pieces you'd like to pick up and dust.

> People (we are told) "got a kick out of meeting" Kennedy. Members had "been kidding around" at the Club. Kennedy's investigations had been so successful that Walter can't understand "why he should lay down now."
> "They are ... rum-runners to society."
> "Get out your flivver."
> Her lips had been rouged a brilliant red.

Less harmless tendencies show in the diction, grown unexpectedly slovenly. Sentences meander, linked by series of "that" clauses, blurred by inexact word choice.

> "... a dripping perspiration was oozing from my pores."
> "I felt a revulsion."
> "There was nothing he missed that seemed strange or that was misplaced."
> "Orchid after orchid we passed until they beggared description."
> "It was satisfactory to find that nothing had been disturbed, that it might leave Kennedy fresh trails...."

The sentences develop echoes.

> "This confirms my suspicions, gives me a clue."
> "The dog was tired, too, showed it in his increasing irritability."
> "He would have paid up, taken an extension on the mortgage."

Not all the prose contains such particles of uncooked dough. Walter tentatively develops a lighter touch and experiments with anticlimactic wit:

> (After sitting up all night) I was glad to see ... dawn ... the stirrings of nature, the twittering of birds, and signs of activity in the kitchen.

By 1928, a few of Walter's objectionable stylistic tricks have melted away. In the cases written for *S&S Detective Story Magazine* during that year, the narrative pace is brisk, the dialogue fresh, bright, contemporary. The prose bounces along, rich with the idioms of the time. There is still the tendency to beat a description absolutely to death:

> Veronica was of a rare type of beauty, with a great mass of heavy, shiny-black hair, a creamy-white skin, and beautiful, big blue eyes. Her slender figure showed every graceful line as she leaned back against the piano
> ....

The quotation is from "Craig Kennedy and the Model" (August 11, 1928). If the description depends overmuch on adjectives to describe every boy's huggie-bunny, that is made up for by dialogue as vigorous as Reeve ever got onto paper:

> (A participant describes last night's party in Greenwich Village): "If some of the girls wore all their earnings on their backs, it looked as if most of them were out of work. Um-mbabie! wild party—plenty of bum hootch—everything! I fell in with a Lady Golconda, or something, with no clothes but a wad of money—then the singing began... I don't think even the jazz band could tell a very straight story after two o'clock.

That's nostalgia.

The story concerns murder discovered the morning after that wonderful party. In one room, a man lies dead; his companionate wife is sleeping it off in the next room, cradling to her bosom the fatal pistol. The landlady absconds with the gun, calling in Kennedy. He begins interviewing those

*Flynn's*, December 13, 1924. In the foreground, with glasses, is Arthur B. Reeve, peering toward a new Craig Kennedy series expurgated of most scientific detection.

*Detective Fiction Weekly,* December 22, 1928. Later Craig Kennedy cases omitted scientific detection, reflected the slang and foibles of the Jazz Age. The cover reflects the perils of rum-running.

party-goers who can pry their eyes open. By this time, Detective-Sergeant Lynch has arrived on the scene, found a second gun, and makes ready to arrest the girl. Walter rather argues that she is guilty because she is "fast." But Kennedy has a clue. Producing the first gun (he has withheld it from the police all this time), he proves the girl could not possibly have done it. Evidence involves firing-pin marks on cartridge cases, plus fingerprints of the real murderer.

Who is in this very room, and there he stands . . . .

The story ends on a high note of accusation. Likely this is nothing to what Kennedy later received from the police, when they advised him of their objections to evidence being carried from the scene. It's a shame that Walter didn't record that discussion.

"The Dead Line" (*Detective Story*, October 13, 1928) describes how Kennedy manages to revive a young man dead for an entire hour. Brings him back without brain damage, too. Unlikely, perhaps, but no more so than Reeve's other fiction of this period.[17]

It must be admitted that his late 1920s work is woefully defective stuff. The science is spurious, the action unconvincing. Reeve seems to have exhausted either his technical references or his imaginative resources. The cases occur in a world queerly distorted, fantasy and reality inharmoniously blended. It is as if Reeve no longer cares what he places on paper. And pity poor Kennedy. Fundamental character changes have occurred. His scientific rigor has vanished, leaving behind only a sticky black residue of pseudo-scientific nouns. Repeatable laboratory evidence, concrete legal proofs, all are ignored. It is a sorry spectacle.

At this low point in Kennedy's fortunes, Mr. Hugo Gernsback brought forth a new magazine. In December 1929, the *Scientific Detective Monthly* hit the news stands, just as the economy lurched forward upon its knees. The *Monthly* is in the familiar Gernsback magazine format—a hefty publication measuring 8 1/2 x 11 3/4 inches, containing 96 pages of soft pulp paper and double columns of text. It sold for 25¢.

Wrote Mr. Gernsback in his lead article, "Science and Crime," for that first issue: "I confidentally believe that in the not-so-distant future the professional criminal will become practically extinct." This by reason of scientific treatment of captured crooks and scientific detection of uncaptured ones.

Since Arthur B. Reeve (the "American Conan Doyle") was known nationwide as the scientific detective man, there is small wonder that his name graced the new magazine's masthead. He was billed as "Editorial Commissioner," a title of considerable grandeur.

Each monthly issue of the *Scientific Detective Monthly* featured a reprint of a Craig Kennedy story drawn from the back issues of the 1910-1912 *Cosmopolitan*. No whisper or hint was given that the stories were reprints. It is a pleasure to report that the first Kennedy story in the initial issue (January 1930) was an original. "The Mystery of the Bulawayo Diamond" describes how the famous diamond was stolen and how Kennedy, aided by a heat-measuring device named the bolometer, tracks the gem down.[18]

Five Kennedy stories were published in *Scientific Detective Monthly* (January through May 1930), after which, the magazine shuddered delicately and changed its name to *Amazing Detective Tales*. This publication offered five more *Cosmopolitan* reprints (from June through October 1930). But even with the addition of some sprightly covers and mildly updated prose, *Amazing Detective Tales* did not prosper and the October 1930 issue was the last published.

After *Amazing Detective Tales* vanished, a reduced number of Kennedy stories trickled into the pulp market. Typical is "Murder on the Mike" (*Argosy,* December 3, 1932), written in about the same vein as the 1928 *Detective Story Magazine* series. The action is quick, the dialogue bright, the ending as weak as tissue paper. An actress is shot to death during a radio broadcast. Kennedy requires barely three hours to snare the murderer, using a parabolic reflector microphone (an "electric ear") as this issue's device.

Again the story is packed with the slang of the times:

> You can sure shove the chatter.
> Kennedy ... was a wow!
> (They) put the scene over with a bang.
> Harriet, that's a deep one.
> "... as soon as we finish this radio stunt ...."

It is a reasonably satisfactory case up to the ending. But how he expects to get a conviction on the available evidence ....

The October 1, 1933, *Dime Detective* contained a Kennedy novelette, "The Golden Grave—A Craig Kennedy Thriller." And here we go, whooping down the main street of the major pulp magazines. At this time *Dime Detective* had two years of publication under its belt. The editorial policy had shifted from an initial bias toward weird mystery adventure stories, filled with dark figures, mysterious cripples, and sudden flares of lightning. By 1933, the magazine was heading toward the cold clear air of the hard-boiled school. The Kennedy novelette is an uneasy compromise between the two fiction types.

Someone has been killing gorgeous redheads and dumping their nude bodies in the river. Kennedy is called in by an old friend, Natalie Webb. She reveals that her husband is deep into a Devil-worshipping cult. To prove it, she takes Kennedy and Walter to a meeting held that night at the Red Lodge.

It is one sensational meeting, the participants dropping their clothing and grabbing each other. After a suitable interval, they attack Kennedy and Walter, who take refuge in a small photographic laboratory. Instantly, this begins filling with chlorine gas.

So far so good. Kennedy neutralizes the gas with some jugs of sodium thiosulphate sitting around. Then a break-away floor dumps them down into a chute and they are hurled into the river.

Down-down-down we were being shot into pitch darkness! Into an
abyss—faster-faster-faster! (p. 104)

The police haul them out of the river amid a great deal of coarse
humor—both being naked. A raid on the devil-worshippers' temple proves
unsuccessful. Kennedy and Walter return to their apartment on Riverside
Drive. While bounding about the Red Lodge, Kennedy has found thin glass
fragments, bits of an ampule; now he sets about analyzing the material that
is dried on the glass. He is interrupted by Stuart Webb, reporting that
Natalie has vanished. Off bolt Kennedy and Walter, hot on the chase.
Which leads them straight into a trap—their car is wrecked and three thugs
attempt to blackjack them. Walter is knocked cold, but Kennedy beats them
off single-handed, of which feat Walter remarks: "Pretty nervy, I'll say."

By now the devil-worshippers are slaying red heads right and left,
stacking nude corpses high. Learning that the latest victim lies pitifully at
the foot of the Palisades, our heroes rush forth once more.

To reach the girl (meeting all specifications of nudity and red-
headedness), Kennedy climbs a rope down the face of the cliff. Part way
down, he discovers a cave in the cliff, ending in an iron door. Certain
obvious relationships tingle his mind. Far below the cave opening lies the
unfortunate nude. Above the cave, back from the cliff, hulks a huge, castle-
like affair known locally as The Chateau.

Instantly determining that this is the headquarters of the devil
worshippers, Kennedy bribes the Irish cook to admit him to the Chateau
that very night. A posse of police come with him—rather tame police, they
are, willing to lurk in the bushes waiting for his call. Once inside, Kennedy
and Walter creep softly about until they locate Natalie. She has been locked
into a basement cell block, patrolled by a huge snake. Just as Kennedy kills
this, with heroic vigor, they are attacked by a horde of male nurses. A
delirious climax follows, reflecting the magazine's belief that peril and
menace are most interesting when piled high. Thus the nurses seize
Kennedy and Walter and:

> —hurl them through another trap door.
> —They land upon a providential ledge.
> —Then grope down stone stairs leading into slimy blackness.
> —To the bottom of a huge rock tube, inside the iron cliff door.
> —At which point, the tube rushes full of water.
> —From which they barely escape by floating up.
> —And struggling free through an inlet into a small lake.
> —Following which the police raid the Chateau.
> —Natalie is saved, after all.
> —And Kennedy now explains.

Those delicious red-heads were murdered by injections of *crotalus
horridus* (rattlesnake) venom. The cult leader did it. He was, however,
dominated by Stuart Webb who did not really love Natalie, in spite of what
you thought. He only wished to kill her for her money, which was to finance
his life with a new little love-pot. His diabolic iniquity exposed, Webb leaps

*Dime Detective*, October 1, 1933  1930s mystery action fiction, hot with weird menace, torture, and hardboiled violence, offered no real place for Kennedy, whose long series was to end in two years.

through a trapdoor to instant doom.

Thus the more usual conventions are observed: The least likely person is the concealed mastermind, the suspected head fiend isn't, and death comes for the evil of their own action, thus leaving the hero's hands unsplashed by guilty blood. (Not that clean white hands mattered much by 1933.)

"The Golden Grave" is far distant from the former adventures of our Professor Kennedy, calm and steely-eyed, working grave miracles in his Coolidge collar. Dusted thinly through the narrative glitter shiny bits of science fact, like memories almost lost. A sprinkling of fact does not make a scientific detective story, however. And, really, who cares about the Latin name for rattlesnake, as the nude corpses pile high and Kennedy rushes up the street and down the street.

In the true scientific detective story, the science must be real. It must achieve something, resolve something. Its function is to shed light, not merely to be decorative, in the manner of a fan-dancer's tassels. There is little science detection in "The Golden Grave"—only the pretend of it.

By 1933, Craig Kennedy had become something other than a scientific detective. Those *Cosmopolitan* days were twenty years and one war in the past. New fiction styles crowded the magazines. The marketplace demanded fresh wares, regardless of the writer's glorious past.

Reeve's name is signed to "The Golden Grave," but it does not read as if he had much to do with the story. The presence of a ghost writer is strongly suspected, if not proven. The novelette, itself, shows obvious carpentry work, particularly during the Chateau scenes. At that point, much additional copy seems to have been added to transform a short story into a punchy novelette. An irresponsible guess is that an unsatisfactory Reeve short story was thoroughly rewritten and expanded by hands unknown.

Not that "The Golden Grave" fails. It works nicely on its own terms, a joyous melodramatic cavort. It is pure pulp adventure, loose-jointed, furiously paced, no more realistic than a plastic whale. It is wild, nutty, superficial. It is charming.

A more sedate Kennedy adventure was published in the February 1934 issue of *World Man Hunters*. "Doped" tells of murder among the wealthy, horsey set, with scenes ranging from a night club in Hell's Kitchen to a race track. Walter does not appear. No mention is made of Kennedy's university affiliations. Now a private consultant, he is hired to cleanse a vicious mess between friends and lovers that involves seduction, debauchery and revenge. Here is a drug-ravaged ex-mistress, there a race horse suffering from the injection of fatigue toxin ("kenotoxin"). And now the horse's owner complains that he is bone weary ....

Kennedy fingers the killer in an old-style seance, the story being a mild rewrite of one published around 1916. It was updated to concentrate the action, eliminate Walter, and show how the morals of the main characters have gone to hell.

A later Craig Kennedy series then began in *Popular Detective*. About five stories were published, from "Craig Kennedy Returns" (November

1934) to the April 1935 "Craig Kennedy's Strangest Case." These adventures were ghost-written by Ashley T. Locke from Reeve's stock of unsold Kennedy cases.

The final Kennedy story to be published appeared in the May 1935 *Weird Tales*. Titled "Death Cry," it does not read as if Reeve contributed anything to the manuscript but his name.

Out there in the heart of the Catskills squats the Three Pines Hotel, grim and silent. Gaiety has flown. Guests burst forth in hysterics. Others awake to find a hulking black figure hunching in their rooms. Nights are split by screaming, "inhuman, terrifying." And Philip Coulter has just roused from sleep to find blood on his throat—yet, the door is locked, the window up only a few inches.

All this reasonably points to an infestation of vampires. Since a specialist is wanted, the manager immediately calls Craig Kennedy, who smiles a cold, bitter smile, straps on two pistols, and drives forth to battle. His apartment is left in care of his man, Parker. What has become of Walter is not mentioned.

No sooner has Kennedy set foot in the hotel than wild violence explodes. A man lies murdered, and on his throat are two small black holes. From this point the action goes Hurrah and flies round and round, fluttering madly.

Kennedy finds two pieces of black leather. The police find poison in the dead man. And the hotel guests find chaos. Every third minute, the huge black thing is seen. Screams split the silence. Something horrid attacks in the blackness of the cellar. Something horrid materializes during the spiritualist's seance.

From this point matters become ever less scientific. Kennedy slips off to a nearby graveyard to investigate and gets socked, very hard, on the head. But now he has a clue. Promptly he flies back to New York City. There he breaks into an apartment, with the lighthearted casualness of a magazine hero immune to the law's petty constraints. He finds more clues (undisclosed) and has an inconclusive tussle with a figure who vanishes with a "dry, inhuman laugh."

Back he rushes to the Catskills, the case clear in his mind. Within two more chapters, his merciless intelligence reveals the true criminal and the weird murder device. Or creature, rather, the hotel horror being a giant, blood-sucking cat from Asia—the Sino-Cat, cited in a book Kennedy borrowed from the Police Academy. Thus the whole fantasy is validated. All this flim-flam was to get rid of those standing between the murderer and a fortune.

"Let's go out to the bar," says Kennedy at the end, "and have a night-cap." Well, let's.

What a long way it has been from *Cosmopolitan*. Science detection, popular acclaim. Kennedy's name internationally known. Heady golden opportunity. Moving pictures, Hollywood, radio, uniform editions. Hard to know when the long slow gentle decline began. When the popularity first showed grey on its edges. The story content waning through the quality pulps, the lesser quality pulps, the reprint pulps. Tinker with the prose and change. Nothing worked too well, really. Modify the series here, feel it skid there. All the promotion, all the manipulation of publishing rights didn't really help that much. The quality of the work steadily shriveled. It must have worried Reeve. He adapted to the times. He lent his name and character to other hands. In the end, he junked everything.

Nothing helped; nothing recaptured that elusive bird that sang so easily in the slick magazines, way back then.

At last it turns to ash blowing in the wind of opportunism. You wonder what Kennedy would have said about it all: Professor Kennedy, the laboratory man who knew what real evidence was and how to read men's hearts.

You might catch him at the door of the Quan Lab and ask.

(But don't expect much; he was not quick to express personal opinion.)

"What do you think of those final stories, Professor Kennedy?"

The tall figure stiffens very slightly. He places one hand on the door, anxious to be gone. "Arthur was writing fiction. He did it acceptably well. There's really little more that I can say."

"Do you regret the way it ended?"

"I regret all ends," Kennedy says. He steps into the laboratory and moves away among the transparent complexities of equipment until his white coat vanishes from sight, and you can no longer hear his voice.

## 4-

For all its popularity, the scientific detective movement lasted about as long as one of those dime store roses that blooms on Monday and falls to pieces on Wednesday.

With the exception of that brief revival during 1930, the scientific detective fad essentially ran its course from 1907 to 1923. Thereafter, numerous stories were published which purported to be in the science-detective tradition. But few were.

The form was difficult to handle. It required considerable factual information worked into the context of a crime problem. It was far easier to write a mystery over which a few science facts were scattered. Such stories dot the pulps, their science often concentrated into the final lines:

> "But what he didn't realize, Chief, is that when you exhale, you exhale nothing but $CO_2$—that's just plain old carbon monoxide!"

The original form of the scientific detective quickly softened and blurred. As used during the mid-1920s, a "scientific" investigator seemed to mean any fellow who could look through a microscope without falling in. It did not necessarily follow that what he saw solved criminal cases.

More successful fiction was represented by stories employing pseudo science. These would begin realistically enough, then bump into a crime problem unsolvable in this world, and so, over the fence into science fiction, using principles yet unarticulated and equipment never to be built. Dense clusters of these stories grew, like cattails in a swamp, among the serials of *Argosy* and the advanced illustrations of *Amazing Stories*. Still later, this story form crept into the single-character magazines of the early 1930s, lending a special savor to *Doc Savage* and the *Spider* novels, where science-fictional devices were the rule.

Another successful variant of the scientific detective was the doctor-investigator. Evolving directly from Dr. Thorndyke, this specialized detective form still lives in paperbacks and television. At first, every detecting doctor dragged along a few scraps of science to be displayed, like banners in the window, when it came time to overawe the reader. For the most part, few of these doctor-investigators retained their scientific rigor, and it is extraordinary how few of them ever bothered with laboratory work. Their only professional necessities were a Harley Street address, a stethoscope and the collected works of Sherlock Holmes. Essentially they were dedicated amateurs, splendid fellows detecting for a hobby. They read criminology, quoted the less controversial Freud, and reveled in endless personal eccentricities. Most enjoyed friends holding high position in Scotland Yard—for, at the beginning, most of the doctor detectives were British. Their ranks include fat Dr. Hailey (amateur) and Dr. Reginald Fortune (one of the few professional investigators in the group).

Rather earlier, a second specialized form developed around the doctor who was, also, a psychic investigator. Members of this group were adept at handling fiends, human and inhuman, and include John Silence and Jules de Grandin. Their adventures usually occurred within an opalescent bubble of fantasy. For that reason, we will not meet them until a later chapter. All are fascinating fellows. But few employ science recognizable at Georgia Tech.

We must admit that Dr. Wycherley did.

Dr. Xavier Wycherley neatly fuses the scientist and psychic sensitive. In his own distinguished way, he represents a group of science-oriented, minor, series characters, whose adventures paralleled those of Thorndyke and Kennedy, without being spoiled by the acclaim given those two giants.

5-

The adventures of Dr. Wycherley began in *The London Magazine,* March 1911. Three months later, they leaped the Atlantic to *Blue Book,* June 1911, under the series title of "The Strange Cases of Dr. Wycherley," by Max Rittenberg.

Dr. Wycherley is a very early representative of the professional psychologist who detects on the side. Not only is he a psychologist but a mental healer and a psychic sensitive. He possesses the gift of sensing those emotions that compose the mental aura glowing about each person. Yes—that mental aura.

While this particular glow can neither be seen nor measured, Dr.

Wycherley is able to perceive it. He can heighten that perception by throwing himself into a light hypnotic sleep, thus drawing from his subconscious all those impressions which have eluded his conscious mind.

Although a modest man, benignly depreciating this accomplishment, the doctor simply blazes with aura. His personal magnetism is a tangible force, compelling you to open your heart and spill out your secrets for his inspection. Since Wycherley is also versed in the techniques of psychoanalysis (although his remarks about the subject would have astonished Freud), he is one formidable fellow.

At intervals he finds himself baffled. In that state, he begins a compulsive rolling of cigarettes with his left hand. This continues to the end of the tobacco and paper, or until he has integrated his mystical and scientific fractions. Then it is time to fetch out the scientific equipment and verify what he already knows. It is by these prosaic, solid, physiological measurements that Wycherley joins the ranks of the scientific detective.

In "The Supreme Test" (*Blue Book*, March 1912, No. 10 in the series) Wycherley's task is to determine whether a man is a true heir or a fraudulent claimant. The fellow has been gone for forty years and the immediate family rejects him entirely. Only a poor relation, who loved him once, knows him on sight. But who would listen to her vapor about a long-ago waltz that they shared.

Wycherley has listened. Shortly afterward, the claimant's blood-pressure response jags the truth across a "revolving 'drum' wrapped with soot-blackened paper (against which rests) a very light metal pointer connected electrically with . . . a battery of Bunsen cells."

Like the scientific equipment, the Wycherley stories are period pieces now, dense with Lords and Ladies and strangling doses of English manor houses and characterizations to lengths more appropriate to novelette-length fiction. The introductory pages of these stories often seem longer than either the middle portion or the end. The adventure, itself, is interesting, once you work to it through the rind of words.

In 1914, Rittenberg created a far more realistic hero—the 45-year old Magnum, Scientific Consultant to Scotland Yard. "The Message of the Tide" (*Blue Book*, March 1915) begins with an empty Benedictine bottle floating in the Thames. Inside the bottle is a note spelled out in needle pricks—rich Mr. Oakeshott, kidnapped for over a year, pleads for rescue. Each month, the kidnappers force him to sign a 600-pound check. They allow him most creature comforts. but he wants out from wherever he is.

Puffing his curved briar, Magnum puzzles the problem, his reddish eyebrows bristling. Analysis of the saline content of the bottle's corks, and comparison of this against river samples, indicates that the bottle entered the river where it meets the sea.

Over that area, Inspector Callaghan throws a police dragnet. The kidnappers are flushed out. By pure accident, Callaghan falls into the river. Magnum, numb with tension, blundering wildly, confronts three crooks who, in their excitement, stumble and bungle in their turn. It appears to be a highly accurate description of violent action.

Magnum fires a shot, hitting no one, and all three surrender.

As time passes (remarks the author in a lovely, wicked paragraph at the end), Magnum came to remember that he had done the rescue and the arrest of the three men all on his own. "Callaghan's share in the work receded into the dim background."

It is a sound, realistic story, full of deft touches, measurably superior to the Wycherley series.

A busier group of stories, in American settings and featuring an American genius, were published in *The Popular Magazine* during 1912. Additional adventures have been noted in 1918-1919 issues. These concern the cases of Calvin Sprague, "Scientific" Sprague. Written by Francis Lynde, these brisk shorts rush intricately along, full of secondary plots, and easy-to-identify-with characters, and Sprague, himself, a strongly developed lead. The initial stories were collected in *Scientific Sprague* (1912).

It is questionable whether Sprague should be included in a discussion of scientific detectives. A detective, he was not. An explainer of peculiar circumstances and twisted situations he is.

Just what Sprague's profession is remains cloudy to this day. "There is," he says, "a certain nameless intelligence department, of which I have the honor to be chief . . . ." You notice that the Chief spends more time in the fields than his agents. Sprague, however, craves action.

He is an immense, huge-framed man, built like an outsized football player. His face is round, genial and seems incomplete without a black cigar stuck into it. He is a manipulator and plotter extraordinary: ". . . man!" a friend remarks, "there's nothing to you but one big plot."

Correct. As a somewhat vague representative of the US government (the stories reflect the ardor or World War I), Sprague is out to see the best interests of the United States upheld.

"Potassium Sulphate" (*The Popular Magazine*, December 20, 1918) reels with misdirection. Sprague (inadequately disguised by a false name) is out among the western mountains talking learnedly about new chemical processes for developing local potash beds. He is spied upon by a sneaking runtish type and beautiful daughter. He is opposed by the regional railroad representative who refuses to authorize building a branch line out to the deposits for any reason whatsoever. Then Sprague's assistant, Chadwick, rides into the mountains to collect samples and is fired upon from ambush. After all these elaborate windings, the reader finds himself muddled. Not so Sprague. After crafty maneuvering, he gets that branch line built, captures a claim jumper, then saves the face of the railroad agent and secures an entire mountain of ferromanganese for the war effort.

No German spies were involved. All the spying-shooting-double-crossing-sneaking was to keep the ore out of the hands of the Eastern exploiters, a rotten bunch.

"The Terror in the Timanyoni" (*Popular*, January 7, 1919) occurs out in the Nevada mountains. There a valley community is wracked by inexplicable accidents—four railroad wrecks, a leaking dam, miscellaneous arson, a transmission line melted.

Sprague analyzes a gummed oil cup and finds sabotage. Enlisting the aid of a demoralized young man, Sprague traces the trouble to a band of hobos who are being manipulated by a Bolshevik mastermind; he plans a nation-wide reign of terror. Upon these unAmerican skulkers, muttering in an abandoned mining camp, descend Sprague and the US Army. There follows a brisk fight with rifles, machine guns and a new type of gas invented by Sprague which gives those exposed to it the sensation that they have been plunged into boiling water.

Interesting as the Sprague stories are, they are essentially adventures rather than mysteries. Action and dialogue are realistic. A strong secondary plot, carrying love interest, is used, adding both dimension and complexity to the story. At the end of each adventure, Sprague explains all, while the characters cluster admiringly about. It's sound fiction, lightly dusted with some scientific facts, but not heavily enough to interfere with the action.

A new series, even more successful than Scientific Sprague, began in the 1919 *Street & Smith Detective Story Magazine*. This series featured Dr. Bentiron, a psychiatrist, an ardent realist, a powerful and compelling figure. Written by Ernest M. Poate, himself a doctor, the stories are vigorous wonders, many of them hardly touched by time.

The series lasted a long while. Dr. Bentiron appeared frequently in *Detective Story* during 1919-1924 and occasionally thereafter until at least 1928. His cases are usually formal mysteries, bristling with complexities based on character, and carefully composed to emphasize atmosphere.

Poate's technical skill is often remarkable. He specializes in developing an atmosphere of strangling supernatural horror, gradually building, gradually edging toward the intolerable. At which point, Bentiron is allowed to demolish it all with his brutal good sense.

Many stories read as if John Dickson Carr had written them: Impossible situations, an exquisitely timed build-up, the sudden smash of sanity. In 1919, however, Mr. Carr was only 13 years old and his work lay some 17 years in the future. Still, the resemblance is startling.

Dr. Bentiron is a scientific detective who does not use devices. Indeed, he even refuses to use the telephone, but hires a nurse to sit by the devil's instrument, receiving and relaying messages. He insists that she relay exactly what he says: "Dr. Bentiron says that you are a fool."

What this irascible paragon does use is the scientific method, combined with a deep technical knowledge of psychiatry. Almost alone among the crowds of detecting psychiatrists, Bentiron has a solid grip on his profession. The others fake it, little or much. Bentiron and Poate don't have to.

Dr. Thaddus Bentiron is a professional's professional. Harvard, 1879. Heidelberg, 1882. A medio-psychologist and psychiatrist. At the Columbia University College of Physicians and Surgeons, he is a full professor of abnormal psychology, an associate professor of medical jurisprudence.

(Thus, the Thorndyke touch.) He is a Master of Arts, a Doctor of Philosophy, a Doctor of Law.

In person, he is a tall slouching man, thin to emaciation. His assistant, Dr. Blakely, describes him as having thin arms and legs. His hair is thin and streaked with gray, his beard a nondescript mousecolor. The forehead, very wide and high, slopes to a narrow face and a high-bridged aquiline nose.

This scarecrow figure is dressed in clothing worn to the threads. It is littered with ashes and cigarette burns—for the doctor is a chain cigarette smoker. (As Freud once mentioned about his own cigar habit, this is, in itself, indicative of unresolved neurotic conflicts.) Wherever Bentiron travels, he carries a fat pack of cigarette papers and a sack of tobacco. He is constantly employed rolling his own, even in his favorite positions—that of a deep slouch in his chair, a cigarette drooping from his beard, as he stares, apparently lifeless, at the far wall.

The Doctor's affectation is exhaustion. Like other amateur detectives of the time, Bentiron professes an all-engulfing weariness. He is forever sleepy and languid. He yawns repeatedly, thus indicating extreme interest. He seems too exhausted to move. Under this, as usual, he is all lightning and raw energy and competence:

> Dr. Bentiron stood in the wide doorway. His rough coat hung open, his battered, disreputable hat was pushed far back. Thumbs in belt, head cocked to one side, he regarded us in silence, one eyebrow whimsically elevated. (His face was) wearily expressionless, inscrutably wise .... His dull gray eyes, widely spaced, incredibly long and narrow, took in the entire scene in one brief, comprehensive glance.[19]

As another character reports: "He never looks at anything in particular; he never raises his voice; he never makes a quick move. But he sees everything."

Blakely reports that Dr. Bentiron did not look him in the eyes more than five times during their association together. It is fortunate for Blakely. The Doctor's full gaze congeals blood and freezes the brain. No one can endure it; they wilt, mumbling incoherently. It is a gift worth cultivating.

In other ways, the Doctor shows mannerisms as abrasive as those of Philo Vance.

He can, for instance, hardly speak without uttering a sound spelled by Mr. Poate as "Umphf!" This ejaculation may be groaned, repeated, replied, or said, having about as much variation in meaning as the laugh of The Living Shadow some eleven years later. Dr. Bentiron also revels in the annoying habit of lecturing in a dry, didactic way to those around him, speaking to them in such patronizing words that you long to do him harm:

> "Observe, Blakely, my son, how infectious is fear."
> "Observe, my children."
> "Umphf! Rot!. You are two fools."
> "It's all explained, child."

He slashes so rapidly to the heart of matters that the others—police and those standing about mystified—do seem a bit childlike. Given a fine murder to view and a houseful of supernatural impressions to dispel, he slouches about, "ostentatiously weary" until all evidence is examined. Then: "I—have—a—hunch."

In another instant follows: "Umphf! So that's how it was done! I—see."

It is a display of mannerisms gloriously annoying to those who have been on the scene all along, shivering with supernatural dread. Also annoying to the reader who hasn't the least idea of what's been going on, a condition of ignorance that will be cured, with appropriate ceremony, in the next chapter.

The central point of these stories is Dr. Bentiron's residence at 500 Madison Ave. It is a big, modern, 4-story home privately licensed for care of selected insane. His personal office is large enough to accommodate three stenographers and a clerk. The great man occupies a bare interior room, stripped to the walls and painted white. It contains two immense revolving bookcases, between which is a reclining chair in which Bentiron is wont to slump and cogitate and smoke the hours away. There are no other furnishings. Nor are there any seats for visitors. If a guest interests him, Bentiron punches one of a score of buttons on his chair arms and a chair is brought in. Otherwise the visitor stands. It's a little technique to keep people from wasting his time.

The Bentiron stories are unified in time, occurring over a number of years. Loosely pulling these together is Dr. Blakely, narrator and Watson of the series. Blakely begins as a young ambulance doctor at New York City's Bellevue Hospital, having recently graduated from Johns Hopkins. He meets Bentiron and his future wife immediately, marries about seven months later, has a marvelous child who grows up through the series, while her father puts on weight and slowly becomes bald, a not unusual consequence of fatherhood.

The first Bentiron adventure seems to have been a five-part serial, "Behind Locked Doors" (January 7-February 4, 1919) in the *S&S Detective Story Magazine*. (It was later published as a book in 1923.) The story begins in August 1913. Major George Carrington Conford, a most peculiar man, lies dead within a locked suite, a bowie knife stuck through him, and his niece Mildred Conford, bent over his remains. The police find her position inexcusable and arrest her. Blakely appeals to the famous Dr. Bentiron, who clears her within three chapters.

The mystery, nicely complex, bounces along, brimming with fascinating characters. Most of these will become series regulars. Mildred, herself, is about the size of a dime, a tiny, fragile little dear, yellow-haired, with big violet eyes, and the appearance of a pitiful helpless infant girl. Over the years, she shows unusual skill in handling both Blakely and Bentiron, manipulating them in her sweet wistful way to get exactly what she wants.

The series continues with a group of short stories that swarm up, like morning glories around the old home door, immediately after favorable reader response to the serial. In the May 20, 1919, "Without Resistance" (all stories being published in *Detective Story*), Dr. Blakely begins the psychologically arduous job as Bentiron's assistant.

"I want your protection," Bentiron tells him, grinning sardonically, "for I am a timorous man."

This is roughly the same speech that the saber-toothed tiger made to the fawn. What Bentiron seems to want is a combination colleague, chief clerk and full-time son. He treats Blakely with a rough affection that is half irony. To him Blakely is still a "cub psychiatrist," not to be allowed out of doors without umbrella and mittens.

This half-humorous, half-patronizing smother leaves purple weals on Blakely's self-esteem. Understand that Blakely is astute, well grounded in his profession. And he would be at least of normal competence if the spectre of Bentiron didn't hover over his shoulder, pedantic, fatherly, firm, eternally right.

> *Blakely*: "Dr. Bentiron possessed . . . a mental force, a dominance of character, which I have never seen approached."

The trouble is, Dr. Bentiron is a shade too dominant. His heat wilts Blakely's candle. The younger man feels that he can not possibly measure up to his senior's intolerable perfection—his mind, his skill, his personal magnetism. In the face of these, what can a young, rather inadequate, stripling, fresh from Bellevue, possibly contribute?

Consider Blakely after an evening in a possibly haunted house:

> I could have wept with relief. By his mere appearance . . . the chief (i.e. Dr. Bentiron) had snatched me out of a shadowy, dreadful half country of ghosts. . . .")

The reaction is juvenile. Blakely badly needs to pack his bag and scratch out of Dr. Bentiron's range. Watsoning is one thing; psychological dependency is another. It is a curious plight for a pair of psychiatrists to wallow in.

If his interior is partially baby fat, Dr. Blakely's exterior is that of a large young man, physically powerful in the hefty manner of a football center. But as far as his actions in Bentiron's presence, he might as well be a ninety-pound weakling with soft bones.

Another recurring character, almost as peculiar as Blakely, is Detective Inspector O'Malley. We first meet him as a detective in "Behind Locked Doors." O'Malley comes across sharp and clear, although he is most unlike those detectives down at your local station-house. His manner is diffident and mild. He resembles a small, elderly bird, hopping from one foot to the other, his tiny eyes darting, his movements jerky. Where his hair is not gray, it is red. He is about the most hyper-imaginative cop to ever get on paper.

On the other hand, the Medical examiner, Dr. Bernstein, is a hard-nosed, tough-minded fellow, with the personality of a sun-cured hide. His face is heavy and darkened by an "undercoat of close-shaved, blue-black beard." Also, he is Jewish and given to extravagant racial gestures.

(Well, it could have been worse. Before you get annoyed by Bernstein's gestures, consider the gross Jewish stereotypes peopling the Jimmie Dale stories and the older dime novels and the older silent movies. These racial stereotypes were conventions of the period, infesting the popular media like roaches in an unclean kitchen. The remarkable thing about Bernstein is that, although Jewish, he is given sufficient character traits to suggest a distinct personality. It is not a particularly charming personality but it isn't constructed from rubber stamps, either.)

Dr. Bernstein does not much like Dr. Bentiron: The unsuccessful egoist resents the successful egoist. Bernstein relieves his envy of Bentiron's professional status by a succession of sneers (oily) and remarks (caustic). All these roll harmlessly off Bentiron's airy arrogance.

Bernstein doesn't like Blakely, either. And he cares so little for O'Malley that he mercilessly elbows this small mild man off into a corner of his own investigations.

We can, at least, thank Poate for including Bernstein in the stories. His antagonism is the bitter salt that makes bearable the general adoration of Bentiron the Splendid.

All these characters stand on their own feet, for Poate is a conscious craftsman. It is odd that a writer so careful in narrative construction and atmosphere development should have assigned three of his five characters names which begin with "B." It is a peculiar oversight.

The cases through which these people move are twisting oddities.

In "Bad Blood" (June 3, 1919), a nurse is accused of accidentally poisoning a playboy patient with arsenic. It is not that simple. He died after being transfused with the blood of an arsenic eater. The affair was engineered by an Armenian, the hospital resident, who burnt with unrequited love. In this story, Blakely is to marry Mildred in three weeks. (This case was reprinted in the December 1930 *Best Detective Magazine*, a Street and Smith publication thriftily composed of fiction selected from well-aged issues of *Detective Story Magazine*.)

The wedding takes place in May at The Little Church Around The Corner, the story being "Questioned Sanity" (July 22, 1919). The title does not refer to this happy event but to an unfortunate young man who seems to be insane. And so you too would seem, if you had ingested the quantities of sodium bromide he had. It's all an attempt to break up his impending marriage and ends with no one very satisfied.

By the September 23, 1919 "False Teeth" Mildred has already learned the technique of manipulating Bentiron. (She murmurs "Daddy Bentiron" in his ear and looks helplessly dainty.) It has been a long time since Bentiron had a woman around the asylum. His wife died thirty years before and he still maintains her room, locked, in his quarters. He is, then, sentimental and more than a trifle neurotic, under that omnipotent exterior.

The police work in "False Teeth" is nothing short of incomprehensible. In a Bentiron case, the police never exhibit the least ability. It is the primary flaw of the series. Their failure in this matter is outlandish. You see, a horribly burned corpse has been found, the upper body and head virtually destroyed. In the mouth shines a set of false teeth, fresh and clean. True sons of Inspector Lestrade, the police look blankly at this clue. The corpse is identified as a man who is insured for $100,000. Even then, the official mentality does not function. As for Bentiron, he takes one look at the teeth, detects toothpits in the gums, and knows a body has been substituted. From that point, it's all routine.

"Phantom Footsteps" (March 23, 1920), is, however, admirable. In this story, Poate elaborately constructs an atmosphere of supernatural fear, then blows it all to rags with a brisk influx of Bentiron's common sense.

That fierce old social tiger, Mrs. Nicholas Ruyter van der Duynck, Sr., brings her daughter, Marianna, to be examined by Bentiron. Since he is out of town, Blakely does the examination. And much intimidated he is by the old girl, who is hell on wheels. Marianna, who gives the impression of being almost transparent, is languidly fading out of life. Neither of the women wishes to tell Blakely anything and he, in turn, refuses to prescribe, and they part inharmoniously.

Shortly afterward, there arrives Mrs. Nicholas Ruyter van der Duynck, III. She is a sensation named Gloire, a vivid young man-killer. She had married the battle-axe's only son, Nick, who immediately got killed while being a hero at a fire. Lost his leg at the knee and his life simultaneously.

The old lady bitterly hates Gloire. Gloire despises both the Mrs. and Marianna. And they all live together in the same house.

At this point, Blakely begins praying for Bentiron's return.

Now the build-up begins, neatly buried in Gloire's conversation:

> "Nick ... used to say, if I forget that I belonged to him forever, he'd come back, even *from the grave.*"

That remark is tossed out in a flood of hard, specific detail of life at the van der Duynck's. Then later:

> "... that dark gloomy house, doctor, and the noises at night! Such dreadful, creepy noises—creakings and whispers, and rustlings down the hall .... And the old woman humped over an ouija board, with the walls cracking and knocking all around her."

Vivid, brief pictures that are followed by a rush of realistic descriptions and the solemn profundities of psychiatric name-dropping.

Now a few weeks slide by. Mrs. NRvdD, Sr. and Marianna return. Blakely begins collecting a family history that includes paresis, manic-depressive psychosis, puerperal depression, psychic palsy, hysterical stigmata, and double ptosis—which last is dropping of the eyelids.

The only thing that he can pry out of Marianna is that she's worried about Nick. "Do the dead come back?" she asks. Seems she is wondering if "poor, dead Nick, out in the snow" might not be returning to see his wife.

One single touch of latent horror. Then they leave. The chapter changes. Gloire returns in a terrible state.

At this point, you may begin to feel oppressed, since all the action has been talk and hearsay, at that, and Dr. Blakely has had four consultations, in four chapters, with these dreadful people. What saves the story from folding up in its tracks is the rapidly increasing black mass of something terribly wrong, as if smoke were pouring into a closed room.

Now begin the phenomena. In the night, Gloire looked out the window of her second-floor bedroom to the snow-covered roof:

> "There were footprints in the snow! Footprints, as if somebody's stepped on that roof, right out of the empty air, and walked up to my window . . . . Doctor, the man—that thing—that left those marks hadn't but one foot! . . . —and on the sill the snow was all packed, as if somebody had put his knee there—or maybe the stump of a leg that had been cut off at the knee."

The method here is to describe precisely a phenomenon while, at the same time, ascribing a cause for that phenomenon. The resulting double image paralyzes the reader's brain. To state an opinion as if a statement of fact were being made creates an impossible situation. It is pure sleight-of-hand, a method developed and polished by John Dickson Carr all through the 1930s.

After this brief glimpse of the horrible, Poate immediately swamps the reader with almost one full chapter of solid, unemotional descriptions of the real world: a little girl sleeping, snow squeaking underfoot, the familiar, precise detail of normal life.

That night, Blakely is called to the van der Duynck mansion. Marianna is worse. And Gloire has been murdered, slaughtered in her bed with a trench knife. Outside her window, in the snow, show three footprints of the left foot.

The police are baffled. Blakely is shaken, Marianna is hysterical. The old lady is abstracted. The doors to Hell are open and the night reels with fear. But Bentiron is returning this very night. A call is placed for him. While they wait for his appearance, the policemen:

> peered about continually, gripping night sticks as though they expected some mysterious attack. The . . . servants huddled near them . . . . An air of suspense, of half confessed fear of the unknown, of the supernatural, pervaded the whole house.

Early in the morning, salvation appears in the guise of Dr. Bentiron. He has taken long enough to arrive, allowing Poate to milk every possible cold shake and to present Bentiron with a grand, symbolic entrance.

His first action is to throw back the shutters, open the windows, let in the sunlight.

> Beneath the crude, bald light of day, the candle failed . . . . The corners started out of the darkness; the room became commonplace, material, a stiff, severe room clustered with ugly, old-fashioned furniture. And old

Mrs. van der Duynck ... was no longer a pythoness, a sybil, but a weary,
pathetic old woman whose false teeth did not fit her ....

Bald common sense, with crude sunshine, now spreads through the
story. That horrific atmosphere rips to rags. Again they investigate, review
the evidence, and, in two chapters, Bentiron has-got-it.

It is a case of multiple personality, a psychopath tortured by "the
feminine counterpart of the Oedipus complex." Resulting in hysterical
somnambulistic self-hypnosis, followed by homicide, followed by brain
hemorrhage and death.

The old lady did it.

She recovers sufficient mental clarity to confess, just before the
hemorrhage carries her off. By that time, Bentiron has hypnotized her and
she has repeated, step by step, the entire murder process—using a rod to dip
a shoe into the snow, taking down the trench knife. And, in a scene of horror,
stalking the bed where Gloire had slept, preparing to stab the empty air. The
abnormal has been substituted for the supernatural. The goose bumps
remain the same.

"In Self Defense" (April 27, 1920) is another long story. It is complicated
by people and their effects on one another, rather than by events. Off in a
small town, some human demon has beaten an old man with a chair, killing
the first and wrecking the second. A thick-headed rube sheriff has arrested
the old man's son. Bentiron sends Blakely forth to investigate. As Dr.
Watson before him, Blakely gathers most of the facts and none of the correct
conclusions. No sooner does Bentiron arrive than things snap audibly into
place. The end is in a jail cell. Following the immortal footsteps of Luther
Trant, Bentiron has brought in a sphygmomanometer and a Parkinson
volumetric apparatus:

> Though the lay reader may not know it, emotions produce easily
> measured changes not only in the pulse and blood pressure but also in
> the size of the soft tissues. Our bodies actually expand and shrink in
> sympathy with mental processes.

Which was Trant's point, precisely, back in 1909 in "The Man Higher
Up."

All this equipment is not really necessary, since Bentiron already
knows the truth. Still, the instrumented response causes the murderer to
break down and confess, much to the sheriff's delight: He had the right man
after all.

It is appropriate to mention, at this point in the series, that the Blakelys
now have an exquisite little dear girl child named Janet, just the brightest
sweet you ever did see, she would break your heart with her cute ways.

"For External Use Only" (July 27, 1920) leaps four years in the story of
Bentiron and company. The great man has served throughout the war as
head of the British Commission on Military Psychiatry. Returning to New
York City, he seems "aged and saddened .... It was as if somewhere within
him a bright lamp had been turned down." But his mind is as piercing as

ever. It takes hardly thirty minutes for him to see through a problem of murder, strychnine being administered in a rub-on ointment, "for external use only."

The "Vials of Wrath" (September 28, 1920) are plague cultures. A maniac is mailing them all over New York City. The case is a high-tension suspense thing that ends in a hand-to-hand struggle with a religious paranoic whose left hand grips a shattered culture of plague bacilli.

The September 6, 1924 "Deadwood" is another long story in the formal murder mystery tradition. Deadwood is the name of a crumbling mansion of the architecture and atmosphere of the House of Usher. The parallel is drawn in the story. Blakely, vacationing with wife and marvelous child, is drawn into a murder where packs of cyanide fly in all directions and every single suspect is a textbook case of advanced neurosis.

"Yellow Jack," a three-part serial (March 24-April 7, 1928) begins with attempted murder in an overheated New York City apartment. The time is winter. The weapon is Stegomyia Calopus infected with Leptospira Icterosus, i.e., mosquitoes with Yellow Jack. Bentiron was never better. Blakely, growing old, bald, fat, is so slow that everything must be explained to him twice.

The Bentiron series is one of the most successful in the 1920s pulp magazine. As in the Sherlock Holmes stories, from which they descend, the atmosphere and personality of the main character, the interchanges between Bentiron and Blakely, all are as important as the stories, themselves. The writing is clear, tight, informed, although occasionally marred by sentimentality (usually Blakely's) and unbelievable police incompetence.

The stories build leisurely, their detail, carefully selected, reflecting a strong medical-psychiatric orientation and assuming that psychiatric insight is an acceptable substitute for Professor Kennedy's electro galvameterscopes.

## 6-

A popular fiction type rarely ends grandly. Not for it the ultimate procession of priests and trumpets and orchestra massed toward a mighty terminal C Major chord. Rather there is a bland melting away in the manner of a Debussy prelude. Fewer characters appear in ever shorter stories. One day, the stream of fiction glides shining along, displaying no evidence that caped avengers, sex-ridden spies, or scientific detectives had ever enticed the public interest.

At some point immediately preceding extinction, it is common that a final major character rise. However brief his appearance, he summarizes the field and lifts it to new life. He is the final grand statement. After him swirl lesser characters only, minnows in the wake of the pike. Then oblivion for the form.

Those fretted by the need to classify may pick endlessly at the problem of the final major scientific detective. Bentiron, perhaps? Taine, that unabashed little man? Doc Savage, himself. Or perhaps the *Scientific Detective Monthly*, substituting a magazine for an individual in the tradition of a technological society.

Strictly speaking, the final, old-fashioned, brass-bound authentic scientific detective of a series seems to have been Dr. Daniel Goodrich, medical examiner and, as we learn, famous criminologist. He was followed by three different avatars of Craig Kennedy, severely confusing what would otherwise be a simple chronological exercise.

Whatever his position in pulp fiction history, Dr. Goodrich is indisputably of the scientific detection brotherhood. His eventful life was recorded in a six-story series that appeared in *Everybody's Magazine* from December 1921 to June 1922. The stories were written by Stoddard Goodhue after reading Nick Carter, Dr. Thorndyke, Craig Kennedy, Dr. Bentiron and an organic chemistry laboratory manual. A different mix of ingredients appears in each story. No two stories have the same mix. They can hardly be said to be predictable.

The first of the series was titled "The Phantom Auto" (December 1921). In the course of 41 pages, Goodrich must explain, cope with, or use such a galaxy of technical marvels as:

> —a driverless red car that races furiously about Long Island,
> —silenced aircraft engines,
> —a remote-controlled boat,
> —a radio antenna inserted inside a woman's garments in such a way that, when she receives messages, she must lift both arms, thus seeming The Bride of Auld Hootie,
> —radio-operated locks,
> —an automobile that electrocutes those touching it,
> —signals given by lights operating at frequencies beyond human sight,
> —a combination laboratory/drawing room within a Connecticut cave, wherein a ferocious German schemes and plots, his mistress reclining languidly in an adjacent chamber.

All this material is rammed into a long short story, thus burning up sufficient devices to operate a normal series for a year. The driverless automobile first attracts attention, as well it might. Then it is necessary to discover why men are found sprawled about electrocuted. From this point, action piles upon action until Dr. Goodrich, concealed in the German's sinister cave, watches a double killing, and ends fighting for his life, as well. An exhausting story. Nick Carter fancied up for the slick-paper magazines, but written so ineptly that even the highly informal Carter series would have spurned it.

"Test Tube Necromancy" (January 1922) fails totally. This seeks to imitate Thorndyke's didactic manner. The narrator is nameless and just as well. He is a boob beyond salvation. He begins the story by asking Goodrich if the microscope or test tubes are more important in a laboratory. Unfortunately, the amiable doctor does not promptly kick him down the stairs, but explains, page after page after page, how to perform a test for human blood. At intervals, the author puts aside his laboratory manual long enough to explain that a young woman has been murdered on board a steamship. The bloody knife has been recovered. The bloodstains are being tested.

On and on the tedious sentences drone, gray, gray, gray. Eventually the chief suspect is tied to the murder knife because he once lived in Australia and on the blade remain ancient stains of kangaroo blood, exciting a galaxy of enthralled ejaculations from the audience.

"The Magic Wheel" (February 1922) describes how Goodrich detects and foils a crooked roulette wheel. In "The First Stone" (March), a minister, boiling with paranoia, accuses a fellow of murder and sets the town tingling against him. "The Accusing Voice" (April) is excessively slow and dull. By heroic exertions, the author lumbers into the narrative on page 5, gets a young woman stabbed and a young man falsely accused. In a court room scene indistinguishable from a minstrel show, Dr. Goodrich interviews a disembodied feminine voice. The real murderer assumes it is a ghost returned and breaks down, coldly shaking, confessing in a loud voice. Very dramatic. The voice was that of a young woman speaking at the other end of a wireless telephone, scientifically packed into a suitcase.

Putting odds and ends together, it is possible to report that Dr. Goodrich has extraordinarily keen gray eyes and a face, frank and open. "Its aspect was benevolent." He is also said to have a "powerful synthesizing imagination." The descriptions are vague as to age, weight, background. He has a country place at Roxbury, Connecticut; he is a New York medical examiner and is versed in matters scientific, although he is not sure that Freud is on the right track.

> *Dr. Goodrich:* "Psychology is only common sense in polysyllabic attire."

That remark is from "The Locked Room" (June), a complete novel, 39 pages long. The doctor is called in to consider the problem of a man found dead in an apartment with all doors locked. No sooner has he arrived than Goodrich assumes the classical position remembered by Nick Carter lovers:

> [Dr. Goodrich] stood just within the entrance, with his hands in his pockets, his head forward a little. Every faculty was alert, and within twenty seconds he had seen things that another eye might have failed to discover after an hour's scrutiny.

Since the right-handed dead man holds the fatal automatic in his left hand, Goodrich senses murder. Then enters the wife, a morphine addict, just returned from Oyster Bay. And so the story proceeds with little movement, much dialogue. After a long while, and considerable self-conscious misdirection, the guilty one is discovered. It was the wife, all the time. She concocted her alibi by calling in on the extension phone downstairs and *claiming* to be in Oyster Bay.

At this point the series drops dead. No scientific detective will penetrate the pages of *Everybody's* for fourteen months, until the brief Craig Kennedy series begins, September 1923.

When Dr. Goodrich departs the literary scene, you experience no sense of anguish. His stories are buried in undramatized prose—always excepting "The Phantom Auto." Elaborate backgrounds of scene and character are provided at the beginning of each new case, burying the true opening that can usually be located by systematic pawing through paragraphs piled on pages 4 or 5. Once the deed of violence is discovered, then it is talked about casually for the remainder of the story. Much scenery is described. The furnishing of many rooms is detailed. Narrative movement does not trouble the pages. The fiction is as inert as a ledge of slate. You can only wonder that Dr. Goodrich lasted as long as six stories.

Formal scientific detectives grew ever harder to find after the early 1920s. That means (as you will remember) those individuals who customarily used the tools and techniques of science, the villainies of their fellow man to learn. Of detectives using an infrequent scientific fact to close his case, there was an over-supply. It was the fashion. Every writer who knew a fact of medicine, or how a word association test was conducted, promptly wrote a long long narrative, featuring his fact. The jackdaw is supposed to make whole nests around some glittering bit of waste it has found. Why wonder then that men write fiction around a fact: Real, glittering scientific fact.

In constructing *his* nest, Ray Cummings created The Scientific Club, a group of pundits gathered to work out interesting criminal problems. In writing about The Club, Cummings (who would also shine in *Argosy* and the science-fiction magazines) saddled his prose with a hateful stylistic trick. It is a ripple from Robert Louis Stevenson, through Wells and Doyle. He names his characters in terms of their professions.

For this reason, members of The Scientific Club are known as The Chemist, The Banker, The Alienist, The Astronomer, The Big Business Man and that stock character The Very Young Man. (He is included to arouse smiles of warm nostalgia and affection.) Each individual has a first and last name and these are given, but in such an intermixed and fragmentary style that notecards are required to keep them straight.

The initial activities of The Scientific Club were pure fantasy. They appeared for the first time in *All-Story Weekly* (March 15, 1919), peering into a golden ring to see, way down there among the molecules, "The Girl In The Golden Atom." The success of this adventure, which introduced Ray Cummings to the world of fantasy fiction, spawned sequel after sequel. The Scientific Club, however fascinated by coming and goings between atomic worlds, found time to become involved with other fantastic activities.

One of these adventures was recorded in a 2-part serial, "The Thought Girl," published in the May and June, 1920 issues of *Live Stories*. The idea here is that concentrated thought can bring a mental image to life. With the aid of several hundred scientific minds, all focusing together, a man's dream girl is created from the stuff of thought and becomes real.[20]

During 1925, The Scientific Club took a sharp jog toward more traditional scientific activities. Through a series of stories published in *Flynn's*, The Club turned to detection. As in "Telling What He Knew"

(March 21, 1925). The problem, simply stated, is that Mr. Ober's wife has vanished; the poor fellow went gently off to bed and, when he got up, she was gone. The police—as often happens in 1925 *Flynn's*—have discovered nothing. Ober relates his doleful tale to The Chemist who whisks him off to meet other members of The Club.

They feed him some fascinating rigmarole about one of the members being a telepathy expert, able to use Ober's mind to focus the thoughts of the wandering wife. Agreeing to the experiment, Ober is fed a complex word association test. Close analysis of the results indicates that he has murdered the poor woman and buried her away. Before the word association test is worked through, The Club advise the police and they locate the body. Quick work and an ingenious job.

"The Man In the Bath" (June 20, 1925) was a fussy old fellow who gobbled sleeping pills every night and bathed with a pair of thermometers—one for water temperature, one for air temperature. As we get old, we get funny. One day he is found face under the bathwater. Accidental death? Not really.

The Club adds and subtracts and finds that it is murder. The solution, you see, is based on the cooling rates of that volume of water in the tub, using before and after data derived from the thermometers. (At this point, it becomes evident that we are not dealing with fiction; Cummings is offering us a dramatized problem from his first-year Physics book.) And more marvels impend. It seems that the murderer took a bath first, only later deciding to kill the poor old boy. Look around the edge of the tub and there, black on white, is the ring of the murderer's bath water. Calculate how much water (in pounds) you need to add to reach that ring again, and you have calculated the murderer's weight. Eureka! The murderer is, therefore ....

Another 1925 *Flynn's* character who dabbled irregularly in science and detection was Ex-Inspector George F. Hopper. The stories were signed Bertrand Royal, almost surely a pseudonym hiding the author's real name.[21] The cases have the content of an air sandwich. Huge volumes of words, wallowing gustily, puff 500-word anecdotes to 5,000-word giants. The inflation of the text is materially assisted by Hopper's tendency to hurl Significant Sayings into his remarks, blithefully indifferent to syntax, word meaning or sense:

"Life and dreams are leaves from the same book."
"I can't pour conjecture into the empty mirror of my mind."
"The only time I'm aware of is in my brain."
"A white bubble of truth in the dark waters of suspicion."

The man should have been a poet. Instead he is a former inspector of the Queen City detective bureau. He has recently married, which may account for much.

The Hopper case, "White Bubbles" (February 21, 1925, *Flynn's*) illustrates how the scientific detection story had hardened to formula. A snarly rich man is accused of killing his chauffeur. This unfortunate is found stiff, stark and pink-cheeked in the garage, his head cracked. In 7 1/2 pages, Hopper knows the answer, although it takes another 10 pages to pry it out of him. First there is endless fiddling, hollow conversation, a courtroom scene. Even a plan of the garage is provided, all dimensions given and such salient points identified as Window, Bench, Vise, Door.

Since science must be served, Hopper secures some "aseptic glass vials, freshly corked" from the local drug store. In court, he performs a test proving that the chauffeur really died from carbon-monoxide poisoning. He calls in an expert witness for a technical demonstration: A strong beam of light is passed through a blood sample in a direct vision spectroscope, producing a deviated spectrum resulting from the monoxide-saturated oxyhaemoglobin solution. Now that's science. Hopper triumphs. General applause. And not one word as to why the Medical Examiner did not identify the cause of death in five seconds or less.

A more concentrated story in the December 4, 1926, *Flynn's* features Douglas Greer, one of those faceless 1920s detectives who differs from his fellows chiefly by the way his name is spelled. Greer is not usually a science detective, preferring the methods of Sherlock Holmes. However in "The Liquid Bullet," he uses a word association test to capture a murderess, first having deduced the significance of a fire-blackened enamel spoon, a stain on the rug, and a tiny funnel, coated with paraffin. (She poured melted solder down the sleeping victim's ear. Imagine her disgust when she discovered that she had accidentally not murdered her husband.)

Far different from this bland, English-flavored prose, is "Earmarked for Doom" by Roland Johnson (*Flynn's*, September 4, 1926). Here is a true 1930s pulp action story, only slightly misplaced in time. The hero, Dan Martin, is the confidential investigator for the English Southland Aircraft Company. They have implicit faith in him, so much so that his only asignment is to work at his own discretion.

Southland has a problem more grave, even, than assuring that their investigator stays busy. Two of their aircraft have burst into flame while in flight. Both were totally destroyed, no small loss since these were giant two-man aircraft. Something must be done, for Southland's stock values are collapsing.

Dan Martin sits whittling in his sitting room. He is a tiny little man, calm and precise minded, with a passion for air relics having criminal associations. Thus his walls are decorated by a fragment of a propeller that killed a man, the flying helmet of a murderer, and such scarlet memorabilia.

To this point, the reader has assimilated sufficient background data to support a full novel. Now Dan rises from whittling, goes forth to investigate the latest smouldering wreck. He learns that the plane flared up instantly and came blazing down. The remarks at this point are an interesting commentary on 1926 aviation technology:

> An inflammable structure of wood and canvas painted with airplane dope, fanned by a hundred mile-per-hour wind and charged with gasoline, does not last long when once properly alight.

While investigating, he learns that a third plane has gone down blazing. He has a chemist analyze the ashes, learns that metallic oxides are present which should not have been. His nimble mind instantly makes the bridge: A fiend has been doping the fabric with ferric oxide and aluminum oxide in suspension. This makes thermit and, when dry, any slight pressure will ignite the whole thing.

The fiend is caught with these sinister oxides in possession, and is carried off, howling imprecations, amid the wreckage of his plot to get rich by selling dear old Southland stock short. Five murders, three planes destroyed, and an agreeable pseudoscientific fact around which to build the story.

7-

The final formal stand of the scientific detective occurred in the *Scientific Detective Monthly/Amazing Detective Tales.* By that time, the form, as a school, was dead. Gernsback's attempt to revive it only made the corpse twitch.

In addition to Luther Trant and Craig Kennedy, at least six other detectives appeared in series of two stories or more. For the most part, these gentlemen luxuriated in magnificent titles—Doctor or Professor. High in the councils of the mighty they towered, mere police deferring to them. All problems melted before the scour of their mighty intellects.

Of these investigators, Dr. Bird and Professor Cauldwell concerned themselves with cases over the line into science-fiction. The other characters draw perilously close to that strange boundary, and it requires an act of will to include them in the same chapter with Thorndyke.

Professor Armand Macklin is reasonably typical of the group. A full professor of Police Practice and Crime Investigation at Roger Williams College, Williamsburg, he "holds the first chair of its kind ever established in America." (Reeve thought Craig Kennedy was the first, but never mind.)

Professor Macklin's achievements are narrated in the first person by his secretary, a shallow dullard named Sabre. Their initial case, "The Campus Murder Mystery" (January 1930, *Scientific Detective Monthly*), begins October 4, 19--, if that fact is of interest. To wit:

An immense explosion staggers the campus. In its aftermath, numerous pieces, later identified as fragments of a Professor Kapek, are found scattered about. Examination reveals no trace of clothing. Large quantities of glass mingle with the remains.

On this evidence, Professor Macklin deduces that Kapek has been slipped into a gigantic tube of liquid oxygen, "the glass being of a special nature." As indeed it would be. Once the victim was frozen, the killer attached the tube to a balloon, sailed this over the campus and dropped it. The poor frozen fellow shattered like glass.

Moments after these revelations, Macklin tracks the killer to his lair. There the wretch cackles in muddled glee: "I have already squeezed a little needle into one of my veins, that releases me from any terrors your clumsy law might have for me."

Increasingly scientific adventures follow. In "The Impossible Crime" (July 1930), a woman is hypnotized into stealing her own diamond necklace, creating a locked room mystery. "Death In A Drop" (October 1930) combines such proven ingredients as a new deadly poison, a shatter-proof bottle that shatters, foreign agents, and a fearsome sonic projector. Barely has Macklin revealed all when the killer commits suicide (once more), turning bright green in the process.

The author of these stories is Ralph W. Wilkins, whose prose sounds as if it were written by a wind-up toy.

Miller Rand, the Electrical Man, was introduced in Neil R. Jones' May 1930 story "The Electrical Man." Rand is still yet another criminologist, an active fellow, ever ready to break into a crook's home to tap the telephone and plant dictaphones. In "Shadows of the Night" (October 1930), Rand is cooperating with the police and the Treasury Department to hunt down a gang of counterfeiters. As the forces of Law engage Crime in a rousing shootout, Rand slips in behind the thugs and taps each with a little wand. This is connected to powerful storage batteries carried beneath his coat and gives them such a shock .... As the story closes, he is pondering the idea of a bullet-proof suit, an idea whose time was not yet.

The adventures of Blackstone Kent were written by Ralph Milne Farley (in real life Roger Sherman Hoar). "The Flashlight Brigade" (June 1930, *Amazing Detective Tales*) opens with a man shot dead in his office. The inventor in the next building is accused. This is because the police can't decide whether a bullet flew into the office or flew out of the office, which is about par for the police in this fiction.

In the murdered man's desk, Kent discovers a flashlight that is blinking in code. Immediately he deduces that it is rigged up as a radio receiver. In a jiffy, he and the police are using radio directional finders and triangulating radio signals, and there, at the intersection of three lines, skulks a nest of infamous stock manipulators.

During the case of "The Vanishing Man" (August 1930, *Amazing Detective Tales*), Kent investigates the mystery of the thief who strikes, steals and vanishes into thin air, right out there in the sunlight on the street. Turns out that he has a paraffin nose and paraffin cheeks, enabling him to mould his face, a la Cleek, as he darts away.

Blackstone Kent is only a part-time detective but a full-time lawyer, a "great Lawyer," as Mr. Farley remarks. At the same time as these stories were appearing in *Amazing Detective Tales*, Kent was also featured in "The Radio Menace," a serial published during June-July 1930 in *Argosy* and another science-fantasy. His activities left him precious little time for the pursuit of Law.

Perhaps the most interesting character of this semi-scientific detective group was Doc Singer, gambler and surgeon. His adventures were written by Eugene DeReszke (or de Reszke—take your choice—it was spelled both ways.) During the Great War, Singer operated on his own son, wounded at the battle of Argonne Forest. The boy died. Crushed, Singer renounced surgery to run a silken gambling nest frequented by ritzy losers.

*Amazing Detective Stories*, June 1930. A retitling of *Scientific Detective Monthly*, *Amazing Detective* featured mystery fiction fantasies and remarkable covers. The disturbed lady has green hair and a red face and catches the eye.

When not manipulating the pasteboards or preventing suicides, Doc Singer investigates crimes that have a medical touch. "The Painted Murder" (August 1930, *Amazing Detective Tales*) is one of these, an elaborate bit of foolishness. The rich old uncle has died, leaving an oil painting of himself to the wastrel nephew. All else goes to the portrait painter. It is a most peculiar portrait. In the right light, you can see that the artist has drawn in the skeleton, nerves and circulatory system, over which is painted the old man. The way Singer figures it out, the artist used the painting as a physiological road map to help him locate the vargus nerve, controlling the heart action. Once zeroed in, he pressed down hard upon that nerve and became an heir. Since the murder is totally impossible to prove in court, it is necessary that the wastrel nephew enter raging and shoot the artist and all ends well.

"The Clasp of Doom" (October 1930, *Amazing Detective Tales*) features a handful of 10¢ a dance tickets that kill you dead at a touch. Through the story pass numbers of hard citizens, painted floozies and floods of bootleg hootch. All are intermixed with such wonders as an oriental rug soaked in lime juice, experimental procedures with laboratory rats, and emergency surgery to remove a man's arm—without his permission, either. But malpractice insurance rates were lower then.

It should be mentioned that the great detective, Taine of San Francisco, was also featured in *Scientific Detective Monthly* and *Amazing Detective Tales*. In deference to this extraordinary man, discussion of his career will be deferred until a later chapter.

The cancellation of *Amazing Detective Tales* creates one of those useful stopping points, like a scenic pull-off on a mountain road, where the reader can pause and take a long overview of the history of the scientific detective story. On one hand rears the shining granite of Thorndyke; on the other boils a curious pink mist through which huge figures struggle.

In less symbolic terms, the scientific detective story began with real laboratory equipment and realistically drawn characters and ended with science-fantasy and characters like cartoons. The genre formed from the initial successes of Dr. Thorndyke, combining two separate elements. One of these was the investigator who was a doctor and used his medical training in the solution of crimes. The second was the technically trained investigator who used real scientific equipment and techniques to collect evidence admissible in court. Initially bound closely together, these elements soon loosened and began to diverge.

The doctor detective has proved the most viable of the two strands. Thorndyke was an early representative, although not the prime mover, for both Doyle and Freeman, himself, had published earlier mysteries in which doctors played a leading role in the solution of crimes. After Thorndyke followed such major brilliances as Dr. Fortune, Dr. Hailey and Dr. Bentiron, part of the 1920s Golden Age. To varying degrees, all used scientific knowledge to advance their cases, although their professional expertise and common sense were of greater importance.

The scientific detective line budded off directly from Thorndyke's use of technical equipment, not to mention Polton's craftsmanship. The initial purpose of that equipment was to collect and verify data. During the Luther Trant stories, however, the technical equipment became a means of demonstrating guilt. The Craig Kennedy adventures magnified this tendency, so that the equipment, like devices of magic, became essential to the resolution of the problem. Much of the story interest transferred to the specific apparatus used.

The emphasis upon technical performance placed severe demands on most writers. Neither education nor experience had equipped them to deal with the realities of laboratory apparatus. And few writers were so conveniently placed that they could easily learn of new applications in the law enforcement laboratories, where these existed.

Obvious applications of known apparatus were soon exhausted. But fiction demanded ever new wonders. It was not the first time that a literary fad had exhausted experience's well.

By the early 1920s, the public passion for scientific facts wrapped in lukewarm narrative was plainly cooling. By necessity, writers gradually edged their fictional investigators toward scientific-tinged fantasy. Their apparatus steadily advanced past technology's limits. Their cases were more frequently sited in that filmy border between reality and dream.

This division clearly shows in issues of the *Scientific Detective Monthly* and *Amazing Detective Tales*. The older figures, Thorndyke, Trant and Kennedy, practice science; the newer figures, 1930 creations, practice science-fiction.

In whatever world they practiced, these science-oriented detectives directly influenced the action-adventure pulps of the early 1930s. Already that influential practitioner, Lester Dent, toyed with the image of a big, hard man, loving action, who actively fought crime from a suitcase crammed with scientific gadgets.

Down through the 1930s, Dent spilled out a stream of series characters (hardly ever formal detectives) who used devices from the leading edge of technology. Foster Fade, Doc Savage, Click Rush all demonstrated that the scientific detection still exerted its ghostly influence. The action fiction of the 1930s, however, is substantively different from that of the 1920s, as stained glass differs from pewter.

By the 1930s, the scientific detective had essentially mutated to the detective-adventurer who used science and its tools as part of his normal investigative routine. Scientific techniques had begun to merge with formal police routines. While science still fascinated, it was no longer an alien tongue. As ballistic comparisons, fingerprint files, soil analysis, blood spectrums, lie detectors became conventional adjuncts to the Technical Police Laboratory, then the science detective melted insensibly into the mainstream detective fiction.

It is a customary phenomenon. Yesterday's miracles, neatly dried, crackle quietly in the file marked "Routine."

What miracle awes us today?

# The Dream Men

The brave man meeting violence with violence has a long history. You can trace his lineage back across the generations, each hero emerging from the last. He predates Nietzsche, the Iron Age, the Bronze Age, goes sliding out of written history to surface on painted walls in Spanish caves, glimmers in legends told and retold until the little dot of event, buried at the story's center, vanishes within a glowing haze of myth.

We assume the Cro-Magnon told of heroes. Perhaps the Neanderthal did. Origins of the hero figure are back there in time, lost among European forests and Asian valleys, deep within hot plains of grass in Central Africa, back to the very childhood of man, where time, like a great artery, throbbed out the generations and the shapes of living creatures flowed, unstable as dreams.

Whether beneath African heat, or sailing the wine-dark Aegean, or whirling through a gunfight in New York City alleys, the heroes are from the same great stock. During the years of the pulp magazines, some extraordinary variations appeared, brightening the sober edges of the world. Among these characters you could find one who:

> —thought best while listening to a recording of "Raggin' the Scale."
> —investigated mysteries while disguised as a dead man.
> —was physically held together by scar tissue and steel plates.
> —branded enemies with the print of a scarlet spider, having first shot them dead.
> —had no identity at all, only a series of perfect disguises, leaving the character only a mellow whistle as his basic personality.
> —was a practicing Lama from Tibet, adept at paralyzing foes with electric shock administered through his finger tips.
> —was employed by a ceramic toad to solve mysteries at $10,000 a case.
> —moulded his paralyzed face like bread dough, when disguise was required.

The heart celebrates them, the odd, the strange, the peculiar. All marvelous, each operating in a world more or less sharply realized, with friends and assistants of an oddity even more extreme. For the reader should be able to identify with the hero, but the sidekick need only be unusual.

The single-character pulps, in which so many of these characters performed, were one branch of the great mainstream. During the 1930s, the hero theme was so prevalent that some believe the field to contain nothing but Captain Captains or Colored Masks or Fearful Avengers blazing away at the underworld. But no. Even when the single-character magazines flamed in white-hot success, they represented only a single log in the fire. Innumerable other series characters glowed as heroically, if more modestly.

These characters appeared in the final magazine folios behind the main novel, and they appeared again and again. Their adventures were followed by faithful readers who wrote to the editor, praising and blaming with equal fervor. These series characters—that is, characters featured in long strings of stories—touched virtually all the pulp magazines, from long-run general publications, such as *Argosy* and *Short Stories*, to such hyper-specialized ephemerals as *Scotland Yard.*

A few of these characters escaped from the magazines to become briefly immortalized (a matter of five or ten years) in hard covers. Others spread exuberantly through a tangle of magazine titles, decades of them, amassing an ultimate total of printed pages far in excess of better known figures.

While each figure stood alone, each was also linked to the past by theme or character type. Behind each wound a long history of loosely similar figures. For the moment, each was the newest detective, the latest cowboy, the most up-to-date adventurer. But he enjoyed blood connections with the detectives, cowboys and adventurers of the past. He was influenced by them, as he would influence the detectives and cowboys and adventurers of the future.

Each figure was unique. But the demand for heroes continues unslacked. Those we read now, freshly contemporary as they might be, are not the last. The road continues.

# II-Strange Days

**1-**

We live in a pleasingly concrete world. We are accustomed to reality's firm surfaces and find, in sunlight on old bricks or the shining metal of an automobile, a comfortable rightness.

These are known things, details of the detailed world that beats and foams at our senses. Our time is spent in familiar routines among well known sights and shapes. We enjoy orderly lives in a world where gravity pulls down and, occasionally, hearts fly up.

There are times when all this detailed, precise beauty catches in our throat. We stand at the door staring out, hot with eagerness to get behind the things we see, to open reality like a door and step through into some emerald-tinted singularity.

To see how things would be if they were otherwise.

To work magic and compute the baleful excesses of the stars.

To eat Cro-Magnon bread and taste King Arthur's beer.

To battle terror behind the ragged mountains where evil is shaped and tusked.

To look at familiar things in an unfamiliar way, seeing in them qualities unseen before. Once learn to look with that special sight, and the day freshens about you and becomes strange. The substantial world abruptly contains something more, undisclosed till now.

The senses open to new possibilties.

All around you the landscape is familiar.

But what stirs?

**2-**

London, England, 1908.

Down Picadilly waddle horse-drawn buses. On their advertisement space, in challenging red letters, the words:

### JOHN SILENCE

On the kerb, a 37-year old man, staring after the buses, in pleasure and a delicious apprehension. His name is Algernon Blackwood, at the moment torn between a career in writing and a career in dried milk. As he said, "a lucrative, yet utterly uncongenial career ...."[1]

71

*John Silence* is Blackwood's third book. Like his first publications, it is a collection of short stories about hauntings and supernatural terror. His name already rides high among writers of that story type.

It will ride higher. He does give up the dried milk business (and the assurance of a fortune) and becomes a full-time writer. Over a long life (1869-1951) he will publish largely, most of it fiction, most of it fantasy and supernatural. Among the stories will be three or four still ranking at the top of the field.

The supernatural story is a well-defined branch of English literature. The category includes more than ghosts, routine bleeding skeletons, and misty ladies come back to press an icy kiss on their lover's brow.

These were popular apparitions of the stage, the story papers, the popular magazines. Popular then, popular in *Weird Tales* decades afterwards.

Less obvious, and proportionally more effective than these horrors, were themes developed during the last half of the 1800s and the first decade of 1900. In these, the shock was contained less in a specific thing—a detached hand, a walking corpse—and more in evil as a powerful and malignant intrusion into our reality. Behind reality, as we see it, lie churning powerful forces, vast and often hostile to man, at best indifferent to him. These may be natural forces, or intelligences whose passions persist behind the wall of death, or evil that is the antithesis of the spiritual in mankind. All pry grimly at the edge of reality, seeking to strike through into the concrete, detailed actual.

Sometimes an opening occurs accidentally. Sheridan LeFanu's "Green Tea," for example, tells of a young man who drinks too much of that poisonous beverage, grows intensely sensitive to psychic phenomena, and finds himself hounded by a demon.

Sometimes evil penetrates the world through an object of force that serves, at once, as a focus and a gateway, as in Bulwer-Lytton's "The Haunted and the Haunters." Or, more conventionally, a concealed body (or parts thereof), or a murder weapon, or mummy artifacts serve to concentrate the spawn of Hell.

Blackwood began writing at a time when most of the conventions had been laid down for this form of story. Over the next thirty years would be published a large amount of that fiction presently anthologized as classics, including work by Arthur Machen, M.R. James, Oliver Onions and E.F. Benson.

These writers, Blackwood included, were consciously literary men, story-tellers deliberately evoking mood and building atmosphere. By present standards, their stories move slowly and are over elaborate. They mature against densely visualized backgrounds, realistically done, only slowly deviating from the normal, diverging by hints and whispers, by crafty play on spiritual unease, until reality drops away and the pages burst with white terror.

The stories are of astounding artistry. And most of them move deliberately as a Handel oratorio.

In 1908 such material was highly popular. The reading public was receptive to things supernatural and things mystical: Thought transmission, psychic residue, astral bodies, aura glowing for any Wycherley to see, vast natural forces beyond man's comprehension. Forces from the outside, wherever that may be. Black outgushings of evil preying directly on the soul, so that it was not merely a matter of being rent to atoms, as in earlier tales, but of being spiritually fouled or obliterated by strengths prenatural.

All the subjects, in fact, which, simplified and accelerated, filled *Weird Tales, Ghost Stories, Strange Tales, Uncanny Stories* during the era of the pulp magazines.

Blackwood's contribution to the pulps was entirely accidental. He was hoping to earn a living writing and his publisher suggested the name "Silence" for a hero who would tie together "separate imaginative studies of 'psychic' themes."[2] As far as is known, John Silence appeared in only five stories in the book bearing his name. (The 1909 American edition was titled *John Silence—Physician Extraordinary*.) He was another medical man— recall the popularity of doctor characters at this period—and, although the originality of the character can't be assessed, he did focus a number of characteristics into a single personality. From 1908 on, most psychic investigators included at least a dim trace of Dr. John Silence. Although the prose was rarely as elegant as Blackwood's.

In person, Silence is past 40, a sparely-built man, with brown eyes and a closely trimmed beard that conceals his mouth without hiding the firmness of his lips or jaw. "... the face somehow conveyed an impression of transparency, almost of light ...." He possesses quite a steely self-confidence.

Independently wealthy, he chooses to doctor only those unable to pay. His clinic seems sparsely attended. He is at least as interested in "psychical afflictions" as rashes and broken bones. "The Psychic Doctor" he is called. And for good reason.

At some time in the past, he voluntarily submitted himself to five years of "long and severe training, at once physical, mental and spiritual." Where is not known. Silence, himself, was not particularly communicative on the subject.

"Learn to think," he said, "and you will have learned to tap power at its source." A statement of stupendous ambiguity, on a par with "Learn to be wealthy and you shall never be poor."

Silence's first case, "A Psychical Invasion," has been reasonably popular with anthologizers and has appeared often in book collections of ghost stories. In 1968 it was also reprinted in two parts in the May and June issues of *The Magazine of Horror* (Nos. 21 and 22).

The story concerns a professional humorist who lost his ability to write humorously after sampling hashish. The drug increased his sensitivity to forces of ancient evil resident in his house. With the aid of a cat and dog, Silence contrives to divert the evil through himself, seeking to purify and cleanse it: "He understood that force ultimately is everywhere and the same;

it is the motive behind that makes it good or evil."

His struggle against the Intruding Personality is powerfully described. The air thickens. The collie, snapping furiously, retreats snarling to a corner. The house seems full of smoke.

> [Silence] could recall nothing consecutively; a mist lay over his mind and memory; he felt dazed and his forces scattered....
> It was ... the strong glamour thrown upon his imagination by some powerful personality behind the veil.

After an extended nightmare of effort, he is able to divert and control the flow of evil. At length, he recovers sufficiently to employ a mystic chant, restoring the integrity of his soul, the room and the animals.

Conventions of the time required a rather full explanation for all these goings-on. After the narrative climax follow several additional pages in which Silence explains all. "The forces of a powerful personality may still persist after death in the line of their original momentum." The conversation at the end provides an undramatic end to a story of exhausting emotional tension, giving it that old-fashioned flavor which the next generation of writers would labor so hard to eliminate.

The following story, "Ancient Sorceries," is told to Silence. The narrator has had the singular ill fortune to visit a town in North France where his psychic memories of a former life have been accidentally awakened. To his horror, he finds himself engulfed in a town-wide celebration of the Witches' Sabbath. From this he escapes only by sheer luck. Or did it happen at all? Objective and subjunctive times do not agree. What remains is swelling horror, so brilliantly handled that it seems entirely natural for the town population to be rushing through the night, changing to gigantic cats as they run.

"The Nemesis of Fire," the third story, has also been widely anthologized and was reprinted in *Bizarre Fantasy Tales*, No. 2, March 1971.

Silence is actively engaged in this, aided by a unnamed narrator, his confidential assistant for years. More theatrical props appear than usual, including a fire elemental, a stolen mummy concealed in a burrow under an English manor house, and a particularly disagreeable sequence where the investigators are trapped in the mummy's cave as something scrabbles toward them along the only passage out.

"Secret Worship" is laid in Germany and most of it is told-to-Silence narrative. In the final pages, he takes an active hand, saving a fellow from fiends that infest the ruins of a school where monks once worshipped Satan.

"The Camp of the Dog" is told by the confidential assistant who is camping with friends on an island in the Baltic Sea. Silence is off in Hungary but arrives on the island just before the end of the story; he is in time to deal effectively with a problem in lycanthropy. The werewolf is far from usual—for Blackwood is not obvious and his stories have peculiarly modern psychological overtones. In this instance, the werewolf is an astral double, the raging id of a man which separates from him in sleep and goes storming about, a sort of materialized dream.

Again the story builds slowly to a climax of force, mixing terror and sympathy. An unlikely mixture but it makes the heart ice.

The adventures are far, indeed, from the grayer round of pulp fiction. However, each story contains elements that later found their way into the magazines.

—the common-sense professional man whose background includes mystical training of some severity.

—the fact that supernatural manifestations are subject to their own special laws.

—the relationship between the supernatural disturbance and the human psychological condition.

—realistic and detailed backgrounds and naturalistic dialogue.

—the use of mystical chants whose sounds (that is, sequences of vibrations per second) effectively cancel out evil's discords.

—the application of rational intelligence to situations of the utmost irrationality.

**3-**

Immediate variations of the John Silence figure began appearing. The most important of these was William Hope Hodgson's Carnacki, a Psychic Investigator who appeared in nine short stories, 1910 to 1947.

Hodgson's life and works are considered in detail in Sam Moskowitz's long critical biography, included in the collection *Out of the Story* (1975). Hodgson was born in Essex, England, in 1877 (or 1875, depending upon the reference you prefer). He ran away to sea when he was thirteen. He was a short, strikingly handsome man, self-educated, strongly developed in body (the discipline of his physical training rivals that of contemporary muscle men). In the life of a seaman, he found not freedom but concentrated misery. Eventually he gave it up—remaining permanently outraged at the brutalities he had experienced—and opened a school of physical culture. He continued to develop his considerable talents in photography. In 1903 he sold several articles, gradually moved into professional writing. From then until his death at Ypres, in 1918, he published a mixture of poetry, short stories and novels, many with sea themes, most of them uncanny and fantastic. Modern horror fiction, action-oriented and emphasizing physical awfuls, begins with Hodgson.

Most of the Carnacki short stories seems to have been written during 1910. Beside the rich texture of the novels, they appear thin and indecisive. Critics have treated them harshly, as critics will, kicking them for being what they are, scorning them for what they are not.

What they are seems to be a hybrid form, the supernatural story in the context of the scientific detective story. Enough of that latter form is maintained so that Carnacki does investigate odd circumstances, although these are as far from Dr. Thorndyke as the subject will permit. Carnacki also uses mounds of apparatus, including cameras, pseudo-scientific gear, and many fine articles of 14th-century occultism. It is the detective story slewed sideways, so that the subject is not crime but fantastic horror, a subject proper for a psychic investigator.

Of the nine Carnacki cases, four deal with outright horrors; one requires straight-forward detection; two reveal that the supernatural elements have been faked to conceal criminal activity. The remaining cases combine spurious and actual supernatural elements, side by side.

In only two stories does anything appear remotely resembling the conventional ghost. "Ghost" is altogether too mild a word for the ravening monstrosities Carnacki uncovers.

These are far from misty images. They are shockingly physical entities, struggling to rip through into reality, as dangerous to the spirit as to the body. Some of them may be contained by occult defenses—but with no real assurance that their brute vitality will not hack past and come screaming in, predatory, terrible, lusting for the "psychic entity of the human."

In "The Hog," Hodgson develops a loose background to explain some few of these monsters. The explanation is fragile as a dried leaf and you are afraid to examine it, for fear the whole thing will collapse. Without pressing coherence too far . . . .

A swarming psyshic world surrounds the earth, as a peach surrounds its seed. In that invisible world, which rings the earth out to 100,000 miles, swarm savage monsters of intelligence and bitter hungers. They are immense clouds of force: The Outer Monsters, Carnacki terms them. Persistent and hatefully aware, they seek doorways into reality through which they may seize the psychic energies for which they scald.

Fairly intangible forces oppose the Outer Monsters. These forces are distinctly ill-defined, since it is easier to think up monsters than forces for good. The Opposing Forces protect only in moments when men are in deadly peril. If the danger is merely physical, they do not intercede, and The Grisly Whatever may dismember you, alas. Only if your soul is threatened are safeguards interposed. You can never be sure of this protection, and some of it lasts only briefly—as when, somehow, something utters The Unknown Last Line of the Saamaa Ritual: That's good for five seconds.

The earth as seen by Hodgson resembles a tiny Ego entirely surrounded by Id. As behooves a writer who was a physical culture specialist, the emphasis is pragmatic and material. Interdimensional interactions are assumed. Force counters force.

No matter how irrational the manifestation, it is subject to its own discipline. Even horrific energy clouds conform to a sort of natural law, that assumption of controlling rationality being a comforting Twentieth Century belief.

So the vacuum penetrated by the Apollo spacecraft is populated by unmaterialized monsters and starving intelligences. It makes for a world under siege. The safeguards are few and they are heavy on simulated occult words and phrases. Yet the vigor of Hodgson's view is unquestionable. The terror it generates is real and the appalling dream stuff of its texture touches the reader in his secret deeps where pallid images shimmer and crawl.

Whether H.P. Lovecraft and the later *Weird Tales* writers were directly influenced by Hodgson cannot be immediately demonstrated, but he undoubtedly contributed directly to the narrative conventions which fed their work.

Carnacki's experiences,then, vary wildly from slobbering nightmare to the mundane criminal case. As a basic rule, he views "all hauntings as unproven until he has examined them."

His examinations are in detail, meticulous as those of Thorndyke. Carnacki may test a haunted site for three days to three weeks, suspiciously probing for secret passages and mechanical devices. He relies heavily upon the evidence of photography.

Rather less routinely, he uses information obtained from the Fourteenth Century *Sigsand Manuscript,* a document packed with valuable insights, obscurely spelled. As a routine precaution, he protects himself by chalking out a pentacle on the floor, around the edges of which he swabs garlic, a specific since the time of Bram Stoker. (Carnacki hates the odor.)

Adjusted about the pentacle is such mystic paraphernalia as candles, hairs, little vases of complex water, mysterious ribbons, *et al.* To these he adds a modern innovation—an electric star, sized to fit inside the chalk lines. The star is powered by a storage battery and is composed of vacuum tubes which glow a thin and eerie light.

Later he will experiment with concentric circles of glass rings, each shining a different color, a multi-colored target, himself in the center representing the bullseye. Later he will test, almost fatally, a machine that emits vibrations distasteful to certain of the Outer Horrors.

The first Carnacki story—the scientific detective turned inside out—is "The Gateway of the Monster" (*The Idler*, January 1910).[3] It is the first of five stories to appear in that publication. We begin in an ancient mansion. There the door to the Gray Room slams violently all night long, although constantly kept locked. Each day, the bed clothing is found heaped on the floor. Over the years, three people have died strangled in that bed.

After extensive checking, Carnacki becomes convinced that something dangerous truly occupies the room. He isolates himself there, crouched behind his defenses, leaving a caged cat in the main room. And now begins a night of appalling terror.

Into the room materializes an immense black hand—an "abnormal monster." It spends the night hurling itself at him, clutching, grabbing, attempting to slam itself through the protective force. The cat is killed at once, then battered against the floor at intervals.

Worse, Carnacki finds he must watch himself intently. The hand seems to have some influence over involuntary actions. He discovers that he is making unconscious movements which threaten the integrity of the pentacle.

After the horror has subsided in the morning, he discovers a peculiar metal ring concealed in the room. This he takes into the pentacle that night. Almost too late, he discovers that the ring serves as the doorway by which the hand materializes into the room.

Suddenly looking up, he sees the hand towering over him inside his defenses. Carnacki makes one long dive, barely escapes. The thing is trapped inside the pentacle, however. Next morning, he destroys the ring and the haunting ceases.

"The House Among the Laurels" (February 1910) is a more conventional story. This one concerns an old isolated mansion where doors close when they feel like it, the fireplace flames out, candles dwindle away, and blood drips from the ceiling. All this is elaborately faked by a gang of miscreants using the place as a headquarters, their sinister plans, unspecified, to accomplish. A time exposure reveals the fraud, but not before Carnacki and a number of burly police are panicked into flight.

The story is effective up to a point. Just how these phenomena were caused is very hastily slurred over. It is at this same point that other Carnacki stories grow weak, giggle and fall down.

Hodgson wrote these stories, outre as they are, within a conventional fiction device of the period—the story frame. That is, Carnacki says to a circle of friends, "Let's us all sit down and I will tell you a story. It was a dark and stormy night . . . ."

The arrangements are simple. At irregular intervals, Carnacki invites four close friends, Jessop, Arkright, Taylor and Dodgson, to his home for dinner. (Dodgson actually writes out the story that Carnacki narrates, giving unlimited opportunity for quotes inside of quotes.)

The four arrive at 472 Cheyne Walk, Chelsa, and converse socially about matters not related to Carnacki's work. After diner, they adjourn to the study and, amid a pungent fuming of cigars, the story begins.

This type of narrative structure lends perhaps a hair of verisimilitude. Once into it, the action part of the story is stripped and taut. Unfortunately, the frame slows not only the beginning but causes the climax to fall several pages before the end of the story. In 1910 that may have been considered no problem. Certainly the same technique is used in some of the John Silence cases. Into those final pages, the author tucked all the loose ends, partial evasions and excuses required to chink up holes in the main narrative. The structure, however, makes it impossible to peak the story on the final page (unless a double surprise ending is used) and the effect is strongly anticlimactic.

Because of this framing, the Carkacki stories all tail off from whatever heights of fear they have achieved and they end with what resembles the question and answer period after the lecturer has closed his notes. This is hardly tolerable, even when A Great Detective is explaining how the murder really happened. In a Carnacki episode there are enough questions left unanswered that he must arbitrarily terminate the discussion. This he does with the "genial" formula: "Out you go. I want a sleep."

And shakes their hands as they step out into the darkness, facing a restless night's sleep and the tendency to sit up in bed, round-eyed, at the slightest sound.

"The Whistling Room" (March 1910) must have wrecked their sleep wonderfully.

From an upper room in an Irish castle droans a huge whistling, foul and persistent. Investigation reveals no physical causes. The atmosphere is nerve-shattering. While Carnacki works within the room, he finds it filled with a purposeful, malevolent silence—"the beastly quietness of a thing that ... thinks it has got you."

Carnacki eventually decides that it is a haunting by a Saiitii manifestation. (Hodgson did enjoy words with numerous vowels.) This is akin to a spiritual fungus that can alter wood, stone, brick, any matter, to its own purposes. That is, the inanimate reproduces functions of the animate.

Practically, this means (as Carnacki finally discovers) that a vast mouth can form in the floor or walls of the room. He observes this at close range, since he is lured into the room and finds himself staring at a pair of monstrous lips bulging from the floor. Only the intervention of a benign Protective Force saves him.

The story is wonderfully effective, particularly if read at night with not many lights. A modern reprinting may be found in the June 1965 *Magazine of Horror*, No. 9.

Dodgson's choice of stories to publish (through his literary agent, W.H. Hodgson) is unfortunate. He has a plethora of splendid material to draw from. Certain of these cases are casually mentioned as Carnacki talks along: The Gray Dog Case, the Buzzing Case, the Moving Fur, the Silent Garden, the Nodding Door, the Grunting Man (which may have been published as "The Hog"). Instead of these lost splendors, the next story was "The Horse of the Invisible" (April 1910).

The story is effectively built and sustained. In this fine old family, there is a legend that the first girl will be haunted by a horse during her courtship. Sure enough, she gets engaged and a horse begins galloping around the house and through the house and inside rooms of the house. The tension builds beautifully, then collapses when the haunt is revealed as a rejected lover dressed in a horse head. At the end, a possibly real horse haunt is introduced. But by then, anticlimax has destroyed the atmosphere and "Out you go. I need a sleep."

"The Searcher of the End House" (June—not May—1910) occurs early in Carnacki's career. He is living with his mother in a rented cottage where doors slam and a rotting stench rises. Two ghosts appear—a fleeing child, which Carnacki sees, and a woman, which he doesn't. The ghosts are incidental to other manifestations caused by human agency, apparently a smuggler who is attempting to regain possession of the house for professional purposes. The case is, as usual, interesting, but contains so many loose threads that it resembles an unraveled sweater.

"The Searcher" is the final Carnacki case to appear in *The Idler*. Several years later, "The Thing Invisible" was published in the January 1912 issue of the *New Magazine*. The case concerns a dagger that flies at intruders who enter a private chapel after dark. Turns out that it is all the action of a mechanical device. In spite of that, the story contains a superb description of Carnacki's rising terror as he sits alone in the black chapel. It is an evocation of fear at a level with the best of Blackwood, and an interesting foretaste of later detective novels in which the dark swirlings of the supernatural are conjured up by the writer to conceal the human hand beneath.

As far as is known, only three other Carnacki stories were written. "The Hog" appeared in the January 1947 *Weird Tales*. That same year all the stories mentioned, plus "The Haunted JARVEE" and "The Find," were collected in the book *Carnacki The Ghost-Finder*.[4]

"The Haunted JARVEE" borrows certain touches from Hodgson's novel, *The Ghost Pirates*. It tells of a voyage Carnacki makes on an old sailing ship, the JARVEE. The ship is pursued by barely visible shadows that come sliding in across the ocean, followed by violent squalls and persistent loss of sailors up among the sails. Carnacki gathers the remaining crew inside the electric pentacle and tries to combat the Forces by a vibration mechanism. The ship is almost capsized before the mechanism is shut off. No defenses work. The JARVEE sinks. Just what was going on remains unclear. Carnacki thinks that the ship had become a focus, its natural resonance frequencies turned to "psychic waves," drawing terrible forces to her. Something like that.

In "The Hog," the case evolves from fear to horror to terror. The development is sustained to the bursting point. To begin with, Mr. Bains is having horrible dreams. He seems to leave his body and drift inexorably downward toward thickening horror through tunnels ringing with squeals and grunts.

He wakes—but his soul remains below, lost in the deeps. By willpower alone, he must draw it back, struggling passionately, always on the verge of failure.

He consults Carnacki about this difficult situation. Carnacki's diagnosis is straight to the point: Bains has a gap in his spiritual insulation from the Outer Monstrosities, a disorder covered by relatively few health insurance plans.

Carnacki decides to explore the situation, using his new spectrum defense, a grouping of seven concentric vacuum tubes, each a different color. It is an almost fatal miscalculation. Before the night is over, both men are subjected to concentrated attack. Around the exterior vacuum tube forms a writhing whirling cloud of black, squealing with rage. Snouts probe out. The room shrills with sound.

A huge transparent pit has formed in the center of the defense. Down in the pit's immensity appears the slowly rising figure of an enormous hog, gradually expanding, thrusting up, at last, a gigantic snout into the room, lifting the inner ring of the defense.

The ring begins to melt ....

The story is an extraordinary tour de force. Carnacki is entirely defenseless, burdened by a mindless man grunting and fighting him, forced ring by ring back into the defenses. To be saved only by the intervention of an exterior Protective Force, a shining mound of blue striped by three green bands.

It blunts a story to have the hero saved by exertions not his own.

Carnacki has fought the good fight, however, and there is just so much one man can do against a million-mile energy cloud. It is possible that we can excuse the appearance of a Protective Force.

It is much harder to excuse the flaccid anticlimax occurring as the adventure ends and we switch back to Carnacki and his friends.

There follow pages of explaining occult trans-dimensional energy masses in terms of objective reality. It is turgid, unconvincing doubletalk, leaving the impression that someone toothless is eating bones.

But in spite of the story frame, in spite of pseudo-technical equipment, in spite of incoherent explanations, in spite of the fleshy theatricalism of the horrors,the story works powerfully.

It is the stuff of nightmare. If your unconscious contains the right repressed material, Hodgson's images leave you embarrassingly uneasy. In some manner, he speaks directly to those elements of hidden rage and fear of retribution concealed, in various intensities, beneath the sunshine of the conscious mind.

These stories leave you shaken, against your judgment. They speak fear across half a century and leave in your mind echoes that linger and disturb.

**4-**

The manuscript that arrived on the Editor's desk, one day in 1911, was evidently titled by amateurs. "Semi Dual" it was headed, a collaboration between J.U.Giesy and J.B. Smith. As the Editor later remarked: "The contents and their nature had never greeted editorial eyes before. Here was a story different ...."[5]

The novel, rechristened "The Occult Detector," was published as a 3-part serial in *Cavalier*, February 17 through March 2, 1912. Immediately it was followed by a second serial, "The Significance of the High 'D' " (3-part serial, March 9 through 23, 1912).

So began the fictional career of Prince Abduel Omar of Teheran, Persia, an astrologer, mystic, telepathist and practical psychologist. Transplanted to America, he practiced his profession from before the first World War into the heart of the Depression. It was a long run over sociologically broken ground.

Prince Omar was more familiarly known as Semi-Dual, an atrocity of a name. It reflects—or was supposed to reflect—his habit of solving criminal problems by "dual solutions—one material for material minds—the other occult, for those who cared to sense a deeper something back of the philosophic lessons interwoven in the narrative."[6]

With dreadful impartiality,the authors referred to him as Semi Dual, Dual or Semi. Not even that dimmed his popularity. For twenty-three years, his adventures appeared in the pulp magazines: Six serials and two novelettes in *Cavalier* (1912-1913); ten serials and one novelette in *All-Story Weekly* (1914-1920); four novelettes in *People's Magazine* (1917-1918); one novelette in *Top Notch* (July 1, 1918); and eight serials in *Argosy All-Story Weekly* and *Argosy* (1920-1924).[7]

*Cavalier,* July 5, 1913. The Semi-Dual adventures reflected the national interest in the occult, combined adventure, astrology, and detection by occult means.

*Argosy All-Story Weekly,* August 9, 1924. Suitably robed and knowing, Semi-Dual searches heavenly angles for the human story.

As far as is known the character never appeared in hard covers, although the equivalent of more than twenty-four books received magazine publication. Taken all together, it is an imposing narrative mass.

Both Giesy and Smith contributed substantially to the pulps during the 'Teens and 'Twenties, under their own signatures or in collaboration with others. Giesy (1877-1947) was a practising physician in Salt Lake City, Utah (another of the writing doctors). He held a number of official posts, including Assistant City Physician, Assistant County Physician and Acting Police Surgeon. Junius Smith was born in Salt Lake City, 1883. His grandfather was a brother of Joseph Smith, founder of the Mormon Church. An attorney by profession, Smith practiced in Salt Lake City until 1944. During the early lean years, he wrote exclusively for the pulps, with Giesy and without.[8] Both men were Fellows of the American Academy of Astrologicans, which possibly explains the depth of Dual's technical explanations. These leave you vibrating with the infinite hours later.

Above all, Dual is an astrologer—as well as an exponent "of many other esoteric angles of thought and the application of higher laws of force." In his world, astrology is not merely an amusement filling five inches of daily newspaper space. It is a technique for predicting the interaction of personalities and calculating their subsequent actions. All he needs to begin is the specific birthdate—month, day, year and, if possible, the time. From this information, he casts the horoscope, an intensely mathematical process which would clearly benefit from the availability of computer time. He can predict not only actions but an individual's movements at the other side of the world.

> ...if we know which planet represents the thing we seek, and which planets stand as symbols for themselves ... the time and place when these planets will come to conjunction will indicate the time and place when the various actors in the human drama representative of those planets will meet .... By constant checking of planetary positions, I am enabled to determine that point upon the earth's surface which is indicated by the latitudes and longitudes and declinations of the various planets involved. And as the planets themselves shift in the zodiac, so must I constantly check and recheck, to follow their wanderings in the heavens (from "The Compass In the Sky,") *People's Magazine,* May 1917).

The paperwork is staggering. It involves masses of detailed calculations, a tangle of lines and symbols, an arabesque of astrological equations—"a blending of Old World superstition and modern mathematical precision" is the way the series narrator explains it.

Shocking as it may be to you materialistic, scoffing Americans, to whom nothing is sacred but the Almighty Dollar—shocking as it may seem, Dual is continuously correct. Once that horoscope is cast, then out the future ravels. His accuracy is appalling. In this wicked world, it is so easy to forget that there is such a thing as perfection.

Not that we are nose to nose, here, with predestination, that comfortable excuse for doing your will. Not at all. At various crisis points, each invididual must make decisions determining his spiritual health.

Whether a good decision alters planetary orbits, or a bad one causes Pluto to bump Venus, is outside the scope of these comments.

Just why Dual involves himself in all this labor is not explained. A considerable amount of his time is spent saving women from the toils of evil, and, given that as a hobby, you can see why his days are full:

> ... woman is the keeper, the guardian of the flame of life, itself—the worker, in the workshop of the world, whose work is new life. Therefore ... woman should be guarded and kept pure that her life may flow unsullied to the generations to come. ("Compass In the Sky.")

The assumption that Woman has some worldly function other than serving as corporation president is now unfashionable. But it's interesting to see how they thought back in 1917.

At any rate, nothing galvanizes Dual to action more rapidly than some young guardian of the flame of life hovering over a pit full of sin.

In addition to defending woman, his other major function is to redress evil's balance in the world. In early stories, he several times is able to save the world from disastrous consequences. Later he battles major forces seeking to enshrine the Devil. Still later, when the story scope has contracted, he will be instrumental in crushing gangsters' elaborate plots.

Primarily Semi-Dual is concerned with people. He will make every effort to save them from crime, or from themselves. He provides the opportunity; they do the saving themselves.

Dual is reasonably accessible. To reach him, go to the Urania Building and ride the elevator to the 20th floor. From there walk up the massy bronze and marble staircase leading to the roof.

You exit into a garden, a place of shrubs and blooming bushes. Beds of flowers glow. A fountain plays over lily pads and goldfish rise slowly in the light. Overhead arcs a roof of green-yellow glass, restraining winter.

At the garden's center bulks a white cube tower. A path leads from this back through the garden to the fancy staircase.

As you enter the garden, from the stairs, you step on a metal plate. This is inlaid with colored glass, reading:

> Pause and consider, O stranger: for he who cometh against me with evil intent, shall live to rue it, until the uttermost part of his debt shall have been paid; yet he who cometh in peace, and with a pure heart, shall surely find that which he shall seek.

Pressure on the plate causes a chime of bells in the tower—"soft, mellow as temple bells in the shrine of some half-forgotten god," the authors remark, enthusiastically.

At the tower, Henri (Dual's companion and servant) escorts guests across a reception room decorated in shades of brown, and into the office.

It is a large room crammed with Persian delights: a glorious rug, an ancient bronze Venus, life-size, converted prosaically to a clock-lamp (the light glows from the golden apple held in her hand; a splendid example of

Persian kitsch). Venus looms beside a massive desk loaded with papers.
Behind it, Semi Dual.

He is a large man, leonine of head, powerfully built. Assurance and
competence radiate from him, an almost visible outpouring of personality.
His features are calm, strong, well-formed. The nose is strongly bridged,
rather hooked. His eyes are deep gray, the color signifying his position as a
lead fictional character. He wears a close-cropped beard.

(The whole description is hero as demi-god. Dual is an early example of
that physical-mental excellence which would reassert itself in 1933 in the
*Doc Savage Magazine*—and in all those other hundreds of handsome,
powerful, wealthy geniuses who chose pulp fiction as a way of life.)

Unlike most characters, Dual wears white robes bordered by purple. He
is the son of a Persian noble and a Russian princess. That blood fusion
produced an individual disconcertingly omniscient, in the manner of a tall
Nick Carter. His personal wealth, his command of languages, his technical
expertise, and, above all, the deference accorded him by the characters, are
shining realizations of those wishes meandering hazily in the reader's
secret heart.

Dual's interface with the outer, material world is on the seventh floor of
the Urania Building—the firm of "Glace and Bryce, Private Investigators."
A private line connects them with the white tower. Dual was largely
responsible for the formation of this agency and it stands constantly ready
to aid him.

James Bryce, retired Inspector of Police, is half the firm. A substantial,
tough old-timer, he is heavy-set, wears a stubby brown mustache, and
grinds away at a black cigar. He is neither stupid nor incompetent. Behind
him is a life of successful police investigation in big-city law enforcement.
He is hard-nosed, discerning, has city-wide contacts.

Gordon Glace, narrator of the stories, is younger than Bryce. Solidly
built and competent, he was formerly a reporter on the *Record* (whose editor
first named Dual "The Occult Detector"). While a reporter, Glace met Dual,
assisted him in certain early cases to clean up "police tangles." At Dual's
suggestion, Glace changed his vocation to detective. He is married to the
charming Connie, met in an early novel.

These three characters and Dual are the continuing core of the series.
Other minor characters appear at intervals, but the regulars provide the
continuing frame about which Dual's enchantments twine.

From first to last, the series covered such major astonishments as
World War I, Prohibition and the Jazz Age, and the Depression. Distinctive
times. They flavored the prose. The earliest stories move with crisp tension.
They are told by Glace, at that time an unmarried reporter who consults
with his strange, predictive friend. The action is usually seen through
Glace's eyes. His solo flights into peril are monitored mysteriously from
afar by Dual, hovering off the edge of the page, peering in. "The House of the
Ego" (*Cavalier*, 3-part serial, September 20 through October 4, 1913) tells of
a young woman who wishes to do good good good. She has fallen into the
talons of Bhutia, a crooked swami. Bhutia operates a mansion of

instruction (The House of the Ego) which is filled with thin-witted seekers of Mystic Symbols and Occult Meanings, all slowly bleeding into the swami's bank account.

Glace insinuates himself into the house as a student of the swami's lore. The mansion is straight out of Nick Carter—or perhaps, Old Cap Collier. It is a house within a house, the space between filled with secret passages, secret stairs, secret levers, secret switches. Extra added attractions also include magnetic door locks, secret panel controls, mystic hangings, a deadly cobra, a pair of evil schemers, and a fine death plot against Glace, whose connection with that noted cop, Bryce, has been discovered.

It hardly seems possible that Glace can save either the girl or himself. But the swami has reckoned without Semi Dual ....

"The Compass in the Sky" (*People's Magazine*, May 1917) is one of those lavishly detailed adventure stories stamped by the African romances of H. Rider Haggard. Little seems drawn from the works of Edgar Rice Burroughs, although the story includes a beautiful girl abducted and carried across Africa, a situation Burroughs had already exploited lavishly.

The girl is Madeleine Lemaire, daughter of the French Commander at Fort Grampel. Alas for her. She is lusted after by Lt. Jean Marsal. He lusts also for German gold and has stolen important papers which will precipitate an international incident if the Germans get them. Off heads Marsal across Africa, papers under his coat, Madeleine tied to an adjacent horse.

In 1917 it was not proper for a young lady to accompany a man across the trackless veldt. Sleeping in his tent, unchaperoned—my dear, I could die with shame! This revolting state of affairs is glossed over by Madeleine's flat statement that, if he lays a finger-tip on her, she will kill herself.

That defers, if it does not quench, Marsal's zealous ardor. He doubles his efforts to seduce her with smiles and winning words. And so onward they ride, a decidedly uncomfortable pair, as ....

...across the seas, in the Urania Building, Semi-Dual summons Glace telepathically. ("You ought to get your brains insulated," growls Bryce.) They are leaving immediately for Paris. The French people need them. Poor Connie is left to her cold, solitary dinner, and off they go to Paris, where the Chief of Police and the Head of French Secret Service ask Dual's aid in averting world catastrophe.

Matters are hardly so grave. The stolen papers reveal a French scheme for extending their influence in Morocco, reprehensible but hardly disastrous. But you know how those Frenchmen carry on.

Dual dazzles them all by displaying knowledge that he could not possibly have, right down to the fact that Marsal has stolen the girl:

> *Dual (In a Matter-of-Fact Voice)*: "...each man has some planetary force which governs the thing we call destiny. If one knows the ruling sign and the planet and the planetary influence in operation at a certain time, one may forecast what the future may hold.... It is no more than the application of a proved and existing natural law, based on the interchanging moves of magnetic force between star and star...."

Even in this 1917 astrological statement, the occult is no more than an expression of natural law. It is not magic but rational science, dressed in white and purple robes.

Now begins one of those splendid trips across the face of the world that the pulps did so well: from Paris to Algiers, by train to Tunis. There Glace infiltrates a small group of German agents, who accept him rather more readily than they would do in the real world. Thence to Khartum.

At this famous place, Dual shows up in the company of a big tough native named Shemba. The lead German is captured, tied, and tossed into a boat before he can gasp "Vaterland." Onward the travelers go, up the Nile to the Lost Land of Ophir. Dual checks planetary progress by the day, calculating, calculating. The German sweats. Glace makes notes for the book he will write.

According to the stars, they will intercept Marsal and Madeleine up ahead. But something is awry—the planets diverge. Madeleine has escaped, taking refuge in a vast ruined city, a colossal wreck of gigantic walls and vast brooding avenues and frowning ruins, the immense temple glimmering evilly in the fading light.

Down among the catacombs, in a cavern decoratively stocked with skeletons, hides the girl, hardly to be extracted even by astrology. By this time, Dual and company have captured Marsal. As they bring Madeleine up away from the skeletons, the evil Frenchman escapes with a triumphant cry.

Shemba shoots him dead, then turns his attention to repelling Marsal's minions, now shrieking down upon them.

Even this Dual has foreseen. Per his instructions given weeks ago, Algerian troops arrive, just at that instant, and with a blast of rifle fire obliterate all final traces of evil. The story ends in a spasm of fierce joy: Virginity has been preserved, the Kaiser checked, French imperialism unfettered and astrology, the glorious science, vindicated. Up the planets.

After the conclusion of the First World War, this positive tone falters and is greatly subdued. The serious literature of the period showed distinct tendencies to sever all connections with former generations and their works. It was not that these connections were evil in themselves, but that spokesmen of the previous generation had been so conspicuously wrong in so many things. Men who have been launched on frontal attacks against massed machine guns, entrenched and sited in depth, are not apt, afterward, to applaud the wisdom of their leaders.

The war introduced all manner of neurotic symptoms into fiction. There was general disillusionment with everything that one might be illusioned with. There was also a calculated search for gratification, personal and immediate, and a vehement denial that contemporary social structures remained relevant. There were equally strong feelings that some sort of conspiracy lay at the foot of it all.

Some blamed the Jews, some the munitions makers, or the Wall Street capitalists, or the Huns, or sinister plotters lurking within the British Empire. The paranoic whimperings were further reinforced by a sharp economic depression following the cut-back of government contracts at the end of the war.

Even the studied optimism of popular fiction wavered. The story of adventure tended, more frequently, to become a story of single struggle against shapeless evil, concealed and vastly powerful, sitting erect in the darkness, black teeth slimed, and waiting.

Which is neurosis. And which (to shrink our horizons to the issue at hand) may possibly explain certain elements in the Semi-Dual novels published during 1918-1921.

At first you notice little change. "The Black Butterfly" (4-part serial, September 14—October 5, 1918, *All-Story Weekly*) seems as barren of clues as some of Nero Wolfe's cases, years later. A celebrated beauty is found murdered, dressed in the costume of a black butterfly. Upon this enigma, the detectives batter in vain, until Dual reveals the truth, using psychometry (or perhaps manipulative psychology) and the interpretation of paintings by the insane.

The post-war emotional sickness begins showing itself through the next serials. These form a series within the Semi-Dual series, and pit Dual and his friends against the Black Brotherhood, representatives of the Devil on earth, worshippers of Erlik, Commander of the Hosts of All Evil.

By embracing evil, the Brotherhood has relinquished personal souls. Death is a total stop for them; they die and cease to exist. Very disagreeable. Their battle with Dual gradually escalates through the serials, employing ever more extraordinary devices—psychic bombs, telepathic spying, mass hypnotism, and what would pass for out-and-out magic if it weren't so deftly explained.

The sequence of four serials begins with "The Ivory Pipe" (3 parts, September 20—October 4, 1919). (All were published in *All-Story Weekly*.) Next followed "House of the Hundred Lights" (4 parts, May 22—June 12, 1920); then "Black and White" (4 parts, October 2—23, 1920); and "Wolf of Erlik" (4 parts, October 22—November 12, 1921).

By "Black and White" Dual has so interfered with the Brotherhood that it sends an assassin after him. She is Lotis Popoff, daughter of a "Red" who committed suicide in the previous story. Lotis comes against Dual with evil in her heart and, as his glass-inlaid plate promised, lives to rue it.

He immediately captures her, then hypnotizes her, hoping to save her soul (for she has performed no overt evil deed and can still be saved). The Leader of the Brotherhood, a fiend named Otho Khan, now turns all his skill to destroying both Lotis and Dual, and our hero has a busy time of it keeping the girl alive; either her vital energies are being drained away or she is attempting to leap from the top of the Urania Building. Always something.

Echoes of the recent war, weirdly reshaped by the general atmosphere of psychic-occult wonder, bang and rattle within the action. Dual is attacked by Otho's psychic bomb. This appears as a sort of singularity in the air, amazing Glace. The bomb allows remote reading of minds and has the added advantage of exploding with immense violence, exactly like the Western Front.

That scheme is foiled without much trouble. Then Otho begins a major attack. Dual's rooftop is assailed by three men. Smoke bombs are exploded and through the haze appear two killers disguised as firemen. Their assignment is to chop Dual up with fire axes.

The effort fails. Dual gestures hypnotically in the manner of Mandrake the Magician, causing the axes to writhe into giant snakes. The hit men stand transfixed. The third man, Otho's second-in-command is driven from the scene by Lotis, who jets fire at him from her dagger.

This is the action climax of the novel. It is a rather trifling affair. Four long serial parts build to this shrunken climax; it is a Fourth of July celebration climaxed by a single firecracker. "Black and White" barely waddles along, laden by tons of description and talk. Particularly talk. Everyone jabbers at everyone else: Dual soothes Lotis, Lotis is desperate, everyone talks apprehensively and peers over his shoulder. How slowly this action story drags. What Giesy and Smith intended was to show all the action occurring on a spiritual level, only occasionally translating into action in the material world.

It drags.

"Wolf of Erlik" is a trifle busier and contains many good scenes, most of them involving Lotis. She is married now, fighting at Dual's side to smash the power of the Brotherhood. This organization has gathered unto itself many voodoo worshippers. They are all concealed in a cave, and there they chant and sweat, while Otho, sloshing with evil, schemes and snarls.

The fight between Dual and Otho is excessively astral. It employs "thoughts—the dynamic lances and swords and spears of the human mind."

Illusion is meant. Lotis faces a yowling mob of voodooers—on this occasion, Otho has descended to physical violence—and drives the rascals off by changing yarn bits from her knitting into flaming serpents. When you are a voodoo worshipper, this transformation violently unsettles your mind. It's mass hypnotism, Glace assumes, or conscious thought projection. It's wonderful.

Afterward, Lotis allows Dual to send her astral form out and away to Otho's cave. There she spies on his plans and reads his lieutenant's mind and has a perfectly splendid time, a sort of living psychic spy satellite.

Through all these stories, each action has a double meaning. Every event is swathed in mumbo jumbo, until you feel the walls begin to move around you. Afterward a perfectly rational explanation is given. Thus, in "Black and White," Lotis and knife appear mysteriously and get a great build-up as the striking force of Otho appearing from nowhere. Sensation. Later it develops that she was smuggled up in the elevator, causing the wonder to reel and go dim. In "Erlik," a major psychic attack is launched against Dual, presumably by concentrating all those voodoo minds. Then things turn around. We learn that everyone was uneasy, not because of focused minds, but because the ceaseless pounding of drums was bothering them. Dual explanations all: all forced.

Two new characters have been added to the cast. Inspector Johnson,

City Police, has become the series' official contact with the Law. And Danny Quinn, the office boy for Glace & Brice, has developed sufficient characteristics to begin carrying plot responsibilty. A former newsboy, red-headed and clever as all newsboys are, he matures through the rest of the series and, by "The Ledger of Life" (1934) is a full operative in the firm.

After "Erlik," the series swings from post-war gloom and devil plotters to the more homey fields of the gangster. "The Opposing Venus" (*Argosy All-Story Weekly*, 4 parts, October 13 through November 3, 1923), concerns a mob-based blackmail ring that is not above using women to ensnare men. Dual predicts and manipulates from afar, laboring to save a girl far gone in sin—but not too far gone. At the end, Glace and Johnson race about the city while the whole criminal plot comes unglued. Gangsters have livened up the story. There is even a running shoot-out with the mastermind, who dies by his own hand. Dual rarely participates directly in these exciting adventures; he appears in the final chapter to speak fat paragraphs of comfort and spiritual solace:

> "So in the end is the measure of a man's sin returned upon him, to crush him into nothingness. For it is written that as one soweth so shall one inevitably reap, and he who sows the wind shall reap the whirlwind, and he who sows good deeds shall reap—peace."

For those interested in the technical side of astrology, let it be known that Dual identified the mind behind the blackmail ring by casting his horoscope (after much delay in securing his birth data) and discovering conclusively that only this one fellow, of all the participants, had exactly the right characteristics to qualify as head of the ring.

For after all, "All force is one—and matter but its expression in a concrete way." Even so.

"The Green Goddess" (*Argosy*, January 31—March 7, 1931) is a six part serial concerning the strange events at the night club The Green Goddess, a dope distribution center and gangster hideout. "Oriental mystery and the horrors of a hasheesh-maddened mind ... shroud the disappearance of an American heiress in a night club." So advises the *Argosy's* editor, shaking with excitement. Matters in the serial quickly become so frantic that Dual, himself, makes a public appearance in his own identity, Prince Abdul Omar, all splendid in robes and full turban with giant ruby, dazzling the patrons of The Green Goddess. The story was illustrated by John McNeil, who did all those interiors for the Land of Oz books.[9]

"The Ledger of Life" (*Argosy*, 4-part serial, June 30—July 21, 1934) was published almost three and a half years after the "Green Goddess." This case also involves a night club. A woman is murdered there under strange circumstances. She was a blackmailer and surrounded by people who wished to do her in. Almost as many sinister characters are involved in the mystery as appear in a Raymond Chandler novel, all tough and slangy and linked one to the other like urban cockleburrs. Crooked real estate deals are disclosed, and fresh bodies, and one-way rides in closed touring cars in the grand Chicago style. Grace, Bryce and Inspector Johnson team up and spend time, gasoline and the reader's patience driving earnestly about. Semi-Dual spends a lot of time off-stage, considering that he's the lead character, but his hand is everywhere.

The finale is one of those ancient Craig Kennedy seances where all the characters gather to listen to the lead detective explain what all the serial parts have been about. Dual does so, thus justifying inclusion of the story in his series.

The case ends with gunfire (off scene), suggesting that mystic trappings needed to be jazzed up with something more hearty by 1934. As the echoes die away, Dual rose impressively: "It is ended. From the Court of Cosmic Justice there is no appeal."

The mastermind was a positively snaky lawyer, you see, so the remark is appropriate.

Dual now approaches the girl of this final adventure. She has been through the storm and, glorified, has found her man. As she clutches him fiercely, Dual stands over them and, in a ringing voice, pronounces his final words: "Daughter of Life, you have served. The Balance is in your favor. It brings you your reward."

You can distinctly hear the authors pant as they struggle to pump mystic overtones into a gun-blazing crook story.

The Semi-Dual series stretches across more than twenty years. When it began in 1912, spiritualism sought to communicate with the dead by solemn inanities; when the series ended, the New Deal, in its own occult way, struggled to communicate with a dead economy. Between these points flowed the adventures of Semi-Dual, an extended series that was at least as rational as the world around it. Like any other succussful series, it changed with the times. The occult detective coped with hateful Germans during the First World War and the forces of Erlik immediately afterward, the Devil being the cause of post-war distress. When the gangster and the bootlegger superseded the Devil's legions, the series shifted adversaries and continued the good fight.

Whether the theme was adventure in foreign lands or thought combat or gangster plots, the Semi-Dual series produced its own distinctive interpretations of the world. It emphatically presented a universe operating to laws misunderstood or ignored, modified by tides of significant force never sensed by the players in reality. This is a coherent world, shockingly close but inaccessible to few other than Persian mystics. Whatever your niggling prejudices against the bright white truths of astrology, they must fall silent before the achievements of Prince Abdul Omar. His successes speak for themselves.

Tremble unbeliever and come in peace, or Mars will prod Jupiter and you will long regret your cynical ways.

5-

While Semi-Dual labored to correlate shifting astrological angles with mundane crime, an even stranger investigator shuffled about in London.

To meet him, you ride out by train from London's center. At Wapping Old Stairs, leave the train, walk down among the derelict streets and buildings slumping amid a stink of river mud. Go through a chattering slum into a dingy street. To the right, a nailed-up doorway, a blank wall. To the left, boarded windows and a crazy fence behind which spread the Thames tidal flats. At the rear of the court stands a decayed curio shop, broken, fetid. Before it litters incomplete chairs, broken pedestals, furniture ancient, peeling, stained.

Inside the shop, dank darkness, the odor of packed trash. Animal stink thickens the air. Stuffed birds, rotting books, swords, lamps tangle in dusty heaps. Rubbish, litter and dirt.

From the rear a parrot shrieks.

"Moris Klaw. Moris Klaw. The Devil's come for you."

From where the shadows blotch thickest, from the darkness, shuffles a ridiculous figure: A tall, gaunt man, deeply stooped. A very faded blue dressing gown hangs limply about him. His eyebrows tangle. Skimpy beard strings about a massive jaw.

"Ah," he says, in a voice deeply hollow, booming as barrels tumbling in a cellar. "How nice of you to come about that most interesting murder."

A hissing sound and the penetrating sweetness of verbena. Mr. Moris Klaw is patting his high bald forehead, which he has just sprayed with scent from a small container. "Most refreshing. A Roman custom. It so cools the hot brain."

Moris Klaw, antiquarian, enigma, was created by Arthur S. Ward, more familiarly known as Sax Rohmer. Klaw was featured in a series of English magazine stories during 1915. Of these, at least four appeared in *All-Story Cavalier Weekly* under the series title "The Methods of Moris Klaw." These stories were "The Tragedies in the Greek Room" (February 13), "The Potsherd of Anubis" (February 27), "The Ivory Statue" (March 13), and "The Blue Rajah" (March 27). All dates are 1915. Later, ten stories were collected in *The Dream Detective* (1920), which has remained available through the years.

The stories continue to fascinate. They are unaged, almost outside of time, unique dreams, vividly colored and uneasy.

Each is a mystery. Some impossible thing has happened. Clearly supernatural forces have struck. The investigators crowd close together, baffled. The scenes shine with detail sharp as that of a steel engraving. Strange curios gleam within the paragraphs, relics best known to Egyptologists and seekers of occult ways. Behind these cluster ancient horrors, vast shadows and shapes pregnant with evil.

"There is here the smell of dead men," booms Klaw.

As through the museum drifts a white figure by night, leaving watchmen contorted corpses.

As laughter, frigid and cruel, shocks a room each night.

As a carved ivory statue rises from its seat, paces deliberately away.

As a battle axe, untouched, smashes out its owner's life.

Horror presses in. The air saturates with fear. And in its midst, Klaw stretches out full length, placidly resting his head upon a red silk cushion. He sleeps, an instant immersion.

Into his mind crowd images—past thoughts whose emotional charge has printed them on the air as surely as a fist prints itself in wet sand. Odic negatives, he calls them. Post-telepathic recovery, the series narrator remarks, no less cryptically.

Klaw awakes. He has seen ambiguity.

A bare-footed girl on tip toe.

Twelve peanuts in a parrot cage.

A figure stepping from a gigantic chimney.

It is enough.

At this point, the story gives an almost visible shake. And abruptly, those carefully constructed, lovingly carved, artfully devised terrors shiver and grow still.

Klaw explains, his voice rumbling hollowly.

As he does so, the real world emerges from among those terrible shadows and sanity reasserts itself. These effects, these images, these suggestions that thickened you with terror are all the work of human beings, only human beings. How strange to sense Old Egypt in this bright room's corners.

It is—we see—the same twist that ended so many of the Hamilton Cleek cases. Rohmer is a more powerful author than Hanshew and the trick works more efficiently for him, as it will work for Ernest Poate and G.K. Chesterton and John Dickson Carr at various dates in various books.

The method was old before 1900. During the first decades of the twentieth century, it was polished skillfully, and today it shines brightly silver in the romantic-gothic paperback novels lined across your daughter's bookshelf.

All four major characters of the series are presented in the first story, "The Tragedies in the Greek Room." The narrator (the stories are all written in the first person), we recognize as a functional character without knowing anything about him. Searles is his name. Most narrators bulk importantly in the other fellow's story, but Searles is so self-effacing that hardly a shadow marks his presence. It is his self-imposed duty to write up the cases and assemble all possible information about Moris Klaw. Searles has been deeply impressed, although he personally believes that Klaw's curio store would be improved by burning. What are Searles' first name, his career, his position in society? It is all omitted. He is as slippery as Klaw himself.

As the first case opens, the head of the Menzies Museum, a personal friend, invites Searles to come see a great outrage. The watchman is dead, and the case containing that wondrous antique, a Greek harp, has been opened. The harp remains within.

Also present at the scene is Detective-Inspector Grimbsy, New Scotland Yard, the youngest member of the C.I.D. He is forceful, a smooth manipulator of people, a cheroot fiend, a man of great competency fumbling now.

As they examine the dead man, word comes that Moris Klaw is at the museum door, desiring entry. During past weeks, Klaw has been hanging around Scotland Yard, an amateur criminologist seeking crime. He is full of hard sense and sharp observations and has lightly impressed Scotland yard, as much as that iron-plated organization can be impressed.

And so, in that fine old 1915 way, Klaw is admitted to the scene of the crime.

Grimbsy has the misfortune to snort at some of Klaw's statements. For the duration of the series, Klaw regards him with chilly amusement. He will aid Grimbsy only because, in doing so, he gets access to crimes from which he would otherwise be debarred.

Klaw is accompanied by his daughter, Iris—the extraordinary Iris Klaw, a slender dark brunette whose beauty hits Grimbsy like a hammer. From this point on, she fills his mind. For her part, she looks at him and gurgles with laughter. That situation never changes.

The slender Iris, red-mouthed, lovely, aloof, glides cryptically through the stories. How superlative she is, how inaccessible. That confident self-possession leaves her only once. She alone holds the key to Klaw's secrets and, more practically, to his notebooks. She is his indispensable partner, his cook and colleague, his thief, his joy most glorious.

It hardly matters that she carries cigarettes in a small, gold case and smokes them in public, a sign of moral turpitude in conventional circles. Her speech is French accented and the French are more worldly that we. She has a fondness for furs, jewelry, clothing of advanced cut and color. She could wear barbed wire gracefully. Searles wonders where the money comes from to dress and ornament her. Surely not from that rotting shop at Wapping Old Stairs. Surely not.

But that matter is never explained. Almost nothing is explained.

Iris adjusts the odically-sterilized pillow and Klaw stretches out to sleep. His dreams show a white figure at the harp case. After he awakes, the investigators sprinkle plaster of paris around the case and leave. It is a most accommodating museum.

Other nights. Another guard dies and Grimbsy grows desperate. The lead characters plan an ambush, huddle together in the Museum after dark. Impending evil thickens the air. High-tension sentences flit molten by.

A shriek. A flash of white.

Grimbsy senseless on the floor.

But a white-clad girl is gripped in official hands.

It is the somnambulistic daughter of the Museum Curator, come to play upon the Greek harp. And the deaths? They were caused by the harp, itself, a Borgia trap. Lift it from the top and out a needle stabs containing enough poison to hurl a man into convulsions. And so they died, there in the darkness, picking up the harp that the sleeping girl had dropped.

Grimbsy closes the case. But Iris remains to sear his heart.

"The Potsherd of Anubis" tells how Klaw, in disguise, recovers a valuable pot fragment. Disguising Klaw would seem to be a problem equivalent to disguising an elk. But it is done. "The Blue Rajah" is a huge Indian diamond that is stolen from a closed room from under the noses of a committee. Not only does Klaw rapidly deliver the thief and his method to us—he also reveals a secret flaw that lies concealed in the hearts of most blond women.

"The Whispering Poplars" is a revenge story, densely atmospheric, in which an American detective is stalked by an American crook armed with a Sioux war-bow. Several new facets of Klaw's personality appear: he is a marvel with a handgun and has written a notorious book, *Psychic Angles*, about haunted places.

"The Chord in G" is actually a chord in G minor, virtually unplayable on the piano. This much Klaw reported as he rose from slumber in the strangled man's room. The odic negative was of a sound, not a picture. That doesn't help Grimbsy much. He is so far at sea that he doesn't recognize a hashish cigarette butt when he sees one. Being a sensible man, he relies on Klaw—although he must listen to still another iteration of Klaw's Theory of Cyclic Crime. (This seems to be that when a relic has a criminal history, the type crime involving that relic tends to be repeated.)

"The Headless Mummies" tells of the methodical decapitation of mummies around London. Even Klaw's home is invaded and his mummy violated. Searles finally accompanies the Klaws to the rear of the curio shop.

From Klaw's book-jammed office behind the store, go through a door, up thickly carpeted stairs to a landing, black-oak paneled. It is liberally studded with suits of armor and Chinese porcelains. Beyond lies a huge room, a combination study, workshop and warehouse. And beyond this— the place is a Chinese box of rooms—is concealed Iris' boudoir, a white silk fantasy appointed with silver and roses massed in shining bowls.

As is evident by this time, Klaw is a clairvoyant. He backs up his perception of the intangible by hard common sense. In hands other than Rohmer's, the series would lose its rich occult patina and appear in the more unflattering light of routine criminal problems displayed against fancy backdrops.

In only one case does the frankly occult intrude. This occurs in "The Veil of Isis," an adventure rather than a mystery. A scholar seeks to recreate an ancient Egyptian ceremonial. He succeeds too well, conjuring up Isis, herself, in a materialization of quite terrible personal danger. Klaw saves himself, if barely.

"The Veil" is a satisfying addition to the series. As in Klaw's odd establishment, the material world contains doors behind doors. Not all of these open to our reality. The story series contains at least one door that swings wide. Into what sort of place, you are not quite sure.

**6—**

The slightest reading in 1918 magazines discloses, at once, how greatly police work was assisted by amateur investigators. Official police memoirs are silent about these contributions. You can easily understand, professional pride and professional jealousy being as they are. If a policeman cannot compete with a pipe-smoking amateur knowledgeable in fish hooks, how much less could he compete with investigators drawing upon occult forces?

These forces certainly gave an advantage. As practiced by Semi-Dual and Klaw, occult detection began at the end of the problem. First, the criminal was identified. Then followed the real difficulty, for identification is one thing and evidence is another. It seems unfortunate, but the most precisely predictive astrological chart has no status in the courtroom. Therefore since the occult detective is rather above evidence, this must be laboriously gathered by the tame police of the series.

This emphasis on crime and criminal detection was a major deviation from the initial form of the occult detective. John Silence, Carnacki and the later Jules de Grandin, all used occult techniques to diagnose spiritual disorders and correct supernatural intrusions upon reality. Vestiges of similar activity can be found in Semi-Dual's cases. In the bulk of his work, however, the emphasis has shifted from spirit land to worldly crime problems. Dual uses occult methods as investigating tools, just as Trant and Kennedy used scientific equipment. In Dual's world, the occult is not a churn of chancy forces, misty with phantoms and non-reproducible events, but a rational portion of reality, unexplored and undefined, yet fully subject to natural laws. It is a point of view which reduces Hodgson's hungry force clouds to an unwritten chapter in advanced physics.

These remarks suggest that occult detectives can be more neatly categorized than is the case. Most writers held individualistic, not to say inexact, notions about the occult. Each series differed radically from the next, and each detective sensed different perceptions. These sensitives were in touch with the infinite. But they responded to remarkably different vibrations.

An interesting representative of this group is Godfrey Usher, noted investigator of psychic phenomena. Usher appeared in S&S *Detective Story Magazine* during 1918 and possibly slightly earlier.

"Usher" is a dark plush name, filled with ominous boomings and hints of movement behind curtains better undrawn. That part is the Poe heritage. Even an uninspired guesser might suspect that the name is borrowed from Poe, together with a few of the milder Dupin characteristics. Add a healthy draft of the English ghost story, and graft the result on small-scale mystery stories and you would assume that the result would be dismal.

It is not. Quite the contrary, the stories are brief little conceits mixing what passed, at the time, as realistic scenes with chunks of fantasy. Much dialogue is used and ambiguous endings.

The stories were written by that busy fellow Herman Landon, whose work would saturate *Detective Story Magazine* for almost two decades. You will find no rigorous mystical background here. Landon doesn't really care whether his effects are consistent. His concerns are those of the professional mystery writer: color, atmosphere, hints of wonder. The prose is ingratiating and Landon develops atmosphere effectively. Usher is even slightly characterized, although not sufficiently to impede narrative flow.

In person, he is the familiar psychic investigator: that is, Dupin through Holmes and John Silence:

> There was a suggestion of the mystic in the lean, lank figure, the pale and almost ascetic face, and the flashing eyes that always seemed to be looking beyond the curtain of the unknown. His mind was a cauldron in which simmered strange and weird philosophies, but they were seasoned with an engaging and vitally human personality, a total absence of the characteristics of the poseur, and an almost boyish interest in life and its mysteries. (from *Twin Shadows*, Feb. 5, 1918)

Usher is tall and slender and his hair has gone iron-gray at the temples. His eyes are gray and capable of the usual changes in color and brilliance that so warmed readers' hearts. When considering occult problems, they are "soft, dreamy, and wonderously deep"; for mere human crime, they grow steel gray and cold.

Inspector Sebastian is a specialist in these eyes. Not because of unmanly emotions, you understand, but every talented amateur needs a high police official to pal around with. Sebastian is Usher's friend, confidant and stooge.

He seems to be an important figure in the New York City Police Department, that maligned organization. Fifty-years old, heavily built, heavily jowled, he is a "picture of close-knit strength and abounding energy, yet his face bore a look of subtlety that differentiated him from the typical police officer."

He is also slightly dense and overlooks clues that would set even Dr. Watson to wondering. However, Sebastian has a speculative mind. "Twin Shadows" begins with his reflections on Transmigration of Souls. This has virtually nothing to do with the story, but it starts matters off in a pleasantly queer frame of reference.

The story is nine pages long. The first two-and-a-half are spent in conversation between Usher and Sebastian, rambling about recollections of previous existences. Usher reveals his own recollections of having seen, someplace, somewhere, a man with two shadows. It is all exquisitely vague. End of Part I.

Part II is four-and-a-half pages long. Acting on a premonition, Usher leaves his jowled friend, goes to the home of an ex-girl friend. Once they almost wed, but a silly lovers' quarrel, etc. etc. She married stupidly and lived to regret it. Now, feeling that Edna needs him, Usher hurries to her house. "Somewhere a clock was doling out twelve reluctant strokes." And there is Edna Rossiter's home and there, inside, is Edna.

"You, Godfrey. Strange—I was just wishing you were here."

She has her reasons. In the library sits the body of her left-handed husband, the pistol clutched in his right hand. Behind him looms a lifesize statue of Alexander the Great whose eyes seem to look derisively upon the dead man.

Rossiter has conducted "an extensive trade in stolen goods" under the guise of being an art connoisseur. Apparently he got what he deserved.

Usher firmly advises Edna that she has arranged the scene poorly. He has detected the artifice of the pistol. She confesses. White-faced, stern, he calls poor old Sebastian, just into bed. (The sidekick of a hero gets little rest.)

Sebastian comes immediately, a murder case this small not being worth the time of a squad of police. Usher sends Edna after her coat. They wait in the hall, an "enigmatic smile playing over [Usher's] lips."

When she returns, they pretend to leave. Usher and Sebastian slip back into the library. And ...

> Suddenly the Inspector gripped Usher's arm, and a whisper that was little more than a flutter slipped through his lips. Usher himself felt a tingling, maddening chill coursing up and down his spine, and he suppressed a cry with difficulty.

The shadow of the statue has suddenly become two. The inspector whips out his automatic. The lights flash on, revealing a tiny man crouched by the statue. "That's the murderer!" Usher cries.

Part III: One and three-quarters pages and two hours later. The little man has confessed. He was Rossiter's partner in crime. The statue was hollow and used to hide stolen goods. Rossiter had sold the goods, attempted to cheat the partner, who hid inside the statue to lurk and wait until he could revenge himself. Edna thought that her son Edwin had killed Rossiter. (Edwin is introduced in the next to the last column of the story.) For that reason, she tried to make the death look like suicide.

> *Usher:* "You did what every noble mother would have done. When you learned that the suicide scene had been staged faultily, you loyally shouldered the guilt and conveyed the impression that you yourself had killed your husband."
> *Edna:* "... You acted so strangely. I didn't understand."
> *Usher:* "...I wanted the man in the statue to betray himself."
> *Edna:* "But, Godfrey, you did not know at the time that any one was in the statue."
> *Usher:* "No. I didn't know. I simply felt it."

That will be the motif of most Usher stories. He does not really reason out matters but he feels them. It is intuition at its finest.

"A Post-Mortem Appointment," February 12, 1918, begins in Usher's library. This is the usual mysterious room, being dimly lighted and stuffed with art objects, curios, and "a sullen-visaged Buddha" with purple eyes squatting on a table. In this case, Usher is consulted by a nut. Or, if you prefer, a gentleman of insignificant intellectual competence. His story suggests that he shouldn't be out walking the streets.

His first wife died (he tells Usher), and he married her look-alike, thirty years younger. But—but—and yet (he wonders), does his wife in Heaven approve? Really approve?

There is a way to find out. He has met this young medium named Mills. The poor fellow feels himself near death and has offered to go promptly, after death, to his first wife and learn her feelings. He will then advise the husband within 72 hours.

We may as well admit, right now, that it is all tricksters' plot. The weak-witted husband also has a weak heart and he is to be murdered by terror.

Which brings us to part II of the case, an effective ghost scene done in early English style—moans, shrieks, muffled black figures, creaking footsteps advancing up the stairs, blood pool under the door—all those delicious old gothic trappings that still work when the right author deigns to handle them. Unfortunately for the stage managers of these manifestations, Usher has seen through the fraud from the beginning, and a large number of policemen put an end to the theatricals.

"Soundless Melodies" (February 26, 1918) takes place in Grandmother Mears' haunted house. Usher and Sebastian stand vibrating in the dark while "Annie Laurie" vibrates in their psychic ears. Thus convinced that the nephew murdered the old lady, Sebastian arrests him and, sure enough, he did and he confesses. Very odd.

During "Whispers from the Dead" (March 5, 1918), Usher plays amateur sleuth. He solves a murder that has been hopelessly bungled by Sebastian, clearing the young man on death row. They can't get word of his innocence to the proper authorities in time, but that's OK. The young man falls down in a trance exactly resembling death by heart attack. Later he wakes up, murmuring the vital clue which no one knew but the dead man. And Usher, of course.

"A miracle," mumbles Sebastian.

Usher smiles cryptically.

"The Purple Terror" (July 16, 1918) presents two strangers who perhaps remember a former life together. He killed her. To jog their memories, Usher ignites an unearthly liquid. This, burning with a purple, poisonous flame, accidentally kills a lurking wretch who was blackmailing her. "There is," murmurs Usher softly, "such a thing as compensation in the universe."

The July 23, 1918, "Told in Shadow," features a possible ghost beckoning a girl to come seek a concealed grave. It is not hers. Usher arrives at the last moment, after the ghost story atmosphere has been piled to the skies, and confronts the entity with a gun. As far as can be understood, it was a ghost calling attention to itself.

"Three Wishes" (July 30, 1918) is about a ring that might be magic. It belonged to a rich man (deceased). The gimmick is that, if you had bad thoughts about the rich man, and put on the ring, it will kill you. This consequence makes his beneficiaries uneasy, since to qualify, each must put on the ring. There is also a conniving lawyer who gets his, perhaps by magic. Or was it guilty conscience? Who can tell?

Other Usher cases have not been traced. They are interesting trifles, curious enough to hold your attention. They are not quite detective stories, not quite weird stories. Mainly, they are odd.

7—

The Usher series is a pleasant variant on the occult detective theme. It is blithely inconsistent, mixing ghost with detective stories and rather amorphous melodramas with both. No central point of view unites the stories. No central purpose or belief drives Usher's character. The series is a set of changes rung on a theme only casually addressed. The changes are often imaginatively handled, but they are gripped by the iron hand of formula in which every amateur investigator is a penetrating fellow and every policeman is a clod. Neither Usher nor Sebastian is developed as a character. They are familiar decals pasted onto a series of bizarre circumstances. The fiction is exploitive and shallow, but the situations, the interesting core problems, catch the attention. You read to the end, pleased in spite of yourself.

Usher was a product of the fad for the occult dizzying the 'Teens. Spiritualism and thought transference, mystic truths and astral consciousness, all whirled together, a confetti of supernaturalism. Like other characters in other magazines, Usher toyed with occultism. He barely touched its inner possibilities.

That penetration remained for a later character, a figure vivid and engaging, crisply drawn, who perched splendidly at the interface between the supernatural and the real. There all was possible, and most of it (in the high tradition of Carnacki) could be handled by practical knowledge and common sense, liberally seasoned with violence. His name was Jules de Grandin, the most successful and the most beguiling of the occult detectives.

**8—**

Curious it is, *n'est-ce-pas*, the psychic investigator's life? Not so normally does he live. *Parbleu!* In his nights, he must himself accustom to the undead drifting at the window, their dry mouths wide, scraping the screen. Yet some, they, those creatures, come by the good sun also. *Dieu et la diable.*

By day, *mon ami*, regard you that lovely red-headed girl, all smiles. But yet, her shining eyes, stone dead they are, like stones so polished, smiling you to the heart. Ah, thinks she, tonight that throat I bite away and tear the bloody heart.

Fifteen thousand blue turkeys! Even one so clever as Jules de Grandin, even he, that extraordinary one, must wonder why flock these naughty fellows here. To Harrisonville, New Jersey of the United States. The town she is with monsters crammed, *le bon Dieu* knows why.

1925 it is. *Predicament.* The Prohibition, it raises a great thirst in honest throats. The good people of the town, so dry they are, at every party the whisky she pours out. The soul opens. The monsters, may they not then rush in?

*Regardz, s'il vous plait.* Of a certainty, Prohibition brings out those so panting demons, these dry mummies to stalk the streets, these unrepentant children of Hell so deep and hot. *Morbleu!* Strange things walk. Most surely, in Jules de Grandin, they meet their match. *Mort d'un chat!*

How they fall before him. How he sweeps them away, goblin and voodoo queen, the witch, the walking dead, the so-leering Hindu, the dead woman's curse. May the Devil roast me in flaming sauce, if I put not a stop to them.

*Helas!* They tremble at Jules de Grandin, the very much so clever fellow. Tonight we tweak the Devil's nose and catch him in his lair, and if he struggle, then with one mighty damn thrust, we hurl him to Hell, his home. *C'est une affair finie.*

It is thirsty work, *mon enfant*, even for so fine a fellow as Jules de Grandin. Pour forth the brandy. Let us leave no bottle full.

Harrisonville, New Jersey, about 1925. To this town, few enough miles from New York City, came Professor Jules de Grandin of the Paris Police, the University of Paris, and the St. Lazaire Hospital, a distinguished physician and surgeon, and the possessor of extensive erudition in fields occult, mystic and magical.

He is a tiny man, slender as a woman, with the stamina of a dock-walloper. He is that rare fellow, a blond Frenchman, wearing a mustache waxed to needle tips, wheat-blond in color, which contrasts markedly with his slim black eyebrows. His eyes are round, light-blue, icily direct, penetrating as the crisp mind watching behind a haze of school book French. His skin is pale. His chin is small, rather sharp. Being French, he is, of course, excitable, and is given to storms of rage in which French and English oaths mingle wonderfully. Before one of these spasms hits, his voice becomes low and flat. After which he flares incandescent.

He will drink anything but seems to prefer brandy. He will smoke anything, stinking French cigarettes when he can find them, cigars when he cannot. He is a skilled cook. And he is also an accomplished glutton whose eye moistens at the sight of an apple pie or a particularly sugary fruit compote. Truthfully, his sweet tooth prevents him from being a gourmet. He appreciates fine food; however, he equally appreciates any food, particularly roast duck.

His English is spoken almost without accent, although with severe diction disorders. American slang puzzles and fascinates him. Almost, one might say, it does capture of him his goat.

De Grandin appeared in ninety-two short stories and a single novel, written by Seabury Quinn and published in *Weird Tales* from October 1925 to September 1951, with approximately a three-year break from 1939 to 1942.[10] A limited number of his cases have been reprinted in anthologies, such digest magazines as *Startling Mystery Stories* and the *Magazine of Horror*, and the 1966 collection *The Phantom Fighter,* which contains ten stories lightly updated. In 1976, a series of paperbacks was issued reprinting thirty-two short stories and the novel, *The Devil's Bride.*[11]

The author, Seabury Grandin Quinn (1899-1969), was trained as a lawyer and admitted to the District of Columbia bar. Following service in World War I, he became editor of trade journals in New York City. Among these was *Casket and Sunnyside*, the funeral directors' journal, and it was because of this association that he was later believed to have been a mortician. Not so.

He taught medical jurisprudence—Thorndyke's field—and wrote both technical articles and popular fiction. He appeared in the *Detective Story Magazine* (1918) and *Thrill Book* (1919). In October 1923, came his first appearance in *Weird Tales*, his major market from that point on. His appearances in *Weird Tales* exceed all other authors, totalling 149 stories and 13 articles.[12]

In 1937, Quinn returned to Washington to practice law—first as a lawyer for a trade magazine group, later as a lawyer for the government until after World War II. After a series of strokes during the 1950s, he went into semi-retirement, continued to write on a lesser scale, and died 1969.

Quinn had thoroughly assimilated the lessons of earlier supernatural fiction. The structures of that fiction show dimly in the de Grandin stories, as old walls show under vines. Here appear remnants of Blackwood's story-building techniques as altered by Hodgson—the pitiful victim's cry for aid; the menace of forces past normal experience; the ghost breaker who strikes first at a symptom, then stands face to face with raw power. There the story climaxes, as you may recall, to be concluded by anticlimax as the hero explains all and the real world reasserts itself.

In telling his stories, Quinn abandoned the bulk of the English ghost story technique—that methodical development of atmosphere which was intended to glide you effortlessly from the real to the unreal. That technique used richly ornamented prose and consciously literary devices; and, often, a narrative movement so gradual that it barely twitched.

Quinn's stories are built for rapid movement. The prose is decently pruned, all considering, although it does not display the staccato chatter of later pulps. The length of the story is significantly shortened to fit the *Weird Tales* format. The openings flash to immediate flame. The action hurries. No time to generate a sense of accumulating evil. Begin the evil in full stride. Plunge into the hot heart of the story. Instantly engage death, fear, horror, death.

And now, into this foaming Hell comes the so-clever de Grandin in full cry, mustaches bristling, very French. He will strike and strike again until it is all over.

As was the convention of their time, Blackwood, E.F. Benson and others spent numerous pages seducing the reader from reality to acceptance of the story's central improbability. Like other seductions, this is an extended process.

Most of Quinn's stories begin approximately where Blackwood climaxed. The *Weird Tales* stories required that the reader immediately suspend his skepticism. At the beginning of the adventure, the improbabilities are fully developed and active. Mummies and ghouls are at stage center, already performing. No time is squandered in preparing the reader: This is the way things are. Up and away. The characters of the story may disbelieve; the reader may not.

Acceptance of the premise permits a fast-flowing narrative. Emphasis falls on action, movement, conflict, studded by startling scenes.

For all this, a negative price is exacted. Narrative speed diminishes character development and emotional richness. (Master writers may do both, but there are few enough of these.) Instead, easily assimilated information is provided—obvious character traits, readily recognized nuggets of sentimentality, over-simplified emotional responses, shallow and incredible.

Action has become the chief character, and even the hero is little more than an interesting decoration.

The de Grandin stories are certainly action oriented. They contain no real character development from one end to the other. In the final story, the characters remain much as they began. This does not necessarily imply a fault. The characters are warm and interesting. We enjoy them. But they do not grow.

Most major characters appear in the initial story, "The Horror of the Links" (*Weird Tales*, October 1925). (Since all stories first appeared in *Weird Tales*, the magazine citation will be omitted in subsequent references.)

Dr. de Grandin has arrived in Harrisonville to study American police methods—or some similar feeble reason. Detective Sergeant Costello, the police official of the series, introduces him to Dr. Samuel Trowbridge, de Grandin's future Watson and series narrator.

The three look into the brutal slaughter of a young girl out on the golf links. A dangerous locale: There, a young man has just escaped mauling by what appears to be an ape in evening clothes. With that report, your attention is firmly fixed and the story darts along. The horrors are rather obvious today but they come at you from unanticipated angles, never quite in the way you might suppose. De Grandin is very French. Costello and Trowbridge are appropriately thick. And the case ends in a blaze of gunfire, as the night fiend is shot and his demented creator (a mad German) is ripped from this life.

After which, in the good old style, de Grandin explains to his dazed friends what has been going on, while they slump numbly, punishing the whiskey.

As you have detected, the characters fill those pigeon holes immortalized by Conan Doyle: Costello satisfies the Lestrade requirement; Trowbridge matches Dr. Watson; Nora McGinnis (Trowbridge's housekeeper) fills in for Mrs. Hudson. And the great detective, himself? Well, while de Grandin fills Holmes' slot, he is far far closer to Hercule Poirot, who had already appeared in two novels (1920 and 1923), a 1924 short story series in the *Blue Book Magazine*, and a collection of short stories issued the same year.

De Grandin shares the natty little Belgian's perception and intelligence, his conceit, his fondness for food and sweets, his professional background (although this is dramatically fattened), his love of secrecy, his assumed foreignness to disarm opponents, his mustaches (thinner than Poirot's), and his amazing predilection for peppering his speech with foreign ejaculations.

Regardless .... De Grandin works nicely as an individual. He is his own man, more intense, more violent that Poirot, certainly a master of arts far darker than any Poirot would acknowledge. Under de Grandin's gloss of easy heroism, you note a few shadows and shades startling in a pulp magazine character. Or startling, at least, to those who don't read the magazines.

After "Links," the series leaps to France. De Grandin and Trowbridge meet there by chance and together investigate a chateau where the last six renters have died violently. ("The Tenants of Broussac," December 1925). Rich Oklahomans have rented the chateau. Already their beautiful daughter's body is wrapped in sinister, spiraling bruises.

Name of a little green man, it is all caused by a tremendous green-gold snake with blue eyes, containing the spiritual essence of a former Broussac, deceased these many centuries. De Grandin seizes a sword and slices up that ancient evil into fourteen pieces, thus inhibiting all further activities, let it be known.

"The Isle of Missing Ships" (February 1926) is a furious adventure. De Grandin is employed by Lloyds of London to discover why so many ships are vanishing, finds a nest of ship-wrecking pirates, and fights his way through sharks, criminals, an exquisitely funished villa in the bowels of a cliff, and a gigantic octopus, in that order. The activities end with a fairly comprehensive machine-gunning of the criminals, and well they deserved it.

After the excitement, Trowbridge returns home, while de Grandin moves on to Brazil and another case. After a long absence, he drops in to see Trowbridge one stormy night. Immediately, they are immersed in "The Vengence of India" (April 1926). Evil "Hindoos" have hypnotized a girl into a death-like trance and so she is buried and so, at their bidding, she walks by night. All this is to get revenge on the family. But de Grandin de-hypnotizes her and the Hindoos get theirs to general satisfaction. De Grandin ends the story by getting as tight as rubber gloves; it is the first time but not the last.

In "The Dead Hand" (May 1926), another hypnotizer has enchanted a woman's severed hand. It flies about, quite indifferent to gravity, committing atrocities, until de Grandin puts an end to it.

By this time de Grandin has settled in as Trowbridge's permanent guest. While retaining French citizenship, he remains inexplicably an expatriate—at least until the Second World War.

His extended stay in Harrisonville is initially a result of the rich fees he gleans. In "The White Lady of the Orphanage" (September 1927), he mentions that he will return to France next month with the $50,000 he has earned. But the return is delayed, then deferred, then forgotten. If he strays away for brief vacations in France, his residence remains firmly at 993 Susquehanna Ave., Harrisonville, New Jersey.

It may be that France reminds him too keenly of his own true lost love, sweet Heloise, with whom he walked hand in hand by the Loire, these many years past. Religious differences separated them. She went to a convent. He became a Professor of Medicine, "one of the foremost anatomists and physiologists of his generation." In 1910 he became a member of *la faculte de medicine legale*. World War I lifts him from the University to a life of action. But he never ceases to mourn his lost love—particularly when he gets tight, which is frequently.

Immediately after the war he began working for French Intelligence. He traveled extensively in Africa and Asia. We surmise that it was during this period he assimilated his immense fund of occult and supernatural lore. What began as a hobby soon became the primary interest of his life.

He did not find it necessary to ransack the world for adventure. You could find as much adventure as a man could stand in Harrisonville, the unique town. You wonder how Trowbridge could keep up his medical practice. After the arrival of de Grandin, no one got any sleep.

As the series opens, Trowbridge is about fifty. He is rather stout, a Republican, an Episcopal, a stable member of Harrisonville's upper class. He wears a pince-nez, enjoys a cigar and a drink, Prohibition or not.

Whether he wears a beard is uncertain. In the September 1937 issue of *Weird Tales*, artist Virgil Finley illustrated him with admirable whiskers. The drawing was so right that you feel it could not be otherwise. He is, of course, older than de Grandin, as is proper.[13]

While well versed in his profession, he shows a startling inability to learn from experience. If once a man has seen vampires, zombies, werewolves and poltergeists in full cry, then, we may ask with some irritation, why should he hem and haw about recognizing them again.

Part of that sluggish comprehension, we must chalk up to the hazard of Watsoning. The rest—well, explain it away as the traditional inability of a senior specialist to accept instances of wildly divergent reality. A man who has functioned for fifty years in a world of predictable natural law can surely be excused if he resists belief in murderous mummies or mobile stone statues.

Despite slow comprehension, despite a smothering air of respectability, Trowbridge is an adventurer at heart. He will accompany de Grandin anywhere, into many a horrid rat's nest. Consistently he faces forces against which a pistol is no defense at all.

They are, you see, strong, essentially inseparable friends: The flame and the stone—one whirling, light, eager; the other ponderously solid. It is recorded that Holmes and Watson rasped each other's nerves, and it is true that de Grandin often annoys Trowbridge. Not only does this clever little fellow positively fall over himself to attribute supernormal causes to insignificant events, but he talks incessantly. At solemn occasions, burials, weddings, insurance meetings, the words flow from his lips, a habit that profoundly annoys Trowbridge. He prefers silent solemnity.

For his part, de Grandin flares to passionate rage at Trowbridge's inability to comprehend the evidence before his eyes. De Grandin registers it all in a glance, has tabulated, summarized, understood, and projected a plan of action, while Trowbridge is still methodically adjusting his glasses.

It galls de Grandin! His temper flares. He lashes out. Then, starting, he pounces upon himself, takes his emotions in hand, settles down to explain matters simply to Trowbridge's skeptical mind.

Yet they are friends and respect each other. There have been more peculiar partnerships.

Similar strong ties bind de Grandin and red-headed Detective Sergeant Jeremiah Costello. He will follow his little Frenchman whenever, wherever. And bring along half the police department. Costello is a huge-framed, iron Irishman, oddly graceful in spite of his massiveness. He speaks a travesty of Irish dialect, an unfortunate characteristic of the series. (It is filled with ethnic types and every single one of them speaks dense dialect.) In early stories, Costello is guilty of chewing tobacco, an evil habit learned, perhaps, while at combat in the Philippines.

He is not nearly as phlegmatic and unimaginative as Trowbridge makes him out to be. Certainly he is no stickler for the letter of the law. His interpretation of justice is wonderfully flexible. He assists de Grandin in the commission of several murders and winks at several more. All are justified of course.

Both Costello and de Grandin practice frontier justice—immediate and final punishment. What other kind would apply? What court would try an individual on a charge of vampirism or lock up a sorcerer who has unleashed familiars onto the world?

In these cases, de Grandin is judge, jury and executioner in the best tradition of The Three Just Men. De Grandin is a full-fledged justice figure, punishing those that the law cannot touch. This is a consistent theme. During the 1930s, when every second magazine featured a unilateral justice figure, de Grandin's behavior passed unnoticed. But it was relatively unusual behavior for the 1920s. De Grandin was merrily executing away while other heroes were going all prickly at the sight of weapons.

Three minor characters provide support throughout the series. Coroner Martin makes a number of appearances. He is a professional's professional in the delicate art of restoring mangled victims and neatly stitching wounds. Coroner's Physician Parnell (described by de Grandin as "an old woman in pants") appears more frequently and regards our hero warily.

Nora McGinnis is the most important of the three. Her magic touch conjured up twenty-six years of meals, at least half on an instant's notice. De Grandin was the only man she permitted in her kitchen, and the savory steam of her art still sends you groping from the magazine to the refrigerator's icy bounty.

A series lasting from 1925 to 1951 has powerful vitality. In part this stemmed from the striking variety of menaces faced by de Grandin and the strikingly original methods he uses to put an end to them. To this action is cunningly added a pinch—even as much as a handful—of bright-red sex, licit and illicit, together with certain oddiments of behavior that would not be out of place in a 1935 *Terror Tales*.

Quinn rather carefully varies his stories. Only rarely do similar menaces follow consecutively. Stories of adventure alternate with supernatural manifestations. Although all stories contain outre elements, the variety is consistent.

Traditional themes receive untraditional treatment. Quinn's great strength lies in his ability at variations. The traditionalist may be annoyed at his cavalier flouting of conventions, but the story is always the better for it. Quinn's werewolves may be killed without a silver bullet. At least one of his vampires returns more for love than blood. Destruction is not always the motivation of the possessing spirits.

Not only do these entities vary from the usual, but de Grandin is inexhaustably resourceful in contriving their doom.

His success depends largely on the fact that the manifestations express themselves physically. They form as material in a material world, susceptible to physical countermeasures. There are no dim Usheresque ambiguities here.

At this point, Quinn differs most distinctly from earlier writers. His basic assumption is that all manifestations are subject to natural law:

> de Grandin: "I do declare, we have never seen that which I call supernatural." Nature (he declares) possesses endless possibilities; man has tabulated few enough of these. "If it is beyond experience, it is still within natural experience." (from "The Poltergeist," October 1927)

These remarks are so seductive to contemporary ears it is difficult to see that they are as evasive as the statement that the "supernatural" contains unknowable elements. Both breads are from the same flour.

In the practice of his cases, however, de Grandin amply proves his philosophy. He is perhaps the first man ever to electrocute a ghost ("The Jest of Warburg Tantavul"), kill a werewolf with a conventional shotgun ("The Blood-Flower"), gut a ghoul with a knife ("Children of Ubasti"), or destroy an evil intelligence with a sledge-hammer ("The Silver Countess").

These deeds are violent and direct. But they are most thoroughly effective.

The stories, themselves, can be separated into two loose groups. First are stories of supernatural entities, a rather slovenly category including ghosts, water demons, running mummies, hungry zombies and all their brotherhood. Second are stories of strange adventure, often featuring vengeance-crazed Hindus or insane surgeons; these violate few natural laws, other than those of probability.

To review even a portion of the fiction, or even to select typical cases, is difficult. Each has at least a single unique event demanding comment. The following remarks are offered with due apologies, understanding in advance that all the reader's favorite stories have been omitted.

"The Blood Flower" (March 1927) is a fine werewolf story. Trowbridge and de Grandin are summoned to medicate a woman who howls at night. Seems that she has become infected with lycanthrophy, not by a bite but contact with dried flowers from Rumania, that sinister place. Her transformation is not into any decent-looking wolf. Rather, the change shapes her (and others similarly afflicted) into a creature closely resembling Lon Chaney when the wolfbane blooms.

De Grandin settles the leader of the pack, the male werewolf, by emptying a heavy automatic into him. No silver bullets are required: "I did shoot a hole in him large enough for him to have walked through."

To cure the woman, he places her at the center of a mystic circle and conducts rites and purifications and such with hysop, prayers and a magic brew, the formula of which is given, in the event that you, too, must cast out demons.

"Restless Souls" (October 1928) is a surprisingly gentle vampire story. It is also a Halloweeen story, complete with walking corpse. A young girl, become a vampire, returns to find the love she died before experiencing. Her blood thirst is almost incidental. (De Grandin is of the opinion, by the way, that vampirism is caused by a virus transmitted during the blood-sucking process.) Being a vampire, she must die; but before he drives home the stake, de Grandin gives her a large shot of opiate to dull the impending pain.

"The Curse of the House of Phipps" (January 1930) is a fine powerful curse, indeed, killing all male Phipps before they see their first born. The curse was set by a young girl, brutally murdered by a long-ago Phipps. The case includes one of those Carnacki interludes where criminals haunt a house to conceal their presence, an idea old when Nick Carter used it. These criminals fare less well than usual, since de Grandin pistols down the first white sheet he sees in the inimitable style of shooting first and looking later. Eventually he gets around to breaking the curse, done rationally enough by burying the poor girl's skeleton properly.

"The Druid's Shadow" (October 1930) contains a popularized hash of Jung's less accessible psychological theories. The idea is that ancestral memories may be activated in the presence of emotionally-saturated relics of yesteryear. Which is a far cry from Jung. Nevertheless, memories of a former Druid rite grip a father-in-law and his son's wife, and he also carves her up before de Grandin gets control of the situation.

The evil relics are, in this story, destroyed by fire. This is a customary device. Quinn uses fire to purify as frequently as de Grandin hypnotizes people to forget, forget, forget for all time what they have just been through. That may not be current science, but it worked in *Weird Tales*.

"The Mansion of Unholy Magic" (October 1933) is an entirely satisfying adventure. Crazy Col. Putnam has animated three mummies. These are charging about the countryside, way back in the sticks, gulping the blood of all they catch. And not a word of this gets into the newspapers.

De Grandin, Trowbridge, and a girl taxi driver spend the night cooped up inside a hunting lodge, while the withered fiends chitter and scrape outside, kept from entering only because de Grandin has arranged knives before the door. The pointed steel (another repetitive plot device) keeps them out. The magical protection saves de Grandin's party, although, elsewhere, the girl's father is killed by a mummy.

The following night, the three head toward Col. Putnam's dire mansion, vengeance in their hearts. De Grandin is armed with a pragmatic scythe. Using this, he chops up one attacking mummy, firing the remains. But during this activity, the girl is abducted.

They find her within the mansion, hypnotized and dressed in filmy scraps, groveling before a woman and a huge man. Both these are mummies restored to their former appearances. Both prove flammable.

Up from her shameful trance rises the girl. While the male mummy was still functioning, he had stripped her bare. But instead of clothing herself decently, as any taxi driver would do, she snatches up the scythe and proceeds to chop Col. Putnam into large, irregular chunks. Trowbridge is rather astonished by all this. De Grandin is gleeful and fills the air with French cries of support. Afterward he burns the mansion to conceal the crime.

A justice figure in the fine tradition.

The adventure stories in this series contain a considerable charge of sadistic elements. Not only is there much shooting down of the evil minions—only to be expected—but there are rich jungles of such less routine material as surgical mutilation, erotic beatings, feminine abasement, torture and wallowing in blood.

As in "The House of Horror" (July 1926).

That dauntless pair, de Grandin and Trowbridge, stranded on a dark and stormy night, take refuge in a creepy old place. The owner, a Dr. Marston, is evasive and sly. The beautiful young girl is drugged rather than sick. Observing Dr. Marston slinking through the night, de Grandin and Trowbridge follow him. He destroys their car, a prelude to destroying them. But it is not to be. The storm hurls down a limb, killing him emphatically.

They return to the mansion—and promptly wish that they had not. Down under the foundations in a sub-basement, they find a cluster of man-made monstrosities—the distorted flesh of seven once-beautiful girls whose misfortune it has been to look like the girl who jilted Dr. Marston. He has removed the bones of their arms and legs, split their tongues, widened their mouths, removed noses and chins, diverged their eyes.

About this time, the house collapses because of the rain. This eliminates the author's problem of what to do with seven monsters that must not be killed and couldn't be permitted to remain alive.

Before the house falls in, the drugged girl upstairs is saved. De Grandin's surgical genius will restore her eye muscles, the only mutilation Marston has performed to that time. This thoroughly ugly case is told artfully enough, using all manner of conventional horror images, from weird mansion and mad doctor to storm and mysterious night activities. All these preparations build to a scene of unconventional and uncompromising brutality.

An equally ugly story, although in a different vein, is "The White Lady of the Orphanage" (September 1927). De Grandin is called to investigate the disappearance of children from an orphanage. He uncovers a horrifying case of cannibalism. The story is tightly told, full of misdirection, and ends in a scene of disagreeable specific detail.

"Mephistopheles and Company, Ltd." (February 1928) has a new method of extortion. They convince women that they are the property of the Devil and he is coming for them. To save themselves, they must pay and pay. De Grandin and Trowbridge invade their mansion (which is shielded by an electrified wall), save the lead girl in a raging pistol fight, and escape across the quicksands which engulf a number of minor characters.

"The House Without a Mirror" (November 1929) is another variation on surgical mutilation. This occurs away from Harrisonville, for a wonder, down in the hunting marshes along the Atlantic coast. There, in an ancient ruined house, lives a grim recluse, two blind servants, and the lovely girl whose face has been mutilated since infancy. A vengeful surgeon did it.

This wretch plans to return on her 21st birthday, cut out her tongue and exhibit her in a side show.

By those inscrutable rules governing the plotting of horror stories, de Grandin and Trowbridge arrive shortly before this fiend and henchmen come creeping through the marsh.

The ending is of satisfactory violence. De Grandin captures two henchmen, shoots another dead and the villain is strangled by the old recluse. As usual, Trowbridge contributes little; it is a rare day when he shoots or slugs anyone.

After these stimulating events, de Grandin demonstrates that skill developed as a plastic surgeon during World War I. He rebuilds the young lady's face from the neck up and, behold, she is beautiful. Alors!

The action is equally direct in "The Drums of Damballah" (March 1930). De Grandin leads the police into an underground nest of voodoo worshippers, secure under the streets of Harrisonville. There they writhe and chant, the kidnapped girls hypnotized or drugged and performing vile rites all unaware, the kidnapped infant wailing. Into this homey niche of Hell storms de Grandin and a pair of French Army revolvers, attacking eighty voodoo fanciers. Costello and his boys clean up the rest in a red-eyed slaughter.

Reading these stories half a century later, you get the strong impression that Quinn was carefully testing the taboos of his time, writing stories deliberately violating conventional moral positions. And doing so in such a way that it did not occur to readers to challenge underlying themes.

The pulp magazines were singularly unlikely vehicles for stories dealing with prostitution, cannibalism, lesbianism, incest or such exotic displacements of the libido. Yet Quinn managed to work all of these into his stories. It can't be said that he explored the themes seriously—but he acknowledged them, at a time when such explicit stuff was never exposed to a general audience.

In September 1934, Quinn published "The Jest of Warburg Tantavul," another appalling case thickly plastered with sexual material. Tantavul is a deranged father who strikes at his long-dead wife in a particularly hateful way. (Again the theme of disagreeable revenge.) His children do not know that they are brother and sister. Their father manipulates them into marriage, intended to reveal their relationship after they have had a baby.

Abruptly he dies, but not thoroughly enough. His ghost, a peering goblin face, returns to harry the girl. Learning, at last, that she has married her brother and borne an unholy child, as it were, she falls emotionally to pieces and runs away.

Unable to stand memory, she leaps into a sizzling life of drugs, drink, prostitution and low living. De Grandin and Trowbridge rescue her after she has had two years as a scarlet woman. But almost before de Grandin is able to hypnotize her into forgetting the recent past, the goblin face comes chittering outside the window.

It can't enter because of the iron screen, a specific against chittering faces. Thoughtfully, de Grandin removes that screen, substitutes one of copper mesh. Attaches to this a transformer and power source. As the goblin slides rejoicing through the copper, on goes the power, and the horror is electrocuted.

It was partly material, de Grandin hastily explains, which is why the juice worked. But even so . . . .

Through all of these stories, sexual activity is constantly equated with evil. The punishment is torture, mutilation, dismemberment—a disgusting whirl of images culled from the Freudian darkness. In the May 1930 "The Brain Thief," a strong story, a singular hypnotizer destroys both men and women by converting them to wantons. They don't remember all the fun but come to themselves years later, their reputations exhausted, immersed in hopeless personal messes. It's all for revenge.

The wicked hypnotist is frankly murdered by de Grandin, who holds the rascal's head inside a red-hot stove, while Costello guards the door, ice-faced.

"The House of Golden Masks" (June 1929) contains ever more alluring sexual scenes. Young girls are abducted to a road house in Harrisonville where they are debauched for the South American market. The debauching involves, among other things, erotic dances and garment shedding before cheering tables of young bloods. How the girls were forced to these lusty performances isn't explained. De Grandin and police put an appropriate, if bloody, end to it all.

As for other stories, there are whippings enough, torture scenes enough, and more than enough of that favorite scene, the abasement of the heroine. Fortunate, indeed, is the girl who does not, at some moment during the story, find herself insufficiently garbed in silken wisps, or less, groveling before gloating powers.

The girl in danger is a usual fictional device for maintaining suspense. Even in the chaste pages of Edgar Rice Burroughs, the girl is abducted times without number. Always she is in sexual danger. That element never varied in the Burroughs' novels. He never said rape. And he never meant less.

It is true that such magazines as *Snappy Stories, Pep, Parisian Nights*, et al, struggled all story long to imply what their final paragraphs denied. While these publications maintained a small, if enthusiastic, readership, such general magazines as *Argosy* and *People's* rarely allowed the suggestive situation to develop past dim gray tints.

As you may recall, the heroine of "The Compass in the Sky" retains her 1917 virginity, although she is abducted and forced to sleep in *his* tent. It seems improbable, but there you are.

It is startling then to find in a low-circulation magazine such as *Weird Tales*, the combination of advanced sexual experiences recorded during the de Grandin series. During the middle 1930s, those specialized magazines *Horror Stories* and *Terror Tales* glowed like furnaces with similar material. But such fantasies in jazz-mad 1920s America?

Fantasies they are. And adolescent fantasies to boot. They do not picture love, and in them the sexes do not come together by mutual consent. Rather the woman, bereft of her will, controlled by a stronger mind, yields herself without knowing. It is the stuff of neurotic fantasizing.

Through the fiction, they parade to humiliation: Women forced to become wanton (forced, yes, indeed). Women exposing their breasts. Women forced to dance lasciviously. Women helpless as their clothing is ripped away. Women painted and daring, their lips glaring against white skin. Women made mindless, yielding, sexually available by arcane art.

There are many reasons for the continued popularity of the series.

"The Devil's Bride" is particularly rich in instances of good, strong, out-and-out, provocative sex. The novel was published in *Weird Tales* as a six-part serial, February through July 1932. Long afterward, it was reprinted as a three-part serial in the *Magazine of Horror*, Nos. 26-28 (March-May-July 1969); and was again reprinted as a paperback in 1976.

The novel was the forty-sixth de Grandin adventure to be published and thus lies at the heart of the series. It is a reeling, bloody account of combat with a horde of devil worshippers.

Alice Hume is abducted during her wedding rehearsal by individuals unknown. Hotly affronted by this obvious breach of manners, de Grandin begins a long and difficult investigation, during which almost every woman in the cast is murdered.

A local cult of devil worshippers carried poor Alice off to serve as their priestess. Leads are few. Since, however, the cultists need babies to sacrifice, and murders and mutilations to perform, they are soon tracked to their lair.

During the search, de Grandin is aided by his old friend, Monsieur George Jean Jacques Joseph Marie Renouard, Inspector of the Surete. Renouard brings the news that devil worship is not restricted to Harrisonville but is, in fact, an international disorder. A world-wide organization, headed by a Russian, is growing in strength, preparing for an eventual attack upon all the nations of the world.

These revelations convert a middling novelette to the dignity of a novel. Just in time. The first half of the adventure has reached its natural climax as de Grandin and friends and waves of police hurl themselves upon the devil worshippers. But not before readers are treated to a detailed account of the celebration of the Black Mass. That out of the way, Alice is saved (dosed to the hairline with drugs) and the cult leader captured.

These agreeable events narrated, we reach the hurricane's eye. A second wall of cloud whirls toward us. But for the moment, narrative tension slacks to calm, as Quinn frantically rushes forth new plot elements to support the next part of the adventure.

When becalmed, introduce new characters. The figure now brought on-stage and permanently into the series, is the genial British giant, Baron Haddingway Ingraham Jameson Ingraham, Captain of the Sierra Leone Frontier Police, and penniless nobleman. He is familiarly known as Hiji.

Hiji shows so many personality traits similar to those of Lord John Roxton (*The Lost World* and other Doyle novels) that they might have been cut from the same metal. In spite of that, he is an interesting character, so strong, in fact, that he has the tendency to overshadow de Grandin. He is brought on-scene since the novel is about to veer off to an African climax and a tough experienced African law type was required.

The reason they go to Africa is that Alice has again been abducted. The reason she is abducted, aside from moving the story to Africa, is that a general convention of devil worshippers is to be held there, deep in remote lands. Alice is still to be the Bride of the Devil. Her abductor is either the leader of the Harrisonville devil worshippers—who was electrocuted, autopsied, buried—or a reincarnation of him.

So it's off to Africa. Jungles, sullen natives, thatched huts, spears and enormous quantities of dialogue lifted direct from Edgar Wallace's "Sanders of the River" series. If the swipes are blatant, the source was good, for Sanders is an excellent series and recommended to young and old.

But enough of this literary talk. De Grandin and friends, and a young army bristling with automatic weapons, come to a freshly excavated Roman circus—stone seats around a central area, 100 yards by 50 yards, one end concealed by silken sheets.

The Devil worshippers have apparently appropriated this place from an Edgar Rice Burrough's novel. Anyway, here it is. There they are. Certain bloody preliminaries transpire. The silk curtains pull back, revealing an immense Devil. And Alice enters.

At the moment she is convinced that she has become a damned soul. She concluded this after waking to find two large curving horns projecting from her forehead.

At this, her morale quite collapses. Now, at the climax of the great ceremony, in she struts, quite abandoned to shame, her breasts bare, her hips thrusting seductively, a meaningful smile twisting her painted lips.

At the crucial moment, just an instant before Alice takes that final plunge into ecstacy and sexual degradation, Jules de Grandin strides forward—one small white-dressed fellow, assured, perky, lethal.

The head devil master dies under de Grandin's sword. Alice (feverishly covering her breasts) is saved. An absolute torrent of automatic weapons fire, plus a convenient landslip, eliminates the devil menace.

An interesting story. Some parts are as crude as a Race Williams adventure. So many abductions. So little shaping of Alice as a main character. So many interesting and undeveloped new characters. The narrative parts do not quite integrate—the African adventure is almost an epilogue, rather than a climax.

These flaws aside, it is an exciting, driving story, full of incident and character, overflowing with material, continuously fascinating. Its pulsing vitality grips your attention.

Although it may make the girls uncomfortable.

During the first seven years of the series, 1925-1932, fifty de Grandin stories were published. From 1933 through the series' end in 1951, a span of eighteen years, only forty-three more stories appeared.

By the end of the 1930s and the early 1940s, Quinn's fiction gradually turned from de Grandin, although the letter columns in *Weird Tales* rattled with pleas for his return. We may surmise that more than ten years of writing pseudo-French dialect had left its mark, and Quinn found his interest turning to other aspects of the supernatural story.

Later de Grandin adventures were slighter in content, shorter in length. Many reflect Quinn's fresh interest in historical periods three or four hundred years before, in which he intermingles costume elements and supernatural drama. Situations from earlier cases are occasionally reworked, although Quinn does not repeat more than the concept. From that a new story is built, with new scenes and surprises.

De Grandin remains as effective as ever. You have the impression that he is drinking more. Hard to say, since he cheerfully drank to excess as often as possible at case's end. In earlier stories, he is seen to absorb two pints of brandy while puzzling out a problem and show no obvious effects. This extraordinary ability is forgotten later. When de Grandin drinks, he drinks to purpose and largely.

"The House Where Time Stood Still" (March 1939) reuses the idea of the July 1926 "House of Horror." Trowbridge carries much of the adventure upon his own shoulders, although ineptly. Hiji and Costello begin the matter. Important government papers have disappeared, and so has young Southerby, who was carrying them. Together our four main characters retrace his probable path across the state. The trail leads to still another of those grim old houses that dot the geography of Quinn's fiction. Trowbridge enters this place all unsuspecting to make a phone call. He has a simple heart. Immediately he is in the clutches of still another mad doctor, one Dr. Friedrich Friedrichsohn. (For it was war again with Germany and the headlines dictated the nationality of the popular fiction villains.)

Dr. Friedrichsohn is a monster in the grand old tradition. He surgically mutilates people, partly for revenge, partly for fun. That girl—whatshername?—who rejected him and married another: Now helpless in the Doctor's web, she has been given a shapeless, huge, limbless body, like a rugged sack, at the top of which perches her lovely untouched head. Her husband has gone quite mad since his scalp was grafted over his face. Now he plays the violin. And, yes, the doctor has captured Southerby and girl friend. They will be slowly carved to monsters over a long period of time; this is to inform the annals of science if they will continue to love each other when deformed.

Alas for the evil German doctor. He fails to watch the door. In de Grandin comes gliding and in a brisk display of savate, the German is

*Weird Tales*, November 1936. The poor girl, entranced, faces doom. She will soon be saved by Jules de Grandin, longest lived of the occult detective who employed physical violence to battle supernatural menace.

*Weird Tales,* March 1945. For twenty-six years, Jules de Grandin fought modern monsters and ancient evil. The threat varied. His success was constant and his character barely changed.

down, the mansion is aflame. Those who can be saved are rushed outside:

*Trowbridge:* "Where's Friedrichsohn?"
*de Grandin*: "He could not come."

An interesting story. As usual, the monsters die in fire. A few dim changes mark the surface of this lengthy series, but only a few. Costello's red hair is gray now, and Trowbridge is about sixty-five. In no other way does either show his age.

For those impelled to observe minute imperfections, "The House Where Time Stood Still" is listed on the cover of the February 1939 *Weird Tales*, although not published until the March issue.

The August 1939 "The House of the Three Corpses" is a taut mixture of mystery and adventure, very heady. De Grandin and Trowbridge discover three fresh corpses in an exotically appointed house. When the police arrive, the corpses are gone. Replacing them are two maniacs, male and female. The girl shrieks and beats the floor with her slipper. It is another vendetta case, this time featuring North African Druses equipped with gigantic poisonous centipedes.

Now ensues a thirty-seven-month gap when *Weird Tales* knows de Grandin no more and the letter columns chitter in that prose peculiar to those corresponding with pulp magazines. When the next story came forth, May 1942, the reason given for the long silence was that de Grandin had been at war.

His history: When war broke out in 1939 de Grandin immediately returned to France, served in Syria until Vichy signed the truce with Germany. Then he joined the Free French forces of Charles de Gaulle, eventually becoming a captain. During an attack on Dakar, he contracted enteritis, was reassigned as an intelligence and liason officer in England and America.

(For the record, Hiji became a major in the British infantry. Severely injured during the retreat from Dunkirk, he was discharged from service, sent as an attache to the British Consulate General in New York City.)

The May 1942 "Stoneman's Memorial" reintroduces most of the old cast. Both Costello and Hiji have stronger roles than de Grandin, and Hiji actually destroys the supernormal entity under our hero's very nose. It happened, you see, that this vindictive fellow discovered a magic formula for animating stone statues and making them do his will. He has a statue and his will is murder. It is kill, kill, kill, up to the point that Hiji tosses a hand grenade at the thing. Later de Grandin executes the statue's master— and with Costello's full approval, too.

Now follows another lull. The next story does not appear until July 1944. "Death's Bookkeeper" is a voodoo doctor who can defer a loved one's death. For a price. The price includes the death of another person. The doctor balances accounts with death, takes a cash reward and so the title, obviously. In reality, it is an elaborately staged extortion plot. De Grandin goes to see him, fires off his cane gun, and Deaths's Bookkeeper goes into

Accounts Receivable.

Then off goes Major de Grandin (he has been promoted) to discuss the whole situation, perhaps with Manly Wade Wellman, a *Weird Tales* writer, a friend, an advisor, who is mentioned several times in the stories.

If the cases are fewer, now, they are all interesting. "The Green God's Ring" (January 1945) serves as entry into the world for that malignant force that is Siva. He/It causes all sorts of problems before de Grandin drives him out again. In "The Lords of the Ghostlands" (March 1945) de Grandin faces down the Egyptian Judges of the Dead across the flimsy protection of a mystic symbol traced in pigeon blood.

The background of this story is rather complex. It is a story within a story and to detail it all, one of the characters has a vision of past events leading to the present problem. This device will be used again, a long flashback incorporated at the story's heart. It gives an interesting perspective, although it reduces the culmulative force of the action and considerably lessens de Grandin's presence as the dominant character. Which may have been Quinn's intention.

The year 1946 introduces Ram Chitra Das, tenth son of a disgraced Napalese princeling (married a dancer and fell from favor). Raised in England, a trained professional in the British Indian Police Intelligence Section, Ram Das is a powerful character and an attractive person. His wife is almost eight times as attractive, an exquisite feminine gem. They live in a second floor apartment on E. 86th St.[14] Pelts strew the floor. Rugs strew the walls. The air is languorous with infatuating scents. Their landlord would have a fit at their decorating scheme.

In "Kurban" (January 1946), Ram Das joins de Grandin in saving a fool girl, awash in hashish, who offers herself as a living sacrifice to a pair of cobras and a calculating swami. "Catspaws" (July 1946) brings forth a Hindu killer. Ram Das carries most of the action, explains all the circumstances, and assumes much of de Grandin's function in his own story. They work with Lieutenant Costello in this, promotion having finally overtaken that fine old detective. "Eyes in the Dark" (November 1946) again features Ram and his wife, this time in less forceful roles. With their help, de Grandin uses two glass eyes to maneuver a murderous fakir into death by self-hypnosis.

Other cases are less Hindu-oriented. "Three in Chains (May 1946) features a powerfully haunted house. It contains three ghosts. A medium digs out the background in a long flashback. This provides de Grandin with sufficient information to confront the ghosts and give them rest. They were not bad folk. Just disturbed.

"Lotte" (September 1946) is a strong poltergeist story. The spirit, furiously angry, steals ectoplasm from the wife to torment the husband. De Grandin finally isolates the thing. Greatly weakened, it is able to materialize only in two dimensions and so comes into view, spread across the wall like an evil decal. A fearful climax.

"Clair de Lune" (November 1947), the only story published that year, is a sort of vampire story: The beautiful actress renews her looks by absorbing the youth of luckless girls. De Grandin locks her into a hospital room at her hour of need, and she expires in the mode of She Who Must Be Obeyed, although without dramatic flames.

Another long pause before the next case, "Vampire Kith and Kin" (May 1949). In the course of this, de Grandin catches a vrykolakas in a bottle and burns it in a furnace. At this late date, he is still hypnotizing young ladies by swinging his silver pencil before them. To prove that time flows onward, however, Trowbridge has given up surgery, although continuing in general practice.

"The Body Snatchers" (November 1950) are a man and woman who have achieved a sort of immortality by transferring their minds from body to body down through the ages. Until 1950, at Harrisonville, when their luck runs out.

The final story of the series, "The Ring of Bastet," was published in September 1951. It concerns *aelurophobia* (fear of cats) and Egyptian gods and possession and all manner of delights. A young woman, donning the ring of a priest of Bastet, is overwhelmed by the power of the elder gods. Her soul is saved by de Grandin, who evokes her belief in Christianity at the crisis. After which, as his last published act, he heads toward twelve ounces of brandy, a self-prescribed dose strong enough to terminate the magazine, as well as the series.

By 1951, the old world of the psychic investigator was a bright distant shining in the deeps of time. Electricity had superseded ghosts. The new physics nullified astral bodies. No longer did fashion speak of auras and finger the unsteady ouiji board or tingle weirdly at the thought of residual evil and woman suffrage.

It was a changed world, more remote, crammed with ominous mechanisms and social structures wobbling forward toward change. During de Grandin's span, Western Civilization had not merely altered but transformed itself in steps of successive brutality. The series carried the story of psychic adventure from Blackwood's gaslight to the Jazz Age, through the pulp magazine era and the Depression and the Second World War. At the end, teetering at the lip of the 1950s, de Grandin is as brightly attractive as ever. The stories glow like well-rubbed old pewter, artifacts from another age. They did not essentially change, although the Jazz Age is far distant from the Cold War.

De Grandin and his friends are figures of the 1920s. These times lingered in Harrisonville, even after the repeal of Prohibition, even during the worst of World War II. In Harrisonville, it is now and always 1925. The telephone still calls that admirable Dr. de Grandin to leave his plate of Lobster Diane and hurry forth, carrying with him the weary Trowbridge, toward still another leering horror.

Other psychic adventurers would embellish fiction. None reached de Grandin's stature. Of a certainty, no, surely not. Of him, one only—the incomparable, the extraordinary.

Another bottle, my friend. And bring him quickly forth. I faint, I perish. I am so vilely dry.

9—

It is possible to glimpse a man's heart by long contact with him. Hear him speak. Measure the pauses between his phrases and the sound of his breath. All has meaning. You can tell something of him from his automobile and his gun, more from his dog; and a very great deal from how he handles himself when he is in a position of advantage over his fellow man.

In the case of Robert Ervin Howard (1906-1936) we have almost none of these things. There remain only a few written recollections, some letters (where what is important to know is hedged), a number of published stories, and a large quantity of narrative scraps.

These suggest the man, if indirectly. They richly hint in one direction, lead in another, then melt away in puzzling wilderness.

He was undoubtedly a genius. There are many, most unrecognized, experience suggests. He was undoubtedly saturated in literature. He swallowed this in massive chunks, some digested, some not. He was essentially self-trained, as any writer is. In certain well-defined areas, his sensibilities were atrophied; in others, as notorious, you find grotesque over-development. Both conditions are symptomatic of major emotional discontinuities. You can sense the presence of these without putting a name on them. They furnish the power of his prose; they limited the growth of his genius; and finally, it is surmised, they killed him.

Born 1906, Howard lived in Cross Plains, Texas, in the north central plains of that state. He was the traditional skinny stripling who, like William Hope Hodgson, developed his body by exercise and became a massive young man of very considerable personal strength.

His formal writing began about 1921. *Weird Tales* accepted his first story in 1924. Thereafter, for twelve years, he poured out an increasing volume of material, written for and sold to the pulp magazines, including *Ghost Stories, Action Stories, Oriental Stories, Fight Stories, Cowboy Stories, Argosy, Sports Stories.*

Unlike most powerful young men, he had read immensely. At one point or another in his career, you can ascertain the marks of Poe, Edgar Rice Burroughs, Harold Lamb, C.A. Smith, H.P. Lovecraft and Talbot Mundy.[15] He learned from all of them. He was a student, not a copyist, and no single influence remained dominant long.

He created a number of series characters, most of them after 1930. Two of his most interesting characters appeared just before that date. These were Solomon Kane in 1928 and King Kull in 1929. Neither of these was a psychic investigator in any sense of the word. They were, instead, adventurers in that uneasy region between reality and the other side. They are included here to illustrate the further extension of the de Grandin-type occult adventure story. Both characters are extensions, in odd guise, of literary forces represented, on one hand, by the work of H. Rider Haggard and Talbot Mundy, and, on the other, by the shimmering horror fantasies of Blackwood and Hodgson.

In 1936 as the texture of his work grew richer, more disciplined, increasingly varied, he committed suicide. (This on learning that his mother was dying.) He was thirty years old. In all his published pages, you will search hard to find a mother pictured or a description of warm family life. There is, however, a sufficiency of death.

Solomon Kane, Howard's first major series character, appeared in seven stories, all published in *Weird Tales* from 1928 to 1932. An additional five stories and/or fragments, plus two poems, appeared in the collection *Red Shadows* (1968), later republished as three paperbacks.[16]

The initial story, "Red Shadows" (August 1928) introduces Kane and establishes at least the outline of that contradictory character. He is described, inaccurately, as a Puritan and a fanatic. He is neither, but the words justify his mode of dress and his tendency to declaim in Biblical thunderings during concluding speeches.

Aside from these descriptive whims—which can hardly be taken seriously—he is a justice figure, unleashed across the world, driven to seek out and punish:

> All his life he had roamed about the world aiding the weak and fighting oppression; he neither knew nor questioned why.... If he thought of it at all, he considered himself a fulfiller of God's judgment, a vessel of wrath to be emptied upon the souls of the unrighteous. ("Red Shadows," Chapter IV)

We may suppose that the name Kane is intended to have associative meaning. With some slight effort, we can presume that he somehow embodies man's original blood guilt and wanders about the world, expunging his innate sin by visiting Heaven's judgment upon those deserving it. For this reason, although he wanders without direction, like the Wandering Jew, he always arrives (as he notes in "Blades of the Brotherhood") at a time and place where someone richly needs killing.

In person, Kane is a tall, lean man, large shouldered, long-armed, with steel strips for muscles. Although his skin is tanned, his face is darkly pallid, drawn in dour lines. (Puritans do not laugh, says the stereotype, and Kane rarely does.) His nose is thin and straight, the forehead high, its broadness concealed by dark hair. His eyes are coldly watchful, as are the eyes of most fictional avengers, and are the color of gray ice, unrelenting.

He dresses in unadorned black. It is plain stuff, unfrilled, worn with a dark hat. On one occasion he is described as wearing a bright green sash tied around his waist to support several flint-lock pistols. The sash is not customary. The rapier is.

He is a brilliant duelist, a deadly killer with the rapier. Almost every story details a combat with naked steel. In this fighting, Kane excels. He fights with a concentrated economy of motion, superb defense, a dazzling attack, icy execution.

The reactions along his nerves are significantly quicker than for most men. He is cat quick and moves with feline gracefulness.

It is hard to tell what manner of man he is. His appearance is part corpse, part devil. A curious enough look for a man of God. Such feelings as he has are locked in rigid self control. Rarely does he permit himself emotion, rarely does he swear, rarely will he allow human softness to touch him.

He is as depersonalized as a man can force himself to be. You observe bitter emotional denial, icy objectivity, discipline harsh over a core of blood-mad snarling violence. The extent to which this represents a profile of Howard's personal stresses is not known.

When the first Solomon Kane story was published, Howard was twenty-two, just filling out his massive frame. A nice enough fellow but touchy in small, surprising ways. As the writer, so his story, "Red Shadows," which is vibrant, passionate and not yet well integrated. It is a series of short scenes, the continuity provided by two main characters and their track of death.

France near the end of the sixteenth century. Kane finds a dying girl, raped and stabbed by the outlaw Le Loup. Swearing vengeance on her behalf, Kane locates the outlaws' cave, proceeds to kill them methodically, one by one. After trapping and blowing up most of the gang, he follows a wounded member to the cave. A great quantity of menacing conversation is tossed back and forth (for Kane talks too much in these early confrontation scenes). Then the killing begins; however, Le Loup escapes.

To Africa. With one violent wrench, the scene is transplanted to another continent. The action continues as before. Down there in the jungle, Kane is captured by savages. N'Longa, the ju-ju man, secretly offers Kane assistance if he will kill Le Loup, who has become the chief's right-hand man. That, of course, displaced N'Longa from his position of power and his ego burns.

In a scene containing echoes from sources as various as Joseph Conrad and Edgar Rice Burroughs, Kane is dragged from the hut, tied to a post to be tortured and killed. It appears that he was captured by Gulka, the gorilla-slayer (a female gorilla that he killed dangles from a nearby roof-pole; gorillas, of course, do not live in the jungle, but if you are going to pick and cavil at every strand of plot, we are never going to get through this).

To show how serious matters are, Gulka kills a native and hurls the cadaver upon an altar before an idol. Before N'Longa can do anything to aid Kane, he, too, is seized and tied to a pole. (For Le Loup heard him talking with Kane in the hut.)

Doom is not yet, as N'Longa is a man of resource. He hurls his spirit from his body to that of the corpse on the altar. The dead man rises and walks, flopping and wobbling, and kills the chief.

Panic, as you may well suppose. Kane is released, snatches his sword, bounds away after Le Loup. He catches this evil fellow in a jungle glade and, with some trouble, runs him through. At this moment of triumph, Gulka appears, huge and menacing, stalking forward to rend Kane.

But before this unfortunate thing happens, out of the leaves lunges the husband of the gorilla Gulka killed. In an instant, Gulka is torn to shreds.

Now that almost every character has died of violence, Kane limps back to his ship, stepping very carefully, you can believe.

Thus "Red Shadows": three fragments merged to one narrative, unified by the chase. The part dealing with Gulka is quite extraneous, serving chiefly to add words to the final scene. And so it does, at the expense of obliterating the climax, the death of Le Loup, which has been the purpose of the whole adventure.

In spite of these gross structural crudities, the story generates a passionate forcefulness, a tribute to Howard's emotional intensity. Not his plotting.

"Skulls in the Stars" (January 1929) takes place in England. Out upon the desolate moor, Kane encounters an insane ghost of particular violence. In "Rattle of Bones" (June 1929) he is wandering through the Black Forest in Germany, where, in the course of a single night he meets a murderous landlord, a blood-thirsty bandit, and a sorcerer's skelton that kills. Both adventures are predictable efforts, the chief interest being Kane, himself.

"The Moon of Skulls" was published as a two-part serial in the June and July 1930 issues of *Weird Tales*. The scene is Africa. The story occurs in and around one of those vast ruined cities forgotten in the African deeps. According to H.P. Lovecraft, these were one of Howard's "most effective accomplishments—the description of vast megalithic cities of the elder world, around whose dark towers and labyrinthine nether vaults linger an aura of pre-human fear and necromancy."[17]

Lovecraft's language is dazzling but it omits the word "Burroughs" and is, therefore, mildly inexact. The story contains several scenes embarrassingly reminiscent of Tarzan adventures. To these borrowed bones, however, Howard brings the lightning of heroic brutality. The story trembles with inner tension and menace thirsting in the dark.

Kane has returned to Africa after a long quest. He seeks a kidnapped English girl, Marylin Taferel. After climbing an almost unscalable cliff, he crosses a wooded plateau, battles decorated savages, plunges into a chasm, kills a monstrous serpent in a cave, and discovers a secret way into the lost city. All this in one-and-a-quarter chapters. The city is evidently Opar, populated by a somewhat different fauna. Hard to tell. In any case, the city is loaded with secret corridors inside the megalithic walls.

Kane digs a hole in one and, peering through, sees, voluptuously sprawling on her throne, the Mistress of Doom, The Red Woman, Nakari, ruler of the Land of Negari. Nakari doesn't have on any more clothing than an egg. Kane watches her put a servant to death, but nude women mean nothing to a Puritan. He moves on, discovers a secret door, and, before you know it, comes, entirely accidentally, to the very room in which Marylin is imprisoned. Only the good have such luck.

For a chapter, the action freezes solid, while we are entertained by Marylin's history, which is exhausting. Then Nakari enters to advise Marylin that she is to be sacrificed when "the Moon of Skulls looks over the black crest of the Tower of Death." That is a dandy sentence. Since the story is not half through, Kane is not now able to save Marylin. Instead, he gets heaved into a dungeon.

To this dreary place comes the queen to question him. By the sound of the conversation, she might even seduce him. But he is a dour Puritan and uncooperative. "I am but a landless wanderer," he tells her.

No sense in revealing that he is God's hit man.

She offers her hand, her kingdom. Together they will conquer the world, which suggests that her grasp on geography was tenuous. Repulsed, she leaves, exceedingly irritated.

Next day, Kane escapes, because it is time to get on with the action. While roaming around inside the walls, he discovers the last man alive of Atlantan blood. He is chained and dying but rouses to give Kane directions to the place of sacrifice.

He arrives just before the moon looks over the black crest of etc. Marylin's slim white form is stretched out on the altar. Killing a guard who, by great luck, happens to have Kane's pistol, he slips forward, shoots to pieces the Holy Skull hanging above the altar. This causes the worshippers to begin hacking and killing one another. Nakari goes to death, bright blood on her skin.

Kane escapes with the girl.

An earthquake destroys the city.

The reader tumbles back in his chair, eyes quite glassy at the megalithic coincidences he has just ingested.

Remove your hat. We are in the presence of the Lost City and Its Savage Priestess, that venerable relic. By 1930, Burroughs had worked the idea to death, after Haggard had tired of it. Lovecraft and C.A. Smith dallied with it, as did C.L. Moore and Lester Dent, and so down to the present day, with priestesses and without, with monsters of distorted appetite and an itch for virgins, and, if you care to check today's paperbacks, there it will be again, ruined and menace-shadowed as ever, where the nearest guard always holds the hero's weapons and the girl lies forever, fragile femininity, white upon the altar's stone.

"The Hills of the Dead" (August 1930) are in Africa. The story reintroduces N'Longa, who has precisely the same relationship with Kane as the witch doctor, Zikali, had with Alan Quartermaine in H. Rider Haggard's numerous novels—that of a friendly trickster who uses the hero as an unwitting tool by which to further private plans. N'Longa gives Kane a voodoo stick. This will appear, variously described, in the next several stories. Off marches Kane into the mystery of Africa, there to battle a race of walking dead men hiving in a cliff face. N'Longa transfers bodies to assist Kane and they have a powerfully described struggle with the dead on a cliff top.

The voodoo stick reappears in the later story, "Footfalls Within" (September 1931). Kane accidentally uses it to destroy a monster imprisoned in a stone mausoleum by King Solomon. When a greedy slaver breaks open the door, out rushes a ravening vastness, quite invisible, to gobble him up.

"Wings in the Night" (July 1932) pits Kane against a race of winged Pre-Human monsters lurking in the heart of Africa. The story, the most effective in the series, grows like a summer storm. The extended ending achieves nightmare.

Harpy people have attacked a village, carrying their victims into the air, where they are torn apart and eaten. Far below, Kane rages, glaring up in killing fury. Whatever rage shook Howard, it received full symbolic expression in that scene. It is, at once, the climax and summation of this series.

Solomon Kane, wrapped in gloom and black clothing, moved within a loosely defined historical period. If he never reached the bellowing power of Howard's later heroes, it is because the word "Puritan" has its own connotations and restrictions. Few enough restrictions were imposed upon Kane, he being a buccaneer who considered himself a sectarian.

Still, even these few limitations galled Howard. Almost at once he abandoned historical times in favor of adventures set in remote periods. Two years after the first Kane adventure was published, Howard had formulated his major theme—a barbarian giant hacking enemies in a world before history. A world that also lacked American-style morality, woman's liberation, or much self-restraint.

The absence of such civilized small change is masked by roaring gusto. More wine! More women! More blood for the thirsty sword, by Barry and by Smith!

Here the Id revels naked, swelling its huge muscles. Prancing preening egoism struts rampant. Myself. Me. Gigantic, omnipotent. Swilling gallons of wine to rise with no heavy head. Lying with all women and rising snorting with passion. Battling human enemies, fiends from Hell, monsters most unnatural. Hack and rend magnificently. Stand as a steel-thewed barbarian, savage, splendid, slobbered in blood, slashed in dramatic places that provide a maximum of showy gore and a minimum of pain.

An adolescent dream world. The only social convention imposed was to be the strongest.

Since worlds so obliging are not found in Cross Plains, Texas, nor on the planet Earth, Howard reached back 100,000 years. Antiquity permits all. He constructed an imaginary gaggle of races and civilizations, including the tingling names of Atlantis and Lemuria, siting these in the general vicinity of Europe and North Africa.

These remote civilizations had the advantage of never existing. He could arrange an elaborate and bloody alternate history for them—it is detailed in "The Hyborian Age"[18]—then revel in their excesses, destroy them to the last atom before recorded history, and dissolve their land masses in catyclysm.

One hundred thousand years allows a writer rather much latitude to construct imaginary worlds. And total destruction excuses any excesses enjoyed.

King Kull, the first of Howard's great barbarians, is a direct precursor of the more famous Conan. During Howard's lifetime, only three Kull stories were published. A poem mentioning him was printed posthumously. In 1967 a paperback, *King Kull*, collected thirteen of the fifteen pieces about the character that Howard had written but never published, or never completed. That paperback collection has had its own influence and history. For our purposes, comments will be generally limited to those stories of Kull originally published in *Weird Tales*.

These provide Kull with almost no personal history. Most of that biographical material is found in the fragment (published in *King Kull*) titled "Exile in Atlantis."

To summarize that information, Kull was a feral child found living among tigers and wolves. He was adopted into the Sea-Mountain tribe, one of the small groups clinging to the coastline of Atlantis and preying, like the later Vikings, upon all within reach.

No sooner had he grown to massive young manhood than he became an exile. The cause was a Sea-Mountain girl who had married a Lemurian pirate. For that crime she was to die by torture. To spare her that inconvenience, Kull killed her, fled with his tribesmen raging behind.

Captured shortly afterward by Lemurians, he became a galley slave. He escaped to the ancient land of Valusia. There he became, in swift succession, an outlaw, a prisoner, a gladiator. He entered military service, becoming a successful commander. And now, in that political position enjoyed by numerous Roman generals, he disposes of the despised King of Valusia and seizes the crown.

How soon the crown galls. Still early in his reign, in "The Shadow Kingdom" (*Weird Tales*, August 1929), Kull is grimly aware that he holds power only by force. His Red Guards are his powerful fist, his ruthless will the force welding the society together.

Already that coalition of political and military opportunists which had supported his rise now hiss and mutter against him. (Only an Atlantean exile, how dare he claim mastery of ancient noble Valusia, whose jeweled cities and buzz, buzz, buzz . . . .)

For a young man who never lived beyond a Texas small town, Howard showed much insight into political intrigue. The court he described boils with interacting factions and plots and shifting allegiances, as if Howard had been an attentive courtier from birth, rather than an attentive reader of Talbot Mundy. Or perhaps the Roman historians.

Whatever Howard's literary sources, he works the hot salt stink of politics inside his fiction. Kull sits wary, testing the air, his freezing gray eyes slitted down.

He is warned by the Pictish ambassador that Valusia will remain unified only if he, Kull, lives. The Picts were a favored people with Howard, who expressed the wish of having been born one—they fought constantly and lived far from Texas. It happens that the Picts and the Atlanteans are hereditary enemies. Kull does not much relish receiving secret information from one. But he does so, being a sensible man of powerful and wary intelligence.

Now Brule, the Spear-Slayer, comes by night to reveal that Kull is enmeshed in deadly conspiracy. The palace is hollowed away by secret passages. In a far place, the King's eighteen body guards sprawl limply. Yet they stand outside his door. Before Brule can explain, Kull's chief counselor creeps in, dagger lifted and murder in his step.

Kull slams a sword half through him. As the man dies, his face vanishes. On his shoulders appears a huge serpent's head.

The situation is, Brule explains, that before humanity there existed other Pre-Human races: The bird-women, the bat-men, the wolf-people, the snake-people, the fox-terrier men. All gone now, except the snake people and a few wolf men.

The snake people remain as priests, ruling in secret. Their powers are such that, to humans, the snake head appears as a human countenance. They can be detected by being forced to repeat the sentence:

*ka nama kaa lajerama.*

Which they cannot do, their jaws and mouth not being shaped for such barbarous sounds.

The following day, shaken by these revelations, Kull broods on his throne in the high tradition of a Howard hero—remarkably grim men as a class. Before him blazes the bright-colored court, full of whispers and laughter. Exquisite women pass, marble shines, the golden ornamentation gleams. All this is material and real. Yet it is less substantial than a dream. The under reality is manipulation by inhuman things, standing unrecognized in the familiar crowd. The real is not real. The actual is unseen. He is a King of Shadows.

Kull is given to brooding about the nature of reality. It comes up repeatedly in the stories. The King does not have Samuel Johnson's iron-headed pragmatism; he never kicks a fence, crying: "This I refute Brule!" All Kull's mental probings only serve to muddle him and smear the distinction between the solid Now and the vaporous To-Come.

And now, amid these scented glooms, the hour of Kull's Council is at hand. In a great room, with Brule bearing him attendance, Kull meets with his eighteen counselors. All are snake people.

They set upon him.

For a page or so—blind scarlet chopping in Howard's best style. Blood jets. Heads and limbs tumble. Kull's enemies are as material as any Jules de Grandin ever met, and the King runs amok in that berserker rage that is "the Atlantean way." By the end of the slaughter, his gigantic frame is covered with wounds, and the blood pours down. But those steel arms still have strength.

Back into the throne room they march. Kull stops, confounded. He sees himself seated on the throne, a serpent man in Kull's form.

Not for long. The imposter gets a sword stuck through him. The corpse is hauled into the council room. This Kull seals by ramming his sword through the door into the jamb, a blow which must have paralyzed his fingers.

Then as he swears to hunt the serpent-people from Valusia, he faints. Brule stands guarding him as the story ends.

For all its rugged outlines, "The Shadow Kingdom" has more content than mere blood drench. The prose beats with dark poetry. It generates a deep crawl of horror. Not at the obvious awfuls, the snake heads and the enslaved ghosts. But a graver horror, as if the hard stuff of our material world were shredding away under our fingers. Where nothing has permanence. Where you walk in familiar scenes, knowing them unstable and attack imminent. Where every chair is something waiting with talons, and every window hides a mouth.

It is deadly falling horror. Pre-human monsters are insignificant when you stand amid a reality that has nothing stable about it.

Variations on this theme appear in "The Mirrors of Tuzun Thune" (*Weird Tales,* September 1929). Set late in Kull's reign, it tells how the King grew bored, visited the wizard Tuzun Thune in the House of a Thousand Mirrors. Some of these show the future, some the past. Some reflect indescribable scenes. To these mirrors, Kull returns and returns again. And falls brooding, once again, on the nature of reality. Only by luck does Brule arrive to slash down the wizard, just as Kull, dissolving to a gray mist, begins entering a mirror.

It gave him something to think about in his later years.

The language of the story is full of music, dark-colored, strongly accented. It pounds and throbs and goes rushing through the paragraphs, gravely rhythmic. Howard's emotional pallet was somewhat spartan but incontestably powerful.

"Kings of the Night" (*Weird Tales*, November 1930) belongs both to the Kull and the Bran Mak Morn series. Bran is a Pict, short, dark, tough, living in the time of Rome's invasion of Britain. In the wilds of Caledonia, he faces a Roman Army. To become a King, Bran must defeat the Romans. He has no army, as such—only a collection of guerillas, irregulars, volunteers from scattered tribes. His only hope is to lure the Romans into a valley. Then, if the neck of that valley can be corked by a group of fighters, the Pict forces can strike the Roman flanks.

But the only available fighters experienced in stand-up-and-hew-away tactics, are three hundred Vikings. These refuse to fight unless Bran provides them with a King worthy to lead them. If he does not do this, they will defect to the Romans at daybreak.

At this point, King Kull steps from the sunrise. The court sorcerer has placed on him the spell of deep sleep and, in some unclear way, he has been transmitted across 100,000 years to meet with Bran upon this field. (Bran, by the way, looks much like Brule.)

Kull is described as a gigantic man, massive, grim. He seems built on the order of a magnified Tarzan. His heavy hair is black, cut square, held by a heavy gold ring. His face is clean shaven, the jaw solid, lips firm, intelligence and unwavering will shaping his face.

Kull fancies himself dreaming. He agrees to help Bran against the Romans and, to begin with, kills the fractious Viking leader in a hand-to-hand fight. Having asserted his leadership in the most positive way, he then leads the three hundred to the narrow valley to stand against the Romans.

Twelve hundred Romans come down on them. The battle continues until not even Howard could draw one drop of blood more. It is a prodigious, endless slaughter, page after page of swords falling. Blood frenzy. Death. Dust. The sweating raging stink of men chopping each other to chunks in a killing that is as savagely mindless as dinosaur struggle.

At the end, only Kull remains of the three hundred. Bran's trap has closed. The Romans are destroyed and, as the victors struggle toward Kull's relief, they see him battling the last handful of Roman survivors. When he disappears into the sunset, he is still killing.

Later legends say he lived to wake into Valusia, covered with wounds, wondering greatly about that night's work.

Reality is a most incredibly slippery thing.

## 10—

It is reported that Kull was not particularly successful in *Weird Tales*. Most readers failed to enthuse over metaphysical meanderings and poetic fervor. As we now know from the Conan series, the image was almost—not quite—in focus.

In spite of his position 100,000 years in the past, Kull was still linked to the real world. It was a precarious linkage, to be sure, but he was required to survive in an intensely political situation of rather modern form. He was a King. But the situation of kings is that they are less free in their movements than merry adventurers. They must watch warily for treasons and go carefully enough within the limits of palace and city. It is confining, even when time travel is tossed in to sweeten their bondage.

So Kull's situation was innately rigid, lacking the bright variety that readers craved. And, additionally, Kull was blessed with a large intelligence and sensitivity that drew him to speculate on reality's gleaming colored coat.

This is hardly the fodder for action-starved readers. It may be admirable that a hero wonder about the meaning of a reflection. To marvel at the transience of human achievement. To make semi-cogent observations on time, that corrosive element. But it is careless of a hero to indulge in abstract thought before the readers' eyes.

Poetic speculation slows the action. And Kull was speculative, as he was also a king and limited in his radius of action. These factors retarded the free evolution of the story, and all were carefully worked around or ignored in the coming Conan series.

## 11—

The stream of occult adventure flows on. We have followed only the larger currents, and few enough of those, from 1907 to 1929. From this point onward, change rears gigantically up. The narrative of sex and sadism is soon to appear, wrapped in a feverish husk of ghouls, mad dwarfs and cackling cripples. The single-character magazines would select morsels of the occult experience. And those practicing occult ways would grow increasingly evil, increasingly depraved.

All this the 1930s held, a brimming cup. It was a cup filled by more than two decades of fiction. From a public craze for occultism, spiritualism, and the wonders of Madame Blavatsky, and the Victorian ghost story; from Blackwood's stories of a psychic investigator; from Semi-Dual's applications of astrology to the detection of crime; and from the intrusion of supernormal monsters from another reality, as in the Carnacki and de Grandin adventures; from all these varied sources, the occult tinge penetrated the popular magazine fiction of the 1930s.

One thing in common, all these writers had, from Blackwood to Howard. Their characters might vary and their personal prose styles might soar or crawl. But all shared that fey conviction that behind life, as we experience it, cluster other existences. That doors swing behind unseen doors. That what our senses show masks something more.

That second meanings are found in the most ordinary things. That the familiar jumble of our Now, all lights and edges, conceals a more profound reality that is, at once, exciting, dangerous and strange.

Edgar Rice Burroughs had the same sense. But with this difference: Where others achieved exceptional adventure by allowing the supernormal to peer through reality, Burroughs merely moved his narrative to hard-to-get-to places and treated all the wonders discovered there as if perfectly conventional.

Burroughs is filled with colossal experience. But there shivers no mystic wonderment about it. There it is: A herd of dinosaurs, a multiple-limbed Red Martian, a city lost for half Earth's history. It is strange, strange. Yet there it sits, right in the sunlight, very solid, smelling rather sweaty, leaving prints in the familiar dust. It has always been in this place. Always will be. Nothing strange about it at all. You just haven't been this way before. Forget these common things—tell me, what is Hollywood really like? Now that's a real place of dreams.

So much goes back to Burroughs. He contributed so copiously that it is difficult to realize he didn't contribute all. Some of his more passionate enthusiasts never quite concede that his work has limitations. But let us hasten by them. They bite and scratch when reasoned with.

Let us return to 1912 and the *All-Story* magazine. In that publication, over the course of seven months, arrived two stories that modified the plastic stuff of popular literature as deeply as the creation of Sherlock Holmes.

# Chapter III—BUMUDEMUTOMURO

1—

In the not too remote past, you might observe that small boys at play would abruptly arrest their activities to contort themselves and hammer their sternums and yodel cries of considerable ferocity. The effect was that of assertive sparrows.

The cause was ephemeral: Exposure to jungle moving pictures, complicated by books about Bomba the Jungle Boy and his great precursor, Tarzan.

Parents recognized the cries and casually dismissed them as "That Johnny Weissmuller stuff." They were correct. All these antics were pallid copies of the Tarzan movies, even as the movies were pallid copies of the Tarzan novels.

Second-hand adventures they might have been. But the movies contained wonderous bits: The vine swing, the apeman's cry, the battle with the lion, the dive from a high place. These glories were set, like precious stones, in a tame jungle, self-consciously leafy and intermingled with stock footage of animals. It all stimulated the imagination—and small boys.

The moving pictures reinforced the book scenes, which clung like burrs to the mind's fabric. How well they are remembered: The wild boy growing up unfettered among apes, sans clothing or regular bedtime, a knife of his own, trees for cavorting, delightfully fierce animals. Freedom glorious in Eden, the African jungle.

That jungle was a thing of the mind, not reality. The prototype was the Indian jungle, lifted from the pages of Kipling's *Jungle Stories,* cleansed of cobra and tiger, transported to Africa.[1] (In the beginning, Tarzan's jungle contained tigers, too, although later editions silently blue-penciled them.) Among the tangled vines lurked life forms customarily found only on the veldt. But if lions snarled behind every bush, far far from their zebra herds, it was supremely right. That is what lions did in Tarzan's jungle. These ecological imprecisions made little difference. The jungle was above reality. The illusions lived, regardless of discrepancies, the conflicting details simply melting to a plausible whole. We accept without question, our senses enchanted.

What possible difference does it make that the lions were out of place, that the center of Africa was heavily studded with lost civilizations, that two or three men looked precisely like Tarzan, that no matter how many times you were abducted, you were invariably saved a few chapters later?

It made no difference. The books lived in spite of themselves. The

132

adventures could have been sited in the jungles of New Jersey and readers would have accepted the fact.

What is in the novels is, if not reality, at least what reality should be. Tarzan and Tarzan's Africa are powerful dreams, massy and casting shadow.

Here we stand amid dark shades, men reverted to first principles, free in tough paradise. Civilization's tedious constraints shackle us no longer. Away with interpersonal finessing. Discard discrimination between delicately different modes of behavior. We rip raw steaks from the flank of our kill. We bellow the challenge of the Mangani, the Great Apes.

This is reality—this powerful body, these heightened senses. Read the wind with your nostrils. Wipe the great knife on the pelt of dinner. Leap upward to the second terrace of limbs, perching there so high that faint minds cringe.

But your nerves never falter.

You eat a delicious beetle and watch the leaves move.

Splendor, with all the toothache omitted.

No need to consider the consequences which attend development of a human mind not early exposed to human language or the abstractions of civilization. In the Tarzan jungle, psychological consequences do not pertain. Ignore them. If you accept the jungle, you accept it completely. No quibbling.[2]

2—

The creator of the jungle, Edgar Rice Burroughs, was born in Chicago, 1875, the son of a Civil War major. On graduation from the Michigan Military Academy, the boy enlisted in the 7th U.S. Cavalry. Afterward he held a variety of jobs: cowboy in Idaho, gold-dredge operator in Oregon, railroad policeman in Salt Lake City. He became a department manager for Sears, Roebuck. By that time, he was married, had several children, no particular economic success.

After reading some 1911 pulps—an experience that still tries the nerves—he wrote a story composed of whim, bloody action, phantasmas, and sold it to the *All-Story* magazine—this was "Under the Moons of Mars," the first John Carter serial.[3] He followed this immediately with "Tarzan of the Apes." And so the real Burroughs' career was found and launched.

After the first World War, he purchased a large property in the San Fernando Valley, California. There he established the "Tarzana Ranch." In 1931, he began publishing his own books. In later life, he went through two divorces, saw the bombing of Pearl Harbor, and served as the oldest accredited correspondent in World War II. He died of a heart condition in 1950, at 75, having shaken the world.

3—

The Tarzan series is generally chronological, spanning time from about

1888 to perhaps 1945. Through it familiar characters move, marry, vanish, reappear. Familiar locales host repeated bloody adventures. Human passions tangle in plot and sub-plot, orchestrated by animal cry. If the passions are not complex, they are intense. What the characters lack in personal depth is compensated by the complexity of their adventures.

These adventures interlock most marvelously. The whole forms a single story. You can begin reading at any point. But you should not read a number of the stories close together, any more than you should take a number of drinks close together. Thoughtfully separated, they enthrall.

Crisp summaries of most Tarzan novels may be found in Lupoff's *Edgar Rice Burroughs: Master of Adventure.* Philip Jose Farmer's *Tarzan Alive* contains elaborate renderings of the stories, intermixed with fictional biographical materials and a fine play of imagination. In the face of this double richness, a few general words concerning the series may still be permissible.

It began in the *All-Story* magazine, October, 1912. "Tarzan of the Apes" is a framed story, told to the unidentified narrator by an unidentified man whose facts were exact. All names were changed, a matter customarily overlooked. Lord Greystoke, Tarzan's family name (as John Clayton was his personal name), is a fiction attached to a fiction.

Mutineers land Lord and Lady Greystoke on the African coast. There he builds a hut. There his wife has her baby, goes mad, dies. Greystoke is killed by the gigantic ape, Kerchak, king of the Mangani or Great Apes. These apes have a certain degree of intelligence and vaguely human characteristics. They speak a form of language understood by all in the jungle, which proves convenient to the author later on.

The infant in the cradle is adopted by Kala, a respectable female Mangani whose baby has only recently died. She places the body of her child in the cradle (providing a solid plot complication for later chapters) and leaves for the jungle. There follows twenty years of extraordinary biography, part of which appeared four years later in a series of twelve stories about Tarzan's young manhood.

In time, Tarzan (the name means White Skin) becomes self aware, discovers the hut in the forest, eventually enters. Inside is wealth—his parents' skeletons, his father's knife and diary, his mother's diamond brooch, and a large variety of children's books. Over an extended period, Tarzan teaches himself to read and print. Attacked by a gorilla while he is studying in the hut, Tarzan kills the beast with the knife. With that first letting of blood, the epic of Tarzan is launched.

Afterward he accumulates clothing and weapons from the luckless natives of the jungle. He bends his head wondering about matters as diverse as his own coloration, God, and the reality of nightmares (all covered in the 1916 short stories). Then there arrives on the coast, a shipload of mutineers and their luckless captives.

The sheer number of mutineers off the African coast is beyond all reason. But reason has scant say in these adventures and we must learn to live with coincidence. To continue. The captives are a treasure-hunting party that has discovered treasure. The group includes nineteen-year old Jane Porter, a wonderfully beautiful girl; her father, the absent-minded Professor Porter; and his friend, Samuel T. Philander. Both men are characterized at the same level as a burlesque black-out sketch. Jane's negro attendant, Esmeralda, is ethnic, fat, and played for laughs. All are from Baltimore, Maryland. Accompanying them is young Lord Greystoke, William Clayton, who came into the title when his uncle John vanished at sea.

These good people are prisoners of the mutineers, who confiscate Professor Porter's treasure and bury it themselves. (It is promptly dug up and reburied by Tarzan.) The mutineers sail off, and Tarzan has his hands full keeping the old men alive and Jane and Esmeralda safe. Almost at once, Jane is abducted by an ape, and Tarzan saves her for the very first time. Following this stirring deed, he carries her off into the jungle for a brief, entirely sexless romance. She does not know that he is Tarzan; he does not know that she does not know he is Tarzan; and endless confusion is sown for later chapters.

About this time, the French Navy has captured the mutineers and dispatched a rescue mission under the command of Lt. Paul d'Arnot. Upon this amiable Frenchman turns the balance of the series.

The lieutenant begins, as usual in a Burroughs' adventure, badly. No sooner does he land in Africa than he is captured by cannibals and dramatically tortured. He is rescued by Tarzan, just before the main course is prepared.

While recovering from his wounds, d'Arnot teaches Tarzan French, table manners, and civilized behavior. It is necessary education. From this point on, the feral man becomes the civilized wild man, capable of exerting his influence in both human society and the world of nature and providing Burroughs endless little object lessons by comparing these worlds, invariably to the denigration of civilization. The ape-man is translated to the high purity of that lovely dream, the natural man, uncorrupted by vice or fashion. Unsullied moral principle lights in him. Henceforth, the universal corruptions of civilization will slide harmlessly about him, leaving his inviolate spirit uncontaminated. So much for Western Civilization, that cess pool.

By the time that d'Arnot has fully recovered, the Porters and their party have long since sailed to America. The beloved is gone away, separated from Tarzan forever and he will see her no more alas. d'Arnot, ever sensible, packs Tarzan off to Paris, that famous healer of sick hearts. While Tarzan stares aghast at the evidences of civilization, d'Arnot secures the ape-man's fingerprints to match against the baby fingerprints in Greystoke's diary. The police are still examining these, when Tarzan sails to America.

His adventures there are as tightly compressed as though he were in the jungle. He briskly saves Jane from a forest fire and unwanted suitor, turns over the lost treasure to Professor Porter (saving him from financial disaster), and renounces both Jane and title under the mistaken belief that she loves Clayton.

Renounces title? Yes, the fingerprints in the diary conclusively prove that Tarzan is really Lord Greystoke.

But to claim the title means that Jane would marry a pauper, for Clayton has no money. Therefore, of course, the only thing for a gentleman to do is....

The renunciation scene is flatly understated. Tarzan has just completed a brief, unsatisfactory interview with Jane. She has only just pledged herself to Clayton through a feminine impulse of that irritating type afflicting heroines in older popular novels. At this moment arrives a telegram from d'Arnot congratulating Tarzan on the establishment of his true identity, that of Lord Greystoke. As the ape-man reads this telegram, Clayton enters to shake hands and gush idiotic thanks for saving them all in Africa.

The scene is a calculated set-up. Although the structural iron shows, no dramatic effectiveness is lost. The weight of the novel presses down upon Clayton, the telegram in Tarzan's hand, and Tarzan, himself, caught at the moment of grand decision. At one stroke, Clayton can be stripped of the Greystoke fortune and title. But "it would take them away from Jane Porter also."

The telegram is not shown and Tarzan retires before Clayton. "My mother was an Ape," Tarzan says. "I never knew who my father was."

With these plain words, "Tarzan of the Apes" ends. The excellence of heredity, speaking through aristocratic genes, has lifted Tarzan to superlative moral heights. The nobility of a natural man flames and blazes, emphasized as it is, by the folly, superficiality, and rigidity of behavior displayed by all other characters.[4]

The sequel arrived with some difficulty. Titled "The Return of Tarzan," it was published as a 7-part serial in the Street & Smith *New Story Magazine* (June through December 1913). It did not appear in *All-Story* because an editor rejected the manuscript. There are reasonable grounds for rejection. "The Return of Tarzan" is not really a novel but three loose parts, dimly connected by extraordinary hero and glowering villains.

Whatever its structural faults, the novel hurls wildly along. On the boat returning from the States to Paris, Tarzan incurs the hatred of that evil Russian, Rokoff. Once in Paris, Rokoff's schemes and his own lack of worldly knowledge embroil Tarzan in various scrapes. From these, he acquits himself splendidly, in spite of a momentary affair with cigarettes and absinthe.

But this is getting the story nowhere. To focus the narrative Tarzan accepts the only job in his life—a special agent in the French Ministry of War. He is sent to North Africa to investigate leakage of official secrets.

There is leakage, and Rokoff is responsible. During the second part of the story, the action carries Tarzan across the top of Africa. Once more he frustrates Rokoff's plans, then is ordered to Cape Town. He does not reach that destination. One dark night, Rokoff and a helper hurl Tarzan into the ocean.

Now begins the third part of the novel. By the Burroughs' Coincidence, which permits a story to rage along in high gear, if low probability, Tarzan finds himself cast up on the shore of the identical jungle he so recently left. Chapter by chapter he reestablishes himself: First as King of the Apes, then King of the Waziris. Then he enters the lost city of Opar for the first time.

Incident on scalding incident rushes by. Peril, action, violence, a panting chain. Nothing is developed. Events pile richly up, one after the other, like ingots of rare metals. On Burroughs rushes, hurling adventure upon the page. Another incident. And then another. On and again on.

In Opar, Tarzan is captured and almost sacrificed by the beautiful priestess, La. Through a series of intensely unlikely coincidences, he escapes. She saves him. He saves her. Eventually he leaves Opar with quantities of gold.

His activities are paralleled by a lesser narrative line that is focused on the tribulations of Jane Porter. When last seen, she had unwisely pledged herself to marry William Clayton and, having given her word, she must follow through, although it means heart-break, silent tears and anguish in the uninformed reader's heart.

For his part, William Clayton has changed from a pleasantly superficial nonentity to a weak rascal and a moral rotter. At some point between the ending of "Tarzan of the Apes" and the last third of "The Return of Tarzan" Clayton has learned that the title really belongs to Tarzan, that he, William Clayton, is not a Lord at all. Yet he will not confess, aspiring sweatily for the lovely Jane's hand.

Which she is not eager to bestow. To stall off the matter of marriage, she suggests they all go on a long cruise. As you might predict, their ship sinks. For several chapters, they float around dying of thirst in the company of Rokoff, as Burroughs struggles to link the errant strands of his story. Eventually they land in Africa. And immediately, Jane is captured by the beast men of Opar. (While the women of Opar are glorious sex-pots, the men look like retainers of the Gnome King, only more brutal.) But before the sacrificial knife drinks Jane's blood, Tarzan rescues her. They are married by her father. Rokoff is captured. Clayton confesses (concealing Burroughs' part in his crime) and dies dramatically. All leave Africa for a glorious future.

The novel is properly not a novel at all but a string of events, not particularly related until the final pages, when brute force accomplishes what artistic craft could not. Through the final portion of the story, alternating chapters weave between Jane and Tarzan. Each chapter cuts off at a point of crisis, in the manner of a silent movie serial. You ricochet from excitement to excitement.

True, all manner of cheats are employed to sustain suspense. Characters observe one another's actions and go off in a snit to grieve alone and bite their tongue. This nicely extends the story, although fifteen seconds of conversation would dispel most of the cobwebs. Coincidence is worked to the point where one more accidental encounter cannot be endured. No, sir. Not one more. Then it happens again.

No matter what technique Burroughs uses to develop suspense, he somehow brings it off. You may be enraged at the wheels grating behind the prose. But the story maintains a high degree of tension.

Tarzan and Jane appear for a third time as bit players in "The Eternal Lover" (*All-Story Weekly*, March 7, 1914). They had a baby boy and returned to Africa, the story taking place on their estate and involving someone else's dramatic love affair from a prior life. The next major adventure is "The Beasts of Tarzan," a 5-part serial, published May 16-June 13, 1914, in *All-Story Cavalier Weekly*.

The narrative begins in England. Rokoff has escaped jail. With the aid of the fiendish Alexis Paulvich, he has stolen away Tarzan's baby son, Jack. It is for revenge, revenge. The child is to be sent to Africa and raised as a cannibal.

During all the incidental confusion, Jane is also kidnapped away to Africa. Tarzan follows, reestablishes himself with the apes. A number of these he trains in the unlikely discipline of sailing a boat. He also enlists the aid of Sheeta, the panther—a similar relationship will be explored in greater detail with the arrival of the Golden Lion, a few books hence.

After much inexact chasing about, Tarzan and company board Rokoff's ship. Violent slaughter, gleefully detailed, follows. Sheeta eats Rokoff but allows Alexis to escape, presumably for seed. Once again Jane returns to Tarzan's arms. She has enjoyed some months of adventure, racing through the jungle either as a prisoner or as the pursued and constantly on the verge of being raped by evil men.

Since the novel has reached its climax and is still not long enough, Burroughs fattens it by a coda, *allegro vivace*. The ship explodes in the easy manner of Burroughs' ships and all are cast away upon an island swarming with pirates. Now follows diverse bloody accomplishments. After death enough has been described to fill the necessary pages, they all board the pirates' ship and sail back to England, only to discover that Baby Jack had been there all the time.

This story was reprinted in the *Triple X Magazine* as a 4-part serial (November 1929 through February 1930), under the title "Tarzan Returns."

The narrative of "The Beasts of Tarzan" is slightly less fragmentary than "The Return of Tarzan," but they are both of the same metal, machined on the same lathe. Each is energized by the unfaltering malignity of dependable villains who chase and are chased, who menace and flee and trick and generally keep alive a story which would otherwise disintegrate for lack of a central plan.

During the next year and a half, Burroughs published five serials on subjects other than Tarzan. These were "The Mucker," "Sweetheart Primeval," "Pellucidar," "Barney Custer of Beatrice," and "The Man-Eater." All were serials and all except "Barney Custer" and "The Man-Eater" were book length. It was a rush of fiction sufficient to explain any deficiencies in the narrative structures. Tarzan did not appear again until the end of 1915.

"The Son of Tarzan," a 6-part serial, was published in *All-Story Weekly* from December 4, 1915 through January 8, 1916. The story begins ten years after "The Beasts" and severely mangles the series' chronology. That should distress no one. The Burroughs' time accounting and the Burroughs' jungle do not lend themselves to rationality. "The Son of Tarzan" fits into no formal time sequence; you are invited to read and ignore any discrepancies.

We begin with that sturdy villain Alexis Paulvich, now decrepit, who reappears with Akut, lead ape from "The Beasts." Alexis hungers for revenge, that usual emotional coin. By complex and improbable events, the initial plot thread of "The Beasts" is now carried out: Little Jack is kidnapped to Africa. There he escapes and recapitulates his father's coming of age in the jungle—in case there existed any reader not already steeped in the original story. Fortunately Little Jack is a sturdy, self-sufficient boy, manly as Frank Merriwell, and solidly practical. Among the apes, he becomes known as Korak the Killer and is very magnificent.

Now, for the first time in a Tarzan novel, a fully developed sub-plot is integrated with the primary narrative. This plot tells the adventures of Meriem, a small girl who has been kidnapped from her father, a French officer, by a vengeful Arab. She is spirited away and treated mean and has only this old doll and is exceedingly pitiful.

The Arab and two vile Swedes, who slink about the jungle, give Meriem a thrilling time of it. She is abducted about every fourth paragraph. By accident she ends up with the Greystokes, now living in East Africa. She tells them of Korak, but they somehow don't recognize the descriptionof their son, Jack.

There is no safety for a woman, even under Tarzan's protection. Meriem is lured away by a libidinous Englishman. He lusts for her. Later he repents. But if you lust for woman in a Burroughs' novel, you are going to come to a bad end—one necessarily leads to the other. And so he dies.

At length, Meriem is saved still again by Korak, then both are saved by Tantor, the series elephant. The Arab is killed; the Swedes die. All characters remaining alive are reunited. As Jane weeps with joy, Korak and Meriem are married.

Even this early in the series, the constant abductions, the constant threat of rape, the excessive number of villains produce an effect strikingly similar to the movement of a windup toy. The action is predictable, even when the monotony is varied by a lion or ape growling from behind a bush in the last sentence of the chapter.

The flow of novels is now briskly interrupted by a sequence of twelve short stories published in *Blue Book*, September 1916 through August 1917, under the series title, "The New Stories of Tarzan." Later they were collected as *Jungle Tales of Tarzan* (1919). Written with warmth and charm, bright with humor, they are a high point of the series.

In "The New Stories," Burroughs returns to Tarzan's early manhood before the arrival of the Porters, mutineers and civilization's complexities. Each story is a bright little excursion into self-awareness.

"The God of Tarzan" contains interesting material describing how he taught himself to speak written words—an intricate process that required use of a gender prefix for each separate letter, thus producing words of appalling complexity. If he had much to say, the system would have collapsed for lack of breath.

"He-boy"—the word Tarzan applied to himself—was, for example, spelled "bumudemutomuro." The ape masculine gender prefix "bu" starts matters off; then the feminine gender prefix "mu" appears before each individual letter. (Each letter is represented by an arbitrary sound that is expressed in English as *two* letters.) Burroughs' explanation will go far to assure that Mangani will never be taught in school.

"The Battle of Teeka," another of the stories, recounts the kidnapping of Tarzan's first love and her rescue. The story was reprinted in the May 1964 issue of *Ellery Queen's Mystery Magazine* as "Tarzan, Jungle Detective." It qualifies as a detective story by no logic that is possible for mortal mind to understand.

"Tarzan and the Jewels of Opar" introduces several ideas that Burroughs was to use again and again and thriftily uses other ideas he had already worked hard. The adventure was published as a 5-part serial in *All-Story Weekly* (November 18-December 16, 1916).

To replace his lost fortune, Tarzan returns to Opar. In some amazing way he is trailed by that vile wretch Lt. Albert Werper, Belgian renegade. Immediate complications set in when Tarzan loses his memory after an earthquake. He reverts to the good old days when he was only a simple ape, recognizing neither La (which enrages her) nor Jane. Both women are abducted more times than you could believe possible.

In spite of these obstacles, La enjoys a triumph of sorts. She glides to the place where the amnestic Tarzan lies tied up tight and proceeds to seduce him. Burroughs is careful not to be too explicit, but the conclusion may be drawn that our hero was raped by that wonderful woman. Of course, she is a wild thing, which excuses her; and he has amnesia, which excuses him. If he had been in his right mind, a thunderbolt would have obliterated the series.

Other than this delightful little episode, little good happens to the Greystokes during "The Jewels of Opar." Their estate is burned for the first of several times, and matters look generally terrible until the final chapter. Then corpses are strewn lavishly across the landscape and all comes out just fine.

The March through August 1919 *Red Book Magazine* published the next serial, a six-part story titled "Tarzan the Untamed." In later years, these parts were combined with a 5-part serial (*All-Story Weekly*, March 20 through April 17, 1920) titled "Tarzan and the Valley of Luna." The combined whole was published as *Tarzan the Untamed* (1920).

The *Red Book* segment tells little-known incidents in the German-English war in Africa. The Germans, an arrogant bunch closely resembling a 1917 propaganda poster, destroy the Greystoke estate (the second time) and fake Jane's murder.[5]

Tarzan retaliates by killing Germans in vast numbers. After sundry battle adventures, he reaches the second part of the story—which concerns the lost city of Xuja. This singular place is populated by madmen, their parrots and their cooperative monkeys and lions. After the usual complications, Tarzan escapes in the company of a British aviator and a woman who proves not to be a German spy. Back at British headquarters, he learns that Jane still lives, although in German hands.

This sets off an entire new novel, "Tarzan the Terrible" (*Argosy All-Story Weekly*, 7-parts, February 12 through March 26, 1921). The story may goad some readers to screaming because almost every no-un in the entire novel is hyphenated in an cf-fort to give a primitive so-und to the pr-o-ceed-i-ngs, the subject being prehistoric m-e-n.

This stylistic annoyance accepted, the adventure roars along famously. The Germans have sent Jane far inland, guarded by the brutal Obergatz. So harsh is he that the natives plan to kill him. This he avoids by slipping off into the night with Jane, crossing an impassable swamp, and entering the weird land of Pal-ul-don. There Jane is captured away from Obergatz, who escapes in order to return later on.

Now back to Tarzan. He also crosses the impassable swamp. On the other side, he meets two separate races of prehistoric men: one white, one hairy black, both with tails. These war on each other, as do all opposing races in lost worlds. They battle together in a country swarming with large, fierce reptiles, including a vast beast that is rather like a triceratops magnified. Tucked off in a corner of the lost land is a lost city filled with scheming priests. These instantly clamp upon Jane and imprison her in their most remote citadel.

Tarzan gets within ten feet of her, then falls down a trap door. There ensue the usual escapes, captures and near misses before Tarzan carries Jane away. They become separated in the jungle and she ends up living alone in the wilds, an ape-girl swinging in the path of her son and husband.

For a pampered woman of Baltimore, she does splendidly. At long last, the Greystokes find each other, only to be immediately captured and stretched out upon the grim altar, within one second of being sacrificed.

You may expect rescue and you will not be disappointed. Korak appears, armed with an Enfield rifle he has lugged across the impassable swamp. In a moment, all the wicked folks are shot dead, including Obergatz, who has gone totally mad and was, to the point of his death by .303, considering himself a god.

Readers completing "Tarzan the Terrible" in March 1921 now faced a gap of twenty-one months before another Tarzan serial began. The long wait was scantily filled in by three serials: "The Efficiency Expert," "Chessmen of Mars" and "The Girl from Hollywood." Their patience was ultimately rewarded with the publication of "Tarzan and the Golden Lion" (*Argosy All-Story Weekly*, December 9, 1922 through January 20, 1923, 7 parts).

This serial begins as Tarzan and family return from Pal-ul-don. Along the way they find a lion cub and adopt the poor orphan, naming him Jad-bal-ja or *The Golden Lion* in the patois of Pal-ul-don. The lion grows to large maturity, trained to reasonable obedience, and behaving like no other lion then or later.

"The Golden Lion" reels wildly about the gold of Opar. A band of rogues scheme to plunder the city. Their secret weapon is Esteban Miranda, a wicked Spaniard who is the exact duplicate of Tarzan physically, if not morally. Unaware of the plotting, Tarzan heads toward Opar to replenish his fortune. As usual, he is caught and almost sacrificed but escapes with La (herself a victim of political intrigue).

Just over the brow of the mountain, they discover a lost city. It beats all you ever saw. This place is populated by intelligent gorillas and is at odds with a second lost city filled with the descendants of Atlantis.

Hazard follows hazard; battle, battle. Eventually the narrative winds back to Opar and La is reinstated as the priestess.

## WHAT HAS BEEN GOING ON IN THE MEANTIME!

Miranda and company have stolen a load of gold from Opar, a heinous crime, far different from Tarzan stealing Opar gold, you may be sure. In the course of events, all people uncaptured get captured. Those captured escape but get lost. Everyone who is lost is found and then lost again. Evil days fall upon Miranda; he has such a terrible time that he goes mad, after being captured by natives, and vanishes from the story. He will reappear in the next novel. After a long series of confusions, double-crosses, and blunders, the Opar gold is recovered and ends in the Greystoke vaults.

Worn out by all this realistic adventure, Burroughs next writes a fantastic Tarzan novel. "Tarzan and the Ant Men," a 7-part serial, was published in *Argosy All-Story Weekly* (February 2 through March 15, 1924). The novel is customarily adored as a marvel of science-fiction. It is, rather, an interesting fantasy with strong satiric overtones, distinctly related to the first part of *Gulliver's Travels.*

To begin with, Tarzan goes up in an airplane, knowing full well that anyone flying at the beginning of a Burroughs' novel is going to crash. Tarzan crashes.

He lands behind an impenetrable thorn thicket that surrounds the land of the Alali, Stone Age savages who live, not very happily, in a harsh matriarchy. In short order, he also discovers a race of tiny men, only 18 inches high, who ride wee antelopes, have advanced sorcery (Burroughs considers it science), and make war and love and behave as if they were normal. Shrunk to their size by technological enchantment, Tarzan has a fine, dangerous time of it.

Paralleling all this activity is a secondary plot tracing the further trials of Miranda. Natives have imprisoned him since the last book, thinking that he is either Tarzan or the River God. With much luck, he coincidences from captivity to Greystoke estate. Jane thinks that he is Tarzan, ill used by the world. But before she can kiss him (compromising her moral character), the real Tarzan returns. He has slipped through the thorn thicket while tiny, then resumed his natural size for the excellent reason that the plot required this change.

The next five Tarzan novels were all published in *Blue Book*. With one exception, they contain still further variations on situations and events already discussed. Some stories are highly entertaining, particularly if you happen into the series with these novels. Their general concept is simple:

Tarzan goes seeking someone lost and discovers a lost civilization composed of two warring factions. All stories contain double and triple plots, and such interweaving of abductions, escapes, captures, evil villains and admirable secondary leads that the tongue despairs of singing praise. The essential bone is, however, that of finding the lost and then getting back alive.

Thus:

"Tarzan, Lord of the Jungle" (*Blue Book*, 6 parts, December 1927 through May 1928) tells of action among an isolated batch of Crusaders settled those many generations in a sort of feudal society, complete with armor, jousting and quaint modes of speech.

"Tarzan And The Lost Empire" (*Blue Book*, 5 parts, October 1928 through February 1929) is about a living fragment of Ancient Rome, complete with togas, Colosseum, gladiators, the short sword and satisfying quantities of killing.

The following serial is more ambitious. With "Tarzan At the Earth's Core," Burroughs tries his hand at merging two of his most popular series. In a 7-part serial (*Blue Book*, September 1929 through March 1930), Tarzan joins a rescue mission that flies away to Pellucidar, that violent primitive world existing deep inside the earth. Seems that the world is hollow as a ping-pong ball, its vast inner cavity swarming with dinosaurs, cave men, intelligent reptiles, murderous mammals, and a swarm of blood-mad other menaces, insatiable and incredible. The Pellucidar series began as a serial in *All-Story Weekly* (4 parts, April 4-25, 1914) titled "At the Earth's Core," when hero David Innes and a gigantic boring machine ploughed down through the earth's crust into bedlam. The purpose of the 1930 *Blue Book* expedition is to rescue Innes. Although Tarzan is not really in top form, the action is even more violent than usual.

But even cross-fertilization with Pellucider does not seem capable of restoring youthful vigor to the Tarzan series. The action continues uniformly crisp and rapid, the characters are often interesting, Tarzan constantly fascinates; but the predictability of the story structure is numbing. Burroughs, like Beethoven, was a master of variations. Unlike Beethoven, however, Burroughs worked his wonders within a single, simple form that had by 1930 gone rigid as a petrified bone.

"Tarzan, Guard of the Jungle" was serialized in *Blue Book* from October 1930 through April 1931 (7 parts). In this warmed-up hash of previous ideas, Red Communistic Fanatics plan to raid Opar for its gold, thus financing world revolution. The book was published by Burroughs himself as *Tarzan the Invincible* (1931).

That serial was quickly followed by yet another lost race adventure. *Blue Book* called it "The Triumph of Tarzan" (6 parts, October 1931 through March 1932) and the book called it *Tarzan Triumphant* (1932). The lost race is a tribe of Christians of a particularly degenerate type, festering within an extinct volcano. The proceedings are enlivened by a gangster who lugs his tommy-gun all over Africa.

*Argosy* published the next adventure. In Abyssinia are two opposing

*Blue Book*, October 1935. A faintly immature Tarzan and Nkima view another jungle menace along the way to another lost civilization, that eternal device.

cities: Cathne, the City of Gold, specializing in trained lions; and Athne, the City of Ivory, which trains elephants. The mad queen of the City of Gold gets all shivery for Tarzan, but he doesn't love her, no matter how many people she murders. So she sets a pack of lions after him. Even that doesn't win his heart. After much literary busywork, she dies. The serial is titled "Tarzan and the City of Gold" (6 parts, March 12 through April 16, 1932).

In strict publication chronology, "Tarzan and the Leopard Men" was written immediately after "Tarzan, Guard of the Jungle," although publication of "Leopard Men" was delayed until August 1932. It appeared in *Blue Book* as a 6-part serial, ending in the January 1933 issue. Throughout the action, Tarzan has amnesia. The plot concerns a beautiful blond girl who is searching for her brother. She is captured by the Leopard Men and is to be their priestess, only she is rescued, then captured, then rescued, then captured. This continues for many chapters.

The next Tarzan novel was published by the *Liberty Magazine*: "Tarzan and the Lion Man" was a 9-part serial (November 11, 1933, through January 6, 1934) that blithefully pounces upon the Tarzan formula and strews the fragments about.

The Lion Man is a cowardly actor, part of a moving-picture company come to Africa to film a jungle epic. The expedition swiftly collapses, beset by ineptitude and fierce natives. Tarzan and the feminine lead find their way to a lost city inhabited by gorillas that speak Elizabethan English. They are ruled by Henry VIII and God, in that order. This unconventional situation is the creation of a mad English scientist who was, it seems, an advanced researcher in genetic modification.

If this sounds appalling, it is not. The story is a piece of cheerful foolishness that pokes fun at the movies, Tarzan, Burroughs and, possibly, readers who took it seriously. The dialogue is fresh and contemporary (always excluding the gorillas) and the heroine is a woman of high good sense.

After the adventure is over, a merry little coda is tacked to the end, as if Burroughs were enjoying himself and didn't want to stop. In this part, Tarzan comes to Hollywood, presents himself to be considered for the Tarzan movies, and is rejected as being unsuitable. He leaves rather more swiftly than is commensurate with jungle dignity, after killing a Hollywood lion that runs amok, thus outraging movie management, which sees a valuable property slaughtered under their noses.

This charming spoof is followed by another, different adventure—a kind of murder mystery. Published in *Blue Book* (6 parts, October 1935 through March 1936) the serial was titled "Tarzan and the Immortal Men." In book form it was *Tarzan's Quest* (1936).

Jane is flying back to Africa in the company of wealthy idiots. The plane crashes. Jane takes charge of the party, and does very well, coming through as a strong, interesting personality. As they battle along through the jungle, one of the party turns murderer. There is no way for the killer not to be the Russian, Prince Alexis Shorov, given Burroughs' feelings about Russians.

Suddenly Jane is abducted and carried far away to isolated heights by a young giant, nice but confused. He has been abducting young girls from all over the jungle and has, in consequence, badly smirched Tarzan's name.

Tarzan catches up with Jane and abductor just in time. The young man is a tool of remarkable natives. These are killing the stolen girls and processing them into small black pills which, when swallowed, convey immortality. The ruler of these people is a mad young man who lusts for Jane. She gives him little respect.

At the end of the action, our heroes carry off a large supply of immortality pills. These are shared among cast members. Jane gets some. So does Nkima, Tarzan's helpful monkey. Tarzan receives his quota, although he is already nearly immortal, thanks to the kindness of a witch doctor, some years before. Philip Jose Farmer believes that some pills were fed to the Golden Lion; and we may suppose that Korak and Meriem and their child got some, too.

The background of the next book, *Tarzan the Magnificent* (1939) is mildly complicated. It is composed of two short adventures pressed tightly together until the wound healed. The first part was published in *Argosy* (3 parts, September 19 through October 3, 1936), as "Tarzan and the Magic Men." The second part was published in *Blue Book* (3 parts, November 1937 through January 1938), as "Tarzan and the Elephant Men." The action involves two tribes of warrior women who battle each other, hate all comers, dominate by hypnotic power, the source of which lies in a head-sized diamond and emerald.

"The Red Star of Tarzan" appeared in *Argosy* (6 parts, March 19, through April 23, 1938). The book was titled *Tarzan and the Forbidden City*. Another Tarzan double is featured. This time, the lost city is underwater, prehistoric lake monsters thresh about, and the wicked priests wear diving helmets.

During 1940, Burroughs published a pair of new short stories. While not of the high excellence of the 1917 "New Stories of Tarzan," they are welcome interruptions to the long sequence of the lost city tales. Both stories feature subject matter drawn from the times and both were included in the 1965 book, *Tarzan and the Castaways*.

"Tarzan and the Champion" (*Blue Book*, April 1940) brings to Africa a boorish heavy-weight prizefighter. He copes unsuccessfully with various menaces and is saved by Tarzan's generosity. The prize fighter seems to have been modeled after Tony Galento, a beer-swilling contender who predicted dat he'd flatten Joe Louis wid one punch. (On July 10, 1939, he did not.)

The second story was published in *Thrilling Adventures,* June 1940. In this, "Tarzan and the Jungle Murders," the action occurs immediately before the beginning of World War II. Secret plans have been stolen for a device, beloved in pulp fiction, that can damp the ignition system of aircraft, jeeps and such war-like vehicles. The evil Axis sympathizers are chased from Rome to Africa. Off in the jungle, a crashed plane is found, in it a murdered man. The plans are gone. Zubanev and Pooch did it. But who are they? The Ape Man knows.

The final Tarzan adventure to be published in the magazines was a 3-part serial, "The Quest of Tarzan" (*Argosy,* August 23 through September 6, 1941). It was later included in *Tarzan and the Castaways* as a long novelette.

We begin with Tarzan in a cage. A vengeful Arab has captured him while unconscious and, since he is suffering from asphia, he cannot speak. The brain damage, while transitory, persists long enough for him to be carried to the Pacific. There, in accordance with the good old formula, the ship sinks. Nearby is an island upon which flourishes a lost civilization—Mayan survivals, in this case, practicing human sacrifices.

The castaways from the ship separate into fiends, wild animals from the cargo, and the good guys, who include a high percentage of people with no sense whatsoever. It is an interesting tale, in spite of the groan of rusty gears, and Tarzan is quite effective through the usual captures, escapes and battles with savage this and thats.

While no further magazine stories were published, two additional books later appeared at widely separated intervals. *Tarzan and the Foreign Legion* (1947) is placed on Sumatra during the war in the Pacific. *Tarzan and the Madman* (1964) returns to Africa and another lost colony—Portuguese this time—and features such staple stuff as two evil white hunters, an amnesiac who believes himself Tarzan, a kidnapped girl, *et al.*[6] Tarzan leads a horde of baboons against wicked natives with considerable effect. The writing is unpolished and likely first draft.

4—

This mass of fiction, augmented by motion pictures, the comic pages, and television, carried the name Tarzan internationally. Until Superman arrived, Tarzan was the best known white skin in the world. Even to the present time, the Tarzan figure generates books of commentary or imitation. The familiar adventures are retold in drawings and in paperback reissues with fierce covers that stretch their numbers across the bookracks.

Those ancient pulp magazines carrying Tarzan in whole or serial part continue in hot demand and short supply. Their prices remain at stupefying levels, for reasons difficult to explain. Such deviations from good sense cause untold anguish to that unfortunate who wishes to accrue to his worldly coffers all issues of *Blue Book* or *Argosy*, or, more fantastically, the *All-Story* issues. The presence of Tarzan sorely complicates magazine collecting.

All this would amuse the Ape-man himself. His opinion of civilized man was low, indeed. He rated most men high only in veniality, treachery and self-seeking.[7] It was hardly possible to surprise Tarzan by demonstration of any human failing. What surprised him was to find another human who was courageous and decent.

This grimly cynical assessment of humanity rarely survives the transition from books to other media. In these, Tarzan is consistently shown as a Good—Heart, lacking any trace of introspection, victimized by others.

That image is, itself, false. Nothing startled Tarzan less than men who broke their word, murdered for personal gain, fouled and destroyed what they could not steal, and wallowed lethally through the jungle, sniffing for the spoils of Africa and girls to be abducted.

Nor had Tarzan high regard for the organizations of mankind. Whether in Baltimore or Paris or some lost city past the horizon, he found exploitation of the many by the few—power abused for the benefit of small cliques of priests and war lords. And he observed groups of men locked for generations in combat for reasons inane, trivial and forgotten.

Perhaps Tarzan had lived too long by those iron simplicities of the jungle:

-kill only for food
-do not interfere
-don't fight unnecessarily
-sleep when you can
-wait patiently
-do not yield
-accept the fact of death

The stories give no indication that Tarzan (or Burroughs) ever understood the problems vexing those who must interlock personal existence with that of a community. When civilization and its complex hierarchies of choice pressed too hotly, Burroughs turned to fantasy and Tarzan turned to the jungle. Tarzan had, at least, the satisfaction of raw deer haunch. It is not known what satisfaction Burroughs found.

Not that we can consider Tarzan a simple wild man. Like Semi-Dual, he lived between two worlds. Obviously the difference is substantive. Dual lived in a real world that was a dream and thought in a dream world that was real. Tarzan's dilemma is less sophisticated. He must balance the jungle and civilization. Or, more obtusely phrased, balance between the unexamined life and that life forced upon us by frontal lobes.

He is highly aware of the conflict. For years, he lacks the words to define his hazy emotions. Mangani are not given to abstract thought. Nor do they reason on the meaning of life and the nature of God. The humanity in Tarzan pulls him from the unexamined life (to which recurring amnesia returns him); the animal upbringing fixes him in ways of simplicity, which his intelligence then qualifies.

He is highly intelligent. He speaks three languages, plus ape, plus a smattering of languages of a dozen lost races. After a remarkably brief period, he slides gracefully into the tradition-gripped life of a British lord. He flies. He shoots. He holds the interest of an equally intelligent woman. He thinks, also. Burroughs preserved many of his negative opinions, and perhaps there were more of these than affirmations. The conflict began in his mind before he had human language. The quality of his thought remained dark. Burroughs never resolved it. It is questionable that Burroughs ever resolved his own private darkness, that intellectual bleakness resulting when the best that a man can do yields mediocrity and such trivial fooling as popular writing hurls him to renown and wealth.

## 5—

Back in 1919, Edison Marshall wrote a series for *Blue Book* titled "From a Frontiersman's Diary." One story of that series, "The Flying Lion" (August 1919), tells of a man saved from wolves by a feral human, six feet tall, slender as a panther. White teeth flash. The face is terribly wrinkled, old, old. A strip of fur covers the body. The hand, dark brown and long-nailed, grips like a steel mechanism. Legend says it was raised among cougars in the Far West and had been born a woman.

## 6—

M. Jean C. Tarzan, or John Clayton, Lord Greystoke, is a massive man, a giant in stature, gracefully developed. A lifetime of exertion has toughened his muscles to metallic consistency. His movements are precise, quick. He may weigh about 200 pounds.[8] When long in the wilds, his heavy black hair is hacked short in front, hangs behind to his shoulders. His face is usually clean scraped. The eyes are clear, cold, gray, the face handsome and firm. A thin white line traverses from above the left eye to the scalp, arcs across his head to his right ear. This scar, which flushes scarlet when he is angered, marks where his scalp was ripped loose in the battle with the ape Terkoz.

In the jungle he travels clad only in a loin cloth. He carries a huge, razor-edged knife, a grass rope, a bow and quiver of arrows. When it is necessary to cross veldt country, he will also carry a spear. A small leather pouch accompanies him, his private pocket.

He prefers his meat bloody, nor is he particular about its freshness. Yesterday's meat will do. Or last week's. He will eat fruit, small rodents, smaller bugs, or search the remains of a rotten tree for grubs. He is, in fact, an omnivore, eating anything but man and hyena—and elephant. Got deadly sick on elephant once.

Frequently he travels with Nkima, a small gray monkey, a prodigious boaster and famous coward. When in Tarzan's company, Nkima's heart is bright. Confidence foams in him and he screams defiance. Alone at night, he feels the leopard stalk; his small heart shrinks and terror grips him in the high trees. He is a wonder monkey, this Nkima. He changed the political face of Africa by a timely warning in "Tarzan the Invincible." He has saved Tarzan's life times innumerable. A magnificent record for such a quivering, short-memoried craven.

Two other animals appear regularly through the series. Tantor, the elephant, was in enough moving pictures to be an instant star. Whether he was, in fact, one elephant or many isn't clear. But no matter. Tarzan has an understanding with all elephants, loving them as deeply as he loves the great apes.

Customarily he uses Tantor as a lounge chair. Through the golden afternoon, Tarzan sprawls on the elephant's back, carelessly content among the humid shadows. It is an unconventional posture for an English Lord.

If occasional madness grips the animal—a toothache or sex, those penetrating imperatives—Tarzan wisely leaves for the high limbs. Eventually Tantor will cease screaming and colliding with trees and settle back to his prime function as a couch.

Although at other times he performs as a highly functional killing machine. Tarzan habitually finds himself tightly tied, cannibals prodding his shortribs. Then, his eerie shrieking cry brings rescue. Tantor arrives, raving, to stomp about on the natives. Or a band of great apes appear, all tusks and red eyes. Or perhaps from the foliage springs an immense lion.

That would be Jad-bal-ja, the Golden Lion, acquired as a cub in "Tarzan and the Golden Lion." Training of this beast has worked marvels. By the time the Golden Lion expanded to colossal proportions, it would come, go, guard, fetch and refrain from eating friends of the Greystokes. Since lions lack total trustworthiness, Tarzan is careful to limit Jad-bal-ja's social contacts.

Other animals swarm the jungle, some friends, others dinner. Burroughs attached names to all of these, after the manner of Kipling. Thus the stories brim with Americanized nouns of Mangani origin:

Bara, the deer

Buto, the rhinocerous

Bolgani, the gorilla

Dango, the hyena

Gimla, the crocodile

Histah, the snake

Horta, the boar

Manu, the monkey

Numa, the lion

Pacco, the zebra

Sabor, the lioness (the name having been modified from tiger)

Sheeta, the panther

Tantor, the elephant

The vocabulary includes such natural phenomena as Ara, the lightning; Goro, the moor; and Kudu, the sun.

In the stories, each noun is followed by its English counterpart. The usage—as in Booku, the book—gives the story a tone of artless simplicity favorably comparing with texts about Spot and Jane.

The human members of Tarzan's circle are defined less precisely than the animals. Either they are names without descriptions, or caricatures, or stereotypes. Over many books, many years, some people define themselves by their actions. Their physical characteristics elude us.

Jane Porter Clayton is an exception. During her first appearance in "Tarzan of the Apes," she was the universal sweetie, a slender, little oval-faced darling, whose rich long golden hair belonged on a fairy-tale princess or pulp magazine heroine. Astonishingly beautiful, obviously, and with a perfect figure.

Her golden hair tumbles unbound to her waist. It must be a scalding burden in Africa, and particularly inconvenient for a woman so prone to abduction. We assume that she cut it eventually; the girl of 19 accepts styles that the woman of 28 waves smiling away. (Or we may also conjecture that she cut her hair because of the constant kidnapping; by "Tarzan the

Terrible," Jane has concluded that beauty is a particularly heavy burden.)

Later in life, after abductions by the dozens and near rapes in the scores, Jane's girlish simplicity firms wonderfully. She does not hesitate to shoot one abductor dead. During the events recorded in "Tarzan the Terrible," she supports herself nicely in the jungle, although alone and almost certainly naked. In "Tarzan's Quest," she serves as the leader, woods-wise expert and brains of a plane load of nitwits crashed into the jungle. As these adventures show, Jane is no longer the blond-headed sweetie whose function is to decorate the story, rather like a wall hanging, and to be stolen away when the action threatens to lag. More often in the later novels, her decisions alter the narrative direction. She performs credibly in trying circumstances. She is competent and mature, a personality change of moment when you consider her sugar-paste beginnings.

Through all her adventures, Jane wears the diamond-studded locket once belonging to Tarzan's mother. That exquisite bit of jewelry contains two ivory miniatures of the dead Greystokes. Jane never permanently loses this heirloom during her travels, although it is often a near thing.

While Jane matures to a woman of high competence, other continuing characters remain rough sketches.

The crudest of these are Esmeralda and Professor Porter. Esmeralda, Jane's negro maid, is part companion, part nurse, total stereotype. She might have stepped from an illustration on a box of pancake mix. Equally shallow is Professor Archimedes Q. Porter, a name intended to evoke merriment in the dullest lout. He is the traditional absent-minded professor, elderly, out-of-focus, oblivious, cartoon stuff. His function, like that of a Shakespearean clown, is to provide belly-laughs between blood drenches.

A more defined character is Lieutenant Paul d'Arnot, initially an officer in the French navy. He enjoys more freedom of personal action than any navy has permitted before or after. D'Arnot enters the story as a faceless player. During the violent chapters of "Tarzan of the Apes," he develops into a distinct personality. This change occurs not through Burroughs' art (relatively speaking) but because of plot requirements.

D'Arnot is indispensable. He is the great facilitator, a device in the guise of a man by which Tarzan achieves the transition between the jungle and civilization, between the animal and the human worlds.

At the time he rescues d'Arnot from the cannibals, Tarzan speaks no human language. He eats raw meat, wiping hands on thighs. He utters ferocious growls. He is no more clothed than necessary and believes himself part ape.

How then to transform this child of nature into a man who can cross the ocean seeking Jane? The obvious answer is to civilize him, a chore assumed by d'Arnot to facilitate the progress of the story. In his role as civilizer, he teaches Tarzan French. Naturally, French. It is a mild mistake, since Tarzan already reads and writes English. D'Arnot also instructs our hero in the picky art of knife and fork, explains society, emotional control, and the technique of wearing clothing.

Nor does d'Arnot's generosity stop with these benefits. Possessor of a vast fortune, he willingly halves it with Tarzan. Through d'Arnot's efforts, Tarzan's true identity is established and his first job is secured.

With equal facility, d'Arnot smooths the way for Burroughs, whose story required a reasonably credible means by which Tarzan could enter civilization. During the first two books, d'Arnot is a refreshing convenience to Burroughs, a means of solving frowning technical problems of transition and narrative direction. Later, the Frenchman is reduced to a few casual appearances, his essential work done. Lacking evidence to the contrary, we may suppose that he looks like a French nobleman. You know what a French nobleman looks like.

Jack Clayton, or Korak the Killer, as you prefer, plays a major role in "The Son of Tarzan." Later he is briefly seen in "Tarzan the Terrible." Elsewhere his role is negligible: either he is a baby or he is lightly mentioned as a parent. Once Burroughs had established Korak as an essentially duplicate Tarzan, he discovered that the series had room for only one such figure. Thus the Son of Tarzan was silently decommissioned and subdued.

Meriem faces the same problem: a strong early appearance and correspondingly little to do afterward. If Jane had really died, there might have been reason to bring Meriem to the series' foreground. As it is, she also slips into the background shadows, a lovely, dark-haired young girl with thin, curving eyebrows, the ability to speak Mangani, and daughter to a splendid old French family.

While Meriem is forgotten, La is distinctly remembered. La and the City of Opar—the two are really inseparable.

Opar is out of the Arabian nights by way of H. Rider Haggard's Kor (a ruined city, immense and forbidding, near the catacombs of She-who-must-be-obeyed). Opar was built by refugees from Atlantis. They liked the massive stone effect, piling up walls fifty-feet high. Thus vast avenues, ponderous temples, prodigious piles of stone, ancient and grim. Opar is an immensity overthrown by vegetation, its broken temples gleaming still with solid gold pillars. Beneath its crumbling floors twists a labyrinth of passages and pits. Secret corridors connect these and unknown ways creep within hidden walls and lost rooms wait within the darkness, weighty with gold bars and jewels forgotten by the Oparians.

Opar impressed Giesy and Smith as it would impress Robert Howard and Lester Dent and other builders of facsimile Tarzan worlds. Here bulk dangerous antiquity and wealth, a fascinating vision. Through the frowning ruins move a race of beings closer to the Neanderthal than the Cro-Magnon. For the Oparian men are ugly. Bearded, dark, hairy, short, yellow of fang, receding of forehead, bowed of leg, they scuttle and hate through the stories, ogres of the jungle, terrible folk. They speak Mangani. Everyone speaks Mangani.

The Oparian women, by a common Burroughs' reversal, are of rare glowing beauty. Their heredity is peculiarly selective but they seem to breed true. Every woman is soft and white and wears few clothes more than is absolutely necessary to assure the strict purity of the pages.

La, the splendid, is the most beautiful of all. Upon her tender shoulders depend the titles of High Priestess of the Temple of the Sun, Priestess of the Flaming God. By which you understand that she handles the Sacred Knife when someone is to be sliced up for religious reasons.

In "The Return of Tarzan" (the first appearance of La and Opar), she is described as a young woman of intelligent and shapely face. Her arms and legs are loaded with diamond-studded ornaments. She is dark-eyed, her voice soft and musical. Once Tarzan (trussed for sacrifice) has saved her from a murderous priest, she falls totally under his spell. Passion scalds her. She rages, thirsting for his blood. Then clings to him, weeping, a feminine plaster, honied seduction.

She is imperious. Scornful. Desirable. Ferocious.

All to no avail. A golden-haired beauty grips Tarzan's heart. La has one opportunity to sacrifice Jane but fumbles the chance and it never comes again. She has one good opportunity to seduce Tarzan (as mentioned in "The Jewels of Opar") and likely succeeds. But Burroughs is not one to tell such delicate secrets.

She is a most engaging little barbarian. The royal blood of Atlantis flows in her veins. Tarzan spends much time wandering through the wilds in her company and just what method he used to avoid being seduced twice is more than a simple reader can understand.

Like all priestesses, La has political problems. In "Jewels of Opar" she loses the sacred knife (Tarzan takes it from her) and she must leave Opar with a horde of warriors to recover it. Her love of Tarzan is open scandal. It is proven by endless repetition. He never gets near Opar without being captured. He is never captured without being fetched to the sacrificial altar. He is never stretched on the altar without La evading her duties of sticking the knife into him. It is disgraceful; such unreligious behavior.

The Oparians mutter against her. On two separate occasions, palace revolutions sweep her from power.

But never for long.

At the time of "Tarzan and the Golden Lion," she has married Cadj, the High Priest, the religion requiring that she marry, and Tarzan having made himself unavailable. She does not remain married long. Cadj betrays her in the grand style of High Priests. For his pains, he ends up in the jaws of the Golden Lion.

Much the same thing happens in "Tarzan the Invincible." Again La flees the homicidal fervor of her people to spend months roaming the countryside with Tarzan. On her return to Opar, those who seized power are spontaneously killed by the people. Politically speaking, matters worked out fine. From all other reports, she seems to have had a distressingly chaste hike.


7—


Success breeds imitation. In the dense jungles of pulp magazine publishing paced ferocious editors, testing the air with delicate nostril, alert for any trace of Readu the Reader. Let a new story fad stir, ever so gently, among the clauses and pronouns, and instantly it was sprung upon and converted, by processes best known to editors, into series retaining as much of the original as self respect and copyright law would permit.

The Tarzan series has been honored by an unusual number of imitations. Plagiarists have stolen the character, inserting Tarzan into adventures as inept as they were unauthorized by Edgar Rice Burroughs, Incorporated. More ethical writers have borrowed the essence of the series, setting their own versions of jungle men to battle ravening evil, the plots being break-neck, the source of inspiration being obvious. Some fine adventure stories have been written, in consequence, and no one protests the outline of Tarzan that rises, a bright mist, behind the prose.

The pulp magazines did not begin massive exploitation of the Tarzan story and the Tarzan figure until the early 1930s. During the fifteen years before, however, Tarzan-inspired figures were scattered thinly through popular fiction.

Of these early figures, the most solidly conceived was Polaris Janess, who was featured in three *All-Story Weekly* serials from 1915 through 1917. (This character will be discussed at length in the following chapter.) Written by Charles Billings Stilson, the series tells the increasingly remarkable adventures of a young man who was raised at the South Pole. It is far from the jungle. The father is a cast-away scientific explorer. But the essential situation echoes the plight of Lord and Lady Greystoke.

(Since from this point on, we will follow variations on a theme by Burroughs, let us briefly recapitulate the basic melody: Husband and wife are isolated in some inaccessible wilderness. She dies, leaving a husband bent with sorrow, tending a tiny baby. Years pass. Sooner or later, the father dies. The child grows to young manhood sustained by genetic excellence, becoming literate through self-instruction, developing a superhuman strength and agility by daily struggle in the wilds. Tarzan's story—and that of Polaris Janess.)

The pair of Janesses, father and son, survive for years at the South Pole, fretted by storms and polar bears.[9] After Polaris has become a young Hercules, his father dies. The boy begins the long trek back to civilization, slaying polar bears as he goes. In a few brief pages, he saves the beautiful Rose Emer, menaced in the ice, and he meets other white men and learns about envy and spite and discovers a lost city among the mountains and engages in adventures, desperate and strongly flavored by Edgar Rice Burroughs' other series about John Carter, adventurer on Mars.

Literary legend has it that Tarzan's initial appearance so rattled the magazine world that ape-men promptly began swinging from every paragraph. A cooler assessment suggests that Tarzan's influence was less immediate. It was not Tarzan but John Carter and the interplanetary romance that initially caught the admiration of writers and editors. They expressed their approval in that most positive form of tribute—direct imitation. Of adventures on distant planets, there came a rousing number. Of children raised by animals to superhuman physique and fantastic adventures there were few enough.

But in Burroughs, origins are less important than action. Little enough distinguishes the adventures of Tarzan from those of John Carter or those of David Innes (who battled primitive life-forms in a world hidden within our hollow earth). The adventures are differentiated by the hero's name, his odd friends, the fauna he encounters and slays, and the location of the adventures. The details of the pattern vary largely; the pattern itself is cut from the same basic cloth.

At any rate, the Burroughs' interplanetary story received much attention. While the Tarzan novels were popular, only selected elements of the series entered the fiction of the 'Teens and early 'Twenties. The most immediate effect was to graft the Tarzan figure to that older story line (developed in the early 1800s) concerning the white child stolen by Indians and raised as an aborigine. After Tarzan, the stolen child story was updated by substituting natives for Indians.

"White Savage Simon" by Beatrice Grimshaw is a novel of this type. Cut into bite-sized chunks, it ran as a series in *The Popular Magazine*, February 7 to about April 20, 1918 (twice-a-month issuance). Simon was a white boy captured by New Guinea natives and raised in the mountains. Rescued and carried off to the benefits of civilization, he fought in World War I. Then he returned to New Guinea. There, after sluggish adventuring, he freed and married Grace Gordon, an abducted white girl also raised as a native.

In "The Young Barbarian" by Theodore Seixas Solomons (*The Popular Magazine*, February 7, 1920), the child was not stolen. But he was reared in isolation, way up in the Canadian North Woods. His father, an idealist, wished to raise his son apart from the world's contaminations, nourished by nature. Then the father died, leaving behind the doubtful legacy of a long letter to his son, dense with good intentions. From this point, the story becomes more conventional. The boy, Eric Straive, meets a lovely girl who is revolted by his crude manners, and he is exploited by a group of tricky white men who fulfill Father Straive's most pessimistic expectations.

These novels, representative of the genre, focus on the interface between the child of nature and the civilized world. A more drastic use of Tarzan materials appeared in 1926 with publication of *Bomba the Jungle Boy*. This was the first of a long series of boy's books signed by Roy Rockwood, a house name used by the Stratemeyer writing syndicate. Bomba adventured about the Amazon jungle, borrowing massively from *The Jungle Book* and Tarzan. The pages panted with struggle, carefully sanitized, sympathetic animals, cruel white hunters and degenerate natives, lost cities, treasure in blazing mounds, unending action and danger, and intensely salted with white supremacy. Whatever its faults, that mixture kept the books in print and brought Bomba to moving pictures and comic books, those arbiters of excellence.

In both these latter fields, Tarzan claimed superiority. He had been the subject of a motion picture (silent but ambitious) as far back as 1918. And he had entered the world of the comic panel page in 1928.[10] By then, Burroughs had published eleven books about Tarzan, plus the children's book *The Tarzan Twins* (1927). It was at this point, the threshold of the 1930s, that the tide of Tarzan imitators began to rise.

The whole of this phenomenon should not be credited to the comic page. Great popular enthusiasms are rarely single determined. Tarzan's adventures were certainly broadcast to the nation by hundreds of thousands of Sunday comic pages. But the Ape-Man's appeal was also sharpened by the growing urgencies of the Depression and the brisk struggle for survival that developed among the magazines. As economic darkness thickened, editors and writers scrutinized all forms of public enthusiasm—moving pictures, radio and comic pages, among others—for whatever indications they might offer concerning popular fads.

Whatever else the magazines saw during this time, it is clear that some of them saw jungle men.

"Morgo the Mighty" was a 4-part serial signed by an ostentatiously fake-sounding name, Sean O'Larkin. The serial ran in *The Popular Magazine* twice a month from August 20 through October 7, 1930. Morgo's story was simple. As an English boy, he tumbled down a Himalayan cliff into a cave system. The caves led to a world so extraordinary as to seem fictional. Here were primitive men, flying humanoids with bat wings, and a choice selection of fantasy-fiction creatures, all of brittle temper. Tested by this Eden, Morgo grew to physical perfection. He became large, cool, powerful, handy with knife, bow and arrow, clubs and such other objects as came to hand during moments of lethality. He enjoyed splendid adventures, far, far from the crash of economics.

The following year, 1931, saw publication of the short-lived *Jungle Stories*, issued by *Clayton Magazines*, 25¢ a copy.[11] The shadow of Burroughs loomed over the magazine, staining the pages red. The first issue, August 1931, presented the novel "Sangro the Sun-God" by J. Irving Crump. As a young boy, Sangroo was marooned in the Malay jungles by an airplane crash—that favored method of joining hero and locale. He had a grand violent time of it, growing to maturity, riding elephants, slaughtering tusked carnivores, performing other exploits in devout imitation of the Great Original.

Although *Jungle Stories* swiftly terminated, the Tarzan exploitation had only begun. Earlier in 1931, that prolific fellow Otis Adelbert Kline began two different serials in two different magazines. Both serials featured jungle adventure and, if neither hero was Tarzan, both acted like blood relations.

The first serial, "Jan of the Jungle" (6 parts, *Argosy*, April 18 through May 23, 1931), begins oddly and veers toward the peculiar.

It begins with a mad scientist. Doctor Bracken was once jilted by red-headed Georgia Trevor. It is only reasonable, then, that Bracken will wait for years to steal away her baby, Jan. Revenge and again revenge. Jan is to be raised by a chimpanzee mother. The plan is to create a human with an ape's mind, trained to kill red-headed women. The doctor's laboratory is snuggled away in the Florida Everglades. From this depressing place, Jan escapes when he is sixteen years old. He is accompanied by the chimp mother, Chicma, and a Haitian negro, Borno, who has befriended them both.

They escape in a boat, are caught in a hurricane, are wrecked and cast ashore in South American jungle country. For two years, they hang around the jungle while Jan learns the Tarzan business. Thereafter, Jane appears—or rather, sixteen year-old Ramona Suarez. She lives over there on her father's rubber plantation. Jan saves her from a puma. He will save her a lot. Later he discovers a lost colony of Mu hidden among the leaves. After considerable travail, he becomes a Prince of the Sun and is ultimately reunited with his glowing family. A sequel to this splendid foolishness, "Jan In India," was serialized in *Argosy* (3 parts, January 12 through 26, 1935).

Kline's second 1931 serial, "Tam, Son of the Tiger," was published in *Weird Tales* (6 parts, June/July through December) and managed to be reasonably successful.

Another fairly direct Tarzan copy appeared in *Thrilling Adventures* in late 1932 and 1933. Kwa of the Jungle roamed through a series of short stories bearing such Burroughs-flavored titles as "Kwa and the Ape People" (January 1933), "Kwa, King of Ophir" (February) and "Kwa and the Beast Men" (March). The initial situation is familiar: while flying across Africa, the father and mother crashed in the Valley of Mu, a large, round place ringed with mountains. There, Kwa was born and raised among the apes, learned the speech of animals, and duplicated other points from the Tarzan series. Kwa is not, however, an English Lord—his given name is Nathaniel Rahan. His grandfather lives on a small estate at the fringe of the jungle, and Kwa passes that way regularly as he makes the transition between American society and his jungle kingdom.

The Ozar the Aztec series is a rather more involved version of the child among savages theme. These loosely connected short stories ran in *Top-Notch* during 1933; they were written by Valentine Wood, a house name used, on this occasion, by Walker A. Tompkins. An American scientific expedition, complete with mother and child, probes deep into the Mexican mountains and stumbles upon a lost tribe of Aztecs. The expedition is slaughtered—all but the tiny babe, who may be, it is possible, the predestined ruler of Karnux. (For predictions say that the god will be fair, with a skin of burnished silver.) The baby is spared for twenty years, then is assigned the god-defining mission of fulfilling the Five Sacred Commands of Mexlitl, the Sun God. And, incidentally, to rid the community of all those pestiferous high priests. Before he does so, mounds of dead heap the jungle. It is not stated whether Ozar ever turns silver.

Bright reflections of Tarzan also shine through the extended adventures of Doc Savage, an extraordinary adventurer and near superman, who towered, physically and intellectually, above the rest of mankind. Written for the most part by Lester Dent, under the house name Kenneth Robeson, the series ran from 1933 to 1949. From his skyscraper headquarters in New York City's tallest building, Doc roamed the world, fighting evil, correcting wrongs, having a joyous and violent life with his five eccentric associates. Whenever the story moved into woods or jungle, Doc took to the trees, racing along branches far above the ground, hurling himself from tree to tree, and dropping silently as a bronze shadow upon the evil, hunched in the underbrush, clutching their machine-guns.

In the *Argosy* serial "Genius Jones" (6 parts, November 27, 1937, through January 1, 1938), Dent borrowed a few familiar elements. Jones, a singularly powerful young man, has been raised in the Arctic wastes by a reasonably mad scientist, survivor of a 1916 polar expedition. Jones has educated himself by reading through his father's library, left on their wrecked ship. He is thoroughly bookish, impractical and honest. His adventures in the wicked world, after being rescued, are brightly humorous and the novel is a brief bit of froth.

A more elaborate rendering of these familiar materials was published in *Blue Book* from 1935 to 1938. The story of Kioga, the Snow Hawk occupies three serials and a series of seven short stories. The author was William L. Chester.

"Hawk of the Wilderness" (7-part serial, April through October 1935) works the predictable theme into a solid adventure novel. Mr. and Mrs. Lincoln Rand, and their Indian friend, Mokuyi, are cast away when their little boat strays to a strange land north of Siberia. The climate is endurable, for the land is warmed by ocean currents and a ring of volcanoes. It is called Nato'wa by ancestors of the American Indians who still live there.

The Rands live with the Indians until killed during an attack of a hostile tribe. Their baby son is then adopted by Mokuyi. At the age of six, the boy, Kioga, is driven from the tribe by racial prejudice. He survives the wilderness, aided by his pet bear, Aki, the bear clan, and the benign author. Later Kioga befriends a puma, the silver-coated Mika. Eventually our hero becomes chief of the forest bears and war chief of the Shoni tribe. But first he must save The Girl (Beth La Salle) from mutineers, his tribe from hostile war parties, and himself from dangers of every sort.

Later adventures deal with love and action in these perilous parts. The final serial, "Kioga of the Unknown Land" (*Blue Book*, 6 parts), ran from March through August 1938. The series has a satisfactory firmness, like chestnut wood, and is one of the best of the Tarzan variants.

The Bantan series, which began in 1936, is longer, softer and more superficial. Written by Maurice B. Gardner, *Bantan— God-Like Islander* began a long string of books set in the Pacific and forming a reasonably connected chronology, regularly supplemented through the 1970s. Bantan (Arthur Delcourt) was cast up on the island of Beneiro when a child of three. He was raised by the native chief and educated by the missionary, Father Lasance, who assumes the d'Arnot role as civilizer. When he is eighteen years old, Bantan begins a long set of adventures among the islands, overcoming scores of menaces.

The Bantan series constructs its own coherent world from Tarzan seeds. The brief Ka-Zar series, however, published during 1936-1937, is

*Blue Book,* May 1935. Dozens of variations appeared on the Tarzan theme. One of the best of these was the Kioga series, featuring a boy raised by Indians and bears in a lost northern land.

*Jungle Stories,* Fall 1948. Ki-Gor and his healthy wife, Helene, continued a Tarzan-Jane saga through fifty-nine novels, the most successful series to use these materials.

a shameless rubber stamp. Three stories appeared: two in *Ka-Zar* (October 1936 and January 1937); one in *Ka-Zar the Great* (June 1937), a mild retitling of the magazine.

At this point in the narrative it becomes actively embarrassing to reiterate those formalities beginning the series: death of the noble parents, the tiny child alone, the savage upbringing, the worthy animals, the bow and arrow and massive physique. These conventions have frozen to a ghastly sameness, inflexible, unchangeable, corpses condemned to minuet through eternity with glazed eye and flapping jaw. This brief apology is extended; now forward into Ka-Zar.

The Rands, father and mother, crashed into unexplored jungle during a cross-Africa flight. Their son, David Rand, was three years old. Mother died. Father lived until David was eight, teaching him English, arithmetic. Nono the monkey became the child's companion. He learned the animal language, was befriended by Kar the lion, learned to roar like a lion when making his kill. Father later murdered by fat, evil Paul DeKraft, a thieving fiend. After chapters of struggle, Ka-Zar duels DeKraft on page 81 and slays him. The novel is titled "King of Fang and Claw" and is said to have been written by Robert Byrd.

The story storms along. It is written in the high-adrenaline style of the 1930s pulps. Menace flames to crisis. Before the resulting blood has dried, new menace heaves hugely up. Violence is glazed with sentimentality, rather like a chocolate-frosted cobra. The familiar Burroughs' concepts are trotted out, one after grinning one: Ka-Zar sniffs the wind for danger, kills with the great knife, terrorizes natives, fights deadly animals, enforces justice in his realm, cleanses civilization's corruption from nature's purity. Even so.

For the enthusiasts of jungle man adventures, the period from 1939 to 1942 stands as a high point of literary history. Tarzan, Bomba and Bantan simultaneously pursued their endless adventures, and in the magazines could be found such luminous names as Ki-Gor, Dikar, Matalaa and Jongor. In truth, a Golden Age, supplemented by comic pages, comic books, and moving pictures elating the pulse.

Ki-Gor, King of the Jungle, enjoyed a longer run in the magazines than any character other than Tarzan. He appeared in the revived title, *Jungle Stories*, the first adventure published early in 1939, the last at the beginning of 1954, fifty-nine stories total.

Ki-Gor was the son of a Scottish missionary, Robert Kilgour, who was killed by natives. The boy grew up in the wilds of Africa, becoming a spectacular figure:

He was a blond, gray-eyed giant, his white skin so bronzed by Equatorial suns that he resembled a mighty-thewed lithe-limbed forest god, at home in his surroundings and blending subtly with them.[12]

In the first novel, "Ki Gor, King of the Jungle" (Winter 1939) he saves the life of Helene Vaughn, a society flier whose plane crashes into the jungle. He marries her in the Summer 1940 issue, "The Cannibal Kingdom."

She was a fitting mate to the White Lord of the Jungle. Spot-lighted by a column of sunlight, she was breath-takingly beautiful... The sun struck glints of fire from her long hair, high-lighted every curve of her golden body...laughter was in her blue eyes.[13]

Helene is red-headed, customarily dresses in scraps of leopard skin, and plays the role of Jane with enthusiasm. After their marriage, Ki-Gor spends much of his time rescuing her, and she, in turn, saves him. The rescues occur on almost every magazine cover, where Helen's figure in tight leopard skin enhances the intense action.

As is usual with Tarzan-figures, Ki-Gor has a monkey friend and an amiable elephant. He is also close to the Chief of the M'Balla tribe, the giant negro, Timbu George, once a ship's cook. A second friend of equal worth is N'Geeso, Chief of the Kamazile pigmy tribe.This cast, remixed for each story, faced problems throughout Africa—gorilla men and dinosaurs, fierce Arabs and lost races, Voodoo slaves, mad monsters, beast gods, and such similar difficulties as the writers could present, four times a year. The first novel was signed John M. Reynolds. All subsequent stories were credited to John Peter Drummond, a house name.[14]

The Ki-Gor machinery had just begun to grind, when Arthur Leo Zagat introduced a new figure, Dikar of the Tomorrow series. The stories appeared in *Argosy* from 1939 into 1941. They pounded heavily on the Yellow Peril theme, beginning with the premise that the Japanese had invaded and destroyed the United States, then established a reign of terror among the surviving population. Fragments of the population escaped to carry on a feeble resistance.

One such pocket is concealed at the top of an almost inaccessible mountain. There a group of families had fled, taking their children with them. Some years pass. The Old Ones die away, leaving behind a group of adolescent boys—The Bunch—governed mainly by admonitions handed down from the dimly remembered adults.

Nominal leader of The Bunch is Dikar, a contraction of his former name, Dick Carr. Marilee (Mary Lee) is the sweetheart, object of adoration by others, and delightful gem to be menaced or stolen away as the plot requires. Rebellion drives Dikar from the Bunch. He is expelled into the world below where, at first hand, he learn the horrors of the Japanese occupation. He slowly organizes a local resistance, over the novelettes joins with other isolated groups to battle the enemy.

Dikar performs in appropriate Tarzan fashion, a young, semi-naked woodswise, semi-savage, using primitive weapons against powerful menaces. These menaces are presented in modern terms, automatic weapons and vehicles, totalitarian masses, brutal and sadistic. The struggle is simplified until no complexities remain—only endless set-pieces of cruelty, last moment conversions to heroism, and harsh physical action. Pure evil opposes faltering good. Bestial Orientals contend with morally superior whites whose racial excellence is constantly displayed as they rise from the ruins of their culture.

The theme was a familiar one, played out in a variety of mid-1930s pulp magazines. These included *Operator 5* (1934-1939) and a short series (during 1936-1938) inserted in the sequence of *The Spider* magazine. The story was everywhere the same: The United States is invaded and virtually destroyed by the ravening hordes of ambiguous origins. Through the efforts of the hero, these hordes are ultimately crushed. Then it happens again.

Upon these roots, the Tarzan image was grafted. And so the Dikar series. At least four novelettes were published: "Tomorrow" (May 27, 1939), "Children of Tomorrow" (June 17, 1939), "Bright Flag of Tomorrow" (September 9, 1939), and "Thunder Tomorrow" (March 16, 1940." Two later serials have been noted: "Sunrise Tomorrow (2 parts, June 8 and 15, 1940) and "Long Road to Tomorrow" (4 parts, March 1 through 22, 1941). The series terminated before the Japanese were defeated and driven from America.

During the 1940s there was a sharp decrease in the Tarzan-based series characters entering the magazines. *Red Star Adventures* offered four short novels featuring Matalaa, the White Savage (June, August, and October 1940; January 1941), the magazine then terminating. Matalaa was the only survivor of a shipwreck in the South Seas. He was raised by natives, according to the usual formula, and, in the initial story, "The White Savage," fights and punishes the man responsible for the death of his parents. Thereafter he battled all forms of oriental evil and white trash. The author is said to have been Martin McCall.

The *Fantastic Adventures* magazine introduced two Tarzan-like characters during the 1940s. The first of these, John Gordon—Jongor—was the son of parents whose airplane crashed into Caspak, a lost world at the center of the Australian Great Desert. They die and the boy grows up, a physical marvel, in a world filled with dinosaurs, degenerate descendents of Mu, centaurs, and similar fantasy stuff. Three widely separated novels were published in the magazine: "Jongor of Lost Island" (October 1940), "The Return of Jongor" (April 1944), and "Jongor Fights Back" (December 1951). All were by Robert Moore Williams.

The second figure, Toka, appeared in *Fantastic Adventures* at least during 1947. The adventures, by J.W. Pelkie, follow Toka, a Prince of Sandcliff, as he moves through a cloud of dialogue and characters living in a lost valley. This is filled with immense and improbable life and fierce neighbors and a city borrowed from Opar.

The final new Tarzan figure to appear in the pulps was not male at all, but a golden-haired girl in a tight leopard skin, carrying the long knife and other jungle armament. The orphaned daughter of a white explorer, Sheena grew up in the Congo where she battled wild animals and wilder men. She appeared in three novelettes contained in the single issue of her own magazine, *Sheena, Queen of the Jungle* (Spring 1951). A fourth novelette was published in the Spring 1954 issue of *Jungle Stories*.[15]

The pulps were dying in 1951 and by the end of the decade they were gone. But the stream of fiction runs deeply and is not restrained by alterations in format. As the stream of fiction, so popular character types. The Tarzan figure continued, appearing in digest science-fiction

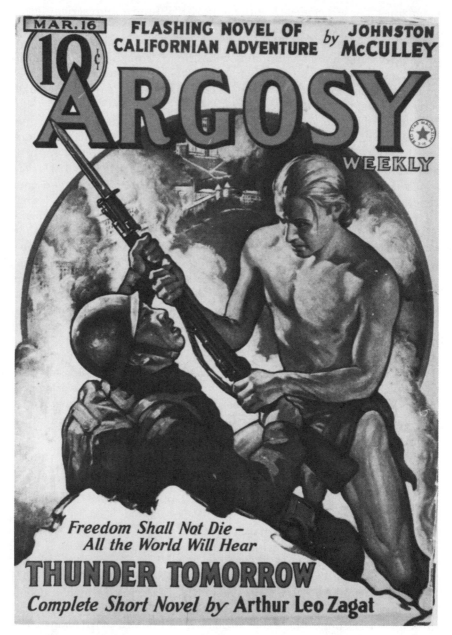

*Argosy*, March 16, 1940. The "Tomorrow" series combined the themes of Tarzan and Yellow Peril, the young hero, Dikar, battling murderous Japanese invaders of a beaten United States.

*Fantastic Adventures*, December 1947. During the final years of the pulps, all the seasoned old themes were tried once more. As in the Toka series, stuffed with lost civilizations, barbaric races, hostile life forms.

magazines, branching out into paperbacks and original novels, comic books and television cartoon productions. Some retold the original Tarzan adventures. Others borrowed the basic ideas and set up for business, themselves. It is a long way from that 1912 *The All Story* but the images still persist. The cry of the white-skinned Mangani rises from modern pages. The end of the adventure is still to come.

8—

Success breeds commentators. Around every successful literary reputation swarm the critics, pointing out all that the author did wrong on his way to fame and fortune.

Burroughs has received lots of this attention. Part of it is his own fault. His work is uneven, often plainly careless. Understandably so. He was no literary man. He was an imaginative pragmatist, a fiction merchandiser offering salable stock.

The world he knew was concrete. It contained books but no writers. That a grown man could support himself by putting words on paper was not even a factor for consideration. Grown men were clerks and cowboys, gold-field operators and soldiers.

His background was non-literary. He seems to have regarded his early work with ambivalent emotions. The stories brought money, yet writing was possibly unmanly, essentially trivial. A pastime.

He cautioned readers not to take the stories seriously. Some did then. Some do now. It was likely more than he expected. His photographs show a large, smooth-shaven, balding man. His face is open, skillfully bland. His intelligence was strong, if neither analytical nor penetrating. Humor warms his work. His opinions, knotty, often narrow, give it bone.

The books are full of opinion:

On civilization, whose advantages he found mixed. On religion which, in his writing, is most often identified with privilege and decadent power structures. On women, fierce under love, who became progressively dehumanized as they attain power and so became opponents of considerable danger. On foreign nationals, whom he treated as caricatures, unless his imagination happened to focus upon a single individual. On humanity, which he regarded, in mass, with skepticism. On conflict, which was the honing edge of life. On courage, which was essential as blood and air. On war, as a spectacle calling forth the noble energies of man. On political figures, as maniacs corrupted by power.

Tough, simple opinions, felt, not thought through. Not for Burroughs the intellectual shading that lends perspective to the African novels of Haggard. Burroughs deals in the immediate adventure. His people do not think abstractly. Rarely do they think. Indeed, they must not. To think would destroy the gossamer of the plot.

A Burroughs' story does not unfold. It progresses in bursts, peculiarly like a Roman candle. Event event event event. From danger, through suspense, toward the golden triumph, dangling like tomorrow behind the next unforeseen peril.

We are going to find a person. Let us trek two weeks to those far mountains. So simple an effort made so difficult by random lions, abductions, frights, confusions, misunderstandings, good-headed people doing wrong-headed things, wicked people doing endlessly selfish things.

No trek is simple. Or short.

The people of the story early take up their separate adventures. Their story lines dart back and forth, bright minnows in danger. Each story line rises to a pounding climax. Is then dropped to pick up another story line. Somehow all these individual threads will interweave. It takes the entire book to tie them all together, the reader panting on and on.

Elaborate variations are played upon this simple structure. The main characters separate. They come together in new groupings. These splinter into still other groupings. Each character shares adventure with each other character. It is as mechanical as a wind-up duck. The story races furiously but barely progresses.

All these combinations occur by the courtesy of coincidence. A Burroughs character could fall from orbit, weirdly sizzling, to tumble safe into the jungle not twenty feet from an acquaintance who is striving against odds.

At such moments, you may feel it all a gross literary swindle. Yet almost always, Burroughs holds your eyes to the page.

Coincidence is a means to maintain story tempo. And because tempo is vastly more important than plausibility, coincidence jangles from every page.

No matter. These are entertainments. These are light fictions by Mr. Burroughs. His obligation is to amuse, and amuse he does. Perhaps he is careless of facts, insensitive to consistency, indifferent to repetition of convenient devices. But in terms of action, movement, color, the sense of wonder tumbling over wonder—there Burroughs builds mightily, indeed.

His was a major narrative talent. Immediate drama flared in his mind. Whole worlds sprang to him in intuitive revelation.

These he mined. He explored them, one by one. At last, his production exceeded the content of these imaginary worlds. And, since his characters were figures of action, rather than of personal complexity, he exhausted the character types possible to him in these worlds.

If his fiction grew repetitive, it remained enjoyable. Let the commentators twitter. His novels are still read. The ape cry has passed into world folk lore. In some far Africa, behind your beating heart, Tarzan still ranges the jungle, magnificent, triumphant, invincible.

# Influence

What the public wanted, the public bought. That being the case, magazine publishers were quick to offer quantities of whatever attracted the public dime. If mysterious crime avengers were wanted—behold, the sea rolled back to reveal legion upon legion of mysterious crime avengers. If tough detectives sold issues, more tough detectives would sell many more issues. Or more violent jungle men were offered. Or more Chinese super criminals.

Writers derive from one another, not only by imitating each other's style, technique and ideas in easily recognizable fashions, but also by catching from one another points of view and effects which they put so completely in terms of their own style and temperament that it is impossible for the reader to detect whence the original suggestion has come. Thus, what seems from the outside a significant movement—a case of a number of different people all arriving at the same ideas and forms independently of one another—may really be only a case of all except the first following the line of least resistance—so that they present the spectacle of a rippled and shadowed field of grain over which a wind is passing, or rather, of a standing file of dominoes of which the first has been knocked over.[1]

There is no reasonable doubt that one series character influences another. Writers read and the case of Tarzan is ever before us. The fiction soaked up when twelve years old has a way of melting into the deeps of the mind, there to nourish fiction written twenty years later.

Each writer is saturated with those images of action peculiar to his temperament and taste. He draws lavishly from the literary tradition surrounding him. For he is one boat sailing a very large river whose head waters are centuries distant. Whether wittingly or not, his sentences are influenced by his particular location on the river. He soaks up those things considered truly valuable, as distinguished from those merely admirable. As a matter of course, he rubs yesterday's values against those of today. From their sparking, he learns about change and the hierarchies of importance. He picks up speech patterns and the patterns of action following speech. He learns the narrative techniques successful in his time. He filters out those experiences and subjects which are of importance to his fellows. And to himself.

All these matters get packed into the writer's fiction. Here are layered his deeper assumptions and here is the fundamental stuff of his experience. From this material, one way or the other, he selects the content of his work. Even when he is recreating Tarzan, something of his private self seeps through. Even when writing to an editor's concept of the market. Even then.

How annoyingly complex. It is very well known than popular literature is simple, shallow stuff.

# IV—Shadows of Other Suns

1—

Imaginative fiction was a staple offering in early pulp magazines. *The Argosy, All-Story, Blue Book, Cavalier* all featured at least occasional bursts of fantasy and primitive science fiction. The Munsey magazines only followed the example earlier set by the dime novels and newspaper fiction. And even such sedate publications as *The Popular Magazine* accepted fantasy into its otherwise impeccable pages.

At different times, and with different editors, this fictional type was identified as scientific romance, prophetic fiction, or scientifiction. The meaning of the words varied with the source. One thing all terms had in common—all were fantasies. The actual scientific content was nil.

To state it bluntly, the science fiction of the early writers had little relation to the science of scientists. However, it had as much relation as it has had since, in the main.... The naked fact is, almost all of what is called science fiction is fantasy and nothing else.[1]

An enormous amount of imaginative fiction was published between—loosely—1890 and 1910 (As Sam Moskowitz has shown in his many collections and commentaries, the history of the form runs deep into the past.) During this time were developed the bulk of those familiar notions that would seem so novel to readers in the 1930s: Interplanetary travel and alien invasion, movement between dimensions, extraordinary devices and inventions, and the social consequences of advanced concepts.

Primary sources were the dime novels—particularly the Frank Reade novels—the works of Jules Verne and H.G. Wells, and various Utopian novels (a burst of these occuring at the end of the 1880s). And off at the edge of the action, quietly and of great influence, radiated the various works of H. Rider Haggard.

Haggard had little to do with science-fantasy but a great deal to do with the novel of adventure in distant, romantic places, where fantastic events alter the face of reality, and the allegiance of the adventurers determines the course of civil struggle.

Back of all the trips of Mars, Venus, Mercury, and less definable points, glimmers the ghost of *King Solomon's Mines*. It is the spiritual ancestor of one hundred years' of adventures far away, in places uncommonly dangerous.

Readers at the turn of the century were deluged by scientific discovery and engineering applications. As mentioned in Chapter I, the scientist-detective resulted from this ferment. One or two of these, more dedicated than the rest, clung to demonstrated scientific principles and hardware that was more or less state-of-the-art. Authors not wishing to write detective stories, however, could turn to the story of invention, or the story of far adventure, and ornament these with bits of scientific nomenclature. The glinting tinsel caught public attention and enhanced the illusion of modernity without limiting the author's imagination.

**2—**

Jules Verne was an outstanding practitioner of the invention story. He kept reasonably close to the technology of the times. He extrapolated from contemporary engineering—bigger guns, more massive submarines, more immense flying ships. In telling his stories, he found it expedient to ignore certain physical laws. Usually not. He was a careful and honest craftsman and many of his fiction sequences, more or less intact, edged their way into the later pulps. *The Mysterious Island*, for example, includes a number of chapters where castaways recreate modern technology on a desert island. As we shall see, those particular ripples spread as far as Venus and Sirius.

Verne's interest in the technical methods of doing things helped fuel the invention fad in fiction. The dime novels reflected that interest. Some of them had reflected it before Verne, and thus we are led, step by step, to questions of influence and counter-influence and so into the Hall of Mirrors.

But let's turn from these scholastic joys and consider the Frank Reade dime novels.[2] The series is a classic example of early science fiction (or technological fantasy, to create a new term that others may now include in their literary summations). Such other dime novel series as the *Wide Awake Library* or *The Boys of New York* intermittently used similar material—submarines, airplanes, hypnotic balls, telepathically-controlled glass aircraft, dusts that permitted mind control, sound recordings, electric eyebrows, and like devices.

On less lofty planes, the wonderful invention flamed through boys' stories. The later Tom Swift series *(Tom Swift and His Miraculous Wonderful)* is a notorious example. Before Tom were legions of preteen geniuses who either learned electricity at Edison's knees or explained it to him. And they invented. Merciful Heavens, they could not be restrained from inventing.

The invention story slipped into the popular magazines as a matter of course. For three solid generations, an entire segment of fiction was device oriented:

—A criminal invents or steals an extraordinary invention. With this he steals and steals, murders and murders.
—A representative of law and order uses astonishing devices to frustrate the above-mentioned criminal.
—A brilliant scientist invents a machine that.... And then...
—A nice fellow is involved in the demonstration of a machine invented by a brilliant

scientist, that.... And then he....
—During the course of a story set in climes far off, a very nice fellow encounters all manner of advanced technology.
—An incompetent inventor attempts a new idea that fails, humiliating him humorously.

In various forms, the humorous inventor is with us yet. He came to his full glory in the 1940s Gallagher stories (*Astounding Science Fiction*). Long before that, he was an object of fun in the archaic comic papers and boys' books. Several series characters performed in this theme for the early pulps.

One of these, Hawkins, by Edgar Franklin, appeared for years in *The Argosy*, 1903-1915.[3] He invented such useful devices as a yacht that was equipped with wheels for on-land travel. But his luck was poor. His magnificent ideas served mainly to engulf him in ever more horrendous problems.

In mid-1919, C.S. Montayne wrote a series for *Top Notch* that featured Mr. Archibald Catfitz, an inventor played broadly for comic effect. Catfitz and Major Hoople (a familiar figure of the comic pages many generations ago) had a lot in common. Catfitz is an ingratiating sponge, hacking up his ideas on top of a packing case in the boarding house bedroom he shares with Bill, the long-suffering narrator. The boarding house is named Proone Villa, which sheds an icy light on the quality of the humor.

Catfitz has invented such devices as the Iceless Icebox, the Coalless Stove, and the Dishless Dish, in addition to other whimsical conceits. In "The Dishless Dish" (*Top Notch*, May 1, 1919), he invents a clay batter that will produce 100 beautiful synthetic porcelain dishes that can be retailed for eight dollars. Unfortunately, the dishes are not waterproof. And so his dreams collapse with the dish bottoms.

Thus providing an opportunity to sell his stain remover formula.

No matter how great the disaster, Catfitz will, by accident, come out slightly ahead.

In the following issue, May 15, 1919, ("Up for Air"), Catfitz has invented a mimeograph process that reproduces color paintings, rather like a messy color xerox. He plans to reproduce paintings in quantity. His process works splendidly, until the reproduction is placed vertically. Then all the colors slide off.

After months of this foolishness, Catfitz becomes a salesman ("Juggling with Jugs," November 1, 1919) and the series veers off in other directions.

A few years later, another science-oriented character was introduced by Ray Cummings, one of the early science-fantasy masters to come, just breaking into the field in the early 1920s. His character was named Tubby. It is difficult to give the exact feeling of the Tubby series, for it is all style, no more substantial than a mouthful of air. Tubby appeared in the *Argosy All-Story Weekly* (1921-1923) and contrived to sound as if he had been transplanted from the boys' magazines of a decade earlier. Same dialogue. Same level of humor.

"The Gravity Professor" (May 7, 1921): At a public lecture, Tubby is

*Argosy All-Story Weekly*, September 6, 1924. Long a major channel in the development of the science-fiction story, *Argosy* had a predilection for the scientific gadget story, as shown by this cover.

*Science Wonder Stories,* August 1929. Intoxication for the space flight fanatic: A "Space House" with solar collectors orbits the Earth, while viewers stare in wonder from a space shuttle. Fiction then: Imaginative fiction, reckless, sensational, and without standing.

accosted by a little withered man who claims to be a Professor of Gravity. In his laboratory, full of wonders, is a black water pool to which a fizzing apparatus is connected. The professor is adding an atom of oxygen to every molecule of water, thus producing a fluid in which nothing can sink. Into this, as an experiment, he tumbles Tubby. He plunges straight to the bottom. And as he sinks, he hears the Professor cry out in alarm that, by error, his apparatus has been adding hydrogen and thus nothing can float in that water and Tubby will remain below forever and ever and ever. At that point, he wakes up.

"The Thought Machine" (May 26, 1923) is less of a cheat. In this, another odd inventor has manufactured a device that seems an innocent pink-white cube. Inside is a diaphram connected to 4,786 feet of wire packed into a box one-fourth the size of a sugar cube.

> *Tubby:* "What is the theory?"
> *Professor:* "Thought is vibration."
> *Tubby*: "Ah!"

The cube permits its wearer to read another's thoughts. Tubby tests the device by wearing it while courting a girl in the garden. He is sorrowed to mind-read the following:

> *Katy:* "This funny little fat guy thinks I'm fallin' for him."

At this, Tubby flies into a passion, breaks the device, shakes the professor. Then he wakes up.

Tubby weighs one hundred and ninety pounds and is about five feet tall. You would think that his stories would have more content than this. Funny dreams, yet.

Most scientific romances required an inventor's services and if the strange fellow was wild-eyed, so much the better. Unstable, these inventors. But someone must create the device. Thereafter, its effects carry you through the story.

As used here, "scientific romance" refers to wonderful adventure and far-fetched incident, lightly topped by a sprinkle of scientific nomenclature. Edgar Rice Burroughs would later include a bushel of love interest and so modify the meaning of "romance." In its most limited form, however, "romance" is limited to the Stevenson use of glorious far adventure.

The early H.G. Wells novels are often referred to in this fashion. Wells, himself, called these novels, "fantastic stories," and incurred Mr. Verne's annoyance by not sticking to devices reasonably related to the technology of the period. Wells was not primarily interested in the possibility or impossibility of invisibility drugs, time machines, and Cavorite:

The invention is nothing in itself and when this kind of thing is attempted by clumsy writers who do not understand this elementary principle nothing could be more conceived more silly or extravagant.... The things that make such imaginations interesting is their translation into common terms and a rigid exclusion of other marvels from the story. Then it becomes human.[4]

A Spartan philosophy. Wells is primarily interested in the impact upon a small group of people when something extraordinary arrives—an invisible man or a worker of authentic miracles or an angel strayed from Heaven. Or a shell filled with Martians. Only occasionally does the device play a lead role in a Well's story, as in *The War in the Air* or "The Land Ironclads." But these are exceptions.

We have met Wells before. Born poor, 1866, rising by personal genius, the social indignities surrounding him impelled him to literature. He sought "...to isolate the conflicts, trends, and threats intrinsic to the late Nineteenth Century; and to project them into an accurate shape of things to come."[5]

If that effort led him to novels that were often heavy with lecturing, it would also produce a wealth of histories, some grimly comic novels, socialist theories, and pursuit of utopia, wherever in the political spectrum it might be concealed.

He contributed, also, to science fiction.

Whole generations of writers would mine Wells' pages. From his imagination came heat rays, views of the earth from space, giant vermin, invisibility, the time machine, scenes from the end of the world and the end of humanity, planetary destruction by stellar bodies, and aliens of admirable ferocity.

All was written in a clear, supple prose, gliding seductively along, smooth as a lover's whisper, full of stings as a cat's paw.

Splendid Mr. Wells. Verne may have been there first, but Wells is the true father of our science fiction, the giant fountain that filled the pitchers of *Amazing* and *Science Wonder* and *Astounding Tales of Super-Science*.

Granted that hordes of clumsy writers did fill these magazines with silly extravagances, so to speak. In imagination, it was easy to flit about the globe having splendid adventures. Or, better still, to flit planetary gulfs and, sword dripping, save the green-skinned queen of the XXXiiiiizzzzz's.

Such stories required little science. That commodity was replaced by bales of imagination and action. And by gadgets galore. Be damned to Wells. Some stories reeled to their knees under the burden of devices.

"Tales of Twenty Hundred" by William Wallace Cook was published as a series in *Blue Book*. It began December 1911 and continued until about mid-1912. The story is set in 2050. The situation is explosive.

Victor Blake, a young scientist who "stood first in the eye of the world," has devised a plan to straighten the tilt of the world's axis. In this enterprise, he is supported by the Quadruple Alliance, a large portion of which appears to be English-speaking. He is opposed by the Federated States of South America. The Federated States not unnaturally fear that fooling around with the Earth's tilt is going to cause large pieces to fly off.

They are probably right. For purposes of the story, however, Federated States members are scoundrels who have assigned hordes of secret agents to kill Blake before he carries his imbecility further. They send our hero a capsule of concentrated energy. When opened, this will fry about 100 square feet.

One of the Federated spies opens the capsule by error. The results are dramatic and fatal to him.

This little story bounds along for seven pages. (It ends as if they hit the bottom of page 7 and quit.) In the course of those pages, the following items appear:

—Personal aircraft which seem to have vertical landing capability.
—A sending/receiving television telephone.
—Automatic hospitals for diagnosis and treatment.
—Colored motion pictures and animation techniques.
—Compressed energy.
—Electric rifles.
—Perfect thermal insulation.
—Package delivery by magnetic-tube networks.
—Total woman's liberation.
—Radium technology.
—Electrical crop stimulation.
—Automatic homes and pushbutton kitchens.
—Automatic food distribution systems.

It is an astonishing number of items. So much material is crammed into those seven pages that the action can barely twitch. No characters are developed as such. Blake has no personality, whatsoever. The Federated States agent is a grinning devil and the treacherous secretary, who sells Blake out, is a whimpering sniveler. It's a wonder Cook got in that many characteristics, with all the other content.

The earth-straightening idea had been used by Jules Verne in his *Purchase of the North Pole (Sans Dessus Dessous)* in 1889. Featured in this novel are the same Americans who fired men around the moon. They now plan to use cannon to tilt up the earth. Verne's narrative plays humorously at the subject, jabbing lightly at various national characteristics. It turns out that the idea won't work.[6]

In his variation of the idea, Cook concentrates on the good guys and the bad guys—and he does saturate the story with devices.

By the conclusion of Cook's series, the serial, "Under the Moons of Mars" was already appearing in *The All-Story* and a hurricane was, entirely without warning, shaking fantastic literature to its roots.

3—

Giovanni Schiaparelli, in 1877, Milan, Italy, peers skyward through his telescope to observe, for the first time, what seem to be *canali*—channels—crossing the planet Mars.

That same year, Asaph Hall, peering through the 26-inch refractor telescope of the Washington U.S. Naval Observatory, sees, for the first time, the two small moons of Mars. He names them Phobos (Fear) and Deimos

(Terror)—the names of the sons of Mars.

Lowell Observatory, Flagstaff, Arizona, 1894. Professor Percival Lowell advances the theory that Schiaparelli's lines seen on Mars are streaks of vegetation following canals built to convey water from the melting polar ice cap. Mars is inhabited.

The theory explodes around the world.

LIFE ON MARS.
NOTED SAVANT SAYS....

Life—but not human life, not familiar Earth life. Mars, after all, was not only parched but more distant from the Sun than the Earth. Summer and Winter are nearly twice as long. Since the planet is half the size of Earth, the gravity is also less. A 150-pound man would weigh about 57 pounds. If that man were a trained athlete, he could leap 20...25 feet.

The Professor argued his case passionately in public with the fervor of a man accidentally committed to an untentable theory.

Theory or not, the public imagination crackled with excitement. As could be anticipated, popular fiction now stepped in.

1894: *A Journey to Mars* by Gustavus Pope. 1898: *The War of the Worlds* by H.G. Wells. 1905: *Lieut. Gulliver Jones: His Vacation* by Edwin Lester Arnold.[7]

(Gulliver Jones is whisked to Mars by a magic carpet. There he finds weird adventures in an exhausted civilization, harried by barbarians. He wins the heart of a beautiful girl, and loses her, and is whisked home.)

In 1907, Mars approaches close to the Earth. Inflamed newspaper and magazine coverage. Excitement. Is Wells correct? Speculation: Will they come *now*? Have flashes of their launching guns yet been seen?

No flashes were seen. They did not come.

1912: a six-part serial, February-July by Norman Bean, begins in *The All-Story* magazine. Titled "Under the Moons of Mars," it is "The Romance of a soul astray." The book was retitled *A Princess of Mars* when published in 1917.

For our purposes, it is in 1912 that these disparate scientific and fictional tracks close.

The scene is Mars. Not the Mars of Lovell or Wells. A blend, rather, of rare old 1912 enthusiasms and a complicated mingling of Burroughs' past reading and present imaginings.

The soul which would go so far astray was that of Captain John Carter, formerly of Virginia and the Confederate Army. His life was a singularity.

He does not seem to age. He can remember no time when he was not 30 years old. As is proper to a man touched by possible semi-immortality, his background is obscure. He has adventured across the world. A Civil War combat officer, he handles men and horses with brilliance. He handles weapons—particularly, swords—with genius.

He is the essence of the hero figure. He stands 6'2" tall, powerfully built in the broad-shouldered, narrow-hipped mould of the fighter. His hair, closely cut, is black, his eyes steel gray. His features have the regular strength mandatory for all such superior figures.

This imposing person is presented as a relative of Burroughs. Not the Edgar Rice Burroughs known to us, but a more successful, rather older individual. Carter is Uncle Jack; Burroughs is the favored nephew.

This much we learn in the Foreword to the first story, which provides a detailed, pseudo-realistic frame against whose sober facts, the wonders to come seem almost possible. We meet Carter, a tall, dark, enigma, occasionally visiting the family, leaving for the Civil War, returning years later, affable but brooding. He leaves again to make a home in New York State on the Hudson River. Dies. Leaves cryptic directions to Burroughs for burial in Virginia. Leaving, also, a mass of manuscript, the text of the novel.

The framed fantasy novel was hardly a new technique in 1912. It was a device already well used when H. Rider Haggard's *She* (1886) opened with an introduction by the author, explaining how the manuscript, actually written by H. Horace Holly, came into his hands and describing the major characters of the novel. The framed opening was a convention provided to slide the reader unsuspecting into the improbabilities that lurked, like toothed reptiles, in the deeps of the novel.

John Carter appears to die on March 4, 1886. His unembalmed body is placed in a Virginia tomb, well ventilated. The casket remains open. The tomb can be opened from the inside. Burroughs inherits.

Now to Carter's manuscript.

After the Civil War, he goes West to prospect. There he discovers a fortune in gold, while in the company of a friend. On March 3, 1866, the friend is killed by Apaches. These fiends hunt Carter into a mysterious cave where he is gripped by an equally mysterious paralysis.

Behind him, unseen, lurks something monstrous, terrifying away the Apaches. (A later book explains that this is a mummified corpse with skeletons dangling about.) Carter does not happen to notice this. He is, instead, regarding his body, limp on the floor, apparently dead. He stands in spirit outside the cave, looks toward Mars.

And is there.

Totally naked, in solid flesh.

Just how this teleportation is accomplished, how he translates from spirit to a physical human body, is never explained. You swallow the wonder and rush on.

Carter recovers his sense near an incubator filled with eggs and newly hatched young—for on Mars, or Barsoom to give it the local name, children are hatched, not born, and come from the egg five years old and furiously active.

Before he has much time to consider this variant biology, Carter is captured by a band of Tharks. These, the green men of Mars, stand about fifteen feet high, huge boned, and with an Earth-weight of perhaps 400 pounds. On Mars they possess only a normal strength and agility. Their eyes are blood red. Two tusks, gleaming like white china, curve upward to points at about eyebrow level. They also have two extra arms growing between shoulders and hips.

These distinctive fellows are equipped with spears, swords, daggers, radium rifles (which fire light-actuated explosive pellets), and ride immense eight-legged steeds, ten feet tall.

Down upon Carter thunders one of these apparitions, Tars Tarkas by name. One day he will be Carter's great friend. Now he is at the end of a spear 40 feet long, charging in the inimitable way of the green men—which is to attack every living creature except those of their own clan.

Carter promptly leaps thirty feet into the air. It is easy for a trained Earth athlete. That so astonishes the Tharks that they carry Carter along as a curious pet, clever at "sakking" (jumping).

He is a lethal pet. Immediately he kills one of the Tharks with a single punch. That amuses the others (who laugh at the sight of pain, misery, or anguish, rather like an underground comedian). Carter discovers that he will now assume the dead Thark's equipment, one of his names, all of his household personnel and responsibilities, and his relative military rank. A later killing brings him high into the Thark's military organization.

First, however, he must learn language and customs, a minor matter. Seems that much of the communication on Barsoom is telepathic. Carter learns to pick up others' thoughts, although his mind is completely shielded. No one can ever read his thoughts. It is another of the innumerable advantages Burroughs confers upon him.

At about this point, Woola is introduced. He is a ten-legged monster the size of a Shetland pony, the head froggish, jaws spangled with rows of glittering teeth. You may consider Woola the equivalent of the family dog. Carter makes friends with this horror. It will follow him all over the planet, faithful, intelligent, eager to have its head scratched.

To this point in the novel, no particular plot has appeared. Much detailed historical and descriptive material flashes by. Brief menaces glare and pass on. It is all necessary preparation. The world of Barsoom functions according to its own laws. Until the reader—and Burroughs—gets the world clearly in mind, the story remains mainly descriptive.

The action tightens and begins to flow with the coming of Dejah Thoris, Princess of Helium. Now the adventure moves toward the escape, capture, re-escape sequences that are characteristically Burroughs' version of a narrative.

Dejah makes her first appearance naked. She has just been captured by the green men. She is a light reddish copper color, her features "finely chiseled and exquisite, her eyes large and lustrous," her hair coal black and waving. Her figure is of the usual graceful proportions. Burroughs does not explain why an egg-laying female duplicates the form of an earth woman. But then, Nature knows best.

The moment Carter looks at Dejah, a strange emotions chase in his heart. And she looks at him with the contempt that a Burroughs' heroine routinely extends to the hero on their first meeting.

Once Dejah is introduced, the problem is to return her safely to Helium, the greatest Empire on Barsoom. The return is difficult enough itself, and is complicated by her perverse misunderstanding of Carter's every action.

Still he remains in voluntary service to her.

Tal Hajus, the Martian equivalent of a dirty old man, and chief of local green men, commands Dejah Thoris hauled before him. Barely does he gaze with undisguised lust, than Carter enters and smacks him about severely. Looking with lust generally results in death to a Burroughs' character, but plot requirements necessitate that Tal Hajus remain alive.

Carter and Dejah escape out across the desert on stolen thoats (those eight-legged, ten-foot high monsters). With them goes Sola, a green woman who had befriended our lead characters. She also happens to be the daughter of Tars Tarkas, although he does not know this. And so the plot threads twine.

After several pages of flight, they are detected by Tharks. In the first of the typical John Carter scenes of self-sacrifice (he is constantly offering up his life for the safety of the woman he loves), Carter sends the women away, turns to hold off the on-coming Tharks. This magnificent gesture will be repeated at least once a novel throughout the series.

The women escape. Carter, captured, is chained in a dungeon for a long period (another thing that keeps happening to him; like Tarzan, Carter is well acquainted with prison cells). Then he is sent to battle for his life in the arena, escapes by a subterfuge.

Fleeing northward, he stumbles upon the Atmosphere Factory. It seems that the Empire of Helium regulates the air and water supply of Barsoom. The air is so thin that it must be continuously replenished. That is done at this factory, standing four miles on a side, faced by walls one hundred feet thick and two hundred feet high. Nothing petty about these structures. The steel doors into this redoubt are twenty feet thick and are operated telepathically. By a fortunate coincidence, Carter mind-reads their combination from the old man in attendence.

From the factory, Carter now heads to Zondanga, capitol of the nation of the same time, for he believes that Dejah Thoris is captive in that city. Aided by Kantos Kan, a red man Carter had saved at the arena, he learns the operation of the Martian air ships. These come in a variety of types, from one-man scouts to battleships. All are powered by the ray of propulsion. The ray is unknown on earth and, since it can be stored, released, or squirted, performs in a manner totally unlike any form of light in the known universe. This is, however, as scientific an explanation as the story offers.

In due time, Carter hacks his way to Dejah Thoris. But now there is another obstacle: She has promised her hand to Sab Than, in this way saving Helium from invasion and destruction by the Zondangian hordes. Being a princess of Helium and a Burroughs' heroine, she cannot recant her word, any more than Jane Porter could recant her hasty engagement.

What is worse, Carter cannot kill Sab Than because, by Barsoomian custom, that means he could never wed Dejah Thoris.

Frustrated on all sides, he steals an air scout and heads toward Helium. He hopes to form a raiding party there, return, and rescue the princess.

Instead he is shot down near a group of battling green men. By a remarkable coincidence, he finds himself fighting by the side of Tars

Tarkas. A few rapid-fire pages later, Tars Tarkas has killed the evil Tal Hajus and become leader of the green men.

Now a march on Zondanga is organized. Just the very instant before Dejah Thoris is married to the Prince, in bursts Carter and his howling hordes. A fine, high slaughter results. The sword deals with all problems, and Carter and Dejah Thoris plight their love amid stacks of bloody corpses.

An air armada now races to aid Helium, under attack by the Zondangian fleet.

Complete success.

Carter restores Dejah to her father.

They are married.

Nine years pass.

Carter has become a prince, fighting in the armies and serving on the councils of Tardos Mors, grandfather of Dejah.

And Mrs. Carter has had a lovely snow-white egg, under incubation for nearly five years.

Before the blessed event, the engine of the atmosphere plant stops.

Rushing to the scene, Carter is able to remember the sequence of thought waves that open the factory doors. Then he slumps unconscious.

To wake in that Arizona cave, very stiff and sore, his clothing in rags, his mind brutally unsettled.

Did the atmospheric pumps begin in time?
Is Dejah Thoris Carter alive?
Did their egg hatch?
How long must readers wait?

Twelve years, fictional time; six months, real time.

January through May, 1913: A five-part serial, "The Gods of Mars" in *The All-Story.* John Carter, not looking a day over thirty, greets his nephew in Richmond, and turns over the manuscript of a new story. He remarks that he has now learned the secret of traversing "the trackless void at my will." Shortly thereafter, he steps back into the burial vault and is lost from sight.

He will return again and again, apparently homing in on his nephew, for he reappears, at intervals, at a fishing camp in Colorado, on the West Coast, and in Hawaii, always with some further account of life and death on Barsoom. All that traveling never ages him a day.

Some of the stories Carter communicates are of his own exploits. Others are of adventures enjoyed by friends and acquaintances. Thus the Barsoom series is constantly refreshed by new faces, new points of view. The rigidity that seems to fall like fog over a series, whose hero returns too often, is, in this way, avoided.

In "The Gods of Mars," all possibilities of the Carter character have not been exploited. And Burroughs has an entire planet to play with. He does so with relish.

"The Gods" begins with Carter having materialized in Heaven. It is the Barsoomian Heaven—the Valley Dor by the Lost Sea of Korus, fed by the holy river Iss.

Barsoomians live about 1,000 years. When they finally feel their vitality ebbing, they set sail down the river Iss to a land so holy and indistinct with faith that no one has ever dared swoop off in a flyer to take a look at it. Once reaching the Valley Dor, they await their loved ones in contentment and joy. Of the many curious philosophical problems this belief introduces, we need not rehearse, for fear that the whole jerry-built myth will fall to pieces. It is sufficient that this is the belief.

What actually happens, however, is that when the pilgrims come sailing down the river, they are each seized upon by plant men and sucked dry of blood. After which, fifteen-foot White Apes tear their corpses to shreds.

The trip is obviously permanent.

Carter lands in this appalling Hell and immediately finds Tars Tarkas battling there. He has decided to go to Heaven. But he carried his sword along, just in case.

Together, Carter and Tars Tarkas cut a bloody swath across the valley, invading the fortress of the Holy Therns—cannibals under whose pious auspices all this flummery is maintained. They escape from the Therns with the help of Thuvia, a red Martian slave girl.

Each escape leads only to further captures. And so Carter is immediately captured by the Black Pirates and taken to their city concealed beneath the southern Polar Ice Cap. In this place, and to his considerable astonishment, he meets his son, Carthoris. This splendid young man has an extraordinary ability to leap and sword fight. Seems that the Earth genes retain their virility.

Now follow an astonishing series of adventures. Hacked corpses clog the paragraphs. Blood and blood and more blood pours out in ceaseless seas. Dejah Thoris and Tars Tarkis arrive, only to be captured. Are saved by a hair. Then Thuvia is captured and saved. Then Carthoris. Each is imperiled and dragged from doom only by incredible exertions and loss of life. Through all this gory prancing about, Carter never falters. In the deadliest situations, his iron resolve holds. "I still live," he says, and hope continues to flicker.

Ultimately a huge naval engagement clobbers all the Black Pirates and Therns. But just as Carter is about to save Dejah Thoris, imprisoned in a gigantic revolving cell block under the Temple of the Sun....

He fails!

The door clashes shut, not to be opened for a year. And as it closes, he sees a dagger slashing downward toward Dejah Thoris' heart.

On this coldly calculated grain of suspense, the book closes. For seven months, obsessed readers dangle in suspense, their faces twitching. The story does not pick up again until *The All-Story* begins the four-part "Warlord of Mars" (December 1913 through March 1914).

It is perhaps needless to say that Dejah Thoris has escaped the dagger.

However, she has been carried far far away. Carter follows hot on her trail, hacking his way through successive walls of flesh to the North Polar Ice Cap and other points across the planet. The slaughter and violent bustling about continues until the last chapter. At that point, the story transforms itself from a dream of action to a dream of glory. High ceremonials begin. Shattering roars of acclaim boom forth. Carter is proclaimed Jeddak of Jeddaks, the equivalent of Don of Dons—the chief leader of Mars.

The scene obviously contains deep appeal. From that time to this, it has been freely borrowed by innumerable writers busily enshrining their particular hero.

Success, glory, the acclaim of fighting men. The love of the only woman. The Dream of Glory, reeling with joy.

If I only had the opportunity, they would acclaim me.

Yes yes, oh, yes, oh, yes.

In subsequent serials, the focus swings from John Carter to others, each battling endlessly singular creatures, at hopeless odds, to win the woman loved. Carthoris wins Thuvia in "Thuvia, Maid of Mars" (*All-Story Weekly,* April 8 through 22, 1916, three parts). There follows a serial about Carter's daughter, Tara, a head-strong little baggage who should have been sent off to bed without supper. Instead, she flies away on a madcap jaunt, thus setting into motion "The Chessmen of Mars" (*Argosy All-Story Weekly,* seven parts, February 18 through April 1, 1922).

Varied adventures fall Tara's lot. She meets a race of bodiless heads and headless bodies and eventually ends up as the Black Princess on a chessboard of living pieces. In spite of her folly, she is saved and wed by Gahan of Gathol, and they have a daughter who, in turn, becomes the subject of adventures.

"The Master Mind of Mars" appeared in the *Amazing Stories Annual* for 1927. (It was the first annual issue and the last.) A new hero is introduced in this adventures. His name is Ulysses Paxton, a sort of diluted John Carter. Paxton gets mangled by a shell while fighting World War I. Instead of dying, he is transported to Barsoom, arriving there miraculously healed, leaving what's left of his body on the fields of Flanders. How this miracle is accomplished is not explained.

Once he is on Barsoom, we are treated to a condensed version of how he learned to walk and jump in light gravity and how he learned the language. As a variation, this Earthman on Mars becomes the assistant to Ras Thavas, an original genius of the slightly-off scientific type. Ras Thavas transplants brains. It's a thing with him. He does it so slickly that there is no residual headache. You wake up in another body.

He removes the brain of Valla Dia, a beautiful princess, giving her glorious body (etc. etc. etc.) to a powerful but wrinkled hag. There follows all manner of to-do until Paxton corrects this mournful situation and marries the wench, who is eager to become Mrs. Vad Varo—Paxton's Barsoomian name.

By 1927, the Burroughs' influence on the popular magazine adventure story was intense. His version of the interplanetary romance swept the magazines. Barsoom seemed to transfix the creative imaginations of that generation. Readers were enchanted. It would seem that editors and other writers were also enchanted. Their stories, bright with different detail, followed the overall Burroughs' concept. While variations were numerous, significant new lines were almost non-existent—at least until the 1928 "Skylark of Space" opened new directions.

> ...Burroughs turned the entire direction of science-fiction from prophecy and sociology to romantic adventure, made the major market for such work the all-fiction pulp magazines, and became the major influence on the field through to 1934.[8]

The Oz novels of L. Frank Baum provide interesting counterpoint to the Barsoom adventures. The Oz story is simply constructed. One or two lead characters set forth on a quest through fairyland. On their way, they meet a succession of astonishing characters, tiny kingdoms, lost communities. They are repeatedly captured and as repeatedly escape, gathering ever more associates in the search. After a climax of some danger, they are successful and return to the Emerald City for a glorious party.

In miniature, that is the structure of the Barsoom novel. Which is not to say that Burroughs was influenced by Baum. The quest through curious lands is a literary form open to all. It does suggest, however, the type of tradition Burroughs worked most effectively in—which is a sequence of separate incidents connected by a single purpose. The result is an episodic narrative that gives the impression of several novelettes grafted together. This is characteristic of both the Tarzan and the Mars stories.

It is, in part, a consequence of writing a story that was serialized in many small bits. Each bit was constructed to contain its own thrills and to end on a chord of suspense. Thus the magazine format contributed to the narrative choppiness. Whomsoever is captured shall be rescued. All those rescued shall be recaptured. Once abducted, thrice abducted. Every new group encountered during the quest is hostile. The novel becomes an extended tissue of aggressive rage. The only interpersonal reaction is hostility, and the only single common act is murderous assault.

> Burroughs' work was "Pop" entertainment writing, nothing more, and seems stilted and dated today, especially in the Martian books.... What was especially bad in Burroughs, in the Martian novels, was the way he had of ignoring background, characterization on an adult literary level, and turning the novel into a running sequence of 'action episodes,' sometimes three or four to a page.[9]

Other repetitive elements in the novels hammer at you. The hero, searching, is taken captive. He is chained in the dark. He becomes a slave. Ferocious doings rage up. These are followed by escape to the next strange culture, where it all starts over again.

More slavery.

More hand-to-hand combat.

Until the reunion and terminal feast at the Emerald City of Helium.

All this adventuring is told in a wealth of circumstantial detail. The chapters bristle with the intricate sociology of Barsoom. Its history grows from book to book, the scene constantly expanding, vivid with color. We smell strange food. Prowl uneasy plains. See hordes of unknown races, in all their multitudes, pressing their business through cities whose strangeness fills us with giddy delight.

It is sweet hypnosis. Burroughs' jewelry may be paste. But such colors, such bright designs, such an enthralling glitter.

Three novels and six short stories were still to come. "A Fighting Man of Mars" appeared as a six-part serial in *Blue Book*, April through September 1930; the adventure does not feature Carter. Four years later, followed "Swords of Mars," also in *Blue Book* (November 1934 through April 1935), six-part serial). The story is a tightly-told account of Carter's battle to stamp out a cult of assassins.

The final novel, "The Synthetic Men of Mars," was published in *Argosy*, six parts, January 7 through February 11, 1939. This is a cheerful piece of foolery, regardless of the slaughter concentrated in the pages. Dejah Thoris has been crippled in an accident. To heal her, Carter and an officer in his guard, Vor Daj, hunt up the super-scientist, Ras Thavas. He is lurking in a hidden city brewing synthetic men from a vat. A fiend is collecting these to conquer Mars, and before you know it, Vor Daj's brain has been transferred to the body of a synthetic man. He spends the novel shambling about, incomprehensibly strong, saving his beloved from perils innumerable.

This serial was followed by six short stories, all published in *Amazing Stories*. "John Carter and the Giant of Mars" (January 1941) is a hasty rewrite of a Big Little Book story and is atrocious. Next came four connected stories (March, June, August, and October, 1941) tracing the adventures of Carter and his grand-daughter, Llana of Gathol. (These were later collected as the book, *Llana of Gathol* (1948). The stories prance along engagingly, bright little sun flecks, slightly flawed by abrupt endings and escapes of high improbability.

The final short story, "Skeleton Men of Jupiter" (February 1943), carries Carter to Jupiter, a prisoner of the Skeleton Men. They wish to invade Barsoom and want all defense secrets. To force Carter's cooperation Dejah Thoris is also kidnapped. Both promptly escape and, when last seen, were organizing planetary resistance.

Jupiter, in every way, is as improbable a planet as Mars.

The story was intended as the first of a new series. The remainder were not written, Burroughs being occupied at the time as a war correspondent and later being in ill health.

It is appropriate that Carter vanish at this point. The romance goes on: the hero, sword in hand, Dejah Thoris at his side, an entire planet to subdue.

And certainly he succeeded. No figure was less capable of failure. None rose higher or shone brighter. He was a first-class fighting man. And, most certainly, a Virginia gentleman.

4—

In 1915, the chromosomes of the major heroes included a gene for good breeding. Geneticists overlook this. Novelists do not. Whether raised among apes or polar bears, the hero's superior heredity makes itself known. By young manhood, he shines with innate courtliness, self confidence, respect for women. Fair play is his code. He stands armored in assurance, competence, self sufficient, generous to the good, fierce to the evil.

In 1912, Burroughs endowed Tarzan with these large qualities. Life among apes did not tarnish his excellence; his instinct for the noble gesture was unsullied by a life-long diet of raw meat.

As Tarzan, so Polaris Janess, reared among polar bears and polar ice, hero of three novels by Charles B. Stilson.

We have briefly met Polaris in the preceding chapter. He is a second-generation Tarzan in an H. Rider Haggard story. Not only is he full of innate gentlemanly instincts, which gush forth at surprising times, but he is a natural and efficient killer. And also the strongest man in the world.

He is, in brief, Tarzan magnified. The magnification omits most of the details that make Tarzan so interesting. Polaris is a character misplaced in time; properly he is the first of the 1930s supermen. He is drawn with the same disregard for physical probabilities that characterizes 1930s pulp fiction. His trail is marked by dead polar bears, dead priests, dead nobles, dead soldiers.

He is a bloody man of peace. Few so spiritual and gentle have killed so many. And, in at least a dozen ways, he prefigures that mighty figure of genius and inhuman excellence, Doc Savage, a major 1930s figure.[10]

Polaris Janess appears in three lost race novels, each involving simplified political manipulations and civil insurrection. The final novel is brimfull of war, reflecting the 1917 era in which it was written: from about 1915 onward, no self-respecting interplanetary or fantastic romance settled for anything less than war. Draw swords and hack.

"Polaris of the Snows" was first published as a three-part serial, December 18, 1915, through January 1, 1916. Then followed "Minos of Sardanes" (three parts, August 12 through 26, 1916) and the long "Polaris and the Goddess Glorian" (five parts, September 15 through October 13, 1917). All serials were published in *All-Story Weekly*. All flow together to make one extended work that is fascinating, derivative, violent.

As has been previously mentioned, the background situation is a variation on the basic Tarzan premise. Polaris Janess, an exceedingly powerful young man, has been raised alone at the South Pole by his father.

(*Father*: explorer, wished glory, expedition to the South Pole, got marooned there with wife. She died. He educates Polaris for years, charges him with The Mission: Take This Packet to the National Geographic Society.)

His father dies. Polaris strides forth into the blizzard and the polar bears, his mission to perform. En route to the coast, he saves Rose Emer's life.

(*Rose*: wealthy, young, beautiful, on expedition led by Captain James Scoland, who wishes to discover the South Pole; Rose makes side trip with brother and companion. Lost three days. Crazed companion kills brother.

*Famous Fantastic Mysteries*, July 1942. Polaris, one of the earliest of the Tarzan-influenced figures, performed amid snow drifts rather than jungle foliage, until his series converted to a romantic science fantasy.

Polaris kills companion.)

Janess Sr., that half-mad explorer, had warned his son against trusting people. Polaris, like any good Tarzan figure, walks warily among men. We note, disrespectfully, that this trait is simply tossed into the story. It is a Tarzan characteristic; therefore, Polaris must also show it. An imitation must, after all, imitate.

Alas for good intentions. Polaris is so much his own character that the author keeps forgetting the bits and snippets of Tarzan selected to ornament the adventure. These borrowings appear once, then drop away, unwept, unremembered.

Now we have Polaris and beautiful girl surrounded by ice and polar bears in the wastes of the world. They blunder about seeking Rose's ship, discover instead a lost colony of Greeks. These live in the City of Sardanes, situated in a valley warmed by a ring of volcanoes. Perhaps they are sister volcanoes to those warming Kioga's Lost Land. Perhaps there is no relationship. Probably not. Most probably not.

At any rate, here we are at the South Pole in a lost Greek colony, just waiting for such explosive elements as an incredibly powerful young man and his beautiful companion.

One glance at Rose's beauty ignites the lust of Helicon, Prince of Sardanes. In complicated ways, this polarizes a division between the Sardanian nobles and the priests. An assassination plot is cooked up against Polaris. It fails. He kills five men hand-to-hand, not being a fellow to trifle with. Thereafter in a bloody, running battle, Polaris, Rose and Kohn (the High Priest) escape the city.

After horrendous hardships (Kohn dies on the trail), they reach the ship. Polaris' reception is chilly. Scoland is knotted with hate. Not only has Polaris kept company with Rose, but he may throw doubts on Scoland's claim to have discovered the South Pole. On reaching New York, Scoland attempts to discredit Polaris. The scene, climaxing the novel, occurs at a meeting of the National Geographic Society. It is properly dramatic. But with all that has gone on before, the only appropriate climax would be the eruption of a volcano in Central Park. This does not happen, and, true enough, the end of the novel rather sags. However, Rose does vindicate Polaris and the true history of his father is revealed.

The second serial does begin with volcanic activity. "Minos of Sardanes" starts with eruptions along the Antarctic coast. These are snuffing out the Sardanian volcanoes. Obviously a rescue mission is required. It is lead by Polaris, Scoland and Zenas Wright, and arrives too late. The entire population of Sardanes—some 2,000 people—have hurled themselves into the sacred volcano. They have been listening to a crazed priest, an unfortunate lapse of judgment. The only survivors are King Minos and his wife, Memene. They are saved at the last moment by Polaris and Zenas, and all return to the ship. But the ship is gone; Scoland has marooned them. Fortunately, they locate another ship abandoned in the ice and set sail in its launch.

Meanwhile, evil cavorts. Scoland has returned to America, professes his love for Rose, is scorned, goes mad. He reveals that Polaris is down there in the icy waste. Instantly, Rose mounts a second expedition. This finds the launch with no difficulty, saving all.

But not for long. In the first chapter of "Polaris and the Goddess Glorian," the rescue ship is destroyed by the disintegrator beam of a second lost race. Polaris and the rest are enslaved. The women are to be sacrificed. Since the narrative demands an escape, Polaris and Zenas escape to the adjoining kingdom, Ruthar, ruled by the possibly immortal Glorian.

As this point, the feeble realism of the series melts away into great rolling clouds of fantasy melodrama. Glorian is a pallid copy of She-Who-Must-Be-Obeyed. All of Ayesha's intellectual force and command of occult powers are omitted, leaving only the usual stunning beauty. In a sequence loosely paralleling a similar situation in *She*, Polaris gets wounded unto death; Glorian nurses him back to health, perhaps using mental power. Interesting. But compared with the power of the original, it is weak gruel.

Once Polaris is healed, it is apparent that the evil kingdom next door, Maeronica, must be invaded. Glorian is willing. Zenas' genius creates a modern high explosive. Polaris leads the invasion forces. At the last possible instant, Rose is saved from death and Polaris dispatches the villain. He and Rose are married under Glorian's authority.

With this odd Epilogue tacked to the end of the novel.

Glorian has fallen in love with Polaris. Zenas Wright suspects that she has made Polaris immortal (by her secret mental powers) and that she will wait patiently until Rose grows old before claiming Polaris for her own. A far-thinking woman. On this unresolved chord, the series ends.

If Tarzan made inhuman strength respectable, Polaris made display of that strength mandatory. Much of the story interest is in the next superhuman act he will perform. Here, he kills an attacker by caving in his chest with one blow. There he batters back a horde of armed soldiers, using an 8-foot metal bar.

The action scenes are interlaced with most familiar descriptive passages:

> As though set on a steel spring, Polaris vaulted into the air, above the clashing talons and gnashing jaws, and landed light and sure on the back of his ponderous adversary. To pass an arm under the bear's throat, to clip its back with the grip of his legs was the work of a heart-beat's time .... ("Polaris of the Snows," Chapter V).

Then he knifes the beast to death. This feat he repeats at regular intervals, blithely disregarding the views of science that there are no polar bears in Antarctica, and that the polar bear is so tenacious of life it is best hunted with a 14-inch naval rifle.

Like Tarzan, the great original, the animal in Polaris growls barely under the surface:

> The impulses in his breast were those of primal man and might not long

be fettered by half-learned lessons of the brain. ("Polaris of the Snows,"
Chapter XVI)

Another piece of Apeman business, strictly unnecessary to the story
and soon dropped.

Polaris has no business being primal. Unlike Tarzan, young Janess has
had human company from birth. His father reared him nicely, giving him a
good education, although we must admit that he allowed Polaris to talk in
an excessively archaic style. This was the result of reading too much
*Ivanhoe.*

As is customary with heroes, Polaris is ever so facile with languages.
Fortunately, or matters might not have gone so well in Sardanes.

In person, Polaris stands about 6 feet 4 inches (the author's vision
wavers on this point). He is twenty-four years old, has topaz eyes (first
described as brown). He is

> ... so broad of shoulder and deep of chest that he seemed short. His
> arms, white and shapely, rippled with muscles at the least movement of
> his fingers. His hands were small but powerfully shaped. [Massive thews
> spread from his neck to his wide shoulders] like those of a splendid
> athlete. His mass of tawny, yellow hair swept over his shoulders....
> Above a square chin were full lips and a thin, aquiline nose.

Given a heavy sun tan and bronze hair, it would be difficult to
distinguish between this young marvel and the wonderful figure of Doc
Savage. Both are strong advocates of physical culture. Polaris believes
firmly that "opposition and trouble must be answered with the strength of
one's body."

Which explains his actions in the first novel. On board ship, returning
to New York, Polaris is recovering from a ravaging illness. As soon as he
can stagger up, he begins rebuilding his strength:

> Up and down the narrow confines [of his cabin] he paced. He jumped
> lightly. He stretched and strained each limb and muscle. Hour after hour
> he endured the severest "calisthenics"—not those taught in the
> gymnasium but anything and everything in the line of motion to which
> his surroundings lent themselves. (Chapter XXI)

His work-out is not yet as rigorous as Doc Savage's exercises, but this is
still 1915.[11]

Given his physique and intelligence, Polaris is a formidable fighter. His
favorite weapon is a long knife. From someplace, *Ivanhoe* perhaps, he has
learned the techniques of sword fighting, a minimum qualification for a
hero in this fiction form. And, naturally, he is also an expert with firearms.
When preparing for action, he belts on a pair of heavy revolvers and slings a
rifle over one shoulder. Then forward to the bloodbath.

He is altogether an astonishing young man. And wealthy in the grand
tradition, for he inherits his father's estate, which was absolutely

enormous.

He certainly dazzles Rose's heart.

And what of gray-eyed Rose, the first woman he ever met?

Her nose was straight and high, its end tilted ever so slightly.

She had full crimson lips and a firm little chin.

Moreover, chestnut hair sweeps her high brow, and she is a delicious little package of delight. She melts at the sight of babies, keeps firm control of herself when facing doom and crazed suitors. Being exceedingly wealthy, she squanders money like dust to assure Polaris' safety. For all this, the action gives her little enough opportunity to develop an original personality. She remains the stock heroine, a darling to be rescued and taken care of.

The two remaining characters are Minos and Zenas Wright.

*Old Zenas Wright*: Geologist and chemist, friend of the Senior Janess. Wright is a little man, bowed with age, whose wrinkled face and sharp black eyes suggest that he will do all the scientific work necessary in this serial. And he does. In spite of wrinkles, he can march all day over Polar ice and never pant.

*Minos, King of Sardanes*: He is equally extraordinary. He fills that traditional role of the pal who starts out as an enemy. He is the last of three brothers—the others tried to kill Polaris and got dead for their trouble.

Minos is nearly a giant. Standing 6 feet 8 inches, he is almost as strong as Polaris. The traditional battle between the hero and the second banana-to-be ended with Minos on his knees. No surprise to readers of popular adventures. At one time, he was known as "The Smiling Prince," but after becoming King he had little enough to smile about. He is a shrewd, quick-witted man of forceful intelligence and he is an uncompromising realist. He believes in natural physical processes, not the will of the gods as interpreted by priests. That makes him a man out of place in Sardanes. As other personality quirks, that one was forced on Minos by plot requirements. He courts the darkly beautiful Memene, who, at first, scorns him as brutally as any Burroughs' heroine. But then she marries him the moment his kingdom goes sour. She battles a bear for him. She is excellent, strong and loving—a superior woman. In the land of Maeronica, she dies after giving birth to a boy—an unfortunate waste of a superb character who could have done much for the story.

The story, however, is severely cluttered with two heroes and two heroines. This state of affairs develops during "Minos of Sardanes," when the narrative focuses on the fortunes of Sardanes as the volcanoes gutter out and the priests run amok. Minos and Memene occupy the central core of the story. By accident, they become as interesting as Polaris and Rose.

That is unfortunate. Double leads are hard to handle. The usual solution is to kill off one set. In "Glorian," Memene goes first, not even receiving the courtesy of a death scene. Minos follows. He dies in action, a scene easier to write: He steals a Maeronican ship and rampages through the enemy navy, disintegrator flaring golden as he wrecks 130 of 150 ships. Then he dies, luminous.

The "Glorian" serial is substantially diffierent from the others. It is a technological fantasy that contains more Barsoom than Tarzan, and more H. Rider Haggard than both.

A Burroughs' romance resembles a bead necklace: Incidents strung along a quest. A Haggard lost race novel is far more formal and, in general, breaks into four main parts: The Introduction in which main characters appear and the theme is set. This is followed by the trip out. Once at the lost civilization, there occur politically-flavored adventures, physically bloody and emotionally violent. And, finally, the novel concludes with the trip back.

"Glorian" is put together, if loosely, after the Haggard model. It is all jazzed up with spurious super-science after the example of the John Carter adventures. The science-fantasy is spread, like frosting, over the Haggard narrative structure.

The disintegrator weapon might have been lifted from *The War of the Worlds*. Makes no difference. The situation is strictly out of Barsoom—a mixture of advanced technology and Alexandrian militarism. Even Burroughs panted making the two match.

The Maeronican naval vessel, for example, is a sea-going flying saucer powered by an atomic (sort of) engine. It is a boat and submarine, and one man can operate it, if he jerry rigs the controls.

Yet the Maeronicans have no aircraft. No electrical knowledge. No means to transmit the messages over long distance. They do have the usual slavery—where would fantasy fiction be without slavery? And they have a military technology roughly equivalent to that of the Roman Legions.

But we must either accept these dichotomies or give up reading this type of fiction. These internal contradictions bump past as you read "Polaris." In fifteen years, these contradictions will become conventions and fill the novels of Otis A. Kline and Ralph Farley Milne. It all goes back to the uneven science of Barsoom.

5-

Edgar Rice Burroughs avoided certain hard problems with skill and grace. Perhaps he didn't recognize them as problems. If he wished to transport his hero across interplanetary space, a mere look did it.

The clay of John Carter lay cold in Virginia, while the body of John Carter, in some way difficult to explain, bounded about Mars, slicing up multiple-armed horrors and kissing Dejah Thoris.

The problem for the next wave of interplanetary novelists was to justify and explain how the hero could be in two places at once. Also requiring impressive triple-tonguing were such Burroughs' conventions as alien females entirely fertile with the human male, and the extraordinary ability of the hero at sword fighting.

Since the hero of an interplanetary romance spent the bulk of his time chopping down hard customers, he was conventionally muscled all over, after the manner of Greek statuary. It helps when you fight killers eighteen feet tall.

Polaris, that engaging fellow, had only to be powerful, hard to kill, and a swordsman. When, however, the lost race was unearthly—or worse, interstellar—then special provisions had to be made.

Dr. J.U. Giesy made them. From 1912 to the end of 1917, Giesy and J.U. Smith had turned out sixteen Semi Dual stories, with more cooking. This was in addition to a constant flow of solo serials and short stories, for Giesy liked to keep busy. He soon picked up Burroughs' idea of a hero transported elsewhere, accomplishing wonderously under an alien sun. From this initial concept, he wrote a series of three novels.

Not Burroughs-type novels, precisely. The Burroughs' episodic adventure does not seem to have been to Giesy's taste. Instead, he wrote a variant of the lost race novel.

To make sure that the race was thoroughly lost, he sited it on the planet Palos, "one of the Dog Star Pack," in the system of Sirius. To transport his hero interstellar distances required no effort at all—particularly to an author so marinated in occult lore as Dr. Giesy was. He merely flicked the hero to Palos by astral projection—that is, projection of the conscious ego.

Behind, on earth, lay the body, stiff, cold, insensitive. You could hardly tell it from John Carter.

But off up there on Palos, the ego roamed around, invisible but aware, and conveniently able to move instantly to any place on Palos that could be thought about. On the other hand, the transition from Earth to Palos, apparently instantaneous, took about 30 minutes.

The valiant traveler featured in this trilogy is Jason Croft. The serials were "Palos of the Dog Star Pack" (5 parts, July 13 through August 10, 1918), and "The Mouthpiece of Zitu" (5 parts, July 2 through August 2, 1919), both published in *All-Story Weekly;* and "Jason, Son of Jason" (6 parts, April 16 through May 21, 1921), published in *Argosy All-Story Weekly.*

All three novels were later reprinted, amid hysterical shouts celebrating their excellence. "Palos" appeared in the October 1941 issue of *Famous Fantastic Mysteries*, with "Zitu" following in the November 1942 issue. "Jason, Son of Jason" was reprinted in the May 1948 *Fantastic Novels Magazine.*[12]

In spite of certain obvious similarities, Jason Croft is no John Carter. Nor are the serials imitation Burroughs. Giesy wrote an interesting, if slow and much ornamented narrative. His fiction generates about 1/10 the cylinder pressure of a Burroughs' adventure. He does not slash back and forth between parallel adventures in the ferocious Burroughs style. Nor is he devoted to the suspenseful chapter ending, which often made Burroughs' work look like spliced-together Saturday serials.

Giesy was writing a novel in the old style. Through the story (as you might expect) the shadow of Semi-Dual falls long. You can hear Dual's voice in the more oracular pronouncements of Jason Croft. Both characters are given to the profound spiritual statement, delivered in hollow tones (like barrels rolling in a cellar) and with the dignity of an elephant lumbering across fresh asphalt.

As is usual, all three novels make a single whole. The basic situation is that the good country, Cathur, battles Zollaria, the bad country, filled with war-mongers and depraved leaders. (In deference to the reader, who has enough burdens, we will not discuss the geography, social customs, religious institutions, political history or economic interrelations which are given in extensive detail and have the cumulative effect of a quart of mandragora.) The social development on Palos is approximately at the Babylonian stage. That permits orgies, sword fights, slavery and all those characteristics pleasing to enlightened readers.

"Palos" begins as a framed story. Dr. George Murray is called to inspect Jason Croft, wealthy young eccentric, who has apparently fallen dead. Croft is a sort of light-haired Tarzan with the eyes of a mystic.

Murray, troubled, sits through the night sending out spiritual vibrations. (He does that sort of thing.) Eventually Croft opens his eyes. He has not been dead but away. And he tells the following tale:

Using mystic secrets learned in India, he has projected his ego to Palos. There he roved about, entranced and transparent, among the fields and glades. There he discovered his soul mate, a bejeweled dear named Naia:

> Her face was a perfect oval, framed in a wealth of golden hair, which . . .
> fell unrestrained about her shoulders in a silken flood. Her eyes were
> blue—the purple blue of the pansy. (Chapter III)

This living dream is all decked out in silks and jewels, showing quantites of "a firm, soft white" skin. Her little toes are jeweled. The description is in prose as evocative as a perfume advertisement.

No wonder Croft "quivered as with a chill."

For reasons of state, Naia is to be married off to that bloated ruffian, Kyphallos. This luxury-loving brute admires her spirit and plans to break it in the fires of his lust, or some such thing. Himself, he is more interested in the sensuous Kalamita, vamp of vamps.

Naia is flesh; Croft is not. He wanders pathetically around until he accidentally encounters Jasor of Nodhur. Jasor is a tall, splendidly powerful athletic type who is pining away because he is stupid. He broods himself to death. As his soul leaves, Jason takes over the body, thus neatly solving the John Carter quandry.[13]

Solving one problem creates another: Croft now has two bodies to worry about. He must forever be flickering across the abyssal gulf to check the condition of his earthly body, much like glancing into the nursery every half hour to be sure that baby is all right.

Croft's first use of Jasor's body is not to rush off and cover Naia's jeweled feet with kisses. Not at all. The first thing that he does to begin inventing things. Croft itches for the easier way, the benign silver gleaming of technology to enhance the estate of man on Palos. Also, he has learned that the Zollarians are plotting aggression. Thus, over subsequent months, the stupid Jasor flowers forth as the most extraordinary of geniuses. He invents:

—alcohol-powered automobiles.

—motorized galleys

These machines are developed and produced with astonishing speed. No problems are experienced in configuration control, metallic embrittlement, porosity, heat transfer anomalies, quality control deficiences, left-handed threads, combustion instabilities, feed control mechanism failures, material process malfunctions, ore purification, or boring mill alignment.

This is why "Palos" may be considered fantasy, rather than science fiction.

While Croft pursues his work, a copy of Jules Verne in one hand and *A Connecticut Yankee in King Arthur's Court* in the other, the reader is not allowed to forget Naia. She is violently brought back into the story by a clever technical device: A team of gnuppas, pulling her carriage, scares, bolts. Her life is endangered (and that of her father).

Croft saves them.

Why, he touches her hand.

They exchange looks.

As love builds to a crescendo of cupids, Kyphallos plots with Kalamita.

Lovesick as he is, Croft returns to Earth to brush up on munitions technology. After two weeks of intensive study, he returns to Palos and invents:

—armored cars
—rifles
—gold alloy cartridges (for lead is scarce on Palos)
—grenades

During those moments when he is not inventing, he slides silently from his body and, transparent as plastic wrap, whisks about spying on the enemy's plans. For the war is about to begin, intrigue having had its creepy way. Fortunately, Croft's 1918 technology has piled up impressive stores of war material. And Croft, in addition, has also invented:

—the tank

This echo from H. G. Wells decisively crushes the enemy. The invasion is obliterated. Kyphallos is exiled. Naia is saved to become the bride of The Prince of Zitra. (That is Croft's newly conferred title; he could have become Emperor but was too modest.)

All this glowing adventure, Croft spills out to Dr. Murray that dark and stormy night. If someone we knew had been deathly sick and then delivered himself of such self-evident wish fulfillment, our immediate reaction would be to call Dr. Freud. Dr. Murray has, however, been toughened by thought vibrations. He believes. He completely believes.

Croft now reports that he is ready to return to Palos forever. He has no further use for his Earthly body and asks Murray to bury the remains. Sure enough, a week later, the housekeeper finds Croft stiff and cold.

The body is buried. Shortly afterward, Croft wishes that it were not. It is time to return to Earth and tell Dr. Murray of later adventures on Palos. Since his original body is no longer available, Croft must enter the body of

No 27, a madman dying in Murray's insane asylum.

This is the frame used to continue the series, the second serial being titled "The Mouthpiece of Zitu."

Returning to Palos, Croft discovers that the priests have declared him a deity in flesh—the instrument through which their god speaks. The declaration leaves Naia not at all sure what she is engaged to marry. She returns the ring and attempts to drown herself in a swimming pool.

Croft, in astral form, meets her astral form and is able to talk her back into her body. This accomplishment so stimulates him that he invents:

—coal mining
—wire manufacturing sites
—power transmission schematics
—baseball
—power transmission lines
—water-wheels
—airplanes
—aerial bombs

Most of these devices are needed immediately. War has once more broken out on the frontier. Croft and Naia marry, aflame with astral kisses. Then he flies off on a bombing raid and any reader of Burroughs knows what happens next: The motor stops, the plane crashes, Croft is captured and loaded with chains.

He is hauled clanking to Kalamita's own personal tent. There she entices him with her gleaming body, her blood-red mouth.

"I can unbind you," she husks, "and—Kalamita's couch is—wide."

He rejects her pleasing suggestion, a hero of the old school. Soon after, he escapes with Naia's astral assistance and a great deal of out-of-the body whispering. Immediately the Zollarian invasion is crushed by 1919 technological war and a world of electrified barbed wire. Once again, peace has been won.

The war has ended none too soon. Naia is pregnant, another result of cultural interaction. Crofts flits down to Earth to let Dr. Murray know the latest, then departs again for Palos.

But not for the last time.

In about nine months, he is back again, intruding into Murray's dreams, urging him to come to Palos and deliver Naia. It's pleasant to have a doctor you can trust. (This is the beginning of "Jason, Son of Jason.")

Dr. Murray is ever obliging. His astral self trips off to Palos, and advises Croft on the latest obstetrical techniques. About a month later, Murray returns for the christening. He remains to visit and admire the blessings of American civilization on this backward planet.

Croft has, in the interim, invented:

—public schools
—wireless
—telegraph facilities

By now, the narrative movement has grated to a halt. To liven matters up, Kalamita engineers the kidnapping of Naia and baby Jason. It is a stroke destined to fail. Croft and Murray track the abductors, hovering nearby as these people mutter together. The Zollarian plan is to burn the baby as a sacrifice to their evil god. How then to rescue mother and child before they are murdered?

Murray suggests a raid by blimps carrying liquid-fire projectors. While these are being manufactured, Croft melts into the sleep of the King of Zollarians and fills his head with prophetic dreams. That shakes the King dreadfully and saves the life of baby Jason.

In a rousing climax, the blimps attack, flame projectors searing forth. Baby Jason and Naia are saved; Kalamita, that Magnet of the Flesh, is burned about the face, losing her lush looks, just punishment for a scheming wanton. And the happy family is united at last.

These are interesting stories, padded with literary kapok. The dialogue is often so exalted that your arteries constrict. The Evil Forces have no real chance to succeed, since Croft's information about their plans is complete. And he can invent a device at breakfast and have it fielded after lunch. For a seeker of occult truth, he is a crackerjack R&D man. And filled with wisdom.

> *Croft:* "Naught is forbidden to the seeker after knowledge...so he see not from evil purpose or for merely selfish gain. All life is a rhythm—even as the sound of the harp given off from a vibrating string...."
> (Chapter VIII)

It is the authentic voice of Semi-Dual, echoing down from Palos its lesson to us all.

**6—**

Between the first and second Jason Croft serials, the *All-Story Weekly* published another adventure into unknown worlds. This was one of those dainty bits of fluff that somehow last like a steel beam and exert influence all out of proportion to its weight.

The story was Ray Cummings' "The Girl in the Golden Atom" (March 15, 1919). It is a long short story, packed with adventure astonishing, that became hotly popular. From it spun off a decade of sequels. It energized a swarm of imitators. It was reprinted until the bibliographer despairs. Among the more available publications, it can be found in *Famous Fantastic Mysteries* (September/October 1939), and in Issue No. 1 of the digest magazine, *Famous Science Fiction* (Winter 1966/1967). It is also available in older paperback reprints.

Raymond King Cummings (1887-1957) was a New Yorker born. In 1914 he began a celebrated employment with Thomas Edison, probably meaning with the Edison Laboratories. There he edited house organs, wrote copy, and, on the side, tried his hand at fiction. Most of this work was tainted slightly with science.

After his success with "The Girl in the Golden Atom," he plunged into full-time pulp magazine writing. For two decades, his fiction appeared in such representative magazines as *All-Story, Science and Invention, Amazing Stories, Argosy, Flynn's Weekly, Astounding Stories of Super Science,* and *Weird Tales.*

Most usually he worked in fantasy adventure. His prose style, clear and straightforward, derived from early H. G. Wells. Cummings' characters, however, are trimmed from one-ply cardboard. Their attitudes are vapid and conventional. His work matured slowly to the end of the 1920s, then stopped. Constant iteration of his favorite themes eventually eroded much of his earlier popularity.

By the mid-1930s, Cummings' 1919 "Golden Atom" idea was thoroughly discredited. Even a fantasy must stand upon a grain of possibility. Cummings' thought was that every atom might be considered an entire universe. Within that universe, every constituent atom contains a lesser universe. And so, down and down, one universe within another, to the limits of patience.

Each universe glares with uncounted suns, planetary systems, diverse tax structures. To visit these alien lands, you need no rocket. Merely a suitable reducing drug. And as "The Girl in the Golden Atom" opens, The Chemist, Rogers, has invented such a drug.

He was motivated. One day while browsing at the microscope (more powerful than any known to science), he examines his mother's wedding ring. Imagine his surprise when a beautiful girl appears in the field of his objective lens.

Most scientists would spray verbena on their foreheads and rationalize her away as a fragment of roast beef or a bit of underdone potato. Not so Rogers. Postulating world within world, he tosses together a cell-contraction drug. This is so effective that it will also shrink clothing and equipment held close to the skin.

Having thus avoided the necessity for plunging naked into a sub-microscopic world, Rogers calls his friends together for a demonstration.

We have already met these friends, The Scientific Club, acting vaguely like scientific detectives. Later they will be indifferent detectives in *Flynn's Weekly*. They are The Banker, The Doctor, The Big Businessman, the Very Young Man. In awe, they watch The Chemist dwindle away into the ring.

Two days later he returns, much the worse for wear.

So far, we are loosely paralleling *The Time Machine*. Admittedly Cummings' prose (he was about 22 at this time) lacks the effortless sheen of Mr. Wells' prose. Rogers dwindles down through matter; the Time Traveler melts off through whatever Time is; the audience marvels and pours tea.

Down within the ring awaits The Girl. She is an extraordinary beauty. You have met her repeatedly under various names. Today, her name is Lylda, that glorious, black-haired dear.

Rogers finds her and hand-in-hand they enter Oroid, the world of the atom. Being an interior world, the horizon curves upward to haze, giving the effect that your astigmatism is uncorrectable. As in Pellucider, discovered by Edgar Rice Burroughs in 1914, there is a central sun. The delirious geometry of Oroid also permits stars. Just where these are situated within a wrap-around horizon is not well explained.

But Lylda is so darling, who speculates about stars when her shining eyes thrill your being to the core? Nor is she insensible of The Chemist's love.

As you may have observed, no heroine of alien culture fails to tremble tenderly when The Alien Outsider, that nice young scientist down the street, comes to visit. This is a curious reaction, for, as is well known, Earth women tend to become hysterical when that nice young scientist, Dr. Zymmirj from Sirius, comes slithering into their presence, his tenacles all bashful.

When Earthmen go exploring, however, they customarily find lots of glamorous Earth-type women out there, all with susceptible hearts. It's only right.

We are now off upon a fantastic trip. This carries us through the first chunk of the story to the city: Strange people, strange buildings, strange customs, marvels galore.

Now what?

Since "The Girl in the Golden Atom" is, after all, another lost race story, we may predict that familiar plot complication, War.

Yes, indeed, War does endanger the peaceful Oroids. At their borders snarl the power-hungry Malites. Their army grinds inward, seizing virgins, singing mocking songs

They are no better than Huns.

They are easier to deal with, however. Rogers merely eats a few enlarging pills, grows vastly, wrecks the Malite army.

The war now settled, Rogers elects to return to Earth and relieve his friends' minds and summarize his adventures, so that Cummings will have something to write about.

Once again the pills are swallowed. Once again "the famiiar sickening crawling sensation" of growth. It is much like the sensation of time traveling. Oroid shrinks away. Walls of metal reel up, endlessly closing about him. He stumbles forward, upward, feet bloody, climbing higher higher in a writhing flowing horror of material in flux.

The descriptions are superb. They would inspire such other tributes to Cummings' idea as Henry Hasse's "He Who Shrank" (*Amazing Stories,* August 1936) and Donald Wandrei's "Colossus (*Astounding Stories,* January 1934).

Up into the lab Rogers comes. Only two days have passed. He tells his story, bids his friends farewell, journeys once more into the ring to fetch Lylda. And does not return. (Neither did the Time Traveler.) Rogers will never return.

Not until the sequel.

Which was published in six parts, January 24 through February 28, 1920, in *All-Story Weekly.* Titled "The People of the Golden Atom," it was later reprinted in the September 1940 issue of *Famous Fantastic Mysteries.*

"The People" is more of the same. Since the serial is much longer than "The Girl," there is much more of the same. Multiplication rules. Four adventurers enter the ring, not one. Two heroes seek our admiration. Two girl friends glow our hearts. Instead of one border skirmish, a full-fledged war rages.

And there is a villain, a real, sneering, scowling, venom in the bloodstream, brutal, rough, sneaking villain. His function is to cause plot complications. Targo, they call him.

In any Cummings' story, you may know the villain by the *T.G.,* and *H* in his name—Targo or Torgh or Turgh or somesuch. These characters stamp scowling through Cummings' fiction, their personalities as subtle as a smashed toe. All are drawn with a superb disregard for human personality and motivation. For all practical purposes, they are grown-up versions of that sneering juvenile nasty that invariably afflicted the boys' book hero.

The story of "The People" is slight. Five years have passed. The remaining members of The Scientific Club meet, learn that the Doctor has the drug formula. After some unconvincing obfuscation—inserted to explain why the enlarging drug wasn't used to smash the Boche—three of the Club enter the ring.

After adventurous shrinkage, they arrive at the socialistic utopia of Arite. And there stands Rogers, older, fatter, and with a son named Loto. Lylda is as sweet as ever.

But crisis is upon them. Revolutionaries of the City Orlog, hipped up by that arch villain, Targo, have polarized disaffected social elements of Arite. This has caused factionalism, street violence, and outcries against magical giants.

Uproar foams everywhere. To further his black plans, Targo steals Loto. He also gets a number of growth-altering pills.

Therafter, the novel is fattened by frantic chases. During these, the sizes of the participants fluctuate violently, as in a Winsor McCay comic page.[14] The Very Young Man finds love and danger, his status slowly altering from that of a simp to semi-hero.

Ultimately the forces of Orlog are crushed. The people of Arite, incensed at giants trampling their world flat, revolt against our friends. Small wonder. Rogers and company elect to go quietly, a sense of service easing their hurt pride.

They gather up wives, sweethearts, families, and set forth. Targo then attacks them, being about the size of the national debt. After a vicious struggle, the Very Young man kills him. They return, singularly battered, to their own world.

It is a pleasing hollow little story. It has the content of an empty box. It presents marvels, unpretentiously. The language is simple. The sentences are brief. You could read six novels a day just like this and feel as refreshed as if you'd had a nap.

Cummings grew mightily fond of this theme. For ten years, he returned to similar adventures, such as the 1929 "The Princess of the Atom." This is considerably more mature than either of the "Golden Atom" stories. This time, the pills are in the hands of the beings of the atom. No one stays the same size fifteen seconds running. It is way up and way way down. Wild rides in size-changing vehicles. The fiend, Torago, destroys a planet, murders ten million people. It is a new popular fiction record. Then, from out of the atom erupt Torago's horde of giants, each as tall as the Empire State

Building and they proceed to destroy America. The descriptions are fascinating and the writing is concentrated and clean. Every chapter splinters another natural law.

"Beyond the Vanishing Point" (*Astounding Stories*, March 1931) is set in 1960 Quebec. It tells how the evil Franz Polter steals kindly old Dr. Kent's secret—something about a chemical means of shrinking into a piece of gold quartz. Before you know it, our heroes and heroines (two each) are down inside an atom. Polter has set up a gang of gigantic criminals who terrorize the helpless Orneans. He gets his. Finally. At the end of a long short story.

It is all interesting and busy. By this time, Cummings is highly skilled at making variations on his theme. But we have been there before.

Let us turn to other matters.

Let us talk about the impact of airplanes and radio on this early fantasy fiction.

But first, a digression.


7—


Memory tricks us.

Memory illuminates yesterday with a mild pale glow. It is a spurious light. The worst is softened, the best elevated. We remember incompletely, lingering over individual tiles in the past's complex mosaic.

These selective memories permit us to deceive ourselves with our own history. Our remembered lives, twenty, fifty, seventy years gone, are glinting bits, like mica in a featureless mass of rock.

How it felt to live in the 1920s is now almost beyond conjecture. We assume that the daily business of living has not radically changed. The smell of cut grass lingers through the decades. So does the glee of a Haydn quartet and the smell of a woman's hair. As it will be in 1999, so it was in 1920.

Aside from these quiet permanencies, the external reality keeps altering endlessly. Yesterday, the saxophone; today the amplified zither. Clothing changes shape and so does the taste in automobiles. Reality has changed its face many times since the 1920s. By now the familiar face of that time has vanished, grossly overlaid by time and legend.

The daily face of the 1920s is now buried heart-deep in blather about flappers, jazz bands, Fords, bootleggers, talkies, gangsters, crashing stock markets, Scott Fitzgerald, the Follies and Charleston, Charleston. It is as if your living room had been piled with tinsel, the familiar furnishings buried beneath a golden carnival sparkle.

The peripheral activities and casual fads of the 1920s receive concentrated emphasis. Yet the gaudy Cafe Society life, celebrated in every television review, touched only a few thousand people. The ukulele and coonskin-coat life affected only a few thousand collegiates. Millions lived who never jazzed away vivid nights. Who never slid into the local speakeasy. Who never lived near a local speakeasy. Who did not toss down synthetic gin or even speculate in a gaseous stock market.

Most stayed at home. Most made one dollar work for three. They raised families somehow (although the children were difficult). They read 2¢ newspapers for staunch Republican assurances and feats of intrepid aviators. And they gathered intently, in listening clusters, about that new, great homogenizer, the family radio.

Radio and aviation were strange intrusions, then—visible evidence of change, stimulating and vaguely improper.

Little boys (forgetting Tarzan) dreamed of plunging cloudward, away from parental strictures. To those slightly older, radio offered another form of escape.

RADIO

...study at home ... in spare time.... Thorough and reliable training ... receive complete laboratory equipment ... easily solve radio problems at home in spare time ... acquire commercial knowledge and ability demanded in radio.

RADIO. MAKE GOOD IN RADIO.

WIN FAME AND FORTUNE IN RADIO!

Don't spend your life slaving away in some dull hopeless job! Let us show you how to make REAL MONEY in RADIO— THE FASTEST-GROWING, BIGGEST MONEY-MAKING GAME ON EARTH.

LEARN WITHOUT LESSONS IN 60 DAYS

TELEVISION in on the way! TALKING PICTURES a great field!

Similar advertisements flaunted their urgent promises in every mid-1920s pulp magazine. And, for the more romantically inclined, other Lorelei songs rose:

AVIATION

LEARN TO EARN $300 to $400 A MONTH

Give me an hour a day of your spare time...prepare for well-paid ground jobs open only to men trained in aviation work... Get big FREE BOOK and Tuition Offer.

(The words "ground jobs" were set in very small type indeed.)

So they dreamed, youth and adult, while about them, the giddy towers of the Jazz Age glinted.

8—

What fascinates the public creeps into public fiction. In the 1910s and early 1920s, magazines bristled with automobile stories, and the fiction reveled in cameras, telephones, moving picture companies.

Series leaped greenly from every subject. These were primarily series of adventure stories, touched by crude mystery elements. Often a series would combine one of these devices with pseudo-scientific elements, usually with jarring effect.

Consider the February 7, 1920, issue of *The Popular Magazine*. In that issue is the first installment of a series titled "Barney of the World Police" by Arthur Tuckerman.

> They had added ten stories to the International Sky Traffic Tower in 1930 .... You could see it anywhere from Newark, New Jersey, to Yonkers up the Hudson, for it towered above all other buildings on the river bank just about a mile above the Transoceanic Airpark, where the bulky triplane liners crept up the harbor on the five-thousand-foot level three times a week ... and disgorged their passengers from London and Paris.

The story is set sometime after 1930 and Cliff Barney, one of "the shrewdest investigators of crime that New York had ever known," is riding an electric elevator up the side of the Sky Traffic Tower to the Pilot's Bureau, World Police.

That is the World Police Air Division, "that brilliantly efficient organization devised as the outcome for (sic) the world revolution of 1925-6." It is an international organization, the air division employing about 2,000 aviators who also possessed "exceptional mental and physical qualifications that made them feared by evildoers in every land."

For this story, "Cape to Cairo," Barney is to investigate why pilots are dying on the Cape to Cairo mail plane run. Over the sea he goes (on the Mediterranean dirigible) to WP Headquarters in Cairo, arriving not quite in time to forestall a third murder. It takes him only a matter of hours to detect that airfield mechanics (in well-paid ground jobs) are doing the dirty work, and an evil pilot is exposed.

Barney has a few more personal characteristics than Victor Blake, that bright young scientist of the future. In addition to being 27 years old, Barney has smooth teeth, is a master of disguise, can speak Arabic, and knocks peremptorily on doors. He also talks to himself when alone, generously allowing the reader to follow his thoughts. And his skill with an airplane is most remarkable:

> *First Mechanic:* "Blime me, if that Yank don't 'alf know 'how to 'handle 's plane!"
> *Second Mechanic:* " 'E's a bit of orl right, 'e is."

By the third episode of the series, "The Bronze Key of Paradise" (March 7, 1920), the world of the post-1930s and the World Police have diminished to pale shadows, existing only to justify Barney's adventures in North Africa.

In "The Bronze Key," he airplanes after wicked men who have kidnapped a beautiful white girl. They are taking her to the hidden villa of a depraved Russian who thieves around the desert in the guise of a native chief. About the only science-fiction here is that Barney's tiny biplane carries enough fuel for ten hours of top-speed flying and can get off a 300-foot flight strip with three people on board.

Yes, Barney does trace the girl to the hidden villa. Yes, he slips inside. Yes, he rescues her in an exciting fight. Yes, his friend lands the biplane on the roof and off they fly.

Without the World Police frame, this is a typical aviation adventure story—essentially the same thing that would fatten the pages of *Top Notch, Triple X* and *Argosy* in a few more years. It is not known what adventures Barney enjoyed in subsequent issues. Most likely, they were not in the company of the beautiful rescued girl:

> A big government biplane came droning toward them ... its twin propellers flashing silver gleams .... Barney rose and waved his hat gaily ....
> *Barney,turning to his companion*: "There, Monsieur, is my first love. Perhaps it will be my last. But they say one never can tell."

The World Police is a minor series whose importance, if we may grant it that, is to point the way of the wind. As predictive fiction, it is of little concern. But still, how useful it is to single out what caught at readers' attention, fifty-odd years ago.

**9-**

The preceding remarks may explain why Roger Sherman Hoar, writing under the name of Ralph Milne Farley, dazzled his audience with stories bearing the general title of *The Radio Whatever*.

Mr. Hoar was author of such books as *Wisconsin Unemployment* (1934) and *Conditional Sales* (1937). These concerned law and legal practice for executive and lawyer. He was a remarkable man, directly related to Roger Sherman who helped draft and did sign the Declaration of Independence.

Born in 1877, Hoar graduated from the Harvard Law School and became a Massachusetts state senator at the age of 23. During the First World War, while serving as a captain in the artillery, he invented a ballistic system for aiming large field guns. Thereafter, he managed a Boston news agency, drew professional cartoons, wrote copious amounts of science fiction. In 1934 he served as a member of Roosevelt's commission to draft the Social Security System. After serving as an assistant attorney general of Massachusetts, he moved to Milwaukee. There he became the chief adviser in the Bucyrus Erie Company's legal department.

He opened his own law firm in 1954, specializing in patent work, and died in 1963.[15]

His science fiction (or, more accurately, science fantasy) work began in 1923. His basic intent was to write something that would amuse his children, and he turned to the interplanetary fantasy, updating it brightly with the aid of that new fad, radio.[16] His "Radio" serials gave *Argosy* readers a pleasurable shock, like three rums in the lime juice.

*Argosy All-Story Weekly* published "The Radio Man" in four parts (June 28 through July 19, 1924). This was followed by "The Radio Beasts" (4 parts, March 21, through April 11, 1925), and "The Radio Planet" (5 parts, June 26 through July 24, 1926). The serials followed the adventures of Myles Standish Cabot, a Bostonian, on Poros—which is to say, Venus.

A later spin-off of the series, "The Radio Menace," was published in *Argosy* (6 parts, June 7 through July 12, 1930). A few lesser stories followed, bearing the word "Radio" in their titles as if to recall greater days. These turned from Poros to more conventional, earth-bound fiction, of which "The Radio War" is the best known example, assuming that it is known at all. (It is a five-part serial in *Argosy*, July 2 through 30, 1932, telling how Russia, Siberia and Japan attacked the United States.)

All the applause and reprinting was reserved for the earlier "Radio" stories. "The Radio Man" reappeared as a four-part serial in the first four issues of *Famous Fantastic Mysteries* (September-October and December 1939, January and February 1940). "The Radio Beasts" was reprinted in *Fantastic Novels*, January 1941; and "The Radio Planet" in the April 1942 *Famous Fantastic Mysteries*. (The cover of that issue gave the title as "The Radio Planet and the Ant Men.")

Long years later, a sequel to the series was published by the *Spaceway Science Fiction* magazine. Titled "The Radio Minds of Mars," this serial had a tipsy history of publication. It began in the June 1955 issue as the first part of a two-part serial, after which the magazine suspended publication. Fourteen years later, *Spaceway* reappeared and in its initial issue, January 1969, "The Radio Minds of Mars" began again as the first part of a two-part serial.

With the next issue (June 1969), more of the serial appeared—Part Two of Three Parts. The final section of the serial was published in the October 1969 issue. Exhausted by this effort, the magazine terminated with its fourth issue, June 1970.

The interplanetary portion of the "Radio" series is a group of framed novels. The text states that they were written by Professor Ralph Milne Farley, Harvard graduate, who lived on a farm on Chappaquiddick Island, near Edgartown, Massachusetts. His great good friend, Myles Cabot, was a radio engineer whose apparatus was spread all over the place—at the RCA television labs, at the GE labs, and in his own private experimental facility.

While perfecting his three-dimensional television, Cabot vanishes from the lab. He is gone without trace, without clues. Years pass. Then an object from space slams into the Farley farm.

Behold! It is a small projectile shell filled with manuscript.

No wonder they found no trace of Cabot. He is on Venus. His 3-D television turned out, by that serendipity common to fantasy adventures, to be a crude matter transmitter. In a moment of inattention off he went.

He went to Venus. This is not the Venus described by current science.

*Fantastic Novels,* January 1941. The interplanetary romance, first popularized by John Carter, told of swords and princesses and high adventure on other planets. Here Myles Cabot, in spurious antennae and wings, applies Earth technology to the internal affairs of Venus.

This world is not a heat-blasted desolation, where the soil shimmers with concentrated heat and the raging sky is dense with clouds of carbon dioxide and cyanide radicals.

Cabot's Venus is rather more benign. The planet contains three continents separated by a boiling sea, its steam forming the clouds. The lands are warmly pleasant and inhabited by such remarkable entities that it is obvious the evolutionary process does not work there.

Here live giant insects, intelligent reptiles, sub-human blue apes, and a charming little humanoid race that closely resembles the illustrations in a book of fairy-tales.

These humanoids, the Cupians, have two little iridescent wings (nonfunctional but aesthetically pleasing). They have two extra fingers and a dozen toes. They lack ears and are totally deaf; however, they communicate by electrical transmission, using small knobby antennae which protrude above their hairlines.

These gentle dears have been enslaved for 500 years by the Formians—gigantic ants, 6-feet tall, proportionately long, intelligent, war-like, fond of rigid organization. They have developed a mechanical civilization that includes aircraft and automobiles, electrical laboratories and weapons. They also communicate by thought transmission, a most satisfactory way of avoiding dull periods of learning an alien language and crisply speeding up the action.

Among all the creatures of Poros exist common speech. It is most convenient, as Burroughs had previously demonstrated.

The planet swarms with outsized bugs. Gigantic spiders spin webs to ensnare unwary Earthmen. Immense bees whistle overhead—these are cultured enough to have a King and to enjoy the benefits of social living. Here fly winged snakes. There glide pterodactyls. And over there in the shrubbery lurks the savage purple Woofus, a magnified tiger-wolf, simply frosted with teeth.

The story trappings are exotic, but the story is the old familiar routine. The action may be roughly summarized as follows:

Capture escape peril peril capture peril escape peril capture....

Once on Poros, Cabot is captured by the ant men. Inside their city (two perils, one escape, one recapture later) he meets the glorious girl, Lilla, Princess of Helium—or rather of Cupia. Princess of Cupia, to be sure.

She is every inch a delight, although she has no ears, cannot hear him, and is revulsed by his ears and facial hair. In addition to a number of extra fingers and toes, wings and antennae, she has: "Dainty cameo-cut features. Frank wide open eyes. Sweet friendly lips. A curly wealth of short blond hair."

To win her heart, Cabot devises fake wings, artificial antennae and lets his hair grow to conceal those disfiguring ears. Soon she learns to love him. How annoying it would be if she did not.

Lilla is the daughter of King Kew of Cupia. He administrates and the ants direct. The reason that Lilla is among the ants is a palace intrigue—she has been abducted by her evil cousin, Yuri.

Cabot helps her escape back to the palace. Enraged, Yuri weaves a plot of evil. There follow thrilling adventures. Fantastic incidents. Unparalleled heroisms. Captures, escapes, perils, betrayals, abductions. Thrills cascade before your enchanted eyes.

After many chapters of this intense activity, Yuri's treasons are recognized by all. Cabot's worth is recognized by all. A successful rebellion by all hurls off the ants' yoke. The resistance is much aided by Cabot's invention of rifles and exploding bullets, for, like Jason Croft, Cabot is an unrelenting inventor.

And, like John Carter, he marries the princess and has sequels.

At some point between "The Radio Man" and "The Radio Beasts," Cabot invents steam engines, coal mining and power transmission. Then he returns to Earth, via a matter transmitter he has tossed together, intending to check out some obscure technical points. While there, he drops in for a chat with that prince of a fellow, good old Farley. This visit is used as the frame of the second serial.

(It should be added that the matter transmitter has a minor flaw. It will not transmit metal. At every use, therefore, it extracts the fillings from Cabot's teeth, so that after each transmission, he must drink very carefully.)

Back to the story. After two years, Cabot and Lilla are married. No sooner has happiness arrived than Yuri strikes. He murders the King, proclaims himself ruler. Cabot is tossed into jail. While he languishes on the straw, word comes that Lilla has had a baby boy. The child is the legitimate King of Cupia.

Here follow a multitude of adventures as Cabot escapes from prison and struggles cross country toward Lilla and his child. Such an avalanche of experiences rarely befalls anyone. After escaping, he:

—battles Yuri's minions
—learns that civil war has erupted
—loses his artificial antennae and becomes stone deaf
—struggles onward toward Lila, 1000 stads away
—is trapped by an ant man
—is saved by an opportune lightning stroke
—falls into the pit of an immense ant bear
—only just escapes
—hi-jacks an ant car
—battles a powerful ant
—wins
—is trapped by the ant hordes in a house
—escapes
—reaches his home, 1000 stads away, only to discover the corpse of his child; Lilla has vanished
—puts on a new set of antennae
—is pursued by ant men, who set a forest afire to roast him
—escapes by plunging into a mysterious river

—is sucked into dark mysterious caverns filled with groping water things and flying dinosours the size of bats.

—is saved by priests from the Caverns of Kor

These adventures comprise the first half of the serial. The final half is as relentlessly active.

To continue: Yuri having thrown in his lot with the ants, Cabot seeks the aid of the whistling bees in battling the enemy aircraft. He is captured by Yuri and company; he is to die in the arena but tames the Woofus that is to kill him there. In a scene faintly showing its Tarzan origins, Cabot and the Woofus win free. A spontaneous uprising drives Yuri to flight. Cabot pursues Yuri. Is captured by Yuri. Escapes from Yuri. Belts Yuri in the mouth, and is then felled by an ant man's bullet.

Yuri escapes by flying machine through the sea steam, and you won't hear from him until the next serial.

After these time-consuming activities, Cabot decides to slip down to Earth for more technical information and some new fillings. Lilla is apprehensive, as well as she should be: *Lilla (to Cabot):* "Every time you ever go anywhere, you get into trouble."

How well she knows her own husband.

About the time that Cabot has finished amazing Farley with this tale, an SOS flashes from Venus.

Lilla is in danger.

Cabot leaps to his matter transmitter.

As it snerrs into life, lightning strikes one of the transmission towers.

What does this mean to Cabot?

What does this mean to Lilla?

How could any writer have the gall to fasten a Burroughs' cliff-hanging ending on a 1925 novel?

The next portion of the adventure, "The Radio Planet," was relayed by code from Venus, like any conventional telegraphic message. The story is in three vaguely related chunks. In the first piece, Cabot materializes on a new continent behind the boiling sea. Yuri is there, having set himself up as the King of the Ant Men. Cabot is taken prisoner, as usual, and attempts a counter-Revolution, aided by a disaffected ant named Doggo. The attempt fails.

After that effort, Cabot seeks refuge with a race of furry humanoids, the Vairkings. With their help, he mounts an enormous technical effort to build a radio—hoping to have the Cupians send an airplane for him. The description of how a radio is constructed from nothing is in the fine old tradition of Jules Verne. Only raw materials are available, and yet, through knowledge and cleverness . . . .

After innumerable complications, both romantic and warlike, Doggo fortuitously arrives in an aircraft packed with supplies. Off they fly over the Scalding Sea, unwittingly carrying with them a stowaway—a new character to the series, Quivven the Golden One. She is a very sexy girl, indeed, covered all over with golden fur.

At this point, the serial is barely half told. Logically, the aircraft must crash. Astonishingly, it does not. The dedicated reader will find it difficult to forgive Mr. Farley for overlooking this usual plot incident. It is as disappointing as cake without icing. However, all of them are soon captured, which makes up for much, and the second part begins.

They are captured by a race of intelligent reptiles—the Whoomangs. The King is a gigantic pterosaur; his advisor an equally immense snake improbably named Queekle Mukki. All seem benevolent folks, and all are simply glowing with soul.

Soul, in this case, has a singular meaning. Soul can be given. They merely slit the skin at the base of the skull, insert a specialized moth grub, and, in about two minutes, the grub dominates your personality. You have become one of the boys, glassy-eyed and smiling intensely.

Both Doggo and Quivven are so treated, henceforth to become willing minions of the Whoomang Empire. Only Cabot escapes to tell the tale.

And, although you may reel beneath the implications, Cabot does not return, sword flailing, to rescue his friends and escape gloriously.

In a most extraordinary example of anti-heroism, Cabot barely escapes the brain-stealing fiends and flies violently off to Cupia, where he crashes. (Yes, finally.) During the third part, he whips up a fresh rebellion and enters Yuri's castle, leading an army of forty-seven supporters.

It is dismaying to report, but there is something about Yuri that paralyzes Cabot's mind. Whenever he faces the arch-villain, Cabot acts like a perfect fool. This time is no exception. He is immediately disarmed because of stupidity. But just as Yuri is about to shoot him down, a dagger flashes. Yuri dies snarling and all the plot threads begin to coil to rest. Yuri has been assassinated by the mother of the dead baby left at Cabot's home in "The Radio Beasts." (Or perhaps you don't remember.)

His way cleared for dramatic accomplishments, Cabot now runs amok. He stamps out sedition, cleanses the land of rebels, sees the bee people annihilated, is reunited with Lilla and his son, and generally cleans up for the final curtain.

The story of Poros, however, has taken on an eerie life of its own and goes rushing onward.

In "The Radio Menace" (*Argosy*, 6 parts, June 7 through July 12, 1930), the Whoomangs set off to conquer the Earth. They fetch along unlimited supplies of moth grubs and plant these in all sorts of skulls—human, cat, rat and dog. They have even brought with them Doggo and the golden Quivven, alluring as ever.

This story is a curious foreshadowing of such major science-fiction novels as *The Mind Parasites* and *The Puppet Masters* which appeared two decades later. Compared to these *tours de force*, Farley's serial is distinctly light weight, making little use of the horror inherent in the situation and developing little of the potential drama. The story blunders genially along through obvious situations and limp complexities to a simplified solution, making a minor fiction of a theme possessing substantial content.

The hero of "The Radio Menace" is not Cabot, but Blackstone Kent, who was, you will recall, appearing at the same time as a pseudo-detective in *Amazing Detective Tales*. You will be pleased to learn that both Doggo and Quivven are eventually relieved of their grubs, and they return to Venus, via the matter transmitter, to join Myles Cabot. He is mentioned in a few paragraphs before the novel ends, but plays no part in this serial.

Roger Sherman Hoar, we may suppose, took no stuffy attitude about his fiction. He produced casual fantastic adventure; the market was avid for it. Poros has no more internal consistency than a bag of rags, but consistency is not what was required. What was far more necessary was marvels mixed with movement, constant surprises, continuous perils.

Cabot, himself, is the first interplanetary non-hero. He is not given the Burroughs' advantages of powerful muscles, an ever-dripping sword, and a commanding presence. He is, on the contrary, a rather average man, given to mistakes, and blessed by showers of luck toward the end of the serial. He is limited by reality in a world where reality has not much meaning.

It is likely that Hoar was consciously limiting his hero. The field was packed with men who accomplished mighty things, their frames blood-splashed, their faces serious.

Little enough is serious on Poros. The very names are facetious. No properly deadly beast is named Woofus. Nor can we regard with awe a serpent named Queekle Mukki. The Cupians and Cupia are uncomfortably close to the familiar Kewpies (who were also equipped with small wings). The series rings with such playful sporting, a mild, self-indulgent joking that is suitable for reading aloud to your children, but which, in the larger context of public fiction, constantly spoils the internal reality of the narrative. "Well, you can't take any of this seriously," Farley seems to say. "I've got a normal bean on my shoulders and I'm just writing this down for fun. The children love it."

Perhaps Hoar was still having fun with "The Radio Minds of Mars." Perhaps not. The serial is no more than an elaborate summary that could easily expand to a piece four times as long. A reasonable guess is that it hung around the Farley farmhouse for years as a draft for an *Argosy* serial that didn't get written. When published, it still was not written.

The story tells how telepathic Martians, resembling octopuses, invade Poros. And how to fight creatures that know your every thought? Myles and his son, Ken (King of Cupia), find a way. Aided by the Whoomangians and their grubs, and the leaves of the terrible Death Plant, the Cabots eventually defeat the Martian expeditionary force.

Ken finds love with the beautiful furred girl, Nardeen.

The sinister Queekle Mukki is finally killed.

Peace is celebrated between Cupia and Woomania.

And Cabot, at last, is united in entire bliss with Lilla, the most elegant of fantasy-land queens.

By the mid-1920s, the fiction line represented by "The Radio Planet" was showing signs of exhaustion. No matter how feverishly you stirred radio and airplanes into the standard Burroughs broth, you changed little.

Much life remained in the formula. Burroughs' Venus novels were still in the future. The Mars/Venus serials of O.A. Kline were five years off. Ray Cummings' Mercury novels were not yet written.

But the interplanetary romance had crested and it would ebb gently away, not to be revived until the 1970s. Already a new story form was shaping—an altogether wilder, more far-ranging, more improbable story form, full of crudities and vigor.

Lay aside the swords. Discard occult-tinged transitions to other planets. Prepare yourself, rather, for plunges into purple exultation, as the crystal furies of space dazzle your mind.

Space opera, the coming king, was rising in *Weird Tales* and *Amazing Stories*, and what a gaudy commotion it brought.

**10-**

From its first issue, March 1923, *Weird Tales*, that magnificent lost cause, reeled forward up a slope of sand. Promising tomorrows beckoned beyond. But significant profit eluded the magazine. And readers, if adoring, were sadly few.

*Weird Tales* embraced disaster almost at once. During its first year, the magazine plunged $51,000 into the red and nearly folded with its First Anniversary Issue.

Publisher Hennenberg, however, liked it. Ignoring conventional business practices, he sold his profitable *Detective Tales* and invested the proceeds to resuscitate *Weird Tales*. The printer ended holding title to the magazine until the debts were paid.

Editor Edwin Baird moved out with *Detective Tales*. O.A. Kline, who had been reading manuscripts for *Weird Tales*, stepped in as temporary editor for the first anniversary issue.[17] Then Farnsworth Wright (who had also been reading *Weird Tales* manuscript) accepted the editor's job. The towering, gaunt Wright was a kind of white magician. He kept the magazine alive until 1939, at which time it passed to another publisher and took on a new editor, Dorothy McIlwraith.

Even that final change didn't seem to matter. Until its final hour, *Weird Tales* struggled up financial dunes.

> *Weird Tales* was the first magazine to be devoted entirely to fantasy fiction. Obviously the emphasis was on horror fiction, but it attracted many science-fiction stories. In this magazine, they were referred to as weird-scientific, but that does not alter the fact that *Weird Tales*, more so than *All-Story* or *Thrill Book*, soon became the major market for science-fiction.[18]

It was science-fiction only by the most lenient standards. Baird used what was available, and that was mainly fiction of careless scientists from whose laboratories sloggered forth blooby awfuls to menace virgins. These tales mingled indiscriminately with sleazy horror adventures that lumbered up and down, making ferocious noises and displaying such titles

*Weird Tales*, November 1929. "The Unique Magazine" from 1922 to 1954, Weird Tales published some science-tinged fantasy from its first issue. Space opera was born in its pages and rockets to the stars and concepts gigantic.

as "The Abysmal Horror," "Tryst with Death," "The Hanging of Aspara" and "Prisoners of the Dead."

Wright gradually developed a cadre of reliable authors. Some few of these occasionally produced a fragile imaginative bubble that might, with effort, be considered science-fiction or science-fantasy. These stories concerned dimly technical people whose adventures were sufficiently immense to override some awful writing.

Unlike Munsey's *Argosy* line, *Weird Tales* concerned itself less with simple prose and distinct ties to reality than with the unique experience. Marvels and monsters. Strange forms. Terror among inconceivable sights. That these were irrational mattered not at all; awe and wonder were the only coin recognized in this realm.

By an interesting coincidence, two series that burnt hotly with awe and wonder began simultaneously in the August 1928 issues of *Weird Tales* and *Amazing Stories*. Respectively, these series were Edmond Hamilton's Interstellar Patrol and the first E.E. Smith "Skylark" serial.

Both series were dedicated to the purple adventure that swaggered grandiose, festooned with rhinestones, among star systems. The conceptions were colossal; the conflicts unparalleled; the science invented for the occasion.

But wasn't it grand and new! You may forget blobby laboratory products. You need fumble no longer with swords. You may turn without regret from astral projections and narrow ramblings within this little solar system.

A new breath stirs and the technological fantasy rises, refreshed, from its doze. But little remains of that approach to the subject matter once used by Verne and the dime novels. No longer is the wonderful invention a matter of magnifying existing hardware. It is all new, now. The science used is yet to be discovered; the engineering principles leap ahead of known, or possible, technology. The gap between is roughly caulked with imagination.

The imagination of Hamilton and Smith burst forth in furies of rays as yet unknown to scientists or H.G. Wells. Aliens astounding moved into view, intelligences of incredible shape. Here lofted alien scenes that tingled along the nerves. Here pounded conflicts across immensities unconfined by maps.

The small coinage of these stories was spaceships, energy weapons, faster than light travel, the destruction of planetary systems, and the glory of the fight bitterly won, you heroes of Earth.

How pastel seemed *Argosy All-Story* adventures among whistling bees and Greek-revival palaces near Sirius. In *Weird Tales* and *Amazing Stories*, the galaxy opened like an egg, crackling with adventure scarlet bright among the "great blooming suns."

As Leigh Brackett remarked, " . . . and if they don't boom, they, by God, ought to!"[19]

**11-**

Walking in the icy Pennsylvania night, 1927, young Edmond Hamilton saw "the great belt of Orion and the Pleiades burning in frosty splendor above the roofs." Future civilizations stirred in his mind. Cultures linked star to star, policed by far-flung law.[20]

It was the beginning of the Interstellar Patrol series, eight stories that appeared in *Weird Tales* from 1928 through 1934. Each story was different and each was grandly the same. They were tales of adventure against unendurable odds, stuffed with heroism and self sacrifice. The narratives rush from height to height, thrusting aside characterization, probability, elegant language. What are these compared to the relentless rush of wonder?

The story situation is this: About 100,000 years from 1928, Earthmen have colonized all eight planets. (Pluto was unknown at the time.) As "Crashing Suns" (August 1928) opens, Jan Tor, captain of a long black interstellar cruiser, is recalled to Earth. The Supreme Council of the League of Planets wants him to do something about that great huge dead star that is headed directly toward the solar system, threatening total destruction.

In the first speed-of-light cruiser ever built, Jan Tor roars off. He lands on a planet circling the dead star, finding swarms of cruel Globe Men. Using a weird ray, they have steered their sun into a collision course with our own sun. The impact, they hope, will reignite their own star.

Jan Tor and company are captured. Closer and closer race the suns. Time is running out. Only a few precious hours remain.

Hope wanes.

Suspense swells.

It is time for Jan Tor to escape with his brave crew, battling hopeless odds. Since the situation permits no reasonable solution, an unreasonable solution is found. This is thickly plastered over with emotion, so that the reader overlooks the improbability and the magician skillfully palms the elephant. The heroism and self-sacrifice of a crewman, Sarto Sen, permits the capture of the Globe Men's ray. With this magical device, the dead star is destroyed. The Sun and Earth are saved.

It is an avalanche of narrative motion, all told in the first person.

To be exact, "Crashing Suns" tells about the *Interplanetary* Patrol. The true Interstellar Patrol appears in the second story, "The Star Stealers" (February 1929). Since the story backgrounds are virtually identical, however, "Crashing Suns" may be considered the first of the series.

By February 1929, the Solar System has joined the Federation of Stars. The Patrol maintains galactic peace the "length and breadth of the Milky Way, patrolling the space-lanes of the Galaxy and helping to crush the occasional pirate ships (which prey) on the interstellar commerce."

The situation resembles the commercial shipping scene of the 1800s when tall ships crowded the seven seas and pirates blighted the Spanish Main, and trade routes were protected by national warships. Although, in *Weird Tales*, the patrol ships routinely sail up to eighty times the speed of light, disdaining contemporary physics.

The Interstellar Patrol is concerned with more than pirates.

In "The Star Stealers" a gigantic dark star hurtles in from outside the galaxy, threatening to sweep our sun completely away. Could you believe that it is a plot by aliens? (These look like upright cones of black flesh, dotted by a white eye spot.) The patrol stops them. Barely.

"Within the Nebula" (May 1929) tells how the galaxy was saved. The nebula was preparing to emit vast sheets of flaming gases, thus raising hob. It was all caused by malicious aliens (shapeless masses of white flesh), using pernicious rays.

In the February 1930 "The Comet Drivers," the galaxy is threatened, again, by an immense comet—the largest you ever did see. It is hollow and controlled by black creatures having two white eye spots. They use a Propelling Ray, and when 5,000 ships of the Patrol arrive at the last possible second, you get goosebumps. The aliens of "The Cosmic Cloud" (November 1930) are tall, blind masses, moving on flap-like limbs. They hate light and keep their world in scientific darkness, huddled down at the center of a gigantic black cloud in the very center of the galaxy. For years, they have been pirating spaceships, catching them with Magnetic Attractor Mechanisms. Now they have collected sufficient ships to invade the entire galaxy and blanket it with darkness.

Just as their ill-gotten fleet swarms away, Dur Nac leads a supreme Patrol effort to energize the magnetism that is the galaxy's only single sole surviving hope....

Perhaps the general idea of the series is now clear.

For all that it was 92.2% fantasy, Hamilton's view of the solar system would prove remarkably influential. He described a community of populated planets bustling with intelligent life, bright with cities, knit by interplanetary commerce.

The concept leads directly to the late 1930s space opera, published in *Planet Stories, Startling Stories,* and *Thrilling Wonder Stories.* Space Opera was part wild west, part circus, and total joy to its readers. It blandly ignored actual planetary conditions, as it ignored the complexities of human life. Space Opera was entirely unruffled by reality.

Nor did reality intrude into Hamilton's Interstellar Patrol world. These stories lie almost outside the English narrative tradition. They are not about people but events. All is subordinate to the wonderous event. Hamilton's mind toys with the gigantic. Immensity fascinates him. Like a three-year old, he bashes suns, hammers galaxies. See them spark. See the wonderful collisions.

Individuals do not appear as such in this fiction. The characters and their relationships are coarsely blocked out, rather like the traditional figures in an oriental play.

The story is simplified as a black and white abstract sketch. *We* oppose *them.* Excellent us against those horrors. Good resists sin—just barely, in fear, with blood, always with success. And new scenes constantly flow by, flaring with cosmic wonder.

## 12—

Approximately the same characteristics informed E. E. Smith's

"Skylark" serials. Smith transferred the lost race novel to deep space, stirred in chases, black villains, and quantities of real and imaginary engineering concepts, and invented at least three characters who remain in the mind. But Skylark and the Interstellar Patrol shared coffee from the same cup. They were infatuated with size. No concept was too immense to be denied their pages.

"Skylark" entered the literature in the August 1928 issue of *Amazing Stories*. That issue effectively confirmed the success of the all-science-fiction magazine, a type of publication which had taken a surprising length of time to develop.

We have already seen that much romantic science-fantasy was published in the Munsey Magazines. A rather separate path was pursued by Hugo Gernsback. He had been including "Scienti-fiction" in his various publications since *Modern Electric* in 1911. His *Electrical Experimenter, Science and Invention,* and *Practical Electrics* all used serials and short stories containing science elements. (Or fantasy lightly powdered with science, as in the Ray Cummings and A. A. Merritt serials that appeared in *Science and Invention.)*

Gernsback was obsessed with the idea of teaching science—hard science—through fiction. The typical "Gernsback" piece of the late 1920s contains almost no narrative movement, only endless drifts of pseudo-scientific conversation, during which the characters vie in naming objects and describing effects. At its best, the story folded in a few nuggets of scientific or technical fact. At the worst, the narrative became simply unreadable.

*Amazing Stories* contained only trifling quantities of this gas, at least at first. The initial issues were top heavy with reprints of H. G. Wells and Jules Verne (those iron men), plus fresher material by Burroughs, Merritt, George Allan England, and other assorted giants.[21] Few of these were willing to suspend the action for an informative lecture.

However, Gernsback soon began developing his own cadre of writers— and a growing coterie of readers eager for a magazine given over to the pleasures of science fiction. Then, indeed, the didactic tone grew brazen.

The first issue of *Amazing Stories* was dated April 1926. The magazine was an inch taller and wider than most other magazines of the time; it measured 8 ½ x 11 inches, and contained 96 pages of thick, rather soft, pulp paper stock. The edges were trimmed. The covers, by Paul, blazed primary colors and glorious mechanisms of skeletal line and mechanical joint. The price was 25¢, costly for 96 pages when competitors offered 115 pages for 15¢.

But competitors were not offering *Amazing's* specialized concentration of fiction. Nor did they offer anything like "Skylark," the New Wave of its day.

It was an oddly old New Wave. Edward Elmer Smith had begun "Skylark" during the First World War. Some slight initial assistance (how much is not known) was given by Mrs. Lee Hawkins Garby.[22] The

*Amazing Stories Quarterly*, Fall 1929. Wells, Burroughs, and Hamilton loosened their imaginations and forth the alien culture rolled, hostile, often as not, and hungering for dainty Earthwomen and conquest, as do the Turtle-Men, shown here on the other side of the Moon.

*Air Wonder Stories,* August 1929. Super-science in raving action. The equipment grew more complex, the weapons more violent, and concepts became galactic. Only the characters never changed.

manuscript was consistently rejected by all markets for about ten years, until Gernsback accepted it, published it as a three-part serial in *Amazing Stories,* August, September, October 1928. It received the cover illustration for the August issue.

It affected readers as water affects metallic sodium.

There is something to be said for their frenzied applause, even today, even by us jaded sophisticates. The details of the story line are inordinately complicated. To summarize the entire series is less wearing: An extraordinary man and his friends use superscience to battle aliens and a particularly competent villain through four novels and more galaxies.

This barren statement resembles the series in about the same degree that the needleless skeleton at the curb resembles the lavishly bedecked Christmas tree.

Consider the first novel, "The Skylark of Space." (The "Skylark" is the spaceship of the series.) Richard Ballinger Seaton—a Ph.D. in rare metals, physically powerful, gray-eyed, square-jawed, incorrigibly slangy, of vigorous and flexible mentality—accidentally learns to liberate and control all energy contained within a copper plate.

In a matter of chapters, he is building a spaceship, "The Skylark of Space." Construction is financed by Seaton's incredibly wealthy friend, Martin Crane, multi-millionaire-explorer-archeologist.

Lurking about the paragraphs is that arch-villain of science fiction, Dr. Marc C. "Blackie" DuQuesne, who plots with a dishonest industrial company to steal Seaton's secret.

DuQuesne, the antithesis of Seaton, is almost precisely his equal in knowledge. Blackie is a tall man, physically powerful, with wavy, thick, intensely black hair, thick eyebrows, and a beard that shows even after shaving. He is in his early thirties. Cold, self-contained, the supreme egotist, he lies as a matter of principle, steals as a matter of policy, and is one of the great geniuses of the human race. Seaton refers to him as "The Ape."

DuQuesne gets part of the secret, then builds a small spaceship. Hoping to extort Seaton's cooperation, he kidnaps Dorothy Vaneman, Seaton's fiancee.

Dorothy is a glorious redhead, with the mental capacity and emotional stability to mesh perfectly with Seaton. She is not to be trifled with, either. Once kidnapped, she promptly kicks one of DuQuesne's minions into the control panel. The spaceship accelerates out of control, out of the solar system, ends lost, 237 light years from Earth.

Unerringly, Seaton and Crane follow, using a tracing device (the first of their many devices), just recently built.

Then a thrilling account of how they catch up with DuQuesne...

...how they escape the murderous attraction of a dead sun....

...how they meet a green homid race on Osnome....

...how they (in the best lost race tradition) plunge into internal Osnome affairs with the subtlety of a football striking the gravy dish....

...how they support the good side (Kondals) against the venialcruelevil Mardonales....

The conclusion is predictable: massively augmented by Seaton's astonishing super science, Good wins.

In immense public ceremonies (riveling those on Barsoom), Seaton marries Dorothy; Crane marries Margaret; DuQuesne sneers.

The Skylark is rewarded with a new transparent hull, five hundred times as strong as steel. All return home wealthy. DuQuesne has received half a tube of radium and, as they orbit the earth, slips quietly away from the honeymooning couples. He is a sly hard genius, most gratifying bad.

Many traditional elements appear here: The good man chasing the criminal, the abducted girl, the menace in space, the civil commotion into which our heroes mix, the public ceremony of acclamation, the unlimited wealth which allows the hero's performance. Familiar material.

The narrative handling is not traditional at all. Smith shows a wry sense of humor, which is shared by his characters. A hard clarity fills his pages. The adventures may be extravagant but they are not sentimental. When abducted, Dorothy does not weep or faint, but scratches/bites/ kicks vigorously and with effect. When DuQuesne's plans go awry, he does not swell with menace; merely adjusts coldly and precisely and continues as before.

Extraordinary optimism prevades the story. No problem encountered cannot be solved—given enough thought and some sort of technical lever. In each novel, the available technology magnifies by four times. So does the size of the Skylark. Its final configuration (in *Skylark DuQuesne,* far down the road) is a 1000-kilometer sphere, not really recognizable as a spaceship. As the ship's power and size expand, so do the capabilities of Seaton. And DuQuesne. And Dorothy. Their minds, variously augmented, fill with the knowledge of thousands of millions of generations—a typical Smith concept, and a typical Smith number. Upon that base of advanced information, they add more—and still more—and yet again more knowledge.

None of them ever lose that ragging cheerful slanginess of speech (frankly, they all talk alike) which brightens the austerities of the long pseudo-technical descriptions. These must have delighted Gernsback.

Each technological break-through in the series is developed in the same length of time required to put on your shoes. The characters accomplish in weeks what would constitute ten-year development programs in the big tough world outside of *Amazing Stories.* Nor do the proverbs of real-world development engineering apply.

Such as:

If it works the first time, something is wrong.

All development programs require twice as much time as you suspect, and four times the official schedule.

The most critical drawing is still in stress analysis.

5% of the cable connectors are never available.

If Quality buys off the welds, the assembly is still warped out of specification.

Procurement never receives a complete list of required attaching parts.

The more critical a sub-assembly, the less probability that it can be installed as designed.

Seaton encounters few such problems. This is because "Skylark" is fantasy. Engineering-flavored, science-seasoned fantasy. But fantasy.

Smith was obviously familiar with laboratory routines. His PhD was earned. That accounts for the authentic scent of the lab that wafts through his fiction. His sentences are salted with enough real engineering to bilk the unwary. He mentions recoil slack in gear trains, a real problem, and follows this by describing applications of fourth-power rays, which is pure magic. The first reference slides you lightly over the second.

Smith calls it super-science. But it is magic, all dressed up in a greasy lab coat. When, in the 1965 *Skylark DuQuesne*, they smash galaxies with psionic force, it all seems quite natural.

Less radical Smith innovations include:

—faster than light accelerations

—movement through the fourth dimension

—routine communication by beaming out a projection of yourself. The projection uses all your senses, so the single, guiding nervous system is coping with two simultaneous sets of stimuli.

—interstellar navigation without maps

—creation of matter by mental force

—beamed energy weapons

—metals that resist any beam

—beams that destroy any metals

—and (we might add) full-systems flights with no ground test

Enough of this niggling. The dialogue is bright, the characters of a tough and resilient competence. The story, crammed with artificial technicalities, hurtles furiously along. The plots tangle ever more complexly. The cast of characters ever expands. The scene constantly enlarges.

The series begins at a laboratory work bench. It ends with an experimental test set-up projected into extra-galactic space, ten light years long, three light years high.

It is splendid.

Unlike other science fiction published during this period, the "Skylark" series has aged gracefully. Traces of World War I fictionizing may be noted in "The Skylark of Space" but the series polishes these away and, by the final novel, becomes wholly modern. (Of course, the blockbuster, super-science novel was obsolete by 1965, but that's another matter.)

In "Skylark Three" (*Amazing Stories*, three parts, August through October, 1930), Seaton and friends join the alien scientists of Norlamin to battle the Fenor of Fenachrone. A crazy leader plans to conquer everything in sight. Seaton's mind is enhanced to the limits of organic capability. He flies the new Skylark Three and blasts the enemy world to a sun. Four hundred thousand tons of uranium detonates the villains from existence—presumably including DuQuesne, presumably to close the series.

Successful series, like vampires, are hard to kill. In 1934, editor F. Orlin

Tremaine, seeking to build circulation for *Astounding Stories,* coaxed a sequel from Smith. This was published as "The Skylark of Valeron" (seven parts, August 1934 through February 1935).

DuQuesne has escaped the general annihilation that closed the last serial. Possessing himself of a captured Fenachrone battleship, and with awesomely augmented intelligence, he proposes to kill Seaton and his associates and become ruler of the Earth—a small enough position for such capability.

Seaton, meanwhile—way out among the galaxies—had met hostile disembodied intelligences, got lost in the fourth dimension, captured by hypermen (looking vaguely like seahorses), escaped to the Planet Valeron. Then the pace of the narrative accelerates as a ruthless Chlorian scout ship attacks.

Within five hours, using multitudes of rays and mental power, Seaton constructs a 1,000-kilometer Skylark Four, powered by cosmic energy. He then wipes out the enemy. As an afterthought, the period added after the sentence.


As we return, now, to Earth, we discover that DuQuesne rules all. Is all lost? Certainly not. Seaton, ablaze with intelligence, solves the problem of the Sixth Order. DuQuesne is captured and, with a group of bodiless intelligences, he is clenched into time stasis and accelerated away on a trip calculated to last one hundred thousand million years.

His journey does not require such a length of time.

About ten years later, Earth-time, *If Worlds of Science Fiction* brought forth the final volume of the series, "Skylark DuQuesne" (June through September 1965, four parts). The plot weaves at least six separate threads together. DuQuesne double-crosses everybody, having escaped from that long trip because of one of Seaton's infrequent oversights. Glibly deft as ever, Blackie tricks Seaton off to a galaxy that has been swallowed up by the Chlorans. (This is as vicious a race as ever tormented the helpless.)

For the rest of the novel, Seaton and friends prepare for the final battle with the Chlorans. They lead a revolt in conquered territory, meet three performing witches of powerful psi talents, then secure and develop a fourth-dimensional device from still another race.

They are finally able to mount a full-scale attack upon the Chlorans, aided, remarkably enough by DuQuesne. One quarter of the Chloran galaxy has been examined and found to contain 149,297,319 solar systems. Unshaken by these figures, Seaton attacks.

For reasons of plot, Seaton and the rest are knocked out of the action early. Blackie DuQuesne goes it alone, using a mind-operated device, plus fourth-dimensional transmovement, plus psionic interpenetration, plus heaven knows what else. Using all this grand stuff, he bombards the Chloran galaxy with suns torn from another galaxy. In a few hours, he kills about 99 trillion Chlorans, reducing their galaxy to a seethe of nova flame.

Blackie remains unperturbed by the immensity of it all. To him, it's just another few trillion deaths. And his action does keep Seaton from becoming a mass murderer, an unacceptable position for a fictional hero.

The series now is ended and Blackie, unrepentant, leaves to become the emperor of his own personal galaxy. Seaton and Dorothy, so intellectually elevated that they are near godhead, face the future. Science has been elevated until it is indistinguishable from magic. The packed math equations supporting the final devices are virtually beyond comprehension by mortal nervous system.

The colossal has triumphed. In the shining manner of Ray Cummings' characters, the series has grown colossal. More colossal. Still more colossal. Ever more gigantic concepts heave up and ever more death on scales so colossal the numbers make no sense.

The culmination of four novels, packed with super science, is the destruction of an entire galaxy. Even granting the necessity, it is singular that the end product of this supreme technology is a quasi-stellar flame mass. Surely the end product of science and technology can be expected to total more than this. We began so optimistically, releasing the energy contained in a copper plate. And now look.

Seaton is certainly a variant on the usual justice figure. He occupies the usual position outside of society (far outside, in this case) and brings his own form of unilateral salvation. His solutions are thoroughly technical and thoroughly permanent.

> [The] idea that science and technology, by extending man's power to the performance of all things possible, will inevitably improve the human condition, [is] an over-simplified view .... [This] unthinking optimism about the effect of science and technology on human life has been the animating spirit of much science fiction.[23]

Which was true until the science fiction of the 1950s and 1960s. By then the form had turned from the story of mechanisms to examine, in detail, such less spectacular matters—social, political and psychological.

The field matured, altering by night in quiet ways until something new and desperate and passionately forlorn stepped forth, the spirit of the times, and began to speak. To discuss the new science fiction is beyond these pages. Enough to remark that, even in the decade of violent change, during the 1960s and into the 1970s, echoes of the great "Skylark" days lingered. You found them in the German science fiction series that featured Perry Rhodan, a direct descendent from Seaton. Rhodan's series gradually expanded as he swept through the universe, his intelligence augmented, his weapons increasingly fearsome, sweeping before him galaxies of leering aliens.

## 13-

That memorable August 1928 issue of *Amazing Stories*, from which so much grew, also included a novelette by Phillip Francis Nowlan. This story, "Armageddon 2419," featured Mr. Anthony Rogers—called "Tony" by his wife, Wilma. About a year later, the novelette would de-evolve into a comic strip, and Buck Rogers would enter the common tongue.

Before embracing these excitements, we should make a brief detour into the past, there to meet a strange sleeper, his strange awakening, and his even stranger influence on Buck Rogers.

Here,then, is Mr. Graham, late of London, sleeping tranced as two centuries fled. He woke in 2100. His investments had so prospered that he owned half the world.

So begins *When the Sleeper Awakes* (1899), another volume in that massive library written by H.G. Wells.

At last awake, Graham stares half stunned at possessions incredible. Around him spreads a bright new Utopia, an Eden of colossal cities, glassed-in, filled with leaping crystal spires and filmy steel webs swooping upward.

All this ruled in his name by a council of twelve. These were dedicated to planning, organization, beauty. Their excellence was enumerated each hour on public communications networks, encouraging the multitudes.

The gray-faced multitudes. Who wore blue coveralls. Who labored among the compacted machines, layer upon layer, piled down under the feet of the city, level after level of them, down in the roaring caves, down down deep among the under corridors.

Down there, the Labor Police carry clubs. They keep order. They enforce, down there among the man-swarm pressed within the winding levels beneath the upper city, whose cool and rose-hued perfection swoops gracefully toward the glass sky.

Mr. Graham has inherited a dictatorship. It is more repressive, more powerful, more tightly disciplined than any known before. That tiny cadre, topside, rides on the backs of slave labor, locked in service to the machines.

This early, then, the familiar question is being asked: How individual freedom is to be preserved in technological civilizations that are increasingly complex, increasingly organized.

Graham found partial answers only.

And the image of that roaring underground city burrowed so deeply into science fiction literature and films that it became the conventional symbol of advanced megascience.

All this preface introduces Anthony Rogers and the world of 2419 A.D.

Rogers was also a sleeper. It is an honorable profession, a way of time travel without equipment. Although it is seriously deficient in means of return. Rogers slept longer than Graham and for a different reason. It happened this way:

The American Radioactive Gas Corporation sent Rogers, two assistants, and a lot of scientific apparatus to investigate the gases in the abandoned coal mines of the Pennsylvania Wyoming Valley.

On the morning of December 15, 1927, while the team was in the deepest levels of the mines, the ceilings collapsed. Rogers' companions were killed. He slept, overcome by radioactive gas.

He slept for 492 years and did not waken to Utopia.

Following the First World War the European nations banded together against America. The following war wrecked everyone. Russia formed a coalition with China and went rushing in over Europe. In turn they were attacked and defeated by the Mongolians. In 2109 Mongolians in limitless hordes attacked both coasts of the United States, using overwhelming airfleets equipped with the disintegrator ray. American power was obliterated. The civilization was essentially destroyed. Small pockets of patriots fled to the deep forests, there to build strength, redevelop science and technology, against "The Day of Hope" when the Second War of Independence would be fought. (It is a more elaborate version of the situation A.L. Zagat would use for his "Tomorrow" series, featuring the Tarzan-derivative, Dikar.)

The Mongolians ignored the shattered remnants of the country. They established strong enclaves in fifteen large cities, converting these to pleasure centers. From these points the Han dynasty in America (a province of the Mongolian World Empire) was administered.

Two major scientific devices supported the Han rule. The first was the disintegrator ray, rather like a searchlight in appearance, that dissolved matter into electronic vibrations; it destroyed all known substances. The second, the repellor ray, was an anti-gravity device and was used to support their air ships.

The Americans, concealed in the forests, live in small, para-military clans (also called "gangs"). Under the forest, they have established buried factories and laboratories. In these they devise their new technology—small rocket ships, rocket pistols (handguns shooting a self-propelled explosive pellet), and two synthetic elements: Ultron and Inertron.

Ultron, an extremely dense solid, is invisible and 100% conductive to light, electricity and heat. Inertron, a disintegrator-proof solid, has no weight, conducts no heat and is of great physical strength. It is made into belts called "jumpers." These reduce your weight to about two pounds, allowing you to jump fifty feet horizontally. An advanced jumper belt called "the floater" is propelled by small rocket motors encased in inertron blocks.

So much for the main elements of science and technology in 2419 A.D. When Rogers appears on the scene, matters are ripe for "The Day of Hope." The Han are weakened by hundreds of years of self-indulgence. The American "gangs" have slowly strengthened. It is almost time to challenge the Han air power.

Rogers awakes. Escaping to the surface, he spends a soul-wrenching two weeks alone in the forest. Then he rescues Wilma Deering from a fire-fight with the Bad Bloods (members of a renegade gang suspected of dealing with the Han).

Wilma is so slender that Rogers first believes her a boy. She has dark brown hair and hazel eyes, stands about 5 feet tall (for the Americans have lost body size during their century-long stay in the forest). Turns out that she is a girl of "studious and reflective turn of mind," who has a reputation of being cold to men.

That assessment is incorrect. She goes after Rogers with irresistible zeal.

She leads him back to camp and soon he is contributing information on how World War I battles were conducted—particularly how a rolling barrage was handled.

On patrol with Wilma, Rogers discovers a method of destroying a Han airship by firing rocket projectiles into the anti-gravity beam and so into the ship's interior. Soon, the gang has ambushed and destroyed seven more Han ships.

The victory sparks widespread guerilla activity. As the Hans prepare for retaliatory attack, the Americans begin to organize nationally. By this time, Tony and Wilma have married. Then Rogers heads a surprise attack into the Han main Nu-Yok information center, seeking information about a traitorous gang of Bad Bloods.

The raid is so successful that the head of the Gang gives over his position to Rogers, amid the usual universal applause.

Now Rogers organizes a raid against the Bad Bloods, using the rolling artillery barrage technique and using low-yield atomic warheads.

The entire camp of traitors is destroyed in a white scald of energy. The holocaust is described in prose as drab as November 17 in New Market, Alabama. On this high point the first story ends.

It is Horatio Alger Jr. all over again. With this difference. The Alger hero must struggle. Rogers does not have to. It all comes showering down on Tony—The Girl, The Success, The Position, The Tactical Triumph. The whole thing reeks of daydream. It is the young man's expectation of how the world will crumble before him—They Recognized My Excellence On Sight!

The story hardly gives a rigorous account of Rogers' rise through the ranks. Experience tells us that rank in guerilla bands is achieved by nightmares of intrigue, political in-fighting and terrible silent psychological struggles. Much the same as in civil life. No trace of these competitions shows in the story Rogers narrates.

No indeed. But it should not surprise us. No tinge of human complexity appears at any point in the story. You may ascribe motives to the characters. It is your own conflict, however, not that of the author.

For instance, Anthony Rogers is 5 feet eleven inches tall and some sort of a scientific technician. We are told this much. The rest we must surmise— that he served in the artillery during the First World War, that he is a strongly built man who has trained a trick memory so that he can repeat, verbatim, what he has heard once.

He has a strong need to shape and manipulate. His personality is powerful, often warmly reassuring. Beneath it lie complex destructive emotions, constantly checked. When these fight to the surface, he is impelled to violent physical exertions. At other times, he seems driven to expose himself to extreme danger. It seems a way of daring Fate to punish his internal stress.

We must read these wise interpretations between the lines. The reader is required to do the writer's work, because the writer is busy inventing extraordinary gadgets.

Gadgets. Not science and engineering. The adventure contains no trace of science as it is practiced, or applied engineering as it shapes resisting material to imagination's direction.

What the adventure does have is indigestible chunks of exposition. These clutter the paragraphs. Reading the story is like traversing a street into which a building has collapsed. Such lecturing stiffened all the Gernsback publications. Most of it is that speculative drivel you hear at 2 am when the boys are finishing the second bottle of Jim Beam and drawing on the backs of envelopes. Words without meaning. Talk without content. Nothing but invented names and statements of function. It makes a senseless yammering at the story's heart. And that heart is hollow enough already.

"Armageddon—2419" is a variant of that familiar scenario used by Wells (and others before him) when writing of the emergence of the perfect state.

The first condition is that present civilization must erase itself. The extinction is accomplished by immense nationalistic wars. Groups of nations hammer at each other with advanced weapons until civilization collapses into its own grit. The world reverts to semi-barbarism, this somehow creating a condition from which enlightened leaders unite to establish a generous-hearted world state.[24] Being technically sophisticated, they do this by use of more advanced technology, which has somehow survived the descent into barbarism. From this point, variations grow madly. In our day, science fiction has concentrated heavily on the negative component—the new world that sophisticated leaders create from the ruins is a dictatorship more rabidly brutal than what has been destroyed.

In Anthony Rogers' world, the collapse has been severe, not total. High technology is still available to the American survivors. The concept is questionable. In our world, high technology has always been a consequence of a highly organized industrial society, not a fragmented one.

"Armageddon—2419"-- doesn't really bother itself with how its scientific wonders arrived. The point is that they have arrived. From that point, the flying belts, rocket pistols and assorted rays are used in about the same way that the Wizard of Oz used his magic tools, those glorious devices that speed the story line. Through their use, the villains will be punished and a splendid new day will dawn.

Perhaps it will. Although Rogers, himself, writing after the completion of the Second War of Independence, notes that men are no wiser than before; he sees a regrowth of customs and thought patterns destroyed for almost 500 years. Folly re-establishes itself and, so we assume, will the Bad Old Days.

The Rogers' story continued in "The Air Lords of Han" (*Amazing Stories,* March 1929). War has exploded across the continent and, in their fifteen cities, the Han huddle under siege. The Americans pound them mercilessly and are pounded in turn.

Both sides gush technological marvels: hand disintegrators, more powerful flying ships, remote controlled television bombs. Each innovation is described to repletion. Every spurious operating characteristic is analyzed.

Among these descriptions of magic tools, Rogers gets accidentally captured. He is taken to Lo-Tan, glistening wonder city in the Rockies. There he is treated with respect and tortured with courtesy. To secure his information, the Han attempt to seduce him with a gloriously fragrant young beauty. In the great tradition, Rogers remains faithful to Wilma.

Imprisoned for months, he finally escapes, assisted by Wilma and a remote-controlled television probe and American troops scattered all over the landscape. Once free, he whirls upon his heel and leads a new assault against the Han. Lo-Tan is wiped out and a complex of underground cities is destroyed. Vicious hand-to-hand fighting, World War I bayonet tactics against disintegrators, obliterates the Han army.

In an Epilogue to the story, Rogers speculates as to the possible extraterrestrial origin of the Han. He reaches no conclusion. By this time, he is a very old man. Wilma has died. He longs to join her. So the series closes.

No Martian Cat-Men. No Dr. Huer. No Asterites. No Black Barney. No space travel. The name Buck is not used once. All this belongs to the comic page. The *Amazing Stories* material is only a plain, future-war novel, split into two parts.

The initial Anthony Rogers adventure is one of many similar fantasies in the Gernsbackian science fiction world. It has a crude vigor about it. Interesting images blaze up unexpectedly, their force enhanced by the slovenly material in which they are embedded, faint lamps in a sprawling swamp.

Characterization, coherent backgrounds, competent prose style rarely appear. If the reader might relish these, the editorial policy stood dead against them.

From this material evolved "Buck Rogers in the 25th Century." The comic strip first appeared in 1929, proved unexpectedly popular, and decisively influenced visual science fiction through at least the next generation.

The strip begins crudely. The drawing is inept, the story line clumsy, the characters immature. Wilma, in particular, is given a childish spitefulness, sometimes rising to self pity, that should have been corrected in her kindergarten.

But the strip does tickle dreams. Adventures cram it, and flying heroes who enjoy exciting times with few enough responsibilities. The situation refreshes the laden heart.[25]

A wry humor is eventually distilled from early crudities. Later will come interesting experiments in creating 25th Century slang. And the drawing improved in time. Things were not hopeless, even at the beginning. Not quite.

The impact of Buck Rogers testifies that the mass market, in 1929, was ripe for visual science fiction. We can only wonder what reception Alex Raymond's *Flash Gordon* would have received had this more sophisticated effort appeared before Buck Rogers.

But now we are tangling leaves with roots.

After 1929, Buck Rogers, future hero, ballooned commercially. From the nattering comic strip leaped Big Little Books, Better Big Books, comic books, radio serials, moving picture serials, dime store arrays of pistols and small metal rocket ships. There came give-away premiums and board games, key rings and watches, and testimonials for cereal. Concentrated commercial exploitation. Until merciful reaction set in and Buck and Wilma faded out, as successfully exploited characters will, leaving a name for the dictionaries, and a vision of high bold glory in young minds.

At that, it was a glorious history to develop from the didactic solemnities of the original novelettes.

## 14-

The Warlords of Mars towers gigantically on one horizon. Against the other, rather smaller, stand Mr. and Mrs. Anthony Rogers. By such clever symbolization, we establish major points of early scientific romance and science fiction. Between them should flap a vast banner, brilliant with exploding galaxies, representing the Skylark saga.

Down on the plain by the feet of these titans, less extreme representatives of the series hero enjoy the sun. Among these potters a thin, little, insignificant man. He looks rather like a feeble boy, standing 5 feet 5 inches tall, weighing only a trifle over 100 pounds. He is muscled as lightly as a mayfly.

He is entirely nondescript. His face, rather round and clean shaven, has not a single distinguishing feature. You could stare at him an hour, then not recognize him ten minutes later. His eyes are a weak blue, his hair an empty color. Even his walk is an apology.

He ambles mildly toward you and diffidently extends his card. In a voice pitched barely above a whisper, he murmurs: "I am the detective you sent for. Taine of San Francisco."

"Oh. Taine, eh? Let's sit and talk. Have a cigar."

"I do not smoke. I find that the nicotine hurts the delicate enamel of the teeth, and once that is gone, the teeth soon decay."

It is the expected response. It appeared in more than half of Taine's adventures, and readers came to feel cheated if the delicate enamel of the teeth was not mentioned at least once a story. It is as much Taine's trademark as his terse card. It is also the mark of all Taine stories: a simple innocence.

The special flavor of the Taine adventures escapes if you read them as straight-forward prose. They are actually colossal jokes told in a soft voice. They are in the same tradition as the Virginian's frog farm, tall stories that begin mildly and inflate to prodigious size. They burlesque the conventional hero, the scientific detective, the hard-boiled detective, the oriental menace and most other obvious science-fiction trends.

When the giganticism of Skylarks and Interstellar Patrols palls, when civilization has been destroyed once too often, when science has become blatantly super, then sample Taine. He makes it all endurable once again.

Taine was the creation of David H. Keller (1880-1966), a doctor and practicing neuro-psychiatrist for most of his life. As dedicated to his writing as to his profession, he contributed to the Gernsback magazines—his first story was published in *Amazing Stories*, February 1928—and pulp magazines during the 1930s-1940s, including *Weird Tales, Fantasy Magazine, Strange Stories* and *Cosmic Stories*. His popularity waned after the mid-1930s, probably because his style hardly changed. Even at its most effective, it contains a curiously obsolete ring.

During the 1960s and early 1970s, many of his short stories were reprinted in the digest magazine *Startling Mystery Stories* together with that interesting series "Tales from Cornwall." Nine collections of Keller's works were published, including *Tales from Underwood, The Homunculus,* and *The Folsom Flint.*

At first glance, Keller's work seems bland. Only later do you feel a sting. Most of his fiction is scaled to human terms—familiar aspirations, everyday scenes. All have gone a little wrong. No horrors loom from yonder galaxy. He is more interested in the horrors concealed between human ears, horrors enough.

Keller did not seem really interested in possible futures. Only two Taine stories are concerned with the future, and that is projected only thirty years ahead. Both stories appear early in the series. Both are constructed on the same framework; both are strongly charged with social materials; both are concerned with minority positions in society—that of negroes in "The Menace" and of women in "The Feminine Metamorphosis." In both Keller uses stereotypes so gross that they obscure his basic points.

The premise of each story is that neither negroes nor women, as groups, are able to reach their effective potential because social organization (established by white men) discriminates against them.

Once that is stated, a facetious assumption is made:

Things would be different if negroes were white.

Things would be different if women were men.

And, respectively, we are given stories in which negroes have found a way to become white, and women have found a way to become men.

In each case, the results are disastrous. In each case, the transformation fails because it is a surface change only. Although both groups perform brightly, they fail because cosmetic modifications have produced only synthetic white men; not superior negroes and superior women.

These interpretations lie close under the story surfaces. They are not difficult to find. But Keller makes it difficult by a patronizing attitude toward women and a dislike of negroes that is strong enough to lead him into the false position of generalizing from a biased particular.

The social material he uses was sensitive then, and is almost intolerably sensitive now. It is virtually certain that today either story would cause civil liberties and womens' lib groups to fall, foaming and shrieking, upon the incautious soul who reprinted them. As soon as an ethical position becomes a Cause, its sense of humor evaporates.

The Taine stories were published in an order having nothing to do with the internal chronology. "The Menace," published in 1928, picks up Taine in mid-career and continues, in vast jumps, for forty years. "A Scientific Widowhood," published in 1930, is his first case. "The Temple of Death," published in 1970, occurs after the third part of "The Menace." "The Feminine Metamorphosis" (1929), takes place in two separate parts over about four years, overlapping part of "The Menace" and other cases.

To reduce confusion, the adventures of Taine will be discussed according to the internal chronology. All known Taine stories are listed in the Appendix by order of publication.[26]

Taine's ancestors were Italian and Spanish. His father was born in California and married a lady from Portugal. It was a mixed enough beginning. Taine's roots set solidly in San Francisco and stayed there. He spent ten years in college, earning an A.B., two law degrees, plus studying three years in science and two in medicine. And one day, he presented himself to the Chief of the San Francisco Secret Service.

(Whatever group Taine worked with was always identified as the Secret Service; this is one of Keller's conventions.)

> "I always wanted to be a detective. Sherlock Holmes is one of my heroes in fiction. Up to this time, I have been so busy that I have had no time to do any real work. But I have to work now, as my money is all spent. That is why I am looking for a position." ("A Scientific Widowhood," *Scientific Detective Monthly*, February 1930)

The speech is pure Taine. Stunning simplicity, causing those who meet him to wonder if he is a total fool or a genius.

The Chief, staggered, is cajoled into letting Taine investigate a woman who has married wealth three times, each husband immediately dying of cancer. Taine accepts the case on a contingency basis, no charge until it is complete, and vanishes from the Chief's sight—and his mind, too, if the truth be known.

Taine then disguises himself as a Japanese, marries the widow, and pretends to come down with acute skin cancer. There follow severe complications, during which Taine either is or is not disguised as the widow, or her sister, or—well, it is not quite clear. The police arrive, as police will. There is the widow and there, on her death bed, is her sister, who has signed a confession that she killed all three husbands. After this we learn that the widow is Taine in disguise and the sister is actually the widow—you are following this, aren't you—and, very likely, Keller is Hugo Gernsback.

The story resembles a Marx Brothers routine. At the end, Taine reports back to the Chief. The husbands, he reveals, were murdered by exposure to X-ray. The widow had a machine upstairs pointing down at the husbands' bed. Taine merely moved it to point at the widow's bed. And so she died.

In "Menacing Claws" (*Amazing Detective Tales*, September 1930), Taine annoys the Chief into assigning him a dope case which has already claimed the lives of two operatives. They died of tetanus, victims of Ming Kow, deadly smuggler.

Taine bets Ming Kow $10,000 that only one of them will leave a room alive. They end up scratching each other's back in a bizarre duel, using disease-impregnated back scratchers. Taine wins.

In this story, we learn that the Chief's daughter, Mildred, thinks Taine is the most unusual man she has ever met. It is a mild understatement. The Chief is hesitant about pitting Taine against Ming Kow, for, if Taine dies, Mildred "will sure be sore at me."

He need have no fear. Taine is Taine. Other detectives (he explains to the Chief) follow certain rules. But Taine has no method in conducting his cases. "I just go alone with the tide until I find out what the Divine Programme is and just what my part is in it. Then I go ahead and close the case."

This is because he is a Presbyterian, and what will be will be.

"Burning Water" (*Amazing Detective Tales*, June 1930) is a parody of science detectives. In this, Taine is employed by a college friend who is President of the World Combustion Machine Manufacturing Co. The friend has gained control over all modes of energy but one. This, invented by a Pole named Paupeneau, is an apparatus "for alternating currents," keyed to the specific vibrations needed to shatter an atom. When he vibrates water, he immediately secures 137 horsepower.

Disguised as a Polish dishwasher, Taine enters Paupeneau's service, but is detected before he learns much. The Pole advised Taine that his identity has been discovered but that he will not be killed. Taine has been mildly useful and, to honor him, Paupeneau will first blow up San Francisco, later everything else in the country.

> *Paupeneau*: "As a man, you are a weakling, as a detective, you are a joke. You are not even worth killing."
> *Taine*: "I ought to have known that you would find me out sometime. Still, I do not see why you take it so good naturedly."
> *Paupeneau*: "It is because you are so damn insignificant."
> *Taine*: "Well, thanks for not killing me. It would have been awkward for both of us .... Are you really in earnest about destroying San Francisco?"
> *Paupeneau*: "I certainly am."
> *Taine*: "I wish you would destroy some other city first. You see, I have a lot of cards engraved. They read: 'Taine of San Francisco.' If you destroy the city, those cards will be a dead loss."

Paupeneau is eventually blown up by a monkey that has been trained by Taine to press the "Destruct" key of the amazing machine. Either that or, perhaps, some Russians blew up the lab with a bomb. The cause isn't completely clear. However, San Francisco is saved, although Taine is not well pleased with his own performance.

In a gloomy mood, he accepts his first (and last) drink from the Chief, characteristically remarking: "My, this is bitter stuff, yet it certainly makes one feel better."

*Chief*: "What about your fee?"
*Taine:* "Oh, send me a check for it. Anything you want to give me."

Later, when accepted as a member of the Secret Service, Taine will earn $200 a week. In addition to this, grateful clients, up to and including the United States Government, will pay him fees ranging from $25,000 to $1,000,000.

"Wolf Hollow Bubbles" is set in Stroudsburg, Pennsylvania, where Keller made his home. (The story was first published as a booklet by the ARRA Printers, Jamaica, in 1934; it was reprinted in the Winter 1968/69 issue of *Startling Mystery Stories*, No. 11.) Taine has been called in to discover why a mysterious millionaire has taken over Wolf Hollow. The reason, Taine learns, is that the millionaire is a mad doctor who has created 15-foot tall cancer cells. He began by feeding them mice, working up to steers, and is about to introduce humans into the diet. But he ends up devoured himself, in a way that Taine's adversaries have, and the wonderful experiment is burnt up. Taine's fee is $50,000, which seems hardly enough for coping with giant cancer cells.

Sometime after "Wolf Hollow," Taine marries Mildred and they have a daughter. In "The Cerebral Library" (*Amazing Stories*, May 1931) Taine foils still another madman. This one plans to collect and kill 500 educated young men. Their brains will then be removed by Wing Loo, the world's greatest brain surgeon, and they will be attached to a machine which will make all knowledge in these brains available on request. We have here an organic computer. Disguised as Wing Loo, Taine frustrates the plan. Not even one brain is collected.

Which brings us to "The Menace." This was first published in *Amazing Stories Quarterly*, Summer 1928; then reprinted in the same publication, Winter 1933. The story is novelette length, in four very loosely connected parts. Rough calculation suggests that it begins around 1919 and ends about 1958. As it opens, Taine is barely middle-aged: he has been in the San Francisco Secret Service for twenty years and his second daughter has been born. At the end of the story, he will be an old, old man, long retired.

In the first part of "The Menace" (the part is untitled), Taine infiltrates a group of negroes who have learned to make gold from sea water and, by injection, how to turn themselves white. A group of 1,000 brilliant negroes, calling themselves *The Powerful Ones*, have organized all negroes in America into a secret society. In the middle of New York City, they have built a 100-story citadel disguised as an office building. From this headquarters, they plan to infiltrate the white race, rise to power, kill all the whites, and conquer the world.

In this laudable endeavor, they are aided by Ebony Kate, a voodoo priestess, who provides tom-tom and snake dance specialties on request and heads their religious activities.

Before *The Powerful Ones* are ready to act, Taine (again disguised) penetrates their inner circle, learns their plans. Detected at last, he is scheduled to be fed to the voodoo snake. By someone's error, however, he is imprisoned in a room where:

—there is an escape chute in the floor

—there is a control panel by which the building may be destroyed

Given these marked advantages, it is no wonder that he escapes and destroys the building, concluding the first part of the story.

From this point, chronology requires that we leap to the first page of "The Feminine Metamorphosis" (*Science Wonder Stories*, August 1929). It is confusing to jump around like this and the cues internal to the stories are not particularly consecutive, but we must do the best we can.

Taine now has three daughters (one married) and the black puppy that he saved at the end of "The Menace" (Part I). Since the first part of "The Feminine Metamorphosis" is six months long, followed by a three-year break, some additional material must be inserted before you learn how it all came out.

Please do not grind your teeth. It may harm the delicate enamel.

In the first part of "Metamorphosis," Taine travels to China to investigate a hospital filled with mysterious women. Disguised as a Chinese girl (and shaving three times a day), he learns that the women at the hospital are performing gondaectomies on thousands of Chinese men (paying each $100) and are sending mysterious liquid extracts to an equally mysterious place in Paris, City of Mysteries.

During this period, Taine enjoys a number of interesting, if unrecorded cases. His wife, Mildred, also spends busy years. She is the President of the Missionary Society to which she donates 10% of Taine's fees. She is also active in the Ladies Aid Society of the church to which she donates most of the rest of his fees. Taine is permitted to keep his salary as a Secret Service detective.

His recorded cases are as odd as ever.

In "The Temple of Death" (*Startling Mystery Stories,* No. 16, Summer 1970), he saves a millionaire and party out in the Arabian desert. They have fallen into the clutches of a woman who is a carrier of epidemic cerebro-spinal fever, so that her kisses are lethal.

Returning to New York City, Taine disguises himself as a Chinese secretary and breaks up the operation of "Euthanasia Limited" (*Amazing Stories Quarterly*, Fall 1929). This organization sells scientific murder at $25,000 a body. (The victim sits in a chair especially rigged to reduce his vital electrical potential and so he dies, leaving no trace of murder.)

During this period, Parts 2 and 3 of "The Menace" take place.

*The Powerful Ones* have invented a way to make artificial gold. They scheme with various sly nations to pay their war debts to the United States in artificial gold (composed equally of mercury, lead and science). After the US has accepted payment, the recipe for artificial gold will be broadcast to the world. This will cause gold to become undesirable, disgracing the US, somehow, and shattering its economy. Learning these details, Taine and a batch of scientists zap the boxes with X-rays, returning the artificial gold to lead and mercury. (So much for Part 2—"The Gold Ship.")

Immediately, *The Powerful Ones* flash back with Part 3—"The Tainted

Flood." In this, they plan to dose the New York City water supply with a chemical that will cause all whites to become permanently black. Taine chases wildly across the country by airplane and taxi cab to locate the barrels of chemicals. He substitutes barrels of flour which are dumped into the water by these inhuman fiends, booming with laughter.

Again foiled, *The Powerful Ones* flee to an island in the Pacific Ocean. There they hatch the most revolting plot of all, which will be revealed several paragraphs from here.

By Part 3, Taine has proved himself of such exceptional value to the United States that the President, warmly grateful, has presented him with an engraved visiting card carrying the President's name. On the reverse side, the President has written: "The Bearer, Mr. Taine, is a direct representative of the President. All citizens are requested to render him any service he needs."

Some years later, in another magazine series, a Secret Service ace known as Operator 5, possessed a similar document, signed by authority as high. When Operator 5 showed this document, you could hear people's spines snap as they leaped to assist.

When Taine shows his card, the reaction is less crisp. The usual response is that he is a crank with a forged card.

What're you trying to prove, buddy? You a wise guy?

It is nearly impossible for a man trying to prevent the population of New York City from being turned black to explain what he is doing. It is difficult to be a Secret Service hero.

Very well. The flour is dumped into the reservoir, *The Powerful Ones* retreat to the Pacific, and Taine returns to San Francisco.

There he learns that a fire has destroyed the Presbyterian church and parsonage. The Missionary Society is going to rebuild and Mrs. Taine feels that she will have to donate $100,000. She is President, you understand, and feels her obligation keenly.

Taine casts up accounts and finds he is worth $110,000, including real estate and insurance. It is therefore necessary to earn $2,000,000, for he does not expect to survive his next assignment and wants to provide for Mildred.

The money comes easily.

Mr. Johnson of Wall Street drops by and gives him a check for a million dollars.

Obviously Mr. Johnson has a problem.

Over the past few years, New York City has been flooded by singularly able young men. Faultlessly tailored young men of extraordinary ability. Working day and night, clever, uncommitted to the New York establishment, they have rocked the city. They threaten to swallow up Wall Street, the banks, the insurance companies, and may even capture the Presidency of the United States at the next election.

They have also built an exclusive building in the center of New York City. There they play bridge and do not invite Mr. Johnson.

Simmering with suspicion, Johnson goes to the Secret Service which refers him to Taine, who gets a million dollar advance from him, and ambles forth to investigate.

Disguised as a red-headed secretary, he penetrates the inner circles of the Bridge Club.

He detects a plot of sinister evil.

The men of the Bridge Club are actually women. By a combination of X-rays, radium, and Chinese gonadal extract treatments, 5,000 women have made themselves over, outwardly, to men.

Over the years, they have focused the resources and scientific genius of their organization to eliminate the world's men. A specially treated food for expectant Mothers has caused the birth of three times as many girls as boys. Soon they hope to fertilize the female egg without recourse to male sperm. Then men can be eliminated.

A grand meeting has been called by top leaders of the organization. Before matters get very far, they learn that Taine is at the meeting in disguise. There follow busy paragraphs during which it appears that every person suspected of being Taine is someone else.

Makes no difference. Taine declares himself. No, they are not going to kill him to keep their secret. Five hundred policemen, he points out, surround the Bridge Club. He is speaking only to announce to them that their plot is at an end. They have made one terrible oversight. They are destroyed.

Seems that ten years ago, when they made up that batch of gonad extract, they didn't realize that Chinese all had a certain disease so mild that it did not show up in a Wasserman test.

Ten years later, however, all 5,000 women-become-men are afflicted with acute paresis and are rapidly becoming hopelessly insane. Your movement, says Taine, will fail because there "will be no brains left to carry the gospel of what you call feminine supremacy to the nation."

With that shattering blow, he leaves and charges Johnson an extra $27,000 for expenses.

It is a frightfully grim ending for a story so strongly comic. But in these stories, comedy and horror are so tightly tied together that they can't be separated without wrecking the entire thing.

At about this time, *The Powerful Ones*, on their island, have begun the final plan to destroy the United States. They have marketed a glass that is "flexible, malleable and ductile, as strong as steel, pliable as copper, and useful as wood." In a short time, six-room houses of glass are available on the market for $100 each.

The houses have only one deficiency. Those living in these houses become insane.

It takes a few years. The houses go on sale during 1935; by 1939, there are two insane people for every sane one. All are incurable. A fortunate scientific discovery, however, allows the insane (violent when awake) to be placed into permanent coma. They can be laid out in rows and cared for. By the mid-1940s, all major US cities have been converted to vast hospitals in which rank after rank of insane citizens are automatically tended.

But this is not the end of the United States. It is also discovered that very superior intelligences are positively affected by the glass houses. They become even more superior. What *The Powerful Ones* have done is to accelerate survival of the fittest. In the United States, the remaining sane have become a race of supermen.

The glass house ploy having misfired, *The Powerful Ones* decide to make one last effort. They will slip over to the Mainland and give those insane sleepers a powerful dose causing them to rouse up raving and destroy civilization.

Off they go, full of plans, leaving old Ebony Kate on the island.

Three years pass.

A ship arrives and from it debarks a little old man. It is Taine, arrived in the very last pages of "The Menace," Part 4: "The Insane Avalanche." Retired from the Secret Service for years, Taine has been assigned by the President to track down *The Powerful Ones*.

No sooner has he arrived on the island than a typhoon maroons him there. Now the remaining four *Powerful Ones* return, their mission a success. They propose to leave immediately for Paris to live the life of wealthy whites. Since Kate is too old and too black, they intend to leave her behind.

This irritates her so much that she poisons them all. When Taine confronts them, his revolvers drawn, they are all dead.

It is now 1958. A ship arrives and Taine boards it for San Francisco. He is accompanied by Kate, who has agreed to become his cook, of all things. Back in the States, he learns that, although the final insanity drug doses were administered, they were so powerful that all the insane were converted to dust.

The problem has gone away. After forty years, The Menace is no more.

So much for one of the more notorious stories of science fiction.

## 15—

Simple minded though they appear, the Taine stories sting with content. Beneath the monochrome prose, behind the rambling narratives, clogged with stereotypes, lie small, exquisitely poisoned teeth that clamp, without warning, on cherished social beliefs.

Social satire and fantasy share a long history of mutual accommodation. From Swift to Wells, writers found the fantasy a useful device for examining the human condition as it is by the light of what it should be. Even Burroughs, that tireless narrator of high action, found occasion on Barsoom or in the jungle to single out the petrifications of religion and militarism and the social preenings of his fellows. As far away as the Land of Oz, pulses of social satire flashed, thin lightnings among the poppies, throwing shadows strangely across the scarlet petals.

David Keller continued this long tradition. Social satire was not his major theme or his primary gift; he touched briefly on delicate matters and passed them to other science-fiction writers as yet unpublished whose work would speak to the 1950s and the 1970s on their own terms, in their own way.

How difficult it was, in 1928, to see any way clearly. The scientific romance still thrust out new green shoots, testing the sun. The space opera had been born. The technological fantasy turned from steam men to electric rifles to flying belts and rocket pistols; and predictive fiction, attentive to the early thunders of Wells, saw glittering technocracy rise, chrome and crystal soaring against the sky, footed in despair and love among the ruins. The Wild West was closed but out past the sky other frontiers lured; at the end of the rocket flight waited strange tentacled beings and their cities, out there among shadows thrown by other suns.

## 16-

Not all science-fiction series burdened themselves with content.

The Dr. Bird series, which appeared during the early 1930s, survived briefly without noticeable social content. Also without scientific content, believable characters, probable events or graceful prose. The series is the tramp art of science fiction, mildly interesting ideas, badly told.

Captain (later Colonel) S.P. Meek (USA) introduced Dr. Bird in January 1930. The doctor stepped forward upon two stages simultaneously: in *Scientific Detective Monthly* ("The Perfect Counterfeit") and in *Astounding Stories of Super Science* ("The Cave of Horror").

"The Cave of Horror" is Mammoth Cave, a place of inexplicable disappearances and grim mystery. Dr. Bird discovers and wipes out the horrid monster lurking in the cave's black deeps.

"The Perfect Counterfeit" relates how a flow of flawless $20 bills is discovered to be privately manufactured. Dr. Bird reasons that each bill is identical—to every wrinkle, blemish and stain. Therefore they are being turned out by a matter duplicator. Merely determine who has been inventing matter duplicators and the problem is solved.

Following this triumph, three additional stories appear in *Astounding* (February through May 1930).[27] In June 1930, "The Gland Murders" was published by *Amazing Detective Stories*. This tells how a Communist plotter spikes bottles of rare old Scotch with essence of murderer's gland. In this way, he strikes directly at the monied classes—the only ones who drink Scotch.

Those who drink fly into a murderous fury. They dispatch loved ones, friends, passerbys. Dr. Bird solves this disconcerting matter, aided by a bootlegger who has faith in the capitalistic system. The police mill around, bumping into walls.

Eight later stories appeared in *Astounding*, one in *Amazing Stories* (May 1931) and one in *Wonder Stories* (May 1932). The story probability never improved, nor did the rough-edged writing. The doctor remained a name on the page, hardly possessing a personal characteristic. But he had a most elastic imagination.

While Dr. Bird performed his gigantic ratiocinations, more interplanetary sword and romance eruped on Venus.

The Interstellar Patrol and Skylark had not, as yet, appreciably dented readers' desire for more Burroughs-like adventures. Those hard-boiled editors at *Argosy* had not published a Burroughs' fantasy since the 1925 "The Moon Men." In fact, no John Carter had appeared since the 1927 "The Master Mind of Mars" and the *Amazing Stories Annual* had got that.[28]

*Argosy* hungered for more interplanetary romance, and lacking contributions by Burroughs, turned elsewhere.

Elsewhere was Otis Adelbert Kline (1891-1946), a professional's professional. Kline provided a serial, a romance set on Venus, in the fine old tradition of menaces, escapes, weird new scenes and weird new creatures.

O.A. Kline, born in Chicago, did many things well: music, writing, business—he was talented in all. During his life, he was telephone lineman, manufacturing chemist, song writer, music publisher, free-lance motion picture comedy script writer. His work appeared in the first issue of *Weird Tales*, and he later contributed to *Argosy, Amazing Stories, Oriental Stories, Magic Carpet* and *Thrilling Wonder Stories*. That list is not exhaustive. His Venus/Mars serials, featuring swords and princesses, were published during 1929-1933. They contain strong Burroughs elements, for which he has received equal praise and condemnation. Closer inspection of his prose also reveals many Verne/Geisy elements which seem to have been overlooked.

During the late 1920s and 1930s, Kline operated a successful literary agency. He moved from Chicago to New York City in 1936, with his wife and three children. During the later part of his life, he suffered with recurrent heart problems, and died at Short Beach, Connecticut in 1946.[29]

Kline's first Venus novel, "The Planet of Peril," was published as a six-part serial (July 20 through August 24, 1929) in *Argosy All-Story Weekly*. The serial has a peculiar history. Originally submitted to *Weird Tales* in 1922, it arrived in Editor Edwin Baird's office simultaneously with Farley's "The Radio Man." Both dealt with Venus, both had been independently written, and both were rejected because of *Weird Tale's* heavy backlog. On Baird's recommendation, both manuscripts were submitted to *Argosy*. However, "The Radio Man" was mailed to the editor's home and thus, barely, beat out "The Planet of Peril."[30]

Whether the novel was remembered and recalled by *Argosy*, or how Kline came to resubmit it, is not known. Nonetheless, it was resubmitted and accepted. Its sequel—after a fashion—"The Prince of Peril," appeared as a six-part serial in *Argosy* (August 2 through September 6, 1930). Later followed "Buccaneers of Venus" (six parts, *Weird Tales*, November 1932 through April 1933). When reprinted this serial was retitled "The Port of Peril."[31]

"Buccaneers" was published by *Weird Tales*, rather than *Argosy* because *Argosy* had, at long last, closed a deal with Burroughs. And the first serial Burroughs produced was an adventure set on Venus. Venus, forevermore Venus. To return the manuscript and so compromise the diplomacy of years, was not to be considered; nor could the contractual matters be set aside, for a contract on a gram of paper binds with the force of tons. The least provocative solution was to return the "Buccaneers" to

Kline. Which explains why the series ended up in *Weird Tales*.[32]

Kline's Venus follows well-established Burroughs lines. Kline was a professional writer, accustomed to giving the editor precisely what he wanted, a sound business practice, if suspect artistically. The serial was an interplanetary romance in the familiar form, full of swords, princesses in danger, carefully webbed about by very odd races and situations that would raise the hair of a marble statue. The hero was reasonably competent, although no John Carter.

The hero, Robert Ellsmore Grandon, is one of those bored young men, after the manner of Jimmie Dale. He is kidnapped by a Dr. Morgan, who is deeply involved in psychic research, astral projection, telepathic communication, and such similar matters as inflame the credulity of believers.

These subjects lay down a solid if not precisely scientific basis for transporting Grandon from Earth to a distant planet. Dr. Morgan accomplishes this by personality transfer. He is able to switch personalities among bodies with the facility of a gambler skidding out cards. Already he has switched a Martian into an Earth body. Now he transfers that Martian into a Venusian body (the Venus personality coming to the Earth body, as is obvious). Now both the Martian and Grandon are sent to Venus, each going to a different side of the planet.

The upshot of this shell game, played with three different peas, is that Grandon moves into the body of Prince Thaddor of Uxpo, a rebellious kingdom in southern Reabon, an empire on Zarovia (also known as Venus). The Prince assumes Grandon's body.

These complications lay the groundwork for the majority of the Kline Venus and Mars novels. These follow the results of each personality switch. These who end up on Earth play no real part in the story line, eventually committing suicide or something to make sure they will not want to reoccupy their bodies. It is all fairly complex, merely because the 1930s were not satisfied by simple 1920s astral projections.

To begin on Venus: Grandon (as Prince Thaddor) wakes in the mines of the Reabonian Empire. He had aspired to the hand of Princess Vernia, ruler of Reabon and a short-tempered little minx. A suitor? Faaugh! To the Mines!

In short order, Grandon escapes to lead a full-scale revolt against Reabon. Being no military genius, he promptly gets his troops into a trap. While escaping from the debacle, he is able to snatch the princess out of the jaws of a gigantic reptile-amphibian with a lizardlike body and a snakelike head and neck. (The princess was there among the horrors because she was being abducted at the time.)

So early in the serial, you realize clearly that there will be no consistency or rhyme or reason to *this* adventure. So either close the magazine or discard your habits of rational thought.

Grandon/Thaddor's responsibility now is to get Vernia safely back home. Off they go, meeting ghastly menaces, large and small. Getting captured. Getting enslaved. Escaping. Crushing the oppressors. Believing each other dead. All these fine suspense devices used by Burroughs in so many other stories.

The conclusion is reasonably predictable. Grandon saves Vernia and her throne and, for reward, receives her hand. He becomes joint ruler with her, honored by the usual cheering multitude.

The story is a competent, professional recasting of familiar elements, precisely what the editor ordered. It is neither deeply felt nor intensely realized, for the form has grown old and custom has staled its charms. The characters seem rather cold fish. They react conventionally to each other and hardly at all to the wonders they pass through.

Descriptions of remarkable alien life abound. Descriptions of action are oddly remote, intensely concentrated, summaries, almost, of graphic scenes the writer did not trouble to visualize.

Suddenly (for example), Grandon is battling blood-sucking terribles. One has clamped onto him from behind:

> ...he gripped his knife firmly and plunged it again and again into the thing on his back, though with no apparent effect .... At last he found a vital spot, and just in time, for his strength was fast passing from the terrific loss of blood. ("The Planet of Peril")

No color. No dramatics. Gray bare words, requiring the reader to clothe these straining figures with blood and horror. The blood loss, by the way, is not bothering Grandon a few lines later.

Another scene: Grandon is trapped inside a glass bell jar from which the air is being evacuated: "Suddenly all went black before him and his head dropped forward. A moment later, he was revived by the sibilant inrush of air."

And with no serious after effects. Other men might bleed from ears and nose. Be weak. Stagger and have to lie down. But not Grandon—those physical responses would slow the story.

Or consider this instance of casual attack:

> But Grandon had scarcely taken fifty steps into the forest shadows when a heavy body fell upon his back from the branches above, knocking him to the ground. It was followed quickly by half a dozen more ... ("Buccaneers of Venus")

In the course of 150 words, Grandon is captured, tied up and freed, the sequence contributing nothing to the story but an interesting event.

Which is the purpose. Every two or three hundred words, up pops a new event. Or a new menace. Or a fresh conflict, assault, escape. The prose resembles a body of choppy water. Something is constantly happening but rarely does anything happen in much detail. Present the incident. Then on to the next incident. It is like reading a drum solo.

There is nothing intrinsically evil about this. Many people adore drum solos. The technique makes for a superficial, busy narrative, admirably suited to hold fast to the reader, after the manner of a giant clam. The *Argosy* serial parts ran about 18 pages each. On every page appeared some sort of surprise. It is sound craftsman's writing, technically aware, professionally adroit, emotionally sterile.

Kline is methodically supplying an exciting interplanetary romance that contains familiar, well-tested elements. His work has nothing to do with the romance of writing, whatever that is. We are speaking here of the business of publishing fiction. The two are not the same and never were. Any belief to the contrary lies in the mind of the unsophisticated reader. The editor knows better. He holds a key position in a commercial effort, and if he gets to thinking about romance per se he is shortly an unemployed editor, a negligible data point.

First and immediately, the commercial writer writes for the editor. He is not responsible to that wilderness of faces out there hovering back of the news stands. The editor buys the manuscript. The editor worries about pleasing those faces. That is his responsibility. The professional writer directs his efforts toward the editor and will write, if at all possible, to specific editorial requirements. If he does not happen to know those requirements, then the manuscript goes out accompanied by a little prayer and return postage. Or so it was in the 1930s. The advantage of an agent, such as Kline became, is that he takes some of the guesswork out of this vaguely irrational process. The less attuned the writer is to editorial requirements, the less probability that he can sell his product in the commercial market.

Self expression is wonderful. But, by definition, a commercial writer supports himself by writing material for sale to available markets.

The Kline novels, those thrilling things, are sound commercial fiction. They follow the Burroughs-Geisy-Farley kind of story, not as imitations but as continuations in kind. It is exactly the same circumstance as that which released a flood of barbarian fiction, during the late 1960s and 1970s, after the Conan series became popular.

"The Prince of Peril" briskly retraces the "Planet/Peril" story line. The "Prince" is the better serial, far tighter, more concentrated, packed with incident and imaginative awfuls. (Kline wrote it seven years later and the additional professional experience shows clearly.) The hero, Borgen Takkar, has been astrally exchanged with one Harry Thorne. (The whole involved matter would be told in the six part "Swordsmen of Mars" *Argosy*, January 7 through February 11, 1933).[33]

But to return to "The Prince of Peril." Takker gets tired of life on Earth and gets himself exchanged with Prince Zinlo of Venus. Through the balance of the serial, he tramps through the Venusian jungles with another fellow's princess. They encounter unending menaces: reptiles, cave apes, machine men and a man and woman who seem to possess 99 dozen bodies between them. In the end, our hero gets the other fellow's princess, legitimizing their long association, as it were.

"Buccaneers of Venus" (or "The Port of Peril," if you wish) is told in the third person, providing a welcome change of pace. Grandon's incomparable Vernia gets stolen by pirates and he has a terrible time getting her back. The story ripples brightly, being all shallows, and Grandon is rather more inefficient than is conducive to long life on Venus.

Three months pass.

It is the twilight of the interplanetary romance, and through the calm, gray, featureless light Ray Cummings offers a new series to the readers of *Argosy*. It will be a brief series, two serials only, set on Mercury, since Venus and Mars were heavily overworked.

The first was the three-part serial "Tama of the Light Country" (December 13 through 27, 1930). Six months later appeared "Tama, Princess of Mercury" (four parts, June 27 through July 18, 1931).

The Tama serials are slight wisps, giving the irresistible impression of your 4-year old daughter wearing mother's shoes and sweater. Given Cummings' predilection for H.G. Wells, you might suspect that the series derives from the Wells' novel *The Wonderful Visit* (1895). This concerns an angel who arrives gloriously, winged and innocent, at an English village, and ends up with her wings clipped, wearing an 1890 dress. The satire is intense enough to melt rocks.

"Tama" borrows lightly from Wells' work, eliminating the realistic scene, the symbolism, the lucid prose and most of the outrage. The wing theme is retained, as it is good theatre.

Tama is a native of Mercury, a planet not usually associated with Heaven. Because the world keeps one face to the Sun, its climate is rigorous. The sun-side is known as the Fire Country. The other side freezes and is called the Cold Country. In both these sides live a scattering of hostile natives and criminals escaped from the Light Country.

The Light Country is a slim belt of light, mild temperatures and constant illumination which encircles the planet. In this area, the women are all born with wings. It is a freak of heredity you will not find again soon; otherwise they seem entirely human. After the ladies marry and settle down, their wings are clipped by the dour, insensitive, heavy-spirited men. They lack wings. Why should women differ? Down from the clouds and into the kitchen. No fluttering around *my* house.

These inequities enrage the virgins (that is, unclipped, unmarried girls), a politically unstable group. Under the leadership of Tama, they cry revolt. As well they should.

Faced by a falling birthrate and rebellious women, the Mercurian leaders make a sensible decision. They will spaceship to Earth and steal a cargo of women. Earth-girls have no wings and will be far more tractable.

Mercurian leaders are much out of touch.

The serial begins in Maine in mystery. Girls' camps there have been raided and young beauties spirited away. In the sky, green-blue flashes, glimpses of UFOs. What can this uproar mean? Reporter Jack Dean comes to investigate and is soon incredulously examining the bodies of a gray-faced man and a slight woman with wings, both obviously extraterrestrials.

To deal with this problem, spaceships are needed and, at this instant, at the Bolton Metal Industries, Trenton, New Jersey, preparations are underway to test the Bolton Cube. This is a large, square spacecraft, the first

*Argosy*, December 13, 1930. The interplanetary romance continued into the 1930s. It is represented here by the winged Tama, heroine of a serial pair that oscillate wildly between Earth and Venus.

ship of space that is not streamlined.

Dr. Norton Grenfall, a powerful man of the Scientist-Genius type, is working on the Cube. Laboring with him is Rowena Palisse, a very tall woman with the "regal aspect of a Nordic queen." Rowena has a personal interest in spaceflight, for her brother, Guy, vanished some ten years prior while attempting to reach the moon.

The Cube functions flawlessly during its first flight test. Thus is avoided the eight to twelve years of ground and flight test that NASA imagines necessary for a man-rated flight vehicle. While swooping around the Earth, the Cube recovers an orbiting projectile. It contains a written warning from Guy Palisse.

Guy writes that he headed for the moon and ended up on Mercury. Forgot to wind his compass, most likely. In the Light Country, he discovered a civilized race that, as usual, was lavishly supplied with artifacts developed by ancient, if forgotten, science. As a result (as usual), they are equipped with a queer mixture of weapons—heat rays emitting blue-green flashes, and swords, and flying ships.

An evil fellow, Roc, has been conspiring with his evil father, Croat (a banished outlaw) to conquer the Light Country. As a first step, they must get the women under control. To do this, Roc plans what, in other years, would be called a "Night of Long Knives." His followers intend to pounce upon all girls over sixteen and cut off their wings. The hellish plot leaks and Tama, our darling, learns of it.

Tama, leader of the winged virgin movement, is at this time twenty years old, five feet tall, and weighs 65 pounds. Dark eyed and "elfin of face," she has a wing-spread of ten feet. The crimson wing feathers contrast wonderfully with her long black hair. Guy Palisse thinks of her as a Joan of Arc type.

Tama's brother, Toh, closely resembles her, although without wings. He comes slipping to Guy one evening to tell him that Tama needs help.

No American refuses a distressed lady, and shortly, Guy is mixed deeply into the rebellion, has punched Roc heavily in the head, and has ended in the company of hundreds of winged women out in the sticks. They are surrounded by Roc's legions, sullen to a man.

Guy learns that Father Croat is flying off to Earth to collect wives. In an effort to warn his mother planet of this danger, Guy scribbles down the story that has occupied the core of this serial and fires it off in a rocket. Its subsequent history we have already learned.

Back in Earth orbit, Jack Dean and Rowena read the message. Overcome by the wonder of it all, they wander out by the airlock and get engaged. That guarantees that she will be kidnapped by Croat, for no writer creates a set-up like this without a purpose. And sure enough . . . .

Rowena is kidnapped by Croat. He desires her tall regal beauty. Unfortunately for him, the kidnapping is of short duration. Jack comes raging after. There is a rousing fight in spacesuits, tumbling all over orbital vacuum, 400,000 feet above the Earth, and Croat is killed. Before the Mercurians can avenge his death, Tama, Guy and company leap from concealment behind bales, and the ship is theirs.

Then the Cube flies up, collects them all, and home they go.

"Tama of the Light Country" is literally two stories in one. It contains two heroes, two heroines, two villains, two spaceships. The Siamese-twin nature of the story suggests that the Introductory frame expanded beyond Cummings' control and devoured large portions of what was planned as the central narrative, Guy's letter. The appearance of Tama, et al, at the conclusion is painfully forced. But she is a nice girl and we would deny her nothing.

The second serial, "Tama, Princess of Mercury," continues as if there had been no break in the action. Bad old Roc creeps down to Earth, kidnapping Tama, Rowena and another cast member. All the characters immediately pile into the Cube and flash off after Roc. But already his sadistic hordes sweep howling into the Light Country.

From this point, we move directly into another science-fantasy war epic. They battle with "crossing rays, of blasting withering heat." They fall limply from heights, escape from death, indulge in deadly struggles. After amazing adventures most remarkable, Roc's forces are annihilated. He is most thoroughly killed. And Tama marries Guy, beginning a new day of peace, prosperity and the tradition of wives with wings.

## 17—

Close the old magazines and look away.

It seems long ago. The moon shone still untouched. Mars glowed with distant possibilities.

If, on Earth, the cities cluttered, self-soiled, fierce with noisy energy, we felt intuitively that, on the other side of the sky, a different freedom waited.

Out there, glory. Possibly, love. Most certainly exertions of a quality richer than those devoted to squeezing nickles from the flint flanks of commerce.

You look out across interplanetary space to the fat, white shining that is Venus, the tinged fleck that is Mars. Or look beyond to Sirius and, on frosty evenings, see Orion spread in mid-stride, as Edmond Hamilton saw him in that Pennsylvania sky, the wind's blade on the face, the heart rising with a cold and solitary joy.

Out along the Milky Way, in that quadrant, or perhaps that one, other eyes look out toward you. Other minds wonder of your face. There is no way to travel to them, yet. Even *Argosy All-Story Weekly* can give no detailed procedure for stripping you from Earth, until the luminous blue globe arcs shrinking away beneath you and, from far miles, come the boom of suns.

There is, at last, always this. The sense of something firm and real existing now and better than we have. Fantasy fiction reaches toward that something. As fiction, it is often shallow, too frequently constructed by rote, repetitive, superficial. It may lack the presence of reality, or it may stumble paragraph to paragraph, unconvincing, inept, lamentable.

Or it may not. It may burn with scented flame, coloring the spirit and lifting it gloriously. For that moment's freedom, much can be excused. The fiction does bear the weight of something more. The Green Star still does call, the sword and princess serial still does promise something more. Perhaps, after all, something waits that is better than we know.

You can almost see it.

You can feel it to your bone.

Mars has a pink sky and treadmarks streak the surface of the moon, and lens caps lie on the stones of Venus. But beyond these, out there, waits glory and love. On a freezing night, your eye seeks out the Pleiades.

# Afterword

The magazines changed and again changed, plastic stuff in the grip of time. They altered physically. You could see it happen, the covers moving from the sentimental constructs of 1905 to rudimentary action and suspense, and illustrations slowly creeping between the covers.

The number of pages trembled between 192 and 208, not including fat pads of advertising fore and aft. Prices ranged from 10¢ to 20¢. The War To End Wars scared prices upward by perhaps a nickel, even as the page count began that inexorable shrinkage to 128, a standard generally maintained into the 1930s.

Specialized publications spun from the general fiction magazines. Where once the family magazine spread its complex web of adventure, mystery, humor, love, western scene, and fantasy, now each category splintered off on its own, and the newsstand, itself, became a web whose strands were *Adventure, Weird Tales, Love Stories, Detective Story Magazine, Sea Stories, Western Story Magazine.* In each of these, letters columns appeared, and readers' clubs, and more, many more series characters.

Less apparent change moved its secret way through these pages, currents intricately interacting beneath the bright surface of the stream. For evolution, once begun, moves in terrible swift ways. During the 'Teens and 'Twenties, both adventure and mystery fiction branched busily, adding new story types like buds along the bough.

That familiar adventure, the quest to far places expanded beyond frontier violence and striving in the Wild West. It turned to Africa and Tibet. It stretched to the Poles and hurled outward toward the planets and the stars. Later it would routinely reach into the future and into the past.

Technology enabled many of these journeys. From the magnified clipper ships and balloons of the dime novels grew space ships, sustained by advanced science, flinging the traveler breathlessly into the void behind the sky. Other travelers, less mechanically inclined, projected their egos or beamed their bodies through space. All came to similar destinations out among the rainbow riot of planets. Out there waited worlds for Earthmen to conquer, with princesses for the winning, glory and social recognition for the thirsty heart, and danger enough for a generation of series.

These adventurers were mighty men, magnificently muscled, lean and agile. They slew and loved and accomplished in alien cultures among strange entities. Just as they slew and loved and accomplished among lost races out there behind the Earth's jungles. For much of the fiction played variations on the lost city, lost civilization theme. Only the location of this far place, and the technique of getting there, varied much. John Carter, Tarzan and Edgar Rice Burroughs opened the way and other writers trampled out a highway.

The princess and sword story thrust out a line of adventurers besieged by monsters and sorcery, while the cutlery ran red. Robert Howard took that step from the interplanetary romance to the occult-touched adventure. He drew, in part, from past reading in *Adventure* and *Weird Tales* and his barbarian imaginings cast a hundred reflections on 1980 paperback racks.

As adventure fiction was modified by variation, so mystery and detective fiction was modified by similar forces. Before the 1900s, the dime novels had presented the urban detective, the darling of the police, the dread of criminals. Sherlock Holmes had brought distinction to the private investigator, a solitary intelligence solacing himself with human problems. Then Dr. Thorndyke added the rigors of medicine and law to the heady stuff of science. From that elixir leaped the scientific detective. The emphasis in these gloriously gadgety stories swiftly turned from professional disciplines to the raw wonders of laboratory apparatus. The story type died in the grip of gadgets. But from it sprang a long line of doctor and professor detectives, their intelligence lightly dusted with scientific fact.

About the same time that Thorndyke began his work, the occult detective rose from the high example of John Silence. Occult detection differed from scientific detection by a studied ambiguity of technique and a certain incorporeity of antagonist. The occultist practiced his profession as an art form. He dealt with a different reality, although one fixed, after all, by firm laws. Semi-Dual wove his wonders along that shifting gray interface between this reality and the other. Jules de Grandin struck at material manifestations of the supernatural. But reason guided both men.

Themes and variations winding in a silent fugue through these early magazines. Each series character adds his trace and falls away in exhaustion, while new characters rise. Thus justice figures and jungle men, occult detectives and cowboys, bent heroes and humorous inventors and leaders of future wars. Their unique story types shuttle busily across the page, a confusion of faces.

Among these, we find that most satisfactory of character types, the criminal hero met earlier in Volume I, of this series: *Glory Figures*. Already established in popular literature before 1900, the criminal lead would develop with explosive force through the magazines of the 1920s.

The series criminal hero, was a child of the dime novels and story papers, both English, American and French. His life was spent furthering plots which showed a distressing tendency to come unstuck in the last chapter. Nonetheless he persevered. At times, he was an emperor of crime, shaking the international structure. At other times, he appeared as a mastermind of crime, organizing armies of underlings to loot the world.

Other criminal heroes contented themselves with less ostentatious activity—a quiet murder, an almost bloodless series of thefts, an amiable sequence of bunko games.

Fu Manchu and Mr. Chang, Fantomas and Black Star and Rafferty. Thubway Tham, Blue Jean Billy, The White Rook and The Ringer.

In the next volume, we will meet these, and a shining stream of others— The people from the dark side, who gave the mystery-adventure story its familiar form.

# Notes

## Chapter I—*Willemite Fluorescing*

[1]Nick Carter, "A Cry for Help," New Magnet Library No. 1042. The story was originally published in 1904.

[2]Baroness Orczy, *The Man in the Corner*, Norton, 1966, Chapter 1.

[3]E.F. Bleiler, Editor, *Best Thinking Machine Stories*, Dover Publications, 1973, p. vi.

[4]Jacques Futrelle, "The Case of the Mysterious Weapon," *Ellery Queen's Mystery Magazine*, Oct. 1950, pp. 105-106.

[5]Futrelle, "The Mystery of the Silver Box," as quoted in an article by Link Hullar, "The Thinking Machine," *Xenophile*, No. 30, p. 133.

[6]A bibliographic history of the Thinking Machine stories was published in the *Ellery Queen's Mystery Magazine*, Oct. 1950, pp. 104-105.

[7]Hullar, *op. cit., p. 133.*

[8]*Ellery Queen's Mystery Magazine*, "The Queen's Quorum," August 1948, p. 89.

[9]Norman Donaldson, *In Search of Dr. Thorndyke*, Bowling Green University Popular Press, 1971.

[10]R. Austin Freeman as quoted in "The Queen's Quorum," *Ellery Queen's Mystery Magazine*, Nov. 1949, p. 99.

[11]Essentially all data cited here were provided by David Arends and J. Randolph Cox.

[12]Anonymous, "The Scientific Detective," *Dime Detective,* Oct. 1, 1933, p. 126.

[13]Reeve, "How Writers Make Good," *Writer's Digest*, August 1930, p. 44.

[14]Sam Moskowitz, "Scientific Detectives," p. 356, an article in the *Encyclopedia of Mystery and Detection*, edited by Chris Steinbrunner and Otto Penzler, McGraw-Hill Book Co., 1976.

[15]Evidence strongly suggests that these stories were published in *Country Gentleman*; however, the magazines, themselves, have not been examined and the matter remains unconfirmed.

[16]Stanley J. Kunitz and Howard Haycraft, Editors, *Twentieth Century Authors,* H.W. Wilson Co., 1942, p. 1157.

[17]J. Randolph Cox, "A Reading of Reeve: Some Thoughts on the Creator of Craig Kennedy," *The Armchair Detective*, Vol. XI, Jan. 1978, p. 31. This article contains a detailed bibliography and a wealth of related information.

[18]Robert A.W. Lowndes, "The Unique Mystery Magazine: Hugo Gernsback's *Scientific Detective Monthly,* Part I," *The Armchair Detective*, Winter 1981, Vol. 14, No. 1, p. 25; see also Footnote No. 6, p. 30, concerning "The Mystery of The Bulawayo Diamond." Lowndes' superb article appears in five consecutive issues of TAD, Vol. 14, No. 1, through Vol. 15, No. 1.

[19]Ernest Poate, "Phantom Footsteps," *Detective Story Magazine*, March 23, 1920, Chap. X, p. 28.

[20]Winston Dawson, "Some Thoughts on Ray Cummings," *Xenophile*, No. 30, March 1977, p. 3. This article gives a more detailed summary of "The Thought Girl."

[21]It is suspected that Bertram Royal was the pseudonym of Florence Mae Pettee.

Similar stylistic incoherencies, bravely flourished, pepper her work. She published several serials in 1924-1925 issues of *Flynn's*.

# Chapter II—*Strange Days*

[1]Algernon Blackwood, *John Silence*, 1962, The Richards Press, London. This book includes the "Author's Note to the 1942 Edition" from which quotation is drawn.

[2]*Ibid.*

[3]The magazine publication sequence cited here follows that given in Sam Moskowitz's biographical article, "William Hope Hodgson," appearing on pp. 80-85 of *Out of the Storm, Uncollected Fantasies by William Hope Hodgson*, Grant, 1975. A later paperback version of this work omits the biography.

[4]William Hope Hodgson, *Carnacki the Ghost-Finder*, Mycroft and Moran, 1947. This collection contains nine Carnacki stories. An edition was also published in 1913 bearing the same title but containing only *The Idler* and the *New Magazine* stories, six in all; the publisher was Nash, London, who had also published *John Silence*.

[5]Editorial introduction to "The Opposing Venus," *Argosy*, Oct. 13, 1923, p. 1.

[6]*Ibid. p. 1.*

[7]William J. Clark, "The Occult Detector by J.U. Giesy and Junius B. Smith," *Xenophile*, No. 17, Vol. II, No. 5, Sept. 1975, p. 55. This article provides a detailed check list of the Semi-Dual stories. The list was amended by Winston Dawson (*Xenophile* No. 30, no volume citation, March 1977), p. 138. These amendments identify "The Stars Were Looking" (*Top Notch*, July 1, 1918) and a story titled "The Web of Circumstance," which may have appeared in the November 1916 *All-Around* magazine. The publication has not been located to confirm presence of the story.

[8]Fragmentary biographical material concerning Giesy may be found in *Popular*, May 1917; *People's*, January 25, 1918; *Argosy*, Feb. 14, 1931. A biographic sketch of Smith was published in the Feb. 21, 1931 *Argosy*. This contains almost no useful information, most of the space being devoted to technical astrological data pertaining to Smith. Other information may have appeared in earlier, unexamined magazines.

[9]McNeil did all interiors for *Argosy* during this period. From the pages, the familiar Oz faces look out, caught in contemporary clothing and situations of violence, looking rueful and dissatisfied with their lot.

[10]A chronological listing of the de Grandin stories appears in issues No. 13 and 15 of *Startling Mystery Stories,* a reprint digest magazine, dated, respectively, Summer 1969, Vol. 3, No. 1, and Spring 1970, Vol. 3, No. 3. An alphabetical listing of all Seabury Quinn's stories, including anthology appearances, is given as end material in the collection *Is the Devil a Gentleman?* Mirage, 1970.

[11]The Popular Library paperback series contains *The Adventures of Jules de Grandin* (Introduction by Lin Carter); *The Casebook of __ (*Introduction by Robert Lowndes); *The Skeleton Closet of __* (Introduction by Manly Wade Wellman); *The Hellfire Files of __; The Horror Chambers of __;* and *The Devil's Bride*. Particular note should be taken of the informative "Afterwords" by Robert Weinberg, which appear at the end of each volume.

[12]Lin Carter's "Introduction" to the Popular Library edition of *The Adventures of Jules de Grandin* provides much material concerning Seabury Quinn.

[13]The portraits of de Grandin and Trowbridge, which first appeared in the September 1937 *Weird Tales*, are perfect representatives of the characters. Most regrettably, both sketches appear to have been lightly adapted from the faces appearing in a laxative advertisement of late 1936. A commentary and comparison of the pictures is given in Chet Williamson's article "The Case of the Moonlighting Physicians," *The Weird Tales Collector*, No. 6, 1980, pp. 14-15.

[14]Harrisonville had a tendency to grow increasingly like New York City. As the series continued, the distinction blurred and merged. The town was supposed to be located an hour away from New York City by car.

[15]L. Sprague de Camp, *The Conan Reader*, Mirage, 1968, Chap. 13, "An Exegesis of Howard's Hyborian Tales," pp. 96-97, discusses Howard's reading and some of the literary influences that touched him. De Camp mentions the particular impact of the 1920s *Adventure* magazine. The longer Howard wrote, the less visible these influences became. Those Haggard-Burroughs scenes, so prominent in parts of his 1930 work, have vanished by 1936, assimilated almost without trace.

[16]The Centaur Press, that excellent and lamented paperback reprint series, separated *Red Shadows* into three smaller paperbacks: *The Moon of Skulls* (1969), *The Hand of Kane* (1970), and *Solomon Kane* (1971).

[17]As quoted in *Imaginary Worlds*, Ballentine Books, 1973, by Lin Carter (Chapter 3, p. 64).

[18]*King Kull*, edited by Glenn Lord (Lancer, 1967), contains about one-third of Howard's lengthy, detailed historical treatment of his imaginary region. The complete article, titled "The Hyborian Age," may be found in *Skull-Face and Others*, first published by Arkham House, 1946, reprinted 1974 by Neville Spearman Ltd., as the *Skull-Face Omnibus*.

[19]The *King Kull* paperback (Lancer) provides a brief summary of Kull's life after he leaves Atlantis. From this information, the text is drawn.

# Chapter III—*Bumudemutumuro*

[1]Richard A. Lupoff, *Edgar Rice Burroughs: Master of Adventure*, New York: Ace Publishing Company (1968), Chap. XV. "Ancestors of Tarzan," p. 223. This quotes correspondence between Burroughs and Professor Altrocchi (Berkeley University) concerning Tarzan's fictional origins. As far as Burroughs knew, the major influences were Kipling's *Jungle Book*, the story of Romulus and Remus, and an unidentified book telling of a ship-wrecked sailor adopted by great apes. Lupoff presents strong evidence that this latter book was the 1888 *Captured by Apes*, written by Harry Prentice. Lupoff's discussion is thoroughly interesting and the conclusions are as specific as we are likely to get.

[2]Philip Jose Farmer, *Lord Tyger*, New York: Doubleday (1970) tells how a crazy millionaire duplicated the Tarzan story—the young boy, the apes, the isolated environment; he used, however, all the current scientific additions to assure that the boy grew to superhuman manhood, rather than becoming a feral thing, unable to talk or think. Human contacts are essential in infancy and early childhood. The infant must receive a steady stream of physical and psychological contacts. Lack of these results in severe preceptive and intellectual aberrations, particularly in language and abstract thinking.

[3]Lupoff and others mention that *Under the Moons of Mars* spun itself from Burroughs' day dreaming. But its development may be described in different terms. Since creative material was involved, and a complex narrative was detailed, Burroughs' state may be more exactly termed a pre-cognitive reverie. This is a specific stage in the creative process, during which materials from unconscious sources are digested and arranged in terms suitable for use by the conscious mind. It is essentially an unstructured interlude, part images, part conscious thought, part perceived emotion. It is a more complex state than day dreaming, which is concerned with immediate wish fulfillment images. The form taken by this creative process apparently startled Burroughs, who had no reason to look upon himself as an artist, at this time. "Under the Moons of Mars" was originally signed "Normal Bean" to indicate the writer's sanity. An editor considerably changed the pseudonym to "Norman Bean."

[4]The renunciation scene was a stock device in popular literature. It was used routinely in magazines, books, plays, boy's papers for generations. By 1905, it had been cliche long enough to be used in one of A.A. Milne's parodies for *Punch*. The situation there is that the hero, not realizing that the heroine loves him, gives up his enormous wealth to benefit her and keep her comfortable forever. In other works, the

situation is often presented in reverse: the heroine is to marry a man she does not love because this, in various incredible ways, benefits the hero.

[5]Sam Moskowitz, "A History of the Scientific Romances in the Munsey Magazines, 1912-1920," *Under the Moons of Mars*, New York: Holt, Rinehart, Winston (1970), p. 428. Moskowitz states that Jane was actually murdered in the *Red Book* serial. Tarzan sees her dead. There is no burnt body obfuscation, as was later introduced into the book.

[6]A complete manuscript of *Tarzan and the Madman* was found after Burroughs' death. It was published in 1964 by the Canaveral Press as a book and received no magazine publication.

[7]Tarzan and such other nature heroes as Whistling Dan Barry characteristically make little distinction between animals and men. They do view life as if it were ranked in steps of increasing superiority, man occupying the summit. Tarzan views life in the mass, seeing in it a tissue of feeling, thinking individuals. Superiority is determined by excellence of mind and body. Whether you are an ape, mule, elephant or man is not material. This point of view is much facilitated by Burroughs' studied humanization of the series' animals (another point in common with *Jungle Stories*). Often the Burroughs animals seem only human beings wrapped in a different skin.

[8]Farmer, *op. cit.*, suggest that Tarzan's weight was 230 pounds.

[9]As readers were quick to point out, polar bears are not found at the South Pole. Nor are lost cities. Both appear in the Polaris series and neither impairs the vigor of the story.

[10]Maurice Horn, "The Magic of Burne Hogarth," *Tarzan of the Apes* (the novel recreated in illustrations) by Burne Hogarth (New York: Watson-Guptill Publications, 1972), p. 6.

[11]W.H. Desmond, "Noble, Yet Savage, Yet Pure," Odyssey No. 5, *Ka-Zar the Great* (Melrose Highlands, MA: Odyssey Publications, 1976), pp. 2-3. This brief survey of Tarzan imitators provides information concerning the first issue of *Jungle Stories*, a magazine difficult to find, and provides many interesting magazine cover reproductions.

[12]John Peter Drummond, "Fane of the Python Priestess," *Jungle Stories*, No. 5, Vol. 10 (Winter 1953-1954), p. 4.

[13]John Peter Drummond, "The Monster of Voodoo Isle," *Jungle Stories*, Vol. 3, No. 6 (Spring 1946), p. 7.

[14]Names of the actual writers are not known, although Robert Turner, a fine mystery story writer, is known to have done the February 1943 "Voodoo Slaves for the Devil's Daughter"; the story was reprinted in the Fall 1950 issue of *Jungle Stories*. Refer to a group of letters by Robert Turner printed in "Letters," *Xenophile* Vol. III, No. 1 (September 1976), pp. 74-75.

[15]Sheena entered the pulps from the comic books. Her first appearance was in *Sheena, Queen of the Jungle*, No. 1 (Spring 1942). The publisher, Fiction House, also issued the pulp magazine.

# Influence

[1]Edmund Wilson, *The Twenties* (New York: Farrar, Straus and Giroux, 1975), pp. 425-426.

# Chapter IV—*Shadows of Other Suns*

[1]Harry Bates, "Editorial Number One," p. xii of *A Requiem for Astounding* (Chicago: Advent Publishers, 1970). Mr. Bates' remarks are selected from a long

paragraph of good sense. A close reading of his editorial is recommended to cleanse the mind of accumulated foolishness.

[2]A brief discussion of some of the *Frank Reade* dime novels may be found in the first volume of this series: *Glory Figures*, Chapter II, Section 6.

[3]Sam Moskowitz, "A History of 'The Scientific Romance' In the Munsey Magazines, 1912-1920," *Under the Moons of Mars* (New York: Holt, Rinehart, Winston, 1970), p. 372.

[4]H.G. Wells, *Seven Famous Novels* (New York: Knopf, 1934), p. viii.

[5]Richard Hauer Costa, *H.G. Wells* (New York: Twayne Publishers Inc., 1967), p. 113.

[6]Richard A. Lupoff, *Edgar Rice Burroughs: Master of Adventure* (New York: Ace Books, Inc., 1965), Chapter III. Lupoff cites the 1894 *A Journey in Other Worlds* by John Jacob Astor; in this story, the Terrestrial Axis Straightening Company has been formed to alter the Earth's tilt from 23 degrees to 11 degrees.

[7]*Lt. Gulliver Jones* was later published as *Gulliver of Mars* (New York: Ace Books, Inc., no date, No. 30600). "The War of the Worlds" was first published as a serial in *Pearson's Magazine*, April through December, 1897.

[8]Moskowitz, *op. cit.,* p. 291.

[9]Frank Belknap as quoted from the article titled "Kline vs. Burroughs Discussions," *OAK Leaves*, No. 7, Spring 1972, p. 4.

[10]Polaris also serves Lester Dent (the primary Doc Savage author) with the root situation in "Genius Jones" (six-part serial, *Argosy*, Nov. 28, 1937, through January 1, 1938. Jones, the son of an odd scientist, is raised isolated in the Arctic regions. He is then abruptly plunged into New York City with instructions to give away thousands of dollars. The result is a brightly comic serial, very merry. For an analysis and discussion, refer to "The Argosy Novels," by Robert Sampson, pp. 45-49, *The Man Behind Doc Savage* (Illinois: Weinberg, 1974); this booklet is a collection of essays about Lester Dent and his work and was edited by Robert Weinberg.

[11]Doc Savage exercised rigorously two hours a day, working each muscle of his body, while, at the same time, solving painful intellectual problems, and testing each of his senses with special devices. A superman's life is hard.

[12]A selection from "Palos" is included in Sam Moskowitz's *Under the Moons of Mars*, pp. 100-124.

[13]The body problem is solved. However, it leaves Croft stuck with the brain of a mental defective, whose structural deficiencies, in our everyday world, could not be overridden by the most enterprising soul. Dr. Giesy blandly glides over this matter and rages onward.

[14]Refer to McCay's *Dreams of the Rarebit Fiend* (New York: Dover, 1973). This book reprints early pages of McCay's superb comic series. No home can count itself civilized without this enchanting—and unfortunately slim—collection.

[15]Obituary, New York *Times*, Oct. 18, 1963, p. 31.

[16]Thomas Sheridan, review of *The Radio Man*, in *Fantasy Review*, Feb.-March 1949, p. 25.

[17]Otis A. Kline in a letter to Dr. I. Howard, reprinted in *OAK Leaves* No. 1, Fall 1970, p. 6. Also refer to Robert Weinberg's *The Weird Tales Story* (Oregon: FAX Publishers, 1977).

[18]Michael Ashley, *The History of the Science Fiction Magazine, Vol. 1* (1926-1935). (Chicago: Henry Regnery, 1976), p. 20.

[19]Leigh Brackett in "Fifty Years of Wonder," *The Best of Edmond Hamilton* (New York: Ballentine, 1977), p. xi.

[20]*Ibid.*, p. 378. In the "Afterword" of this book, Edmond Hamilton describes how the idea for the Interstellar Patrol came to him.

[21]Alva Rogers, *A Requiem for Astounding* (Chicago: Advent, 1964), p. 2.

[22]*Ibid.*

[23]Mark R. Hillegas, *The Future as Nightmare: H.G. Wells and the Anti-Utopians* (New York: Oxford, 1967), p. 152.

[24]Hillegas, *Ibid.*, Chapter IV contains an interesting discussion of how Wells and

others anticipated the supplanting of our present political and social forms by Utopia.

25Robert C. Dille, Editor, *The Collected Works of Buck Rogers in the 25th Century* (New York: Chelsea House, 1969). This collection of early Buck Rogers comic strips and Sunday pages begins with a richly evocative "Preface" by Ray Bradbury, "Buck Rogers in Apollo Year 1." Bradbury's comments glow so warmly that you can hardly believe they were generated by the crudely presented comic.

26A similar bibliographic listing was prepared by Lt. (Ret.) Herman R. Jacks and published in *Startling Mystery Stories* No. 13, Summer 1969, pp. 114-115.

27Michael Ashley, *The Complete Index to Astounding/Analog* (Oak Forest, IL: Robert Weinberg, 1981), p. 125. This listing cites all Dr. Bird's appearances in *Astounding Stories of Super Science.*

28*Argosy* had bargained furiously with Burroughs for about three years (1929-1931), according to Sam Moskowitz. Refer to his article, "The OAK-ERB Feud," *OAK Leaves* #4, Summer 1971.

29Bibliographical information concerning Kline is provided through various issues of David Anthony Kraft's *OAK Leaves,* a publication devoted to that writer's works.

30Darrell C. Richardson, quoted in "Burroughs, Kline, and Farley," *OAK Leaves,* No. 7, Spring 1972, p. 5.

31Donald M. Grant published the first-edition hardback of *The Port of Peril.* The "Peril" series was also reprinted in the early 1960s by Ace Books: *Planet of Peril* (F-211); *Prince of Peril* (F-259); and *The Port of Peril* (F-294). Portions of the texts were severely edited. The internal chronology of the stories was extensively reworked and contain a reference to Burroughs not included in Kline's original serials. An elaborate time-discontinuity explanation is provided to account for why the present Venus and Mars do not conform to Kline's descriptions.

32Moskowitz, "The OAK-ERB Feud," *OAK Leaves,* No. 7, Spring 1972, p. 9.

33The Mars series continued with publication of the seven-part serial, "The Outlaws of Mars" (Nov. 25, 1933, through Jan. 6, 1934) in *Argosy.* The hero was Jerry Morgan, nephew of Dr. Richard Morgan, who shuffled these many personalities from one body to the other. Jerry, needless to say, was briskly sent off to Mars where he won himself a princess.

# Bibliography

Anonymous, "The Scientific Detective," *Dime Detective,* Vol. 8, No. 2 (Oct 1, 1933).

Arnold, Edwin L. *Gulliver of Mars.* New York: Ace Books, undated (No. 30600).

Ashley, Michael. *The Complete Index to Astounding/Analog.* Oak Forest, IL: Robert Weinberg Pubs. 1981.

——*The History of the Science Fiction Magazine, Vol. 1: 1926-1935.* Chicago: Henry Regnery Co., 1974.

Balmer, Edwin and William MacHarg. *The Achievements of Luther Trant.* Boston: Small, Maynard, 1910.

Bates, Harry. "Editorial Number One." *A Requiem for Astounding.* Chicago: Advent, 1970.

Blackwood, Algernon. *The Empty House.* New York: Donald C. Vaughan, 1915.

——*John Silence, Five Stories.* London: Richards Press, 1962.

——*Strange Stories.* London: William Heinemann, 1929.

——*Tales of the Mysterious and Macabre.* London: Spring Books, 1967.

——*Tales of the Uncanny and Supernatural.* London: Spring Books, undated.

Brackett, Leigh. "Fifty Years of Wonder." *The Best of Edmond Hamilton.* New York: Ballentine, 1977.

Burroughs, Edgar Rice. *Jungle Tales of Tarzan.* New York: Ace, undated (F-206).

——*A Princess of Mars.* New York: Ballentine, 1963.

——*Tarzan of the Apes.* New York: Ballentine, 1963.

Carter, Lin. *Imaginary Worlds.* New York: Ballentine, 1973.

Cazadesus. C.E., Jr. "ERB—A Brief American Bibliography," *ERB-dom* No. 39, Oct. 1970.

Chester, William L. *Hawk of the Wilderness.* New York: Ace, undated (G-586).

Christensen, Peter. "William Hope Hodgson, Carnacki the Ghost-Finder." *The Armchair Detective,* Vol. 12, No. 2 (Spring 1979).

Clark, William J. "The Occult Detector by J.U. Giesy and Junius B. Smith." *Xenophile,* No. 17, Vol. II, No. 5 (Sept. 1975).

Cockcroft, T.G.L. *Index to the Weird Fiction Magazines.* Lower Hutt, New Zealand, 1962.

Cook, Michael L. *Monthly Murders.* Westport, CT: Greenwood Press, 1982.

Costa, Richard Haner. *H.G. Wells.* New York: Twayne, 1967.

Cox, J. Randolph. "A Reading of Reeve: Some Thoughts on the Creator of Craig Kennedy." *The Armchair Detective,* Vol. XI, No. 1 (Jan. 1978).

Cummings, Ray. *The Princess of the Atom.* New York: Avon, 1950.

Dawson, Winston. "Some Thoughts on Ray Cummings." *Xenophile* No. 30 (March 1977).

deCamp, L. Sprague. "An Exegesis of Howard's Hyborian Tales." *The Conan Reader.* Baltimore: Mirage, 1968.

Desmond, W.H. "Noble, Yet Savage, Yet Pure." *Ka-Zar the Great* (Odyssey Reprint No. 5). Melrose Highlands, MA: Odyssey, 1976.

Dille, Robert C. Editor. *The Collected Works of Buck Rogers in the 25th Century.* New York: Chelsea House, 1969.

Donaldson, Norman. *In Search of Dr. Thorndyke, The Story of R. Austin Freeman's Great Scientific Investigator and His Career.* Bowling Green, OH: Popular Press, 1971.

Farley, Ralph Milne. *The Radio Beasts*. New York: Ace, undated (F-304).

Farmer, Philip Jose. *Lord Tyger*. New York: Doubleday, 1970.

——*Tarzan Alive, A Definitive Biography of Lord Graystroke*. New York: Doubleday, 1972.

Freeman, R. Austin. *As a Thief in the Night*. New York: Dodd, Mead, 1928.

——*The Best Dr. Thorndyke Detective Stories*. New York: Dover, 1973.

——*The Dr. Thorndyke Omnibus*. New York: Dodd, Mead, 1932.

——*Mr. Polton Explains*. New York: Dodd, Mead, 1940.

Futrelle, Jacques. *Best Thinking Machine Detective Stories*. New York: Dover, 1973.

——*Great Cases of The Thinking Machine*. New York: Dover, 1976.

——*The Diamond Master*. New York: A.L. Burt, undated.

Gardner, Maurice B., "Why I Wrote the Bantan Novels," *The Pulp Era*, No. 62 (Nov-Dec 1965). Reprinted in *The Age of the Unicorn*, Vol. 1, No. 1 (April 1979).

——*Bantan, God-Like Islander*. Boston: Meador Press, 1936.

——**Bantan and the Island Goddess**. Boston: **Meador Press**, 1942.

——*Bantan Defiant*. Greenwich, 1955.

——*Bantan Valiant*. Boston: Meador Press, 1957.

——*Bantan's Island Peril*. Boston: Meador Press, 1959

——*Bantan Incredible*. Boston: Meador Press, 1960.

——*Bantan Primeval*. Boston: Forum, 1961.

——*Bantan Fearless*. Boston: Forum, 1963.

——*Island Paradise and Others*. Boston: Forum, 1964.

——*Bantan and the Mermaids*. Gaus, 1970.

——*Bantan's Quest*. Gaus, 1974.

——*Ancestors of Bantan*. Gaus, 1976.

——*New Adventures of Bantan*. Gaus, 1977.

Goulart, Ron. *Cheap Thrills*. New Rochelle, NY: Arlington House, 1972.

Hamilton, Edmond. *The Best of Edmond Hamilton*. NY: Ballentine, 1977.

——*Crashing Suns*. NY: Ace Books, Inc., 1965. (F-319).

——*Outside the Universe*. NY: Ace Books, Inc., 1964. (F-271).

Harwood, John. "Arthur B. Reeve and the American Sherlock Holmes." *The Armchair Detective*, Vol. 10, No. 4 (October 1977).

Hillegas, Mark R. *The Future As Nightmare: H. G. Wells and the Anti-Utopians*. NY: Oxford University Press, 1967.

Hodgson, William Hope. *Carnacki The Ghost-Finder*. Sauk City, Wisc: Mycroft and Moran, 1947.

——*Deep Waters*. Sauk City, Wisc: Arkahm House, 1967.

——*Out of the Storm*. West Kingston, Rhode Island: Donald M. Grant, 1975.

Horn, Maurice. "The Magic of Burne Hogarth." *Tarzan of the Apes*. NY: Watson-Guptill Pubs., 1972.

Howard, Robert E. *The Hand of Kane*. NY: Centaur Press, 1970.

——*The Moon of Skulls*. NY: Centaur Press, 1969.

——*Skull-Face Omnibus*. Jersey: Neville Spearman, 1974.

——*Solomon Kane*. NY: Centaur Press, 1971.

Howard, Robert E. and Carter, Lin. *King Kull*. NY: Lancer Books, 1969

Hullar, Link. "The Thinking Machine." *Xenophile* No. 30 (March 1977)

Kline, Otis Adelbert. *Jan of the Jungle*. NY: Ace Books, Inc., undated. (F-400).

——*The Outlaws of Mars*. NY: Ace Books, Inc., 1961 (D-531)

——*Planet of Peril*. NY: Ace Books, Inc., undated. (F-211)

——*The Port of Peril*. NY: Ace Books, Inc., undated (F-294)

——*Prince of Peril*. NY: Ace Books, Inc., undated (F-259)

——*The Swordsman of Mars*. NY: Ace Books, Inc., 1960. (D-516)

Kraft, David Anthony. *OAK Leaves* (Reprinting #1 (Fall 1970), #2 (Winter 1970-1971), #3 (Spring 1971), #4 (Summer 1971), #5 (Fall 1971), #6 (Winter 1971-1972), and #7 (Spring 1972). ND: Modern Limited Pubs, 1971.

Laing, Alexander. *The Haunted Omnibus*. NY: Farrar & Rinehart, Inc., 1937.

Lovecraft, H. P. "Robert Ervin Howard: A Memoriam." *Skull-Face Omnibus*. Jersey:

Neville Spearman, 1974.

Lowndes, Robert A. W. "The Unique Mystery Magazine: Hugo Gernsback's *Scientific Detective Monthly*," *The Armchair Detective*, Vol. 14, No. 1 (Winter 1981) through Vol. 15. No. 1 (1982), Vol. 16, No. 2 (Spring 1983).

——"The Cases of Jules de Grandin, Part One." *Startling Mystery Stories*, No. 13, Vol. 3 (#1 (Summer 1969).

——"The Cases of Jules de Grandin, Part Two. *Startling Mystery Stories*, No. 15, Vol. 3, #3 (Spring 1970).

Lupoff, Richard A. *Edgar Rice Burroughs: Master of Adventure*. NY: Ace Publishing Co., 1968.

Lynde, Francis. *Scientific Sprague*. NY: Charles Scribner's Sons, 1912.

McCay, Winsor. *Dreams of the Rarebit Fiend*. NY: Dover Publications, 1973.

Moskowitz, Sam. *Under the Moons of Mars*. NY: Holt Reinhart Winston, 1970).

——"Scientific Detectives," *Encyclopedia of Mystery and Detection*. NY: McGraw Hill 1976.

Nowlan, Philip Francis. *Armageddon 2419 A.D.* NY: Ace Publishing Co., 1962 (#02935).

Orczy, Baroness. *The Man In the Corner*. NY: W. W. Norton & Co., 1966.

Poate, Ernest. *Behind Closed Doors*. NY: Chelsea House, 1923.

——*Dr. Bentiron, Detective*, NY: Chelsea House, 1930

Pound, Reginald. *Mirror of the Century, The Strand Magazine 1891-1950* NY: A. S. Barnes & Co., 1966.

Prager, Arthur. *Rascals At Large; or, The Clue in the Old Nostalgia*. NY: Doubleday & Co., 1971.

Queen, Ellery (editor). *101 Years' Entertainment, The Great Detective Stories, 1841-1941*. NY: The Modern Library, Random House, 1941.

——"Queen's Quorum: Part Five," *Ellery Queen's Mystery Magazine*, Vol. 14, No. 72 (November 1949).

Quinn, Seabury. *The Adventures of Jules de Grandin*. NY: Popular Library, 1976.

——*The Casebook of Jules de Grandin*. NY: Popular Library, 1976.

——*The Devil's Bride*. NY: Popular Library, 1976.

——*The Hellfire Files of Jules de Grandin*. NY: Popular Library, 1976.

——*The Horror Chambers of Jules de Grandin*. NY: Popular Library, 1977.

——*Is the Devil A Gentleman?* Baltimore: Mirage, 1970.

——*The Phantom Fighter*, Sauk City, Wisc.: Mycroft and Moran, 1966.

——*The Skeleton Closet of Jules de Grandin*. NY: Popular Library, 1976.

Reeve, Arthur B. *Craig Kennedy on the Farm*. NY: Grosset & Dunlap, 1925.

——*The Dream Doctor, The New Adventures of Craig Kennedy, Scientific Detective*. NY: The Van Rees Press, 1914.

——*The Fourteen Points, Tales of Craig Kennedy, Master of Mystery*. NY: Grosset & Dunlap, 1925.

——"How Writers Make Good," *Writers' Digest* (August 1930).

——*The Poisoned Pen, Further Adventures of Craig Kennedy*. NY: The Van Rees Press, 1913.

——*The Romance of Elaine*. New York: Harper, 1916.

——*The Social Gangster*. New York: Harper, 1916.

Rohmer, Sax (pseudo of Arthur Henry Sarsfield Ward). *The Dream Detective*. New York: Pyramid Books, 1966.

Rogers, Alva. *A Requiem for Astounding*. Chicago: Advent Pubs., 1967.

Roy, John Flint. *A Guide to Barsoom, The Mars of Edgar Rice Burroughs*. New York: Ballentine, 1976.

Sayers, Dorothy L. (Editor). *The World's Great Crime Stories, The Second Omnibus of Crime*. New York: Blue Ribbon Books, Inc., 1932.

Steinbrunner, Chris, and Otto Penzler (Editors). *Encyclopedia of Mystery and Defection*. NY: McGraw Hill Book Co., 1976.

Stong, Phil (editor), *The Other Worlds—Twenty-Five Modern Stories of Mystery and Imagination,* New York: Garden City, 1942.

Turner, Robert. Extracts from letters. *Xenophile,* Vol. III, No. 1 (Sept. 1976).

*The Weird Tales Collector.* Chicago: Robert Weinberg (Nos. 1 and 2, 1977; Nos. 3 and 4, 1978; No. 5, 1979; No. 6, 1980).

Weinberg, Robert. *The Weird Tales Story.* Oregon FAX, 1977.

——(editor). *WT50, A Tribute to Weird Tales.* Oak Lawn, IL: Robert Weinberg, 1974.

——with Lohr McKinstry. *The Hero Pulp Index.* Evergreen, Co: OPAR Press, 1971.

Wells, H.G. *Seven Famous Novels,* New York: Knopf, 1934.

Williamson, Chet. "The Case of the Moonlighting Physicians," *The Weird Tales Collector No. 6* (1980).

Wilson, Edmund. *The Twenties* New York: Farrar, Straus and Giroux (1975).

Wise, Herbert A., and Phyllis Fraser (Editors). *Great Tales of Terror and the Supernatural.* New York: Random House, 1944.

## MAGAZINE APPEARANCES OF SERIES CHARACTERS

The following section lists magazine appearances of certain series characters discussed in the text. Listings known to be incomplete are so identified; however, given the usual scatter of fiction through the magazines, undiscovered stories about almost any of the characters may yet be found.

Well-prepared checklists are available for the work of such writers as Edgar Rice Burroughs, Seabury Quinn and Arthur B. Reeve, and the listings of their major characters are given as a matter of convenience. Other series characters have been documented in various amateur publications, which are, however, difficult to locate and often of suspect accuracy. The larger number of series characters have never been recorded. The magazine appearances of these, although incomplete, have been validated by direct review of the magazines or confirmation by two sources. They are offered here to make a beginning from which more complete references may be developed.

Your additions to or corrections of these lists are requested and would be warmly appreciated.

## Bentiron, Dr. by Ernest Poate

*in S&S Detective Story Magazine* (Listings are incomplete)

*1919*

| | |
|---|---|
| Jan 7 - Feb 4 | Behind Locked Doors (5-part serial) |
| May 20 | Without Resistance |
| June 3 | Bad Blood |
| Jul 22 | Questioned Sanity |
| Jul 29 | After Forty Years |
| Sept 23 | False Teeth |

*1920*

| | |
|---|---|
| Jan 27 | The Perfect Plate |
| Mar 23 | Phantom Footsteps |
| Apr 27 | In Self Defense |
| Jul 27 | "For External Use Only" |
| Aug 31 | Marked Green |
| Sept 28 | Vials of Wrath |
| Nov 2 | Mental Murder |

*1921*

| | |
|---|---|
| Jan 29 | Inside the Limousine |
| Feb 19 | Dr. Bentiron's Addict Case |
| Aug 13 | Dr. Bentiron Balances Accounts |
| Oct 22 | When the Punishment Fitted the Crime |
| Nov. 19 | Honest John's Millions |
| Dec 24 | Christmas Eve at Dr. Bentiron's |

*1922*

| | |
|---|---|
| Mar. 25 | Dr. Bentiron's Unexpected Patient |
| June 24 | Dr. Bentiron's Blackmail Case |
| Jul 1 | "Out of the Mouths of Babes" |

1923

| | |
|---|---|
| Mar 17 | A Luminous Clue |
| *1924* | |
| Sept 6 | Deadwood |

*1928*

| | |
|---|---|
| Mar 24 - Apr 7 | Yellow Jack (3-part serial) |

*1929*

| | |
|---|---|
| Oct 5-19 | Monsters of Madness (3-part serial) |

*in Best Detective Magazine*
*1930*

| | |
|---|---|
| Dec | Bad Blood |

*1931*

| | |
|---|---|
| Feb | The Cotton Stopper |

*1932*

| | |
|---|---|
| Jul | Dr. Bentiron Cures a Complex |

**Bird, Dr. by S. P. Meek**

*in Amazing Stories*
1931
May                         The Earth's Cancer

*in Astounding Stories of Super Science*
1930
Jan                         The Cave of Horror
Feb                         The Thief of Time
Apr                         The Ray of Madness
May                         Cold Light
Oct                         Stolen Brains
Dec                         Sea Terror

1931
Feb                         The Black Lamp
May                         When Caverns Yawned
Aug                         The Port of Missing Planes
Oct                         The Solar Magnet

1932
Mar                         Poisoned Air
May                         The Great Drought

*in Scientific Detective
Monthly*
1930
Jan                         The Perfect Counterfeit
June                        The Gland Murders

*in Wonder Stories*
1932
May                         Vanishing Gold

**Cabot, Myles by Ralph Milne Farley (The Radio Series)**

*in Argosy All-Story Weekly*
1924
June 28 - July 19           The Radio Man (4-part serial)

1925
Mar 21 - Apr 11             The Radio Beasts (4-part serial)

1926
June 26 - Jul 24            The Radio Planet (5-part serial)

*in Famous Fantastic Mysteries*
*1939*
Sep/Oct, Dec
and                          The Radio Man (4-part serial)
*1940*
Jan, Feb


*1942*
Apr                          The Radio Planet


*in Fantastic Novels*
*1941*
Jan                          The Radio Beasts


*in Spaceway Science Fiction*
*1955*
June                         The Radio Minds of Mars (1st of 2-part serial;
                               2nd part not published)


*1969*
Jan, June, Oct               The Radio Minds of Mars (3-part serial)

## Carter, John by Edgar Rice Burroughs (NOTE Includes associated Barsoom fiction)

*in The All-Story*
*1912*
Feb - Jul                    Under the Moons of Mars (6-part serial, signed
                               Norman Bean)


*1913*
Jan - May                    The Gods of Mars (5-part serial)
Dec - Mar (1914)             Warlord of Mars (4-part serial)


*in All-Story Weekly*
*1916*
Apr 8-22                     Thuvia, Maid of Mars (3-part serial)


*in Argosy All-Story Weekly*
*1922*
Feb 18 - Apr 1               The Chessmen of Mars (7-part serial)


*in Amazing Stories Annual*
1927                         The Master Mind of Mars


*in Blue Book*
*1930*
Apr - Sept                   A Fighting Man of Mars (6-part serial)


*1934*
Nov - Apr (1935)             Swords of Mars (6-part serial)

*in Argosy*
1939
Jan 7 - Feb 11                    The Synthetic Men of Mars (6-part serial)

*in Amazing Stories*
1941
Jan                              *John Carter and the Giant of Mars
                                    (Reprinted Apr 1961)
Mar                              The City of Mummies
June                             Black Pirates of Barsoom
Aug                              Yellow Men of Mars
Oct                              Invisible Men of Mars

1943
Feb                              Skeleton Men of Jupiter

*Primarily written by John Coleman Burroughs, with added material by Edgar Rice Burroughs. (Refer to Lupoff, *Edgar Rice Burroughs, Master of Adventure*, p. 155.)

**Croft, Jason by J. U. Giesy**
*in All-Story Weekly*
1918
Jul 13 - Aug 10                  Palos of the Dog Star Pack (5-part serial)

1919
Jul 5 - Aug 2                    The Mouthpiece of Zitu (5-part serial)

1921
Apr 16 - May 21                  Jason, Son of Jason (6-part serial)

*in Famous Fantastic Mysteries*
1941
Oct                              Palos of the Dog Star Pack

1942
Nov                              The Mouthpiece of Zitu
*in Fantastic Novels*
1948
May                              Jason, Son of Jason

**De Grandin, Jules by Seabury Quinn**

| Title | Published in Weird Tales | Published Other |
|---|---|---|
| The Horror on the Links | Oct 1925 | PF; ADV |
| | May 1937 (rpt) | |
| The Tenants of Broussac | Dec 1925 | SMS #4. Spr. 1967; ADV |
| The Isle of Missing Ships | Feb 1926 | SMS #10, Fall 1968; ADV |
| The Vengence of India | Apr 1926 | SMS #11, Wint 1968/1969 |

| | | |
|---|---|---|
| The Dead Hand | May 1926 | *PF; ADV* |
| The House of Horror | Jul 1926 | SMS #2, Fall 1966; *CASE* |
| Ancient Fires | Sept 1926 | SMS #13, Sum 1969; **CASE** |
| The Great God Pan | Oct 1926 | *HF* |
| The Grinning Mummy | Nov 1926 | |
| The Man Who Cast No Shadow | Feb 1927 | SMS #15, Spring 1970; *ADV* |
| The Blood-Flower | Mar 1927 | SMS #3, Wint 1966/1967; *AL* |
| The Veiled Prophetess | May 1927 | |
| The Curse of Everard Maundy | July 1927 | *ADV* |
| Creeping Shadows | Aug 1927 | |
| The White Lady of the Orphanage | Sept 1927 | SMS #8, Spr 1968 |
| The Poltergeist | Oct 1927 | *PF; HC* |
| The Gods of East and West | Jan 1928 | SMS #5, Sum 1967; *HC* |
| Mephistopheles and Company, Ltd. | Feb 1928 | *HF* |
| The Jewel of Seven Stones | Apr 1928 | |
| The Serpent Woman | June 1928 | *CASE* |
| Body and Soul | Sept 1928 | |
| Restless Souls | Oct 1928 | *PF; HF* |
| The Chapel of Mystic Horror | Dec 1928 Nov 1952 (rpt) | *CASE* |
| The Black Master | Jan 1929 | |
| The Devil People | Feb 1929 | *HF* |
| The Devil's Rosary | Apr 1929 | SMS #16, Sum 1970 |
| The House of Golden Masks | June 1929 | *HC* |
| The Corpse-Master | July 1929 | *PF; CASE* |
| Trespassing Souls | Sept 1929 | |
| The Silver Countess | Oct 1929 | *PF; CASE* |
| The House Without a Mirror | Nov 1929 | |
| Children of Ubasti | Dec 1929 | *PF; CASE* |
| The Curse of the House of Phipps | Jan 1930 | *PF (*as "The Doom of the  .. |
| The Drums of Damballah | Mar 1930 | *SC* |
| The Dust of Egypt | Apr 1930 | *SC* |
| The Brain-Thief | May 1930 | *SC* |
| The Priestess of the Ivory Feet | June 1930 | |
| The Bride of Dewer | July 1930 | *SMS*#17, Fall 1970; *SC* |
| Daughter of the Moonlight | Aug 1930 | *SC* |
| The Druid's Shadow | Oct 1930 | SMS #6, Fall 1967 |
| Stealthy Death | Nov 1930 | *HC* |
| The Wolf of St. Bonot | Dec 1930 | *PF; HF* |
| The Lost Lady | Jan 1931 | |
| The Ghost-Helper | Feb-Mar 1931 | |
| Satan's Stepson | Sept 1931 | |
| The Devil's Bride (6-part serial | Feb through Jul 1932 | MOH (3-part serial), #26-28, Mar/May/Jul 1969; *1* |
| The Dark Angel | Aug 1932 | |

| | | |
|---|---|---|
| The Heart of Siva | Oct 1932 | |
| The Bleeding Mummy | Nov 1932 | |
| The Door to Yesterday | Dec 1932 | |
| A Gamble in Souls | Jan 1933 | *HC* |
| The Thing in the Fog | Mar 1933 | |
| The Hand of Glory | Jul 1933 | *HF* |
| The Chosen of Vishnu | Aug 1933 | |
| Malay Horror | Sept 1933 | |
| The Mansion of Unholy Magic | Oct 1933 | SMS #1, Sum 1966 |
| Red Gauntlets of Czerni | Dec 1933 | |
| The Red Knife of Hassan | Jan 1934 | |
| The Jest of Warburg Tantavul | Sept 1934 | *PF; HC* |
| Hands of the Dead | Jan 1935 | |
| The Black Orchid | Aug 1935 | |
| The Dead-Alive Mummy | Oct 1935 | |
| A Rival from the Grave | Jan 1936 | |
| Witch-House | Nov 1936 | |
| Children of the Bat | Jan 1937 | |
| Satan's Palimpsest | Sept 1937 | LF #9 |
| Pledged to the Dead | Oct 1937 | |
| Living Buddhess | Nov 1937 | LF #9 |
| Flames of Vengence | Dec 1937 | |
| Frozen Beauty | Feb 1938 | |
| Incense of Abomination | Mar 1938 | |
| Suicide Chapel | Jun 1938 | |
| The Venomed Breath of Vengence | Aug 1938 | |
| Black Moon | Oct 1938 | |
| The Poltergeist of Swan Upping | Feb 1939 | |
| The House Where Time Stood Still | Mar 1939 | *25 Stories* |
| Mansions in the Sky | Jun-Jul 1939 | |
| The House of the Three Corpses | Aug 1939 | |
| Stoneman's Memorial | May 1942 | |
| Death's Bookkeeper | Jul 1944 | |
| The Green God's Ring | Jan 1945 | |
| Lords of the Ghostlands | Mar 1945 | |
| Kurban | Jan 1946 | |
| The Man in Crescent Terrace | Mar 1946 | |
| Three in Chains | May 1946 | |
| Catspaws | July 1946 | |
| Lotte | Sept 1946 | |
| Eyes in the Dark | Nov 1946 | |
| Clair de Lune | Nov 1947 | |
| Vampire Kith and Kin | May 1949 | |

| | |
|---|---|
| Conscience Maketh Cowards | Nov 1949 |
| The Body Snatchers | Nov 1950 |
| The Ring of Bastet | Sept 1951 |

The following abbreviations have been used in this checklist:

ADV — *The Adventures of Jules de Grandin,* Popular Library, New York, 1976

CASE — *The Casebook of Jules de Grandin,* Popular Library, New York, 1976

DB — *The Devil's Bride,* Popular Library, New York, 1976

HC — *The Horror Chambers of Jules de Grandin,* Popular Library, New York, 1977

HF — *The Hellfire Files of Jules de Grandin,* Popular Library, New York, 1976

LF #9 — *Lost Fantasies #9* — The Sin Eaters, Weinberg, Chicago, 1979

MOH — *Magazine of Horror,* Health Knowledge, Inc., New York

PF — *The Phantom Fighter* by Seabury Quinn, Mycroft & Moran: Publishers, Sauk City, Wisconsin, 1966

SC — *The Skeleton Closet of Jules de Grandin,* Popular Library, New York, 1976

SMS — *Startling Mystery Stories,* Health Knowledge, Inc., New York

25 Stories — *The Other Worlds — Twenty-Five Modern Stories of Mystery and Imagination,* edited by Phil Stong, Garden City Publishing Co., Inc. Garden City, New York, 1942.

### Dikar by A.L. Zaget (The Tomorrow series)

*in Argosy* (Listings may be incomplete)
*1939*

| | |
|---|---|
| May 27 | Tomorrow |
| June 17 | Children of Tomorrow |
| Sept. 9 | Bright Flag of Tomorrow |

*1940*

| | |
|---|---|
| Mar 16 | Thunder Tomorrow |
| June 8, 15 | Sunrise Tomorrow (2-part serial) |

*1941*

| | |
|---|---|
| Mar 1, 8, 15, 22 | Long Road to Tomorrow (4-part serial) |

### Goodrich, Dr. by Stoddard Goodhue

*in Everybody's*
*1921*

| | |
|---|---|
| Dec | The Phantom Auto |

*1922*
Jan                                          Test Tube Necromancy
Feb                                          The Magic Wheel
Mar                                          The First Stone
Apr                                          The Accusing Voice
June                                         The Locked Room

## Interstellar Patrol by Edmond Hamilton

*in Weird Tales*
*1928*
Aug                                          Crashing Suns

*1929*
Feb                                          The Star Stealers
May                                          Within the Nebulae
Jul                                          Outside the Universe

*1930*
Feb                                          The Comet Drivers
May                                          The Sun People
Nov                                          The Cosmic Cloud

*1934*
Apr                                          Corsairs of the Cosmos

## Jan of the Jungle by Otis Adelbert Kline
*in Argosy*
*1931*
Apr 18 - May 23                              Jan of the Jungle (6-part
                                               serial)

*1935*
Jan 12 - 26                                  Jan In India (3-part
                                               serial)

## Jongor by Robert Moore Williams
*in Fantastic Adventures*
*1940*
Oct                                          Jongor of Lost Island

*1944*
Apr                                          The Return of Jongor

*1951*
Dec                                          Jongor Fights Back

## Kane, Solomon by Robert F. Howard
*in Weird Tales*
*1928*
Aug                                          Red Shadows

*1929*
Jan                            Skulls in the Stars
June                           Rattle of Bones

*1930*
June - July                    The Moon of Skulls (2-
                                 part serial)
Aug                            The Hills of the Dead

*1931*
Sept                           Footfalls Within

*1932*
Jul                            Wings in the Night

**Ka-Zar by Robert Byrd**

*in Ka-Zar*
*1936*
Oct                            King of Fang and Claw
*1937*
Jan                            Roar of the Jungle

*in Ka-Zar the Great*
*1937*
June                           The Hidden Empire

**Kennedy, Craig** by Arthur B. Reeve (NOTE Listing incomplete. The
following information generally follows that presented by J. Randolph Cox
in his article "A Reading of Reeve" *The Armchair Detective,* Vol. 11, No. 1
January 1978.)

in *Cosmopolitan:*
*1910*
December                       The Case of Helen Bond
*1911*
January                        The Silent Bullet
February                       The Bacteriological Detective
March                          The Deadly Tube
April                          The Seismograph Mystery
May                            The Diamond Maker
June                           The Azure Ring
July                           The Spontaneous Combustion Case
August                         The Terror in the Air
September                      The Black Hand
October                        The Artificial Paradise
November                       The Steel Door
December                       The Sand Hog
*1912*
January                        Bacillus of Death

| February | The Master Counterfeiter |
| March | The Firebug |
| April | The Yeggman |
| May | The Poisoned Pen |
| June | The White Slave |
| July | The Forger |
| August | The Unofficial Spy |
| September | The Smuggler |
| October | The Invisible Ray |

*in The Popular Magazine*
1912

| May 1 | The Green Goods King |
| Jul 1 | The Treasure Vault |

1913

| Apr 1, 15 | The Death Thought (2-part serial) |

1914

| Jan 1, 15 | The Scientific Gunman (2-part serial) |

*in Hearst's Magazine*
1912

| Nov | The Campaign Grafter |
| Dec | The Kleptomanic |

1913

| Jan | The Opium Joint |
| Feb | The Vampire |

in *Cosmopolitan:*
1913

| April | The Green Curse |
| May | The Sybarite |
| June | The Phantom Circuit |
| July | Elixir of Life |
| August | The Dream Doctor |
| September | The Death House |
| October | The Submarine Mystery |
| November | The Bomb Maker |
| December | The Ghouls |

*in Adventure*
1914

| Feb | The Abduction Club |

in *Cosmopolitan:*
1916

| August | The Beauty-Mask |
| September | The Love-Meter |

in *S&S Detective Story Magazine:*
1918
July 16 - August 6 Craig Kennedy and the Film Tragedy (4-part serial)
August 27                    The Sinister Shadow
Sept 17 - Oct 8              The Soul Scar (4-part serial)

1924
July 5                       Craig Kennedy's Greatest Mystery

1928
July 7                       Craig Kennedy Gets His Girl
July 28                      Craig Kennedy Gets the Dope
August 11                    Craig Kennedy and the Model
August 25                    Craig Kennedy and the Ghost
October 13                   The Dead Line
October 27                   Craig Kennedy Splits Hairs

in *Everybody's*
1923
September                    Thicker Than Water
October                      Dead Men Tell Tales
November                     The Radio Wraith
December                     The Hawk

1924
January                      The Jazz Addict
February                     The Counterfeit Beauty

in *Flynn's:*
1924                         (Series title: "Craig Kennedy and the
                             Elements")
September 27                 Air
October 11                   Fire
October 25                   Earth
November 8                   Water
                             (Series title: Craig Kennedy and the
                             Compass")
December 13                  North
December 20                  South
December 27                  East

1925
January 3                    West

                             (Series title: "Craig Kennedy and the *Six*
                             Senses")
January 31                   Sight
February 7                   Smell
February 14                  Taste
February 21                  Touch
February 28                  Hearing
March 7                      Sixth Sense

*in Argosy All-Story Weekly*
1925
May 23                          Revenge

*in Detective Fiction Weekly*
1928
Sept 22                         Blood Will Pay
Oct 6                           Radiant Doom
Dec 22                          Craig Kennedy's Christmas Case

1929
Feb 23-Mar 9                    The Mystery Ray (3-part serial)
Mar 16                          The Beauty Wrecker
Aug 31                          Poisoned Music

Sept 7                          The Crime Student

*in Clues*
1929
2nd Nov                         The Mystery of the Phantom Voice
1st Dec                         The House of a Hundred Murders

1930
1st Jan                         The Mystery in the Mire

in *Best Detective Magazine:*
1929
December                        The Sinister Shadow

1931
April                           Craig Kennedy's Greatest Mystery

in *Scientific Detective Monthly:*
1930
January                         The Mystery of the Bulawayo Diamond
February                        The Bacteriological Detective
March                           The Seismograph Adventure (retitling  of
                                "The Seismograph Mystery")
1930
April                           The Terror in the Air
May                             The Azure Ring

in *Amazing Detective
    Tales:*
1930
June                            The Diamond Maker
July                            The White Slave
August                          The Scientific Cracks-
                                    man (retitling of "The
                                    Case of Helen Bond")
September                       The Body That Wouldn't

|  |  |
|---|---|
|  | Burn (retitling of "The Spontaneous Combusion Case") |
| October | The Man Who Was Dead (retitling of "The Artificial Paradise") |

in *Argosy:*
1932

| December 3 | Murder On the Mike |
|---|---|

in *Complete Detective Novel Magazine*
1932

| Apr | The Kidnap Club |
|---|---|
| June | The Junior League Murder |
| Dec | Murder in the Tourist Camp |

1933

| Aug/Sept | The Electric War |
|---|---|

in *Dime Detective*
1933

| October 1 | The Golden Grave |
|---|---|

in *World Man Hunters:*
1934

| February | Doped |
|---|---|

in *Popular Detective:* by Ashley T. Locke, signed by Reeve)

1934

| November | Craig Kennedy Returns |
|---|---|
| December | (Title not known) |

1935

| February | Craig Kennedy Strikes Back. |
|---|---|
| April | Craig Kennedy's Strangest Case |

in *Weird Tales:*
1935

| May | Death Cry |
|---|---|

### Kioga, The Snow Hawk by William L. Chester
in *Blue Book*
1935

| Apr - Oct | Hawk of the Wilderness (7-part serial) |
|---|---|

1936

| May - Oct | Kioga of the Wilderness (6-part serial) |
|---|---|

*1937*

> Short story series titled "One Against a
> Wilderness." After the unnumbered first
> story, the remaining stories take the
> general series title, plus specific titles for
> each.

| | |
|---|---|
| Mar | (Unnumbered) One Against a Wilderness |
| Apr | II. The Dire Wolves' Prey |
| May | III. Unharmed, He Dwelt Among the Forest People |
| June | IV. Flight of the Forest People |
| Jul | V. White Heritage |
| Aug | VI. The Turn of the Tide |

*1938*
Mar - Aug                    Kioga of the Unknown Land (6-part serial)

**Klaw, Moris by Sax Rohmer** (Listing is believed incomplete) in *All-Story Cavalier Weekly* (Under series title: "The Methods of Moris Klaw")
*1915*

| | |
|---|---|
| Feb 13 | The Tragedies in the Greek Room |
| Feb 27 | The Potsherd of Anubis |
| Mar 13 | The Ivory Statue |
| Mar 27 | The Blue Rajah |

**The Scientific Club by Ray Cummings** (Mystery listing only; the following is incomplete
*in Flynn's*
*1925*

| | |
|---|---|
| Mar 21 | Telling What He Knew |
| May 9 | When Rosa Confessed |
| May 30 | What Thought Did |
| June 20 | The Man in the Bath |
| Aug 22 | Memories of Guilt |
| Sept 12 | Ashes of Guilt |
| Sept 19 | The Encyclopedic Sleuth |

*in Best Detective Magazine*
*1936*
April                    A Dark-Room Conviction

**Semi-Dual by J.B. Giesy and Junius B. Smith**
NOTE This list was originally prepared by William J. Clark and published
in his article about Semi-Dual, "The Occult Detector by J.B. Giesy and
Junius B. Smith," in *Xenophile* No. 17, September 1975, p. 55. The format
of Mr. Clark's list has been modified, and amendments by Winston
Dawson included.

*1912*

"The Occult Detector," *The Cavalier,* 3-part serial: Feb 17, 24; Mar 2.
"The Significance of the High 'D'," *The Cavalier,* 3-part serial: Mar 9, 16, 23.
"The Wistaria Scarf," *The Cavalier,* 3-part serial: June 1, 8, 15.
"The Purple Light," *The Cavalier,* 3-part serial: Oct 5, 12, 19

*1913*

"The Master Mind," *The Cavalier,* novelette: Jan 25.
"Rubies of Doom" *The Cavalier,* 2-part serial: Jul 5, 12
"The House of the Ego," *The Cavalier,* 3-part serial: Sept. 20, 27; Oct 4.
"The Ghost of a Name," *The Cavalier,* novelette: Dec 20.

*1914*

"The Curse of Quetzal," *All-Story Magazine,* novelette: Nov 28.

*1915*

"The Web of Destiny," *All-Story Weekly,* 2-part serial: Mar 20, 27.
"Snared," *All-Story Weekly,* 3-part serial: Dec 11, 18, 25.

*1916*

"Box 991," *All-Story Weekly,* 3-part serial: June 3, 10, 17.

*1917*

"The Killer," *All-Story Weekly,* 4-part serial: Apr 7, 14, 21, 28.
"The Compass in the Sky," *The People's Magazine,* novelette: May
"The Unknown Quantity," *All-Story Weekly,* 3-part serial: Aug 25, Sept 1, 8.
"Solomon's Decision," *All-Story Weekly,* 3-part serial: Dec 1, 8, 15.

*1918*

"The Storehouse of Past Events," *People's Favorite Magazine,* novel: Feb
    10
"The Moving Shadow," *People's Favorite Magazine,* novelette: June 10.
"The Stars Were Looking," *Top-Notch Magazine,* believed to be a novelette:
    July 1.
"The Black Butterfly," *All-Story Weekly,* 4-part serial: Sept. 14, 21, 28; Oct 5.
"The Trail in the Dust," *People's Favorite Magazine,* novel Oct 25.

*1919*

"Stars of Evil," *All-Story Weekly,* 3-part serial: Jan. 25; Feb 1, 8.
"The Ivory Pipe," *All-Story Weekly,* 3-part serial: Sept. 20, 27; Oct. 4.

*1920*

"House of the Hundred Lights," *All-Story Weekly,* 4-part serial: May 22, 29;
June 5, 12; "Black and White" *Argosy All-Story Weekly,* 4-part serial, Oct. 2,
9, 16, 23.

*1921*

"Wolf of Erlik," *Argosy All-Story Weekly,* 4-part serial: Oct 22, 29; Nov. 5, 12.

*1923*

"The Opposing Venus," *Argosy All-Story Weekly,* 4-part serial: Oct 13, 20,
    27; Nov. 3.

*1924*

"Poor Little Pigeon," *Argosy All-Story Weekly,* 5-part serial: Aug 9, 16, 23,
    30, Sept. 6, 13.

*1926*

"The House of Invisible Bondage," *Argosy All-Story Weekly,* 4-part serial:
    Sept. 18, 25; Oct. 2, 9.

*1929*
"The Woolly Dog," *Argosy All-Story Weekly,* 4-part serial: Mar 23, 30;
   Apr 6, 13.
*1931*
"The Green Goddess," *Argosy,* 6-part serial: Jan 31; Feb 7, 14, 21, 28; Mar 7.
*1934*
"The Ledger of Life," *Argosy,* 4-part serial: June 30; Jul 7, 14, 21.

## Skylark of Space by E.E. Smith

*in Amazing Stories*
*1928*
Aug - Dec                      The Skylark of Space (3-part serial)

*1930*
Aug - Oct                    Skylark Three (3-part serial)

*in Astounding Stories of Super Science*
*1934-1935*
Aug - Feb                    The Skylark of Valeron (7-part serial)

*in IF Worlds of Science Fiction*
*1965*
June - Sept                Skylark DuQuesne (4-part serial)

## Taine by David Keller

*in Amazing Stories Quarterly*
1928
Summer                       The Menace

*1929*
Fall                           Euthanasia Limited

*1933*
Winter                       The Menace (reprint)

*in Amazing Stories*
*1931*
May                         The Cerebral Library

*1935*
Feb                         The Island of White Mice

*in Amazing Detective Tales*
*1930*
June                      Burning Water
Sept                      Menacing Claws

*in Booklet by URRA Printers, Jamacia*

1934                                      Wolf Hollow Bubbles
*in Science Wonder Stories*
*1929*
Aug                                       The Feminine Metamorphosis

*in Scientific Detective Monthly*
*1930*
Feb                                       A Scientific Widowhood

*in Startling Mystery Stories*
*1968/1969*
Winter (#11)                              Wolf Hollow Bubbles

*1970*
Summer (#16)                              The Temple of Death

*in Wonder Stories*
*1934*
Sept                                      The Tree of Evil

## Tam, Son of the Tiger by Otis Adelbert Kline
*in Weird Tales*
*1931*
June/Jul - Dec                            Tam, Son of the Tiger (6-part serial)

## Tama by Ray Cummings
*in Argosy*
*1930*
Dec 13 - 27                               Tama of the Light Country (3-part serial)

*1931*
June 27 - Jul 18                          Tama, Princess of Mercury (4-part serial)

## Tarzan by Edgar Rice Burroughs

| | | | |
|---|---|---|---|
| Tarzan of the Apes | novel | *All-Story* | Oct 1912 |
| The Return of Tarzan | 7-part serial | *New Story Magazine* | June-Dec 1913 |
| The Eternal Lover | novel | *All-Story Weekly* | Mar 7, 1914 |
| The Beasts of Tarzan | 5 part serial | *All-Story Cavalier Weekly* | May 16-June 13, 1914 |
| The Son of Tarzan | 6 part serial | *All-Story Weekly* | Dec 4, 1915-Jan 8, 1916 |
| The New Stories of Tarzan | 12 part series | *Blue Book* | Sep 1916-Aug 1917 |

| | |
|---|---|
| "Tarzan's First Love" | Sep 1916 |
| "The Capture of Tarzan" | Oct 1916 |
| "The Fight for the Balu" | Nov 1916 |
| "The God of Tarzan" | Dec 1916 |
| "Tarzan and the Black Boy | Jan 1917 |
| "The Witch-Doctor Seeks Vengence" | Feb 1917 |

| | | | |
|---|---|---|---|
| "The End of Bukawai" | | | Mar 1917 |
| "The Lion" | | | Apr 1917 |
| "The Nightmare" | | | May 1917 |
| "The Battle for Teeka" | | | June 1917 |
| "A Jungle Joke" | | | July 1917 |
| "Tarzan Rescues the Moon" | | | Aug 1917 |
| Tarzan and the Jewels of Opar | 5 part serial | *All-Story Weekly Weekly* | Nov 18-Dec 16, 1916 |
| Tarzan the Untamed | 6 part serial | *Red Book Magazine* | Mar-Aug 1919 |
| Tarzan and the Valley of Luna | 5 part serial | *All-Story Weekly* | Mar 20-Apr 17, 1920 |
| Tarzan the Terrible | 7 part serial | *Argosy All-Story Weekly* | Feb 12-Mar 26, 1921 |
| Tarzan and the Golden Lion | 7 part serial | *Argosy All-Story Weekly* | Dec 9, 1922- Jan 20, 1923 |
| Tarzan and the Ant Men | 7 part serial | *Argosy All-Story Weekly* | Feb 2-Mar 15, 1924 |
| Tarzan, Lord of the Jungle | 6 part serial | *Blue Book* | Dec 1927-May 1928 |
| Tarzan and the Lost Empire | 5 part serial | *Blue Book* | Oct 1928-Feb 1929 |
| Tarzan At The Earth's Core | 7 part serial | *Blue Book* | Sep 1929-Mar 1930 |
| Tarzan, Guard of the Jungle | 7 part serial | *Blue Book* | Oct 1930-Apr 1931 |
| The Triumph of Tarzan | 6-part serial | *Blue Book* | Oct 1931-Mar 1932 |
| Tarzan and the City of Gold | 6 part serial | *Argosy* | Mar 12-Apr 16, 1932 |
| Tarzan and the Leopard Men | 6 part serial | *Blue Book* | Aug 1932-Jan 1933 |
| Tarzan and the Lion Man | 9 part serial | *Liberty Magazine* | Nov 11, 1933- Jan 6, 1934 |
| Tarzan and the Immortal Men | 6 part serial | *Blue Book* | Oct 1935-Mar 1936 |
| Tarzan and the Magic Men | 3 part serial | *Argosy* | Sept 19-Oct 3, 1936 |
| Tarzan and the Elephant Men | 3 part serial | *Blue Book* | Nov 1937-Jan 1938 |
| The Red Star of Tarzan | 6 part serial | *Argosy* | Mar 19-Apr 23, 1938 |
| Tarzan and the Champion | short story | *Blue Book* | Apr 1940 |
| Tarzan and the Jungle Murders | short story | *Thrilling Adventures* | June 1940 |
| The Quest of Tarzan | 3-part serial | *Argosy* | Aug 23-Sept 6, 1941 |
| | | | |
| *Reprints of interest* | | | |
| Tarzan Returns (Retitling of The Beasts of Tarzan | 4 part serial | *Triple X Magazine* | Nov 1929-Feb 1930 |
| Tarzan, Jungle Detective (reprint of "The Battle for Teeka," June 1917) | short story | *Ellery Queen's Mystery Magazine* | May 1964 |

## The Thinking Machine by Jacques Futrelle

(Note This listing includes only the final four stories published in *The Popular Magazine,* under the series title, "The Thinking Machine.")

*1912*
Aug 1                          I. The Tragedy of the Life Raft
Aug 15                         II. Five Millions By Wireless
Sept 1                         III. The Case of the Scientific Murderer
Sept 15                        IV. The Jackdaw


**Thorndyke, Dr. R. Austin Freeman**
     **(Note Listing incomplete)**
*in Argosy All-Story Weekly*
*1923*
Sept 15                        The Stolen Ingots
Oct 20                         A Fisher of Men

*in Flynn's*
*1924*
Nov 29                         Little Grains of Sand
Dec 27                         Rex Vs Burnaby

*1925*
Jan 31                         Nebuchadnezzar's Seal
Feb 28                         The Puzzle Lock
Mar 28                         The Green Check Jacket

*1927*
Jan 8                          Written in Blood
Mar 12                         Left by Flame

*in Amazing Detective Tales*
*1930*
June                           The Blue Spangle (retitling of "The Blue
                                  Sequin")

*in Ellery Queen's Mystery Magazine*
*1942*
Spr                            Percival Bland's Proxy

*1949*
May                            The Missing Mortgagee

*in Rex Stout Mystery Quarterly*
*1946*
Mar                            The Puzzle Lock

*in The Saint Detective Magazine*
*1958*
Jul                            The Blue Scarab

*in The Saint Mystery Magazine*
*1962*
June                            The Anthropologist At Large


*1965*
Jul                            A Sower of Pestilence

## Trant, Luther by Edwin Balmer & William MacHarg

in *Hampton's Magazine*
*1909*
May                            The Man In the Room
June                           The Fast Watch
July                           The Red Dress
August                         The Private Bank Puzzle
September                      The Man Higher Up
October                        The Chalchihuiti Stone
November                       The Empty Cartridges
December                       The Odor of Death


*1910*
January                        The Axion Letters
February                       The Eleventh Hour
May                            The Hammering Man
October                        A Matter of Mind Reading


in *Amazing Stories* (reprinted during 1926-1928, listing incomplete)
1926: December                 The Man Higher Up
1927: April                    The Man In the Room


in *Scientific Detective Monthly*
*1930*
January                        The Fast Watch
February                       The Man Higher Up
March                          The Man In The Room
April                          The Hammering Man
May                            The Eleventh Hour


in *Amazing Detective Stories*
*1930*
June                           A Matter of Mind Reading
July                           The Private Bank Puzzle
August                         Vapors of Death (retitling of The Odor of
                               Death)
September                      The Duel In the Dark (retitling of The Empty
                               Cartridges)

**Usher, Godfrey by Herman Landon**
    **(NOTE Listing incomplete)**

*in S & S Detective Story Magazine*
*1918*

| | |
|---|---|
| Feb 5 | Twin Shadows |
| Feb 12 | A Post-Mortem Appointment |
| Feb 26 | Soundless Melodies |
| Mar 5 | Whispers from the Dead |
| Jul 16 | The Purple Terror |
| Jul 23 | Told in Shadow |
| Jul 30 | Three Wishes |

# Index